Online Child Safety

Online Child Safety

Law, Technology and Governance

Joseph Savirimuthu
Liverpool Law School, Liverpool University, UK

First published 2012 by
PALGRAVE MACMILLAN

Palgrave Macmillan in the UK is an imprint of Macmillan Publishers Limited, registered in England, company number 785998, of Houndmills, Basingstoke, Hampshire RG21 6XS.

Palgrave Macmillan in the US is a division of St Martin's Press LLC, 175 Fifth Avenue, New York, NY 10010.

Palgrave Macmillan is the global academic imprint of the above companies and has companies and representatives throughout the world.

Palgrave® and Macmillan® are registered trademarks in the United States, the United Kingdom, Europe and other countries.

ISBN: 978–0–230–24152–7

This book is printed on paper suitable for recycling and made from fully managed and sustained forest sources. Logging, pulping and manufacturing processes are expected to conform to the environmental regulations of the country of origin.

A catalogue record for this book is available from the British Library.

A catalog record for this book is available from the Library of Congress.

10 9 8 7 6 5 4 3 2 1
21 20 19 18 17 16 15 14 13 12

Printed and bound in Great Britain by
CPI Antony Rowe, Chippenham and Eastbourne

To Adaikalam Packiam Pillai – who always believed.

Contents

Tables

Cases

Australia

Crowe v Graham (1969) 121 CLR 375.
Cox v State of New South Wales [2007] NSWSC 471.
DPP v Drummond [2008] NSWLC 10.
Geyer v Downs [1977] HCA 64.
Gibson v Evans [2008] NSWSC 495.
Hitchen v R [2010] NSWCCA 77.
HML v The Queen, SB v The Queen, OAE v The Queen [2008] HCA 16.
McEwen v Simmons [2008] NSWSC 1292.
Paul Savage v R (2010) VSCA 220.
PDA v R S (2010) VSCA 94.
R v Asplund [2010] NWSCCA 316.
R v Carson [2008] QCA 268.
R v Costello (2011) QCA 39.
R v Dragos (2010) ONSC 3093.
R v Flynn [2010] QCA 254.
R v Gajjar [2008] VSCA 268.
R v Gedling [2007] SADC 124.
R v Gent [2005] NSWCCA 370.
R v Lee [2010] NSWCCA 88.
R v Mara [2009] QCA 208.
R v Newman (2010) SASC 82.
R v ONA (2009) VSCA 146.
R v Randall (2006) NSPC 9.
R v Sahin (2000) VSCA 145.
R v Shetty [2005] QCA 225.
R v Thomas (2006) VSCA 165.
Ridgeway v The Queen (1995) 184 CLR 19.
Saddler v R [2009] NSWCCA 83.
Tector v R [2008] NSCCCA 151.
XYZ v Commonwealth (2005) 227 ALR 495.

Canada

Canada (Attorney General) v Leamont 2010 BCSC 1281.
HMTQ v Bock (2010) ONSC 3117.
R v Boudreau-Fontaine [2010[QCCA 1108.
R v Cafferata [2008] YKTC 93.

The United Kingdom

R v Patel [2005] 1 Cr App 27.
R v Pearson [2009] EWCA Crim 1994.
R v Perrin [2002] EWCA Crim 747.
R v Penner [2010] EWCA Crim 1155.
R v Ping Chen Cheung [2009] EWCA Crim 2965.
R v Porter [2006] EWCA Crim 560.
R v Rowe [2008] EWCA Crim 2712.
R v S and another [2008] EWCA Crim 2177.
R v Sang [1980] AC 402, 69 Cr App Rep 282, HL.
R v Secretary of State for Education and Employment and others
    (Respondents) ex parte Williamson (Appellant and others) [2005] UKHL
    15.
R v Sheppard and Whittle [2010] EWCA Crim 65.
R v Smith and R v Jayson [2002] EWCA Crim 683.
R v Smith (Wallace Duncan)(No.4)[2004] 3 WLR 229.
R v Smurthwaite [1994] 1 All ER 898.
R v Solanke [1969] 3 All ER 1383, [1970] 1 WLR 1, CA.
R v Stamford (John David)[1972] 2 QB 391.
R v Stanley [1965] 2 QB 327, 49 Cr App Rep 175, CCA.
R v Stephen Neal [2011] EWCA Crim 461.
R v Straker [1965] Crim LR 239, CCA.
R v Thomas John C [2010] EWCA Crim 1871.
R v Waddon 2000 WL 491456.
R v Walker [2007] EWCA Crim 68.
R v Whittle (Barry Gordon) [2010] EWCA Crim 2934.
R v Williams (1986) 84 Cr App Rep 299, CA.
R v Windsor [2010] EWCA Crim 1660.
R v Wood (1982) 76 Cr App Rep 23, CA.
Rantsev v Cyprus (2010) 51 EHRR 1.
Redknapp and another v Commissioner of the City of London Police and
    another [2008] EWHC 1177 (Admin).
Rotaru v Romania (2000) 8 BHRC 449.
Savage and Parmenter [1992] 1 AC 699.
Shivpuri [1987] AC 1.
T v The Queen [2011] EWCA Crim 729.
Treacy v DPP [1971] AC 537.
United States v Tollman [2008] EWHC 184.
Webster v Ridgeway Foundation School [2010] EWHC 157 (QB).
Wenting v High Court of Valenciennes [2009] EWHC 3528 (Admin)).

The United States

ACLU v Reno, 929 F Supp 824 (ED Pa 1996).
AH v State 949 So. 2d 234 (Fla. Dist. Ct. App. 2007).

Abbreviations

AMF	Alannah and Madeline Foundation
APEC	Asia Pacific Economic Cooperation
AFP	Australian Federal Police
APPCG	All Party Parliamentary Communications Group
ACPO	Association of Chief Police Officers
ABS	Australian Bureau of Statistics
ACMA	Australian Communication Media Authority
BBC	British Broadcasting Corporation
CAIP	Canadian Association of Internet Providers
CCCP	Canadian Centre for Child Protection
CPCMEC	Canadian Police Centre for Missing and Exploited Children
CRTC	Canadian Radio-Television and Telecommunications Commission
CSIS	Canadian Security Intelligence Service
CEOP	Child Exploitation and Online Protection Centre
CRC	Committee on the Rights of the Child
CSEC	Commercial Sexual Exploitation of Children
CWG	Consultative Working Group on Cybersafety
COPINE	Combating Paedophile Information Networks in Europe
Convention	Council of Europe's Convention on the Protection of Children against Sexual Exploitation and Sexual Abuse
CPCLA	Children's Participation in Cultural and Leisure Activities
DBCDE	Department of Broadband, Communications and the Digital Economy
DCSF	Department for Children, Schools and Families
DCMS	Department for Culture, Media and Sport and Department for Business, Innovation and Skills
SSNP	EU Safer Social Networking Principles
SIP	EU Safer Internet Programme
ECHR	European Convention on Human Rights
ECDG	European Commission Directorate General
Framework	European Framework for Safer Mobile Use by Younger Teenagers and Children
EFC	European Financial Coalition
EUROPOL	European Police Office
FTC	Federal Trade Commission
FBI	Federal Bureau of Investigation
FCACP	Financial Coalition against Child Pornography
HRC	Human Rights Council

ISFE	Interactive Software Federation of Europe
INTERPOL	International Criminal Police Organisation
ISTTF	Internet Safety Technical Task Force
ITU	International Telecommunication Union
IWF	Internet Watch Foundation
MSIG	Multi-Stakeholder Internet Governance
NCECC	National Child Exploitation Coordination Centre
Ofsted	Office for Standards in Education, Children's Services and Skills
OfCom	Office of Communications
OECD	Organisation for Economic Cooperation and Development
OSTWG	Online Safety Technical Working Group
PROTECT	Act Prosecutorial Remedies and Other Tools to end the Exploitation of Children Today Act
SWGFL	South West Grid for Learning
UN	United Nations
UNCRC	UN Convention on the Rights of the Child
UNESCO	UN Educational, Scientific and Cultural Organization
UNICEF	UN International Children's Emergency Fund
GAO	US General Accounting Office
ICE	US Immigration and Customs Enforcement Agency
VGT	Virtual Global Taskforce
WC III	World Congress III against Sexual Exploitation of Children and Adolescents
WSIS	World Summit on the Information Society

Foreword

At some point in an indeterminate future, historians will argue about how it came to pass that towards the end of the twentieth century and a little way into the twenty-first, otherwise intelligent people claimed that the Internet was entitled to sit, indeed according to them optimally *should* sit, outside the ordinary discourse of public policy making and law making. Governments, Parliaments, Senates were held to be if not exactly completely redundant then certainly as being of limited use when grappling with both the challenges and the opportunities which this singular and exciting technology was starting to present.

Having fought in some cases for centuries to curb the previously unaccountable powers of Princes by establishing democratic institutions which could bring them to book or force them to act in ways which were more acceptable to the majority, somehow the idea got around that *we the people* should now repose greater trust in the benign operation of large corporations. Even in those countries where politicians are not universally loved and admired, to many this seemed like a much less appealing alternative.

Governments and legislators have a unique obligation to be forever watchful of the wider public interest. This is not an obligation they can resign from or have removed simply because something comes along that is new or difficult. Yet the arrival of the Internet in our midst undoubtedly did create novel demands on the machinery of government. It did make it necessary to look for better designs for the policy and law-making processes which impact upon it. Joseph Savirimuthu's landmark book maps out the early efforts to do that. Moreover, Savirimuthu writes with an elegance and lucidity which should broaden the book's appeal well beyond the community of lawyers, child care professionals and law enforcement officers who are likely to be among the first to buy it.

As I have suggested, some did and still do argue that governments should absent themselves completely from the stage. If there was ever the merest sliver of a possibility such a techno-libertarian vision might become a reality, which I doubt, it quickly foundered. The cases which Savirimuthu discusses in this book are all the proof anyone needs to show that the creators of the Internet had not fully thought through key aspects of their project. The unborn historians referred to earlier will owe Savirimuthu a great debt for bringing together the evidence in the way he has.

The men and women who put together the Internet had no notion it would end up in the bedrooms of 11-year-olds in Birmingham and Benin. It would have filled them with horror and given pause for more than a little thought if they ever imagined their invention would completely transform and hugely expand "the market" for child pornography. The possibility that by building Transmission Control Protocol/Internet Protocol (TCP/IP), they would be paving the way for even one man to locate, kidnap, rape and murder a single child would have propelled some to abandon computer science altogether and take up flower arranging. Yet all this has happened and much besides. The facts are assembled and documented with great care and precision by Savirimuthu, not as a ghoulish catalogue or an indictment but as a scholarly call for us all to do better.

The Internet grew up in and burst out of the small and trusting world of the Academy. It had tootled along for years as an aid to research and communication within communities which, originally, typically were small enough and intimate enough, if not exactly for everyone to know everyone, at least to have a shared ethos that allowed a sense of a self-governing collective responsibility to emerge. Even as private companies started to discover the value of e-mail and FTP servers in the 1980s, we were still a long way from the sort of Internet we have today.

The development of the web in the early 1990s changed everything. It heralded the arrival of a new, heterogeneous, gigantic clientele, including in its midst enormous numbers of children and young people. But the same notions of independence from officialdom and authority persisted, particularly among old hands. "We didn't need government to get us here and we definitely don't need them now." In fact, a large part of the funds which paid for the early research, which paved the way for the Internet, was provided courtesy of different though mainly American taxpayers, but let that pass.

Could the Internet have been constructed in a different way which would have avoided or reduced its potential to do the kind of evil I have outlined and which Savirimuthu analyses? Absolutely. Does it matter that it wasn't? Probably, but we are where we are. We all have to deal with it now. The Internet is an egregious example of the doctrine of unforeseen and unintended consequences.

The Industrial Revolution of the eighteenth and nineteenth centuries has interesting parallels. The benefits of that revolution were and remain overwhelming. Few would renounce them. It was not deliberately designed to pollute rivers and poison the air or generate greenhouse gases in a way which would eventually threaten to extinguish all life on Earth. Eventually we caught on to the downside and began to take steps to address it.

The benefits of the Internet to society in general and in this case to children and young people in particular likewise are immeasurable. It is hard to find anyone who wants to turn the clock back completely even though daily we read how the technology has led not only to the assaults on children which Savirimuthu describes, but also to a host of other antisocial behaviours such as identity theft, breaches of national security, fraud, invasions of privacy and so on. Few if any of these crimes are in and of themselves wholly new but the Internet has recast and promoted them on a completely new scale. Why are things allowed to continue in this way? Can't someone tell someone else to put it right?

Here is where the special circumstances surrounding the Internet forcefully rear their head. Governance. A key theme in Savirimuthu's book.

Famously the Internet is borderless and can collapse time and space. Yet it expresses itself in tangible ways, inside national jurisdictions within particular time zones. This can raise fiendishly difficult questions both about whose law applies and how and by whom it might be enforced. The role the Internet plays in much of modern social, economic and political life and, in this context, the fact that children are in the middle of the mix adds greatly to the sensitivities and tensions.

Henry Kissinger was once supposed to have said "Who do you call to speak to Europe?" Even if the words never actually passed his lips this remains a powerful metaphor. "Who do you call if you want to speak to the Internet industry?"

In the beginning when one spoke about "the Internet industry" it generally meant only Internet Service Providers (ISPs), the companies providing basic connectivity to cyberspace. Pretty obviously ISPs are still massively important players. Without them there would be no gateway. They hold basic information about users' activities, information which is often essential to law enforcement investigations or other legal processes.

Today other kinds of online service providers have come to dominate the value chain and public perceptions of what the Internet now is. Some of the largest, best known, most successful and important online businesses have only a marginal or no involvement at all in providing direct connections to the Internet. They range from giants such as Facebook and Google through to hundreds of thousands of small businesses perhaps being run by individuals in their spare time from their garage, kitchen table or university dorm.

Hardware manufacturers produce ever more inventive and interesting ways of going online. Some of these have a particular appeal to children and young people. Sony, Nintendo, Xbox, Nokia, Samsung and Apple constitute a major part of the modern ecology of the Internet.

Out of this latticework grew an expectation that private-sector actors needed to embrace a larger set of responsibilities. Around the globe a range of self-regulatory and co-regulatory models emerged, sometimes supported or led by legislation and sometimes not, but all specifically designed to address the interests of children and young people as Internet users. How well they are working is discussed with great perceptiveness by Savirimuthu. He provides us with a roadmap and an incisive commentary.

As we survey the terrain of governance we see that one of the key global institutions responsible for the ongoing overall management of the Internet, the Internet Corporation for Assigned Names and Numbers (ICANN), has no direct representation from any governments or any inter-governmental agencies on any of its decision-making bodies although it does have a Government Advisory Committee that provides both with an opportunity to air their views on matters within ICANN's remit.[1] Standards bodies such as the Internet Engineering Task Force and the World Wide Web Consortium have persons associated with them who work for governments or governmental agencies but the narrow, essentially technical nature of the remits of those bodies limits any scope for influencing a broader policy agenda.

This lack of a single point of accountability or reference creates disturbances and eddies which at times have spilled over into evident frustration at the lack of responsiveness to what many national governments feel are their legitimate concerns. The final communiqué of the 2011 G8 meeting made express references to the position of children and young people as Internet users and as potential victims of trafficking or abuse mediated through the Internet. For all that was said at the time about President Sarkozy's alleged grandstanding by bringing such issues to the G8 meeting and making so much of them, the very fact that many of his points were accepted and reflected in the final communiqué was very telling.

The abuse of anonymity is at the root of many of the Internet's enduring problems. A paedophile or someone wishing to exchange child abuse images would be more constricted or limited in what they could do if reliable strong authentication was required before they could sign on or swap files. But any attempt to deal with an issue like anonymity which is seen to have been inspired by a political institution such as a government not unnaturally raises concerns.

Similarly if a government advocates the use of technical tools, for example, filters to block access to age-inappropriate material, might they in truth be preparing the way for a bigger deployment of filtering which had an ideological or other kind of illiberal edge to it? To put it another way, do governments invoke the language of child protection as a cover for an unstated political agenda which might threaten human rights?

Against that it has to be asked if Internet companies on occasion play on and perhaps even play up these fears? Again, to state the proposition slightly differently, do otherwise hard-headed capitalist enterprises sometimes adopt the altruistic language of human rights as a convenient foil to help them ward off demands by governments to put more resources into things which, as they see it, make it harder to make a profit?

Often consumers are asked to put their faith not in governments but in the operation of the market. That might have something going for it as an argument if there was any sign that the markets in question worked at all efficiently. However, it is self-evident that while several Internet companies have been spectacularly successful in getting people to sign up for their services and spend money with them, they have failed, not completely but still on a monumental scale to ensure their customers understand how their products works or what they should do to use them safely. Can't the same magic and sparkle that delivered one also be turned on to deliver the other? If not, why not? The word "proportionality" usually gets an airing about now but, like beauty, proportionality is in the eye of the beholder.

My own view is that it is very much in the longer-term interests of the Internet itself and in particular of the companies that currently dominate it for governments to be fully convinced that their legitimate concerns for the welfare of their citizens, perhaps particularly in relation to children and young people, are taken seriously and are acted upon reasonably promptly. Otherwise there is a very great likelihood that not-so-eventually, governments will conclude that Internet businesses are taking unfair advantage of the lack of any specific legislative or other body which could hold them to account more directly. This will lead to the further and rapid fragmentation of the Internet as different jurisdictions produce a variety of locally grown solutions.

To some extent this is already happening. A number of countries have introduced laws and regulations which they feel better suit their cultural, legal and political traditions because their local "branches" of the Internet industry have not come forward voluntarily to respond in what was considered an appropriate way. Savirimuthu documents many examples in an accessible style that many non-lawyers will greatly appreciate.

The key point, though, is that for all the examples that can be pointed to of local laws and regulation that might exist now, many more governments have refrained from such radicalism in the belief that a co-operative approach will be better for everyone. Should faith in voluntary co-operation finally be shown to be a fruitless path, a proliferation of new national or regional laws and regulations will quickly follow.

In *The Doctor's Dilemma*, written in 1911, George Bernard Shaw famously observed that all professions are conspiracies against the laity. What he meant was that groups of people who congregate around particular disciplines, be they carpenters or astrophysicists, tend to develop ways of working, and above all, ways of describing what they do when they are working, which are more or less deliberately designed to separate themselves from everyone else. Maybe this does not matter very much if you work in a discrete or narrow space but it matters a very great deal if, as with the Internet, your canvass is pervasive and global. Savirimuthu's book will have great value in helping non-techies and non-experts everywhere to understand the nature of the challenges. If, as we might reasonably hope, this leads to better-informed decision-making on the part of companies and governments, children and young people on every continent will be in a much better place.

Part I
Online Child Safety

1
Introduction

On 3 February 2009, it was reported by the Attorney General for Connecticut that 90,000 registered sex offenders were found on MySpace, a social networking site (Office of the Attorney General, 2009). Following the disclosure of the information, a press release issued by the Attorney General claimed that the presence of convicted sex offenders on the social networking site was evidence of

> MySpace's monstrously inadequate counter-measures. MySpace must purge these dangerous offenders now – and rid them for good. Social networking sites must be barred as playgrounds for predators – a very real threat exposed by the response to our subpoena ... Law enforcement officials know the reality: children are solicited every day on line. All too often, they fall prey. Technology companies and social networking sites must do more – and do it now. Blaming the victim is appalling and outrageous. (Ibid., 2009)

Promoting trust and confidence in the online environment continues to be at the forefront of governments' online child safety governance strategies. At the heart of the ever-present concerns of parents and educators are the risks children can be exposed to when using the Internet and communication technologies like mobile phones, laptops, online games and social networking sites (Web 2.0 technologies) when interacting with peers, online communities and social media (Ito, 2008). The popularity of these communities for child's safety and well-being can be compromised. It is perhaps more accurate to say that convergence now creates new spaces for children to use the technological affordances and equip them with tools which can be used to define their lives, identities, audiences and relationships (Fox, 2008). Online child safety governance has to address a complex task: balancing empowerment and protection issues raised by children's access to and use of Web 2.0 technologies. To paraphrase the opening observation of the EC

3

Green Paper – policy decisions now have the potential to shape the way Web 2.0 technologies and social media are delivered to and consumed by children (European Commission, 1996b,c). An imbalance in online child safety governance has immediate and long-term consequences – the overreaching of protective and precautionary impulses can undermine children's autonomy and privacy. Conversely, indifference, apathy and ignorance can result in children exposing themselves and their peers to serious harm and abuse. Getting the balance right is an immense challenge. As Fish J. observed in his opening passage in the Supreme Court of Canada hearing in *R v Legare* (2009), the threats posed to children are embedded in network structures and information flows:

> The Internet is an open door to knowledge, entertainment, communication – and exploitation ... Shielded by the anonymity of an assumed online name and profile, they aspire to gain the trust of their targeted victims through computer "chats" – and then to tempt or entice them into sexual activity, over the Internet or, still worse, in person. (paragraphs 1–2)

Human-centred computing and mobile computing networks make it difficult to ascertain the identity of the participants children are connected with or the invisible audiences connected with them (Casey, 2004: 11). Digital information by its nature can be easily stored, reproduced, manipulated and disseminated without the owner's knowledge or consent. Mobile and communication technologies provide new avenues through which children are exposed to such harms. Individuals and criminal organised gangs now use Web 2.0 technologies to engage in the commercial and sexual exploitation of children on a worldwide basis. For example, in the Canadian case of *HMTQ v Bock* (2010), the offender connected to a peer-to-peer (P2P) network to not only view child pornography content made available by other users but the technological affordances also made it easier for him to share his own collection of pictures and videos with a global audience. In *R v Costello* (2011), the offender used communication platforms like chat rooms and instant messaging (IM) communication to transmit indecent material to minors with the intention of procuring victims to engage in sexual activity, contrary to the anti-sexual grooming provisions in the Commonwealth and Queensland legislation. Phoebe Prince, a 15-year-old teenager, committed suicide after being victimised by peers through text messages and postings on her social network account (Boston Globe, 2010). Patchin and Hinduja, in their study of 2,423 profiles on young adolescents on MySpace, noted the risk-prone behaviour engaged in by many of them – posting of personal information, images and inappropriate content (Patchin and Hinduja, 2010a: 197–216). Policymakers, as a consequence, now have to contend with risks which are not readily visible (Van Asselt, 2005; Jasanoff, 1993). To commentators like Smedinghoff, the safety issues encountered in this area of policymaking are not unique or exceptional (Smedinghoff, 2008). He is right in suggesting that multiple online services and a wide array of communication media platforms create never-ending security problems of integrity, authenticity and reliability (ibid., 19–22; OECD, 2002a). The wide range of platforms for communication, the ease with which information about children can be obtained, the relative low costs for creating, storing and disseminating content and the targeting of potential child victims by online users present policymakers with some hard questions regarding the appropriate mix of direct State intervention, industry self-regulation and individual assumption of personal responsibility. This is hardly a message that policymakers, parents and educators would like to hear – particularly as Web 2.0 technologies continue to be celebrated in glowing terms. Web 2.0 technologies present society with a Faustian bargain. The benefits derived from human-centred computing also bring with it risks of children being exposed to threats and vulnerabilities (OECD, 2002b). The heightened regulatory activity and anxiety about perceived threats facing children in the online environment cannot be disassociated from the role played by the media in shaping public perceptions about the online threat landscape – a testament perhaps to the consequences of living in a post-modern risk society (Beck, 1992a). The Attorney General's reaction is perhaps not an unconventional one. It is also based on some common myths: the online environment is less secure than the offline environment, the safety of children cannot be ensured without a fundamental change in the technical infrastructure and children are less than capable in managing online risks as opposed to offline risks.

Online child safety continues to be a topic that extends beyond the legal domain – children, parents, educators, child welfare organisations and industry are now regarded as having important roles to play in this area of public policy (UN, 2006a). There are some indications that policymakers are beginning to understand how creative use of governance strategies can promote and strengthen the rights of children, in particular, those regarding the freedom to develop and live without fear of violence (Livingstone and Haddon, 2009b). In fairness, policymakers are now increasingly drawing on research and evidence from a number of sources when responding to the governance challenges raised by children's exposure to Web 2.0 technologies (Lenhart *et al.*, 2007a; ACMA, 2009a). Attempts to use the law to enforce legal norms against those using Web 2.0 technologies to distribute illegal or inappropriate content and misusing technologies to solicit minors for sexual gratification and sexual activity and to victimise peers would appear to have been far from a perfect solution to concerns about children's safety in the online environment. Neither will the enactment of more child safety laws and increased surveillance of children and their online activities magically transform the spaces children inhabit into idyllic settings (Jenkins, 2003: 205–21). Many of the governance challenges facing policymakers, particularly in the use of the agency of the State in enforcing its criminal law, can be traced back to decentralised network infrastructures and the indeterminate properties of digital information, which make detection and prosecution difficult (Casey, 2004).

Online child safety governance: Mapping the issues

What is online child safety governance?

The phrase "online child safety governance" can be described as a process whereby various stakeholders now coordinate their activities to promote trust and confidence in children's interaction with individuals and social media. For the purposes of this study, the term "governance" will be used as a counterpoint to regulation by "government" in the sense of describing the process by which three groups of stakeholders engage in the participatory and decision-making processes: (i) those who make the technologies; (ii) those who make consumption of the technologies and services available; and (iii) those who consume the technologies and services. The viability of a Multi-Stakeholder Internet Governance strategy (MSIG) is very much an outcome of the regulatory paradox where

> on the one hand, Europeans want [politicians and institutions] to find solutions to the major problems confronting our societies. On the other hand, people increasingly distrust institutions and politics or are simply not interested in them. (European Commission, 2001: 3)

This approach illustrates how safeguarding children also coheres with the strategy of enhancing trust and confidence in their use of Web 2.0 technologies through dialogue and consultation with civil society (European Commission, 2010e: 15–16). The term "children" will correspond with the definition provided by the UN Convention on the Rights of the Child (UNCRC), namely, individuals who are below the age of 18 years. In this book, the focus will be primarily on the activities of young adolescents, who are within the age group of 13 and 18. With regard to the phrase "online child safety", it will have been observed that there is no comprehensive definition. At best, we can view the phrase as a term of art used to describe the context in which risks and threats to the safety and well-being of minors are encountered (Palfrey *et al.*, 2008). The Online Safety Technical Working Group (OSTWG) adopts a similar view of the phrase "online child safety" by emphasising the safety implications resulting from children's consumption of interactive technologies and social media (OSTWG, 2010: 4). The Byron Report also noted that many of the risks encountered by children should not be seen as being unique or exceptional to the online environment (Byron, 2008: 5). For example, even though peer victimisation through the use of mobile phones or online interactive technologies may suggest that children are exposed to greater risks, this perception may be due to the fact that many of the offline risks experienced by children are migrating to the online environment as communication technologies become mainstream in their daily lives (ibid., 2008: 6). We can, however, agree that online child safety policymaking comprises a "diverse set of issues that are directly or indirectly related to the physical or psychological well-being of children who use digital media" (Gasser *et al.*, 2010: 6). More specifically, these issues originate from the difficulties faced in establishing the nature of electronic communications, verifying the identity of the participants and controlling the flows of communications.

Mapping online child safety issues

It is also important to be mindful of the contingent nature of the issues arising from children's consumption of and exposure to Web 2.0 technologies and social media, since the risks encountered are also influenced by factors like the characteristics of the minors and national and regional variations. The results of the three-year European Union (EU) Kids Online Project (Project) serve as a timely reminder of the need to keep these characteristics in mind when developing policy responses to online safety issues (Livingstone *et al.*, 2009b). The national reports from the 21 European countries who participated in the Project highlighted the effects of variations in cultural attitudes towards adolescent sexuality, risks and parenting on the strategies relied upon by policymakers (Livingstone *et al.*, 2009c: 25–127, 140, 148). To summarise, the term "online child safety" for the purposes of this study can be understood as addressing three categories of information risks faced by children – content, contact and conduct – as noted in *Table 1.1*.

The Australian Government's Consultative Working Group on Cybersafety (CWG), which is an initiative of its Cybersafety Plan, also appears to map the information risks in a similar vein: cyberbullying; inappropriate use of one's own or others' personal information; exposure to and creation of inappropriate content, gaming addiction and sexual predation (CWG, 2010: 13–15). It may be useful to keep in mind that there may be considerable overlaps between actors and information risk categories, and that some of the online activities may be "risk-prone" (e.g. email communications and posting of information online) whilst other activities may be the outcome of children engaging in "risky behaviour" (e.g. sexting, accessing self-harm and suicide websites) (ITU, 2010b: paragraph 78).

This book will adopt the "contact", "content" and "conduct" risks terminology used by the Project with a view to exploring the governance issues raised by children's interaction with the Internet and other communication technologies and the policies, measures and strategies adopted in response. As the Project clearly shows, what is regarded as coming within a high-risk category or as an at-risk individual may not necessarily be

Table 1.1   Online risks

	Commercial	Aggressive	Sexual	Values
Content – *child as recipient*	Advertising, spam and sponsorship	Violence, hate, racist	Pornography and child sexual abuse	Hate, biased or misleading advice
Contact – *child as participant*	Profiling, data mining	Victimisation by peers	Online sexual solicitation	Inappropriate lifestyle choices
Conduct – *child as actor*	Gambling, computer misuse, illegal downloading	Victimising peers	User-generated sexual content	Participant in lifestyle communities (e.g. bulimia, self-harm and anorexia

Source: Adapted from EU Kids Online – Hasebrink *et al.*, 2009.

regarded as such in another country (Livingstone *et al.*, 2009a, b). This is one of many problems that may be faced by those who attempt to provide a comprehensive account of all the online risks encountered by children. From a child protection perspective, a review of the literature from the EU Safer Internet Programme (SIP), and consultation processes in Canada, Australia, the United Kingdom and the United States, suggests that this classification of risks and harms can provide a focal point for governance strategy and development of policies and measures to deal with these – peer victimisation, exposure to illegal or inappropriate content and sexual solicitation. In this study, online child safety governance will be approached from four vantage points: the ongoing and emerging legal and investigatory challenges posed by Internet-related contact, content and conduct risks; the transborder and jurisdictional complexities for regulating Internet sexual abuse and harm; the interaction between civil society and industry and the role of education and safety awareness campaigns as governance instruments.

A number of commentators have examined the regulatory and child protection issues within the discrete domains of peer victimisation, sexual grooming and child pornography and increased our understanding of online child safety (Shariff, 2008; Hinduja *et al.*, 2009; Akdeniz, 2008; Ost, 2009). Akdeniz, in his review of the institutional and regulatory responses, seems less than convinced that great inroads have been made into disrupting the market for the creation, distribution and consumption of child abuse content (Akdeniz, 2008: 278–81). Peer victimisation, which is the subject of Shariff's scholarly work, places the focus on the need to confront the problems at source (e.g. schools) and argues that the legal system should be engaged in a similar process and attend to the unique features of technology-mediated violence (Shariff, 2008: 186). Ost views many of the conundrums surrounding the role of the criminal law in grappling with online sexual predators as being rooted in conceptions of children that perpetuate moral panics and reactive policymaking (Ost, 2009). One of the purposes in writing this book is to assess the extent to which the governance challenges these authors allude to can be explained in part by our ongoing preoccupation with the need to maintain order and certainty, particularly in the lives of children, by virtue of living in a risk society (Beck, 1992a,b). The Internet and communication technologies appear to erode the dominant roles previously played by parents and educators in socialising children (Castells *et al.*, 2007: 161). There is an evolving networked sociability, which is creating new outcomes to the way children develop, socialise and conduct their relations with family, educators, peers and society and consequently

> leads both to an individual-centered network, specific to the individual, and to peer-group formation, when the network becomes the context of behavior for its participants. (ibid., 2007: 144)

Accordingly, the problems of application and compliance in relation to enhancing the safety of children must address this "crisis of the patriarchal" framework that continues to provide the mainstay of childhood (ibid., 2007: 143). The emerging MSIG model best reflects the reconfiguration of the organisational and regulatory milieu, mirrored in continued efforts directed in extending the standards and principles enshrined in the UNCRC to all multiple stakeholders in the "information chain". What is unclear however is how commitment to these values is to be articulated and extended to the various contexts and settings that technological affordances make possible. These aspects receive very little coverage in the accounts by commentators who focus on the strategic role of legal instruments and policy instruments as techniques for regulating online behaviour. Paradoxically, the effectiveness of the legal rules and norms will depend on developing mechanisms that ensure that its standards and principles are fully understood and complied with by all participants in the "information chain" – those who *make* the technologies, those who *consume* technology and those who *make consumption* of the technologies possible. Indeed, it can be hypothesised that the varying competences, knowledge and understanding displayed by children in network publics and their management of information credibility may be relevant to the issue of targeting appropriate safety messages to different age groups and abilities (Flanagin *et al.*, 2010).

The drivers of online child safety policymaking

We cannot fully appreciate the complexity of online child safety governance without an understanding of the diverse factors driving the policy responses and the standard setting agenda pursued by a number of stakeholders (OECD, 2004). The policy issues raised and the responses to them, will incorporate a comparative dimension, using primarily the United Kingdom and countries like the United States, Canada, Australia, where appropriate, to highlight the emerging role of MSIG strategies in addressing some of the shortcomings of national legal systems. As an introduction to the theme of governance – which is developed more fully in later chapters – some understanding of the drivers of online child safety will help us engage more critically with existing international and national policymaking efforts.

The child, the family and the State

The child's safety and its development continue to be associated with the paradigm of the family and the State. These two institutions have long assumed the custodial role of children; the evolving patriarchal framework has provided a fertile ground from which child safety and well-being issues and policies are formulated and implemented. One perennial issue encountered in this area is the constitutional and practical limits on the circumstances when the State can intervene in matters relating to a child's safety and well-being (Archard, 2004). The State, for example, has overall control over the way families and organisations like schools, the private and the public sector and voluntary organisations discharge their obligations towards children (Fortin, 2009). Parents continue to be regarded as having an important role in the development and nurturing of children (Livingstone, 2004a; ACMA, 2007). As the Supreme Court stated in *Morse v Frederick* (2007), both schools and parents have an important role in educating children and preparing them for their participation in society:

> Through the legal doctrine of *in loco parentis*, courts upheld the right of schools to discipline students, to enforce rules, and to maintain order. Rooted in the English common law, in loco parentis originally governed the legal rights and obligations of tutors and private schools... "One of the most sacred duties of parents, is to train up and qualify their children, for becoming useful and virtuous members of society; this duty cannot be effectually performed without the ability to command obedience, to control stubbornness, to quicken diligence, and to reform bad habits... The teacher is the substitute of the parent; ... and in the exercise of these delegated duties, is invested with his power." (2007: 2631–2)

Historically, the benchmark for assessing, developing and implementing child protection policies is the child's best interests. As Baroness Hale observed in *R v Secretary of State for Education and Employment and Others (Respondents) Ex Parte Williamson (Appellant) and Others* (2005):

> Children have the right to be properly cared for and brought up so that they can fulfil their potential and play their part in society. Their parents have both the primary responsibility and the primary right to do this. The state steps in to regulate the exercise of that responsibility in the interests of children and society as a whole. (2005: paragraph 72)

The best interests of the child principle provides a flexible standard that has been used as a foundation for policies and measures aimed at balancing the protective and welfare elements with those of the child's right to autonomy, privacy and self-determination (European Commission, 2011b). It will be observed that many governments demonstrate their commitment to these values as evidenced by States' voluntary subscription to the UNCRC – Article 3 of the UNCRC makes clear that States have a responsibility in ensuring that children's physical and emotional integrity are safeguarded. The online environment does not alter these guiding principles or for that matter the role of the State and parents in fulfilling their obligations in any fundamental respect. Safeguarding children from sexual harm and abuse in the online environment is one of the four priority areas identified by governments in 2002 at the 27th Special Session of the General Assembly on Children (Pinheiro, 2006).

Ongoing tensions

As we seek to fulfil our responsibilities towards children, we need to also acknowledge the complex relations between the State and families, the imprecise boundaries between childhood and adulthood (Madge *et al.*, 2007: 13) and the impact of the media on the role of adults in their relations with children (Prout, 2005: 118–25). The solutions proposed by policymakers and regulators to safeguard children cannot be easily disentangled from the way society has traditionally constructed children and their role in society and which has placed the Judiciary in an invidious position (*FCC v Pacifica Foundation* (1978); *Turner Broadcasting System v FCC* (1994)). Buckingham highlights the presence of not dissimilar tensions, when television and video games became the staple sources of children's entertainment and lifestyle choices (Buckingham, 2007: 76–7). It is not only the content of the broadcasts or media that raise parental anxieties and fears; well before the emergence of the Internet and ubiquitous computing, even public spaces populated by children were problematised (Jenkins, 2003: 26–30; Valentine, 2004: 27). Our traditional preoccupation with children's safety and well-being continue to be shaped by cultural views of childhood and the resulting tensions have never been fully resolved. Furedi, like many scholars who examine the sociology of

childhood, characterises risk-averse attitudes as indicative of our ambivalence towards children and the quest for embedding certainty, security
and order in their lives (Furedi, 2001). Many of the protective and precautionary impulses regarding children's exposure to illegal or harmful content, victimisation by peers and sexual solicitation seem familiar. These
impulses, it should be said, do not discriminate between managing risk
and uncertainty (Van Asselt *et al.*, 2006; Knight, 1921). Consequently,
online child safety discourse appears to focus on addressing the likely
effects of risks materialising rather than those encountered by children
(Van Asselt *et al.*, 2009). History also reminds us that many of the risk
identification and assessment approaches that have been touted by policymakers and authorities have not been infallible (BBC, 2009b, 2010b).
We know, of course, that despite the well-intentioned efforts of parents,
educators and lawmakers, children still continue to be one of the groups
in society who are most vulnerable to sexual abuse and exploitation (UN,
2006b). Victimisation by peers still continues to be the bane of many
children, notwithstanding the many educational and public awareness-
raising campaigns devoted to eradicating this form of deviancy (UN,
2006a). For more than a decade now, these same safety messages about
contact, content and conduct risks and spaces where they have been
located (i.e. playgrounds, school, shopping malls, churches and homes)
are being extended to the spaces inhabited by children in network publics
(Valentine, 2004). For many, the relevance of these safety messages is seen
as being reinforced through media reports of the threat landscape coupled with attitudes towards children's competence and resilience. Stories
about online child predators scouring the Internet, teenagers using the
Internet without parental supervision (BBC, 2009c, 2010a) and risks to
children from exposure to illegal and inappropriate images on websites
(BBC, 2009a) continue to be given prominence by the media and schools
(Grant, 2009). The magnification of children's online activities and society's fascination with their daily online existence has a negative aspect, in
that it tends to fuel a culture of constant regulatory and parental scrutiny
over children's access to and use of the Internet. Consequently, digital
technologies accentuate the tensions that have always existed in the way
the family and the State have been expected to fulfil their obligations
towards children. Enhancing the safety of children is of strategic policy
importance since it prepares them to assume their roles in society as individuals and as citizens (*Bethel School District v Fraser* (1986)). It is worth
remembering that the scope of the best interests of the child principle
may become divisive particularly where the views of young adolescents
relating to the privacy of their online interactions, choices and decisions
diverge from, for example, those of the State and parents (or carers) (*JS v
Bethlehem School District* (2002)).

Structure of the book

Online Child Safety: Law, Technology and Governance directs its focus on the governance challenges raised by the problems of ascertaining the integrity, authenticity and reliability of information flows and network infrastructures for our attitudes towards risks facing children and strategies for enhancing their safety in the online environment. It also seeks to understand the governance challenges facing policymakers and articulates the significance of emerging trends in the way compliance with child safety norms are defined, communicated and enforced. It is often said that the law's role in this area, particularly through the identification of the rules governing acceptable behaviour, has now to be revised in view of the complexity of managing a diverse array of online service providers, applications, and users (Benkler, 2006). This is true, but the significance of the growing visibility of legal standards and the increasing emphasis on the role and continued relevance of UNCRC standards and principles by policymakers and governance should not be underestimated. More importantly, it is not an exaggeration to say that the evolving governance model is well upon us as we witness a range of online child safety policies, strategies and measures being pursued at domestic, regional and international levels, which correspond with the standards and principles embedded in the UNCRC. An understanding of these developments will help provide some clarity and understanding of the MSIG model for safeguarding children. It is beyond the scope of this book to engage in a detailed examination of the cultural, legal, technological and political dimensions of child protection. The topics chosen for this book have been deliberately confined to three areas – online sexual grooming, child pornography and peer victimisation – and primarily situated within the context of England and Wales, so that the governance challenges and responses can be identified and evaluated against those taking place in other jurisdictions. The narrowness of the focus should also enable us to better reflect the online child safety responses to the issues raised by children's interaction with the Internet and communication technologies. Online child safety policymaking is both an intriguing and a distinctive area of study, since most democratic societies adhere to the idea that its regulations are premised on promoting the best interests of children (UN, 2006b; WSIS, 2005). Although the subject of children's rights and the sociology of childhood and child sexual abuse has been the subject of extensive scholarly deliberation and commentary, there has been very little consideration of the way networks and digital information, as pointed out previously, create a trust deficit which consequently implicates all non-State actors and civil society in the "information chain".

The basic argument of the book is that if the strategy of creating sustainable governance models is to be realised, a number of policy objectives will have to be pursued in tandem. First, we need to enable children, parents and educators to manage, as far as possible, the online risks and safety issues at source. Second, whilst it is true that the law is often reactive, in a global and decentralised environment, we need to think more creatively about how best legal standards and principles can be extended to the various actors in the "information chain" so that child safety norms can be embedded into the architecture of the Internet and interactive technologies without compromising the benefits that the end-to-end principle make possible (Lessig, 2004). As commentators like Benkler make clear, software applications and tools can be used to enforce standards and principles:

> The idea is simple to explain, and distinct from a naïve determinism. Different technologies make different kinds of human action and interaction easier or harder to perform. All other things being equal, things that are easier to do are more likely to be done, and things that are harder to do are less likely to be done. All other things are never equal...technology sets some parameters of individual and social action. It can make some actions, relationships, organisations, and institutions easier to pursue, and others harder. (Benkler, 2006:17–18)

Finally, there is a clear need to maintain a perspective when approaching the risks associated with children's interaction with the Internet and communication technologies. It needs to be recognised that in many cases children navigate the online environment safely (Byron, 2010). A number of research policy documents and legal scholars have subjected topics like child pornography, peer victimisation and online sexual solicitation to doctrinal analysis. This book concentrates less on the doctrinal reach of the criminal laws safeguarding children or the normative foundations of non-State actors' participation and regulatory techniques. It instead focuses on how legal rules and judicial interventions together with other regulatory measures provide an overarching strategy aimed at extending standards and principles that enhance the safety of children in the online environment. Too often legal rules and its institutions are viewed as inadequate. Some conversely argue that legal rules have to be extended in dealing with the commercial and sexual exploitation of children in the online environment (Ost, 2009). Others have pointed to the shortcomings in the criminal law in curbing the problem of online peer victimisation and distribution of pornographic user-generated content amongst minors (Shariff, 2008; Akdeniz, 2008). Online child safety provides an invaluable case study of how society as a whole can or should respond to the significance of the trust deficit for policymaking and regulatory efforts. One conclusion reached in this study is that online child safety governance is not a technical or legal problem. Rather, it is in essence a problem of developing and coordinating MSIG strategies aimed at *reducing* the trust deficit that threatens to undermine confidence in children's ability to manage risks as they gain access to and use the Internet. *Online Child Safety: Law, Technology and Governance* offers one perspective of society's response to governance challenges in this area of child protection policymaking. It is also alert to the fact that child protection policies have as one of its aims the better management of online risks – the process of re-examining child safety and security policies and measures also tell us something about how we as a society view, construct and direct our efforts in managing risks in the age of modernity. Indeed, the incident outlined at the start of this chapter seems to suggest that at the root of the governance challenges facing policymakers is our preoccupation with risks and the processes and mechanisms through which society and its institutions attempt to manage them. Law is now only one policy instrument for defining the standards and principles governing individuals behaviour – indeed, it is becoming apparent from the considerable work done by working groups and commissions in the United Kingdom, the EU, the United States and Australia that MSIG strategies can and should be used to secure compliance with legal norms as well as extend it to those spheres of human activity that the law has struggled to regulate (e.g. peer victimisation and the growing practice of sexting).

This book consists of eight chapters. Chapter 2 examines children's engagement with the Internet and interactive technologies and attempts to situate the risks encountered by children within the context of the architecture of the Internet. Attempts to understand child protection policymaking must at a minimum reflect an awareness of the architecture of the Internet and more crucially, the significance of our responses to living in the risk society (Beck, 1992a; Giddens, 1990). More specifically, the significance of the architecture of the Internet for the three risks that concern parents, educators and law enforcement will be explained in the light of societal preoccupation with them: online sexual solicitation, exposure to illegal or inappropriate content and peer victimisation. The premise here is that in seeking to understand online child safety governance as a case study of the role of MSIG as a legal standard setting and compliance framework, we need to address two related matters. First, we need to consider the significance of convergence between technology and youth culture. Second, we need to recognise the extent to which the design characteristics of the Internet can be said to implicate the way we now conceptualise risk and which influence the policy choices, strategies and responses (Giddens, 1991: 123–4; Beck, 1992a: 24). One reason why enforcement and securing compliance with legal standards appears to be problematic is that the free flow of information and the difficulties of authentication and verifiability result in security vulnerabilities operating at different levels and contexts (i.e. networks, virtual worlds, mobile phones, social networking sites and IM) (Casey, 2004). Understanding the role and limits of the law can also be hampered in part by societal attitudes towards risks encountered by children. The chapter concludes with an analysis of the rhetorical significance of concepts like "risk" and "child safety" and describes ways through which discourses on online child safety not only compel responses from policymakers and the law but also reflects evolving parenting and societal attitudes towards children. Notwithstanding the tensions and rhetoric surrounding child protection, the design constraints imposed by the Internet have an added significance, namely, in influencing decisions taken by law enforcement in pre-empting risks and investigating and prosecuting offenders engaged in the sexual exploitation of children. Indeed, one of the issues raised in this chapter is the influence of legal standard setting techniques and UNCRC principles within the MSIG framework.

Chapter 3 looks at some of the legal and investigatory processes that protect children from three particular risks: online sexual grooming, child pornography and peer victimisation. The principal regulatory technique, which forms the focus of this chapter, is the use of the criminal law to proscribe these forms of conduct. An account will be provided of its key rules and principles. A comparison will be made with some of the developments taking place in Australia, the United States and Canada. Often, when issues of managing risk and promoting trust are encountered, the real challenges are not so much to do with the substantive rules but the application of these to varying contexts and the evidentiary and investigatory challenges faced by law enforcement. More importantly, given that the prosecution of individuals of a crime involves, by definition, a criminal act as having taken place (or shown to be imminent), the chapter suggests that, increasingly, information awareness programmes, greater collaboration with the law enforcement authority and industry engagement play an important role in online child safety policymaking. Chapter 4 considers the rationales for rules on extraterritorial criminal jurisdiction. Harmonisation of jurisdiction rules has been put forward as an attractive solution but this is far from being a straightforward process. The chapter concludes that the process of engaging sovereign nations in producing a global commitment towards harmonising child safety rules and norms is not as easy as it might first be thought, particularly as many of the child protection issues also have political, cultural and socio-economic dimensions. Online child safety governance is now a global phenomenon. As Web 2.0 technologies become an integral part of children's education, entertainment and interaction with peers, it seems right that governance strategies be directed towards extending the standards and principles in the UNCRC to all stakeholders at the national, regional and international level. The next three chapters can be regarded as an attempt to sketch this emerging governance landscape. Chapter 5 identifies some of the major developments taking place within three spheres of policymaking: the UN, the EU and the Council of Europe. Particular importance is given to the SIP, emphasising the role political actors can play in extending standard setting rules and norms amongst the various stakeholders in the MSIG framework. Chapter 6 introduces a much-neglected topic in the area of online child safety – the governance aspects of the interaction between the State, civil society and the private sector at the national, regional and international level. Increasingly, the opening up of public deliberative and participatory platforms for interaction between the State, private sector and non-governmental organisations (NGOs) has led to non-State actors and civil society engaging in productive dialogues culminating in the identification of clear strategies for promoting compliance with child safety norms and practices in the online environment (OECD, 2010b). From a policymaking perspective, these interactions illustrate how the converging spaces for governance follow the standard setting agenda of the law (in its expectation of acceptable standards of behaviour towards children) and the UNCRC. The insights gleaned are developed further in Chapter 7, which examines the role and value of media literacy as a legitimate standard setting measure in online child safety policy. Indeed, media literacy has been regarded as an invaluable policy tool in enabling children to better manage risks in the online environment. The chapter explores the concept of media literacy and argues for the need to calibrate our understanding of this measure with the dynamics of network publics and ethical challenges these communities raise for all stakeholders. The particular issue that this chapter highlights and leaves unresolved is that relating to the way children are now to be supported in addressing citizenship and ethical challenges that emerge when participating in network publics or consuming social media. As Ohler correctly observes, our concern with children's interaction with Web 2.0 technologies needs to be set within a broader discourse to "balance the connections and the disconnections offered in digital community and to develop a personal ethical core" (2010: 4). Chapter 8 concludes by summarising the key themes and arguments and assesses their significance for our understanding of online child safety and the evolving MSIG framework for public policy.

2
Regulating Risks and Web 2.0 Technologies: Convergence, Technology and Social Policy

What do news stories of criminal prosecution of individuals involved in on-line paedophile rings, obligations on social networking services providers to address parental anxieties surrounding sexual predatory behaviour on network publics and the Summit on Bullying hosted by the White House have in common? A number of possible answers can be given to this question. One answer may be that it reflects our consciousness about the disorientating features of technology (Ohler, 2010: 77–90). The misuse of technologies taps into our

> primal forces that have been with us for thousands of years. These "forces of the cave," ... range from fearing predators, seeking food and shelter, and nurturing our children to protecting our mate and trusting fellow tribe members. (Dertouzos, 2001: 211)

Another answer might be that these are all responses to the way network infrastructures and information flows distribute risks. These incidents also illustrate how politicians, the mass media, law, industry and society construct and respond to these risks (Garland, 2003). The events do not of course tell us about growing societal preoccupation with enhancing the safety of children in the online environment or even what it is about Web 2.0 technologies and children's interaction with them that bothers us. Neither do they hint at the burdens increasingly shouldered by the State, child welfare organisations, law enforcement, parents and children in managing the security risks accompanying their risk-prone activities (e.g. emails, use of search engines and participation in network publics). The need to be seen to respond to risks in itself becomes a preoccupation of many parents and the communities in which they live. The US President's call for a community response in dealing with one pernicious threat faced by children is emblematic of a perennial dilemma for those living in a risk society. "Risks", as Ulrich Beck defines it, is a "systematic way of dealing with hazards and insecurities induced and introduced by modernization itself" (1992a: 21). This chapter has two objectives. First, it seeks to explain and integrate the salient aspects of Beck's ideas about the risk society into online child safety discourse. In undertaking the task, an attempt will be made to identify how ideas of risk manifest themselves in online child safety policymaking, rule development and discourse. Second, this chapter lays the foundation for subsequent discussions on the standard setting role of law and the extension of its rules, values and norms to all stakeholders with the aim of creating a culture of safe and responsible use of Web 2.0 technologies and social media.

Living in the "risk society"

An overview

Beck identifies risk as a focal point in his study of the impact of the interaction between the State, industry and science on society in late modernity. In *Risk Society: Towards a New Modernity*, he offers us a grand theory, depicting the impact of techno-economic developments on society. He postulates that the risk society is a "catastrophic society" where "averting and managing" risks become norms rather than exceptions (Beck, 1992a: 24). In focusing on the concept of risk, Beck, unlike Marx or Weber, is not particularly interested in addressing the class and economic implications of the capitalist system of production (Lupton, 1999: 1–7). For him, the capitalist modes of wealth creation and distribution not only produce increased benefits and new opportunities for prosperity and development but they also generate negative or destructive outcomes – the logic of wealth creation, he suggests, sets in operation processes by which risks are not only created but they are also distributed to individuals across society. The ideological, technological, economic and political imperatives, which sustain the logic of wealth creation, produce risks that leave no part of society untouched. Beck concludes that advances in technology and science now pose society with a governance dilemma, since we can no longer be concerned

> exclusively with making nature useful, or with releasing mankind from traditional constraints, but also and essentially with problems resulting from techno-economic development itself. (Beck, 1992a: 19)

How society addresses this dilemma is in essence the "risk society" thesis which for our purposes forms very much a part of the challenges confronting the online child safety MSIG framework. Indeed, it is a dilemma that confronts policymakers grappling with the services, products and activities that result from the convergence of networks, communications and information (OECD, 2004). The World Summit on the Information Society (WSIS), in its *Geneva Declaration of Principles*, expressly regards the protection and preservation of children's rights as an important priority in the development of information and communication technology (ICT) applications and operation of services (WSIS, 2003). Paragraph 90 of the *Tunis Agenda for the Information Society* states that the pursuit of economic growth through ICT should also incorporate "regulatory, self-regulatory, and other effective policies and frameworks to protect children and young people from abuse and exploitation through ICTs into national plans of action and e-strategies" (WSIS, 2005). The *Adolescent Declaration to End Sexual Exploitation* emphasises that without appropriate regulatory responses, the threats posed to children are likely to be endemic given

> the continuing high level of sexual exploitation of children and adolescents in States in all regions, and at the increase in certain forms of sexual exploitation of children and adolescents, in particular through abuse of the Internet and new and developing technologies, and as a result of the increased mobility in travel and tourism. (WC III, 2008: paragraph 2)

A failure to respond to risks in a balanced and principled way has undoubted implications for the safety and well-being of individuals and trust generally. As the Organisation for Economic Cooperation and Development (OECD) noted in its policy document, trust is

> one of the central channels through which social identities are constructed in late modernity. Trust is fragile. Typically it is created rather slowly, but it can be destroyed in an instant by a single mishap or mistake. Once trust is lost, it can take a long time to rebuild. In some instances, lost trust may never be regained. (OECD, 2003)

Risks, reflexive modernisation and individualisation

The globalisation of risk with the resulting examination of the governance responses of the State and its institutions for wealth creation is a familiar trope in the discourse on modernity (Lupton, 1999; Beck, 1992a; Giddens, 1990). We will deal with the globalisation of risk in Chapter 6. For present purposes, we need to highlight two other insights from Beck's "risk society" thesis: the techno-economic advances which lead to the emergence of risks and individual and institutional preoccupation with redressing the uncertainty created by its pervasiveness in society (Jarvis, 2007; Giddens, 1991). The emphasis on techno-economic advances is central to Beck's vision of the "risk society" since it allows him to distinguish natural hazards from those categories of risks he regards as man-made (Beck, 1992a: 98). Man-made risks, he suggests, are generated by the logic of wealth creation, and these include pollution, unemployment, accidents in the work environment and breakdown in family and class structures. Sexual exploitation and abuse of children is not a natural hazard but society's preoccupation with child safety issues can be treated as part of Beck's risk paradigm since the regulatory State continues to be one of the proponents in developing responsive regulatory systems (Hood *et al.*, 2001: 4). As Hood, Rothstein and Baldwin remark on the decision by the State to release paedophile ex-offenders from custody:

> What is new about this risk is the degree of recognition and public discussion it has attracted over recent decades... [the] risks presented by released paedophile offenders are of high political and media salience across much of the developed world. Within the UK, that salience contrasts markedly with a lower, albeit growing, level of public attention and concern about child sexual abuse within the home by close family members. (Ibid., 2001: 41)

Faced with the generative nature of risks created by the logic of wealth creation, governments, institutions and individuals are faced with the prospect of being overcome by these negative consequences (ITU, 2009d). Beck argues that society in late modernity is unable to desist from establishing control and reducing the uncertainty that actual (or potential) risks create. However, it may be more accurate to say that government intervention here has to do with fostering public trust and confidence in demonstrating its ability to manage risks. We see Beck's ideas resonate, for example, in the security developments following the atrocities of the terrorists attacks in the United States and London, concerns about nanotechnologies, mad cow disease, severe acute respiratory syndrome (SARS), the anxieties revolving around the increasing sexualisation of young people and release of ex-sex offenders into the community (Wilkinson, 2001; Handmer *et al.*, 2007; Papadopoulos, 2010; Hood *et al.*, 2001: 41–2). Society's desire and need for certainty and control is manifest in the way governments now assume the role as managers of risk through the development of rules and mechanisms for identifying, monitoring and responding to a wide range of risks (Lofstedt, 2005). Individuals and institutions in society engage in what Beck terms as reflexive modernisation; society preoccupies itself with managing risks and becomes constantly dependent on mechanisms which lead to risks being audited, expert advice being sought when formulating policies and measures and regulations being designed to promote compliance with legal standards and obligations (ITU, 2010b; OECD, 2003). There are a number of examples even in the sphere of safeguarding children from commercial sexual exploitation that bring to mind the politicisation of risk and the process of reflexive modernisation taking place. For example, at the World Congress III against Sexual Exploitation of Children and Adolescents (WC III), it was noted that over 129 governments had adopted and ratified the Optional Protocol and an increasing number of countries were ratifying the Optional Protocol to the Convention on the Rights of the Child on the sale of children, child prostitution and child pornography, the International Labour Organisation (ILO) Convention 182, the CPC Convention and Cybercrime Convention (WC III, 2008: paragraph 1). Additionally, a number of countries have prioritised online child safety policies in their national strategies, agendas and plans (ibid., 2008: paragraph 3). We can infer from the politicisation of risk the increasing role played by politicians and civil society in driving forward child safety agendas and risk-based modes of reasoning and policymaking activity (Beck, 1992a: 155–63). For Beck, these are prime examples of risk becoming increasingly secularised and politicised. Risks (and their management) also become very much an important part of public consciousness, particularly as the media provides an increasingly influential avenue through which risks are defined and communicated to a wide audience. Unsurprisingly, in the area of online child safety, the media attention tends to be focused on the extreme edges of technological misuse or "worst-case scenarios" (e.g. online paedophile rings, suicide, self-harm, exposure to pornography and peer victimisation). Such is the anxiety that is generated that "we are left to wonder what else happens in the largely invisible world of the infosphere" (Ohler, 2010: 141). Managing risk in modernity becomes a reflexive process where the development of prudential and precautionary measures is seen as an ongoing process where the agency of political institutions becomes prominent in governance since

> questions of the development and employment of technologies (in the realms of nature, society and the personality) are being eclipsed by questions of the political and economic "management" of the risks of actually or potentially utilized technologies – discovering, administering, acknowledging, avoiding or concealing such hazards with respect to specially defined horizons of relevance. The promise of security grows with the risks and destruction and must be reaffirmed over and over again to an alert and critical public through cosmetic or real interventions in the techno-economic development. (Beck, 1992a: 19–20)

These last references to the "promise of security", the need for affirmation, and a public highly attuned to risks and the "cosmetic" nature of some of the interventions have a lasting impact on the sense in which "risk-based" regulation is understood: the distinction between actual and perceived risks becomes blurred and consequently contributes to society's continued anxiety about managing risks. Increasingly, the governance question is framed not in terms of whether online risks facing children should be regulated but what risk-based systems facilitate deliberative and participatory processes that enable the child safety policies and standards to be attained without compromising public trust (Graham, 2010: 244–5). The latter is particularly relevant as information networks and Web 2.0 technologies are seen as producing risks and benefits that affect certain groups of individuals in society disproportionately. One reason for the "irrationality" of individual's responses to risks in society, sometimes characterised as "moral panics", is that techno-economic developments also transform structures and systems that have previously been regarded as frameworks for security and stability (i.e. welfare state, agrarian society and feudal structures). The transition from "industrial" to "risk society" and the resulting loss in public trust and confidence in the State and its institutions is seen as leading to individuals assuming a greater role in managing their own safety and well-being (Beck, 1992a: 101; 1992b: 127–37). As Beck points out:

> Risk Society begins where tradition ends, when, in all spheres of life, we can no longer take traditional certainties for granted. The less we can rely on traditional securities, the more risks we have to negotiate. The more risks, the more decisions and choices we have to make. (Beck, 1998: 10)

The individualisation of risk subjects everyone in society to turbulence and social conflicts in varying degrees (Beck, 1992a: 134–5). The central point here is not that late modernity creates more risks, rather the changes wrought by technological advances create conditions, which lead to an individual's heightened awareness of risks and the quest for effective responses (Giddens, 1991: 123–4).

The emerging MSIG strategy

The International Telecommunication Union (ITU) in its 2009 Report highlighted the rapid penetration of ICTs across societies (ITU, 2009a). Individuals and organisations now have access to not only a range of information but also a wealth of computing applications. These developments have not escaped the attention of policymakers and governments. For example, under the *Digital Agenda for Europe*, electronic communications are seen as a necessary medium for creating a sustainable and inclusive economy (European Commission, 2010a). It is expected that broadband technology and online services will be made available to all Europeans by 2013 (European Commission, 2010b). Many homes now have access to online networks and the availability of multimedia services is now transforming the way information is accessed (ACMA, 2009a). Under Canada's Economic Action Plan, $225 million was provided to Industry Canada to increase broadband connectivity to areas not currently served (Government of Canada, 2011). The US National Broadband Plan views the networked economy as critical to improving domestic economic and social conditions and global competitiveness (FCC, 2011). The networked economy is seen as central to providing businesses, organisations and individuals with considerable opportunities, but these flows of networked information also bring with it vulnerabilities and threats that undermine trust and confidence

(Garland, 2003; Giddens, 1991). These threats and risks are not immediately identified since they exist in multiple communication platforms and in environments of collapsing national and international boundaries. The transition to a risk society also has important consequences for the way risks generated have now to be managed. For example, governments now have to assess, manage and regulate risks in society (Beck, 2002). Individuals in society, for example, are also vested with the responsibility for managing their affairs as traditional insurance and social infrastructures for maintaining cohesion are gradually loosened. The distinctive features of online safety risks are that the "producers", "managers" and "protesters" of risks are in effect the State, the ICT industry and, indirectly, educators and parents who make the products and services available to children (Van Asselt *et al.*, 2009: 360). This characterisation is important since many of the stakeholders assume an important role in the governance process and make decisions on the risk management strategies to be adopted. At the high level of regulatory theory a number of developments have taken place, which have undoubted implications for the way policymakers think about online child safety governance issues. In Canada, a policy document was produced to look at the effects of risk-based regulation (Government of Canada, 2004). Others have defined risk-based governance in terms of the barriers to developing innovative regulatory responses. Policymakers in the European Commission highlighted the role of the precautionary principle as a touchstone for managing risks in conditions of uncertainty (European Commission, 2000). With children's increased exposure to Web 2.0 technologies, policymakers have also framed responsive risk governance in terms of worst-case scenarios – peer victimisation, children meeting sexual predators, exposure to illegal and age-inappropriate content and children accessing self-harm and suicide websites. These risks are understandably difficult to quantify and, consequently, provide the justification for pursuing reflexive regulatory strategies and measures. The reflexive responses underscore the heightened awareness of the scale and complexity of managing risks and anxiety and the need to ensure that risk management becomes an ongoing policy-making priority. There is concern that such anxieties, if left unchecked, may lead to overregulation or result in policymakers targeting individuals or organisations to assume greater responsibility for managing these risks (Sunstein, 2007). From a governance perspective, prioritising the regulatory agenda becomes a legitimate objective. For example, in response to the growing concerns about the impact of online security threats on user trust and confidence, the Australian government has undertaken a series of studies with the aim of identifying priority areas for risk management (ACMA, 2009c,d). Governments now regard encouraging parents and educators to supervise the activities of children aged 5–7 as a legitimate child safety objective (ITU, 2009b,c). Broadcasters, the Internet industry, Internet service providers (ISPs) and online service providers are encouraged to implement design, technological and educational solutions (ITU, 2009d). Policymakers are provided with statistical indicators of risk-prone activities and risk-prone behaviours, which identify areas for regulatory activity and policymaking (ITU, 2009e). Consequently, we end up subscribing to the

> mean world syndrome [which] says that, because of the media's attraction to reporting the worst in human nature, people think the world is much more violent and dangerous than it actually is. It is certainly more dangerous than how most of us experience it. (Ohler, 2010: 143)

It follows from the preceding discussion that the resulting institutionalisation of risk now brings into the regulatory landscape non-State actors. ISPs, online service providers, mobile phone operators and NGOs are regarded as having important obligations and roles in online child safety governance (Klinke, 2009: 403–4). The Byron Report neatly encapsulates the significance of the individualisation of risks facing children by its three governance objectives:

> Reduce Availability – Reduce the availability of harmful and inappropriate content, the prevalence of harmful and inappropriate contact and the conduciveness of platforms to harmful and inappropriate conduct.
>
> Restrict Access – Equip children and their parents to effectively manage access to harmful and inappropriate content, avoid incidences of harmful and inappropriate contact and reduce harmful and inappropriate conduct.
>
> Increase Resilience – Equip children to deal with exposure to harmful and inappropriate content and contact, and equip parents to help their children deal with these things and parent effectively around incidences of harmful and inappropriate conduct by their children. (Byron, 2008: 62)

Accordingly, as will be discussed in subsequent chapters, the responsibility for assessing and communicating risks will be directed at sector-specific industries (e.g. social networking sites, computer manufacturers, mobile phone providers, and ISPs). The gradual widening of the channels for risk management and allocation brings into the multi-stakeholder governance model a range of regulatory techniques for managing risks: private and public law, insurance and codes of practice. Even though Beck's thesis is not without its critics, his contribution, however, is important for our understanding of how and why risk-based regulation has become a defining characteristic in online child safety governance. We will examine some of the dynamics of risk-based governance systems in Chapter 7. The first matter to be considered is the extent to which the end-to-end design principle creates the techno-economic and social conditions that lead to policymakers defining the roles and obligations of the stakeholders within the MSIG framework.

Children, Web 2.0 technologies and social media

Even though this is not a book about the protocols and architecture of the Internet, some appreciation of its function and design principles is necessary if we are to begin to understand the relationship between the logic of information flows, the new channels for risk distribution and anxieties about children's safety and well-being and the attainment of the three governance objectives. To this end, the discussion will address three aspects in turn: the design and architecture of communication technologies, convergence between youth culture and technology and the policy implications arising from the interaction between the technical infrastructure and design, online security threats and risks and governance challenges.

Design principles and the architecture of the Internet

The Internet is first and foremost a complex network of computers. The original designers of the Internet were not concerned with providing virtual worlds, social networking sites, web streaming or email services (Castells, 1997). Their challenge was to develop protocols that allowed networks to connect with each other (Berners-Lee *et al.*, 2000). As Werbach makes clear:

> Unlike traditional communications networks, the Internet does not provide a particular kind of service. Its designers set out not to deliver content, but to interconnect networks (hence the name Inter-net). Neither services offered nor physical infrastructure nor geographic location determine whether something is part of the Internet. (2002: 47)

This extract highlights two particular aspects with regard to the interaction between the architecture of the Internet and its design principles. First, the design principles and architecture can be likened to providing engineers and programmers with tools and a medium through which information can be disseminated across networks and represented as text, images and sound. The fundamental design principles shaping much of the work undertaken by these individuals in creating a technical communications infrastructure were those of interoperability, decentralisation and non-discrimination – the information space was to be an environment that was capable of being accessed by anyone, from any country and from any computer or communication device (Berners-Lee, 2000: 37; Table 2.1). As we will discover later, the technological affordances and the channels through which information flows can now be accessed owe much to the priority given to design rather than security principles (Dertouzos, 2001: 209). Security principles, like those relating to confidentiality, integrity, authenticity and availability,

Table 2.1 Tim Berners-Lee design principles for the World Wide Web

An information system must be able to record random associations between any arbitrary objects
If two sets of users started to use the system independently, to make a link from one system to another should be an incremental effort, not requiring unscalable operations such as the merging of link databases
Any attempt to constrain users as a whole to the use of particular languages or operating systems was always doomed to failure
Information must be available on all platforms, including future ones
Any attempt to constrain the mental model users have of data into a given pattern was always doomed to failure
If information within an organization is to be accurately represented in the system, entering or correcting it must be trivial for the person directly knowledgeable

Source: http://www.w3.org/People/Berners-Lee/1996/ppf.html.

are concerned with managing the flow of information so that the right information is made available to the right persons, at the right time and at the right place (OECD, 2002a).

The design principles are reflected in the "protocols" now used by on-line intermediaries and mobile phone companies to provide users with opportunities to exchange information and view or experience social media on a variety of platforms (Lane, 2008). "Protocols" are rules, which enable networks to connect with each other. The Internet is in essence based on a number of protocols known as the Transmission Control Protocol/Internet Protocol (TCP/IP). Accordingly, the adoption of protocols enables files to be transferred, emails to be sent and information in all forms to be stored and disseminated. The TCP/IP protocols can be categorised into four functional groups or layers, which enable users to exchange content over networks (Table 2.2). These relate to Content, Application, Transport, Internet protocol, Link and Physical properties like cables and wires (Solum *et al.*, 2004).

Second, many of the innovations and developments that we see today (i.e. Smartphone, portable media devices and multimedia communication platforms) can be traced back to the design principles and the architecture of the Internet (OECD, 2008a). The development of software applications and ready availability of broadband connectivity has contributed greatly to the emergence of a vibrant communication ecosystem (ITU, 2009a; OECD, 2010a). P2P file-sharing technologies, voice over Internet protocols (VOIP), wireless connectivity, mobile applications, cloud computing and next generation mobile phones enhance economic and social activities by enabling individuals and organisations to access, create, store and distribute information. Social networking sites like Facebook, Bebo and MySpace enable

Table 2.2   The layer principles

Application layer

There are user protocols aimed at providing users with online services.

Examples include services for remote login (Telnet), transfer of files (FTP), sending email (SMTP) and exchange of information between a web client and web server through HyperText Transfer Protocols (HTTP)

Other examples of applications include voice over internet protocols, P2P file-sharing applications and web browsers (e.g. Firefox and Internet Explorer)

There are support protocols which address system functions

Transport layer

This layer provides end-to-end communication services for applications.

The Transmission Control Protocol (TCP) provides a connection-oriented transport service

The User Datagram Protocol (UDP)

Internet layer

The Internet Protocol (IP) enables any set of hosts to exchange data packets.

Internet Protocol version 4 (IPv4)

Internet Protocol version 6 (IPv6)

Internet Protocol Security (IPsec)

Link layer

A link layer protocol enables communications on directly connected networks. For example, organisations may have local area networks which implement standards like Ethernet

---

Source: RFC 1122, Available at http://datatracker.ietf.org/doc/rfc1122.

information to be freely accessed, exchanged and created. It is hard not to notice that at the core of the Internet and the evolution of Web 2.0 technologies is the belief that innovation, creativity and freedom of expression thrive best in an environment of free markets, entrepreneurial endeavour and minimal State intervention (Benkler, 2006). As Zittrain recalls:

> From its start, the Internet was oriented differently from the proprietary networks and their ethos of bundling and control. Its goals were in some ways more modest. The point of building the network was not to offer a particular set of information or services like news or weather to customers, for which the network was necessary but incidental. Rather, it was to connect anyone on the network to anyone else. It was up to the people connected to figure out why they wanted to be in touch in the first place; the network would simply carry data between the two points. (2008: 27)

It is not an exaggeration to say that without the four functional layers and its underpinning design principles, we would not have seen the acceleration of a networked society comprising online intermediaries, network operators and commercial product manufacturers (OECD, 2010a). Neither, it should be said, would the absence of the functional layers have created the necessary incentive structures for the ICT industry, online services providers and mobile operators to make available products and services which mirrored consumers' need for immediacy, intimacy, community and information (Lane, 2008: 5–7).

The advances in communication technologies and the ubiquity of computing represent an important paradigm shift in the way the logic of sustaining information flows frames economic, technological and cultural activity (Castells *et al.*, 2007). Mobile phones, for example, now come packaged with software applications, widgets and Wireless Application Protocol (WAP) that have standard web technology components to enable users to engage with the others in online environment (Lane, 2008). One study forecasts not only the growth of mobile social networks but it is also expected that this trend will culminate in transforming the way individuals in society will interact and communicate (ibid., 2008: 15). The OECD Working Party on Telecommunication and Information Services Policy observed that "[c]onvergence in electronic communications is bringing together industries in the communications area which were previously viewed as separate in both a commercial and technological sense, and which have quite distinct regulatory traditions and arrangements" (OECD, 2004: 5).

Convergence in broadcasting, telecommunication and entertainment impacts a wide range of economic and social activities. Consequently, governments and regulators continue to be alert to the public interest issues raised by the ubiquitous computing environment (Schewick, 2010: 20–2, 37–8). Many child safety issues are increasingly linked to the governance implications arising from the ICT industry and online services providers leveraging the capabilities of networks and telecommunications. Children's consumption of new technologies now provides a catalyst for a whole range of technical issues confronting online intermediaries, the Internet Engineering Task Force and the World Wide Web Consortium (W3C) (WGIG, 2005). From a child protection perspective, the interaction between children's consumption habits and the individualisation of risks has also led to a re-examination of how risks can be better managed by the ICT industry and related online service providers (WSIS, 2003). With the convergence of the broadcasting and telecommunication sectors and the emergence of new online services providers, risk-based regulation efforts continue to be directed at promoting sector-specific assessments, standard setting initiatives and improving compliance (ITU, 2009d; WSIS, 2005). This process of reflexive modernisation is depicted in the technical literature as the end-to-end arguments. In a highly influential paper written in the early 1980s, the question of how applications should be incorporated into the technical infrastructure of the Internet was addressed, with the recommendation that the application-level functions be built into the high levels, rather than the lower levels of the system on the basis that

> the function in question can completely and correctly be implemented only with the knowledge and help of the application standing at the end-points of the communications system. Therefore, providing that questioned function as a feature of the communications systems itself is not possible. (Saltzer *et al.*, 1984: 278)

The allocation of specific applications and services away from the core of the system were seen as reducing the demands on the lower-level system and ensuring efficiency, reliability and flexibility gains (Blumenthal *et al.*, 2001: 71). Despite the seeming elegance and simplicity of the end-to-end argument, the premise is clear: the logic of information flows is seen as requiring, if not compelling, the end points (i.e. those who make the technology to be consumed, those who make consumption of online services and technology possible and those who consume the technology and services) to assume ultimate responsibility for managing and allocating responsibility for risks. For example, under the end-to-end principle, the architecture of the Internet in effect vests the responsibility for managing risks, to varying degrees, with the various participants in the information chain. Recall that the applications are situated at the core of the Internet's technical infrastructure and, consequently, the functional layers do not discriminate as to the type of content being sent and neither do the information flows make the characteristics of the senders and recipients immediately discernible to end users. The end-to-end principle, as originally formulated, can also be seen as reflecting an ideological preference for limited State intervention, with market rules and norms being seen as appropriate instruments for regulating the telecommunications and broadcasting industry. The debates that we now witness in online child safety governance regarding the role of online intermediaries involves, in essence, an argument about how the negative consequences of information flows are to be managed by the existing framework for regulating telecommunication services across network infrastructures and content that can be accessed from these platforms. For example, mobile phones and Smartphones now incorporate a bundle of software applications into their hardware. The aim of these measures is to provide consumers with a wide range of services and access opportunities. With these benefits and mindful of the end-to-end principle, mobile and online content service providers are now vested with the responsibility of ensuring that the information accessed through their products and services correspond with national content standards and policies (ITU, 2009d). The end-to-end principle also confronts policymakers with difficult choices regarding the outcomes of managing the uncertain nature of convergence, the speed and scale of convergence and the individualisation of risks (OECD, 2004:14). Risks in short are now socialised and engender a continued process of reflexive modernisation as part of the MSIG strategies in the area of regulatory policy, national coordination and legislative activity (ITU, 2009e).

The digital natives' landscape

The exponential growth of the Internet is transforming the way individuals and in particular children, now interact with communication technologies and social media (Negroponte, 1995: 200–2). Commentators like Livingstone and Bovill have remarked on the significance of the growing convergence between youth culture and technology (Livingstone, 2003b; Bovill *et al.*, 2001). These technologies have become an integral part of children's daily lives and activities (ACMA, 2009b; Ipsos Mori, 2009). The European Commission's *Safer Internet Plus Programme* has funded projects examining the online experiences of children from 21 Member States (European Commission, 2011b: 9). The EU Barometer Surveys in 2005 and 2008 showed that in 2005, 70 per cent of 6 to 17-year-olds in the countries were using the Internet (Eurobarometer, 2005, 2008). By 2008, this number had increased to 75 per cent, with the finding that 60 per cent of children aged between 6 and 10 years were online. Another view of convergence is that communication technologies now enable individuals to interact with each other without the traditional constraints of time, distance and space. Ubiquitous and mobile computing now free individuals from the traditional physical constraints associated with interaction and consumption of social media (Castells *et al.*, 2007: 127–46). As Ito remarks, technological affordances allow children to take full advantage of participating in network publics and negotiate their identities (Ito *et al.*, 2008). Children aged 5 to 12 years not only spend an increasing amount of their leisure activity online but they also use a range of media platforms to access information, play games and interacted with their peers (Staksrud *et al.*, 2010). The Office of Communications (OfCom) noted that during the past five years there had been a gradual transformation in the way young children interacted with social media and technology (OfCom, 2009). Growing interoperability at the application or device levels and the consolidation of telecommunications, media and entertainment have contributed to this shift in children's engagement with technology and their environment. Similar trends have been noted in developed economies outside the EU, including America, Canada and Australia. In the *Digital Futures Report 2010*, consumption of the Internet and communication technologies by Americans was shown to increase as the age decreased (Centre for Digital Futures, 2010). In an extensive study examining the online behaviours of children (grades 4 to 11) in Canada, between 2003 and 2005, communication technologies were found to be well and firmly embedded in children's daily lives:

> Young people, on the other hand, do not see the Net as a distinct entity or environment. It is simply one more space in which they live their lives – connecting with friends, pursuing interests, figuring out what it means to be a teenager and a grown up. (Media-Awareness, 2005)

The Australian Bureau of Statistics (ABS) identified similar trends in its study *Children's Participation in Cultural and Leisure Activities* (ABS, 2009). It was found that Internet use and frequency of use also increased with age. For example, during April 2008–09, 96 per cent of young adolescents (aged 12–14) accessed the Internet, in contrast to only 60 per cent of five- to eight-year-olds; Internet access was now available to children at home, school and elsewhere (79 per cent), and the activities for which the Internet were used included education (85 per cent), playing online games (69 per cent) and downloading music (47 per cent).

Design, cultural convergence and the genres of participation

What is "cultural convergence"?

Terms like "digital generation", "mobile youth" and "digital natives" form very much a part of popular discourse on children and their interaction with new technologies (Rideout *et al.*, 2007). In essence, these terms attempt to capture a radical transformation in children's interaction with their environments in contemporary society (Prout, 2005; James *et al.*, 1998). At a basic level, "convergence" in the age of mobile computing can be viewed as the coming together of information, media and communication. Convergence can also be viewed more expansively (Jenkins, 2006). As many commentators have pointed out, Web 2.0 technologies are imbued with social and cultural meanings (Benkler, 2006). According to Jenkins, convergence

> represents a paradigm shift – a move from medium-specific content toward content that flows across multiple media channels, toward the increased interdependence of communications systems, toward multiple ways of accessing media content, and toward ever more complex relations between top-down corporate media and bottom-up participatory culture. (2006: 243)

Jenkins' description frames the discourse on network publics and technological affordances well. There is of course a "qualitative change in users' experience of everyday life… [which results in a]… technosocial sensibility" (Castells *et al.*, 2007: 141). Cultural convergence can also be represented in another way. Benkler observes that participatory cultures deviate from the norm of hierarchical and centralised models for coordinating interactions and a key aspect of this improvement

> has been the technical–organizational shift from an information environment dominated by commercial mass media on a one-to-many model, which does not foster group interaction among viewers, to an information environment that both technically and as a matter of social practice enables user-centric, group-based active cooperation platforms of the kind that typify the networked information economy. (Benkler, 2006: 357)

Childhood in 2012 is lived in spaces created by information networks. Children's use of mobile phones, the meanings attributed to the building of extensive "friend" lists and the use of social network profiles as tools for self-presentation and admission into online communities are manifestations of what life in a networked society means for individuals, particularly children (ibid., 356–8). The role of Web 2.0 technologies in enhancing children's autonomy has also marked an important shift in what Senft describes as a growing culture of gossip, self-branding and sexual display as leitmotifs of children's fascination with new technologies, social media and celebrity culture (Senft, 2008). Cultural convergence also shapes the way children engage and participate in these environments – not as passive actors but as autonomous individuals with their own identities, preferences and values (Herring, 2008: 71–92). There is perhaps a sense of a new sociability where children now exercise their newfound autonomy through "consumerism, faddish trends, cultural identity, peer-group formations, relationship with existing social institutions" (Castells *et al.*, 2007: 142) Creative uses of technologies have been used to promote civic participation and critical media literacy skills (Goldman *et al.*, 2008: 185–206). Mobile phones now embed these preferences and tastes so as to enable children to enjoy and experience a range of social and cultural opportunities. A study, focusing on the lives of children aged between 8 and 18, found that ownership of mobile phones and Smartphones amongst this group of consumers was on the rise (Rideout *et al.*, 2010). For many children, mobile phones open up opportunities for engaging with their communities, participating in support networks, and entertainment (Ling, 2008: 43, 58, 77). Teenagers use mobile phones for texting, taking pictures and accessing online content. "Cultural convergence", according to Stald, has elevated the wisdom of peer participatory cultures and norms:

> Because of the always there, always on status of the mobile and the pace of exchange of information, and because the mobile is the key personal communication device for so many young people, it becomes important

in establishing social norms and rules and in testing one's own position in relation to the peer group. (Stald, 2008: 143–64)

Her findings correspond very much with the ongoing work by Ling on mobile phone use. In his research, Ling rejects any suggestion that mobile phone use is "exceptional" or novel; rather, he sees the mobile phone as a tool through which ritual social interactions and social bonding take place (Ling, 2008). Communication technologies are instruments for expression, cultural interaction and identity experimentation (Stern, 2007). In her study involving the use of communication technologies by adolescent girls, Stern noted that IM tools were not simply tools for transmitting information or content but that they were also utilised to create communities and establish norms of behaviour. There is also a sense, in reviewing the studies from the Kaiser Family Foundation and the Pew Internet & American Life, that young children view interactive technologies as private communication spheres where intrusions by parents and other persons are kept to a minimum (Rideout *et al.*, 2010; Lenhart *et al.*, 2008). Social networking, regardless of whether it takes place on a mobile phone or personal computer, is the digital equivalent where children

> hang out, jockey for social status, work through how to present themselves, and take risks that will help them to assess the boundaries of the social world. They do so because they seek access to adult society. Their participation is deeply rooted in their desire to engage publicly. (boyd, 2007: 137)

Finally, convergence allows individuals to engage with information, content and users anytime and anywhere – the de-centralisation of networks of communication infrastructure also creates new spaces for communication and interaction (and one which as a consequence erodes the dominant roles of parents and educators and leads to the blurring of the boundaries between childhood and adulthood).

Convergence, participatory cultures and genres of participation

Convergence can also be said to represent a cultural phenomenon comprising not only of participation but also a whole range of activities, which include interaction, formation of relationships, identity expression, community support, and engagement in creative activities (Livingstone, 2005a; Table 2.3).

Discussion forums, IM and social networking sites now provide children with opportunities to form communities and engage with their peers and persons they meet online (Livingstone, 2008b). Many social networking sites have taken advantage of the design and architectural principles to create innovative features on their platforms, by incorporating video, chat and IM facilities. Identity expression, experimentation and peer acceptance are

Table 2.3 Participatory cultures and genres of participation

	MMORPG/virtual worlds	Blogs	SNS	Chat/IM/mobile
Content – *child as recipient*	Identity media literacy and strategic thinking	Identity media literacy	Identity media literacy, writing skills and creativity	Identity media literacy and strategic thinking
Contact – *child as participant*	Social communication	Building communities and relationships	Relationships and social interaction	Social interaction/collaboration
Conduct – child as actor	Citizenship Skills and values	Support peers	Social communication content	Citizenship Skills and values

Source: drawing on AMF, 2009 and EU Kids Online, 2009

very much in evidence in the way children use these sites to interact with each other. Disclosure of information is regarded as part of the process of gaining access to online communities and interacting with others. For example, social network sites allow users opportunities to disclose a range of personal information – identity, age, gender, and address. The decision to disclose personal information like screen names, preferences and contact details may be based on a number of factors: the perception of relative safety of the online communication platform, opportunities to make friends and share similar interests, identity experimentation, anonymity, the accessibility of tools for managing risks and the absence of parents and educators in these communication spaces (Lenhart and Madden, 2007c). Social networking sites also fulfil the need of users to define their communities and to be connected with others. Consequently, search directory services provide individuals with opportunities to seek out friends and lifestyle interests. Identity and sexual experimentation is also very much a part of the network sociability, and the transition from adolescence into adulthood. To some children, the anonymised and disintermediated environment provides them with an opportunity to experiment with different persona and lifestyle experiences. Others use the online environment to seek assistance and support from their peers (Livingstone *et al.*, 2011). Whilst chat and IM create invaluable spaces for social interaction and learning, the Youth Internet Safety Survey 2 reported that children were also using communication platforms and tools to assert their autonomy and identity by engaging in discussions about sexual preferences and lifestyles (Mitchell *et al.*, 2007c).

This overview of the rich participatory culture, which defines childhood in the networked society, contains three important lessons for risk-based governance. First, the very same activities, which are celebrated by Web 2.0 enthusiasts, are regarded as potentially risk-prone activities, even though these may not be readily quantifiable (Asselt *et al.*, 2006). Second, the framing of the "risk-prone" behaviour will inform online child safety governance policymaking and strategies (Mitchell *et al.*, 2007a,b). Third, social constructions of childhood will influence the expansion of the precautionary principle to address not only risks but the resulting "uncertainties" surrounding children's risk-prone behaviour, and perhaps confirm the politicised nature of online child safety governance (James *et al.*, 1997). The latter is of particular relevance as politicians and law enforcement may respond to public concerns about the effects of particular harms and risks by seeking the private sector to communicate and justify their risk management strategies and responses.

It may be useful to spend some time reflecting on how Web 2.0 technologies and affordances lead to businesses and industry becoming "risk producers" and agents in the distribution and individualisation of risk (Van Asselt *et al.*, 2009: 359–60; Table 2.4). In a highly competitive environment, the business models of social network providers like Twitter, Facebook and MySpace and the mobile phone industry recognise the value of innovation. Online service providers and manufacturers of new technologies align their services with the needs of their users. For example, mobile phone operators

Table 2.4   Technological affordances and network publics

Category	Description	Features which are most frequently used	Text	Photo	Video	App
Friending	Forming communities and making friends, sharing interests, and lifestyles	Profile pages, search directory, linking to social media, interactive communication and browsing	Post View	Post View	Post View	
Identity lifestyle	Experimentation, Sharing offline/online experiences friendships, risk taking, creativity, exhibitionism	Games, rating, browsing, use of social and interactive media, updating of profiles, extending friendship circles, gossip, alert features	Post View			

Source: Adapted from Lane, 2008: 10.

now ensure that their services and devices "avoid overcrowding or creating overly complex user interfaces" (Lane *et al.*, 2008).

Mobile phones continue to be packaged with software applications which, allow users to send SMS texts and take photographs with ease. Virtual worlds have become popular online environments for many children. These are applications that leverage the architecture of the Internet and provide users with an online environment. Users of these applications can interact with each other through a persona, known as avatars, and communicate through the use of text and icons. Virtual worlds have also expanded to provide users with entertainment and games, which can involve a large number of players not confined to any particular geographical locality. In a recent report it was stated that more than $1.38 billion was invested in 87 virtual goods-related companies. According to the Virtual World Management (now Engage Digital Media), there are over 200 youth-oriented virtual worlds (which includes those which are planned or in active development).[1] The figures show an increase, when compared with 150 virtual worlds in 2008. The growth area appears to be in the market for children with three sub-categories represent-ing the age groups 7 and below, 8 to 12 and 13 and above. Some examples of virtual worlds for children include Club Penguin, Webkinz, Barbie Girls, Moshi Monsters, Lego Universe and Adventure Rock. The demographics of these sites suggest that the reasons children access these sites are not dissimilar to those we have seen in other mobile social networking environments (Lim *et al.*, 2010). Children are provided with tools to enable them to participate in communities, share interests and make friends, develop their identity and create user-generated content (Jackson *et al.*, 2009; Marsh, 2010).

In summary, the logic of network infrastructures and information flows illustrate the democratic, developmental and social opportunities that Web 2.0 technologies make possible. These are evident in three areas. First, technological affordances create new spaces for communication. Second, communication tools are imbued with social and cultural meaning and these are reflected in the way users negotiate social norms, relationships and their individual identities. Finally, children can exercise their new-found autonomy, which may not be hindered or governed by parental rules and norms. Integrity, reliability and authenticity are assumed to be the ne-cessary pre-requisites for engagement, affirmation and self-validation. Web 2.0 technologies provide society, and children in particular, greater choices and opportunities. More significantly, in the light of Beck's risk society, the expanding networked society now has in place the necessary conditions, which enable risks to be distributed, communicated and individualised. Individualisation also brings with it a heightened awareness of the risks that are generated from engagement with digital content and network pub-lics. More importantly, as children now discover their newfound autonomy, it is important to note that they still continue to engage in these activities within a patriarchal society, which considers them to be vulnerable, risk-prone and which, crucially, defines the rules within which these freedoms are to be enjoyed (Castells *et al.*, 2007: 146–7). In the next section we will identify the different dimensions of risks, how these are related to Web 2.0 technologies and its implications for child protection policymaking.

Online child safety: The individualisation of risks, reflexive modernisation and insecurity

The unexceptional nature of online child safety

Palfrey and Gasser stress that the online environment does not raise any novel safety or child protection issues – indeed, they argue that parents' and educators' perceptions of the online environment as being more dangerous could be attributed to their lack of familiarity with the Internet infrastructure and communication technologies (Palfrey *et al.*, 2008). Whilst not averse to informed parenting and rule making, the authors stress that many of the online risks and threats have their offline equivalents and the root causes for contact and conduct risks are "poor judgment, a lack of concern for the well-being of others, human depravity, mental illness, and so forth" (ibid., 2008: 98).

Policymakers are, however, confronted with an unenviable conundrum when faced with assertions like these (ITU, 2010). Regulating the communications and broadcasting industry is challenging at the best of times, given the volume and reach of many of the risk-prone activities (e.g. email, SMS text, online gaming, social networking) that make children particularly susceptible to online threats. Risk-prone activities include not only the amount of time children spend online but also those risks which emerge from their engagement with technological affordances and social media (Lenhart, 2007). The ABS in its 2009 Children's Participation in Cultural and Leisure Activities (CPCLA) Survey reported that 2.7 million children aged 5 to 14 years (7 per cent) used the Internet (ABS, 2009). Their online activities included educational activities (85 per cent) and playing online games (69 per cent). These activities are also related to their exposure to online risks or suggestive of their tendency to engage in risky online behaviours. In this same study, an estimated 3 per cent of children who accessed the Internet reported experiencing online safety incidents (e.g. approximately 72,000 children). Three per cent of children who have mobile phones (28,000 children) reported similar negative experiences. Sixty-five per cent of teenagers have been contacted by online users not in their peer group (Lenhart *et al.*, 2007a: 35), and 31 per cent have "friends" whom they have never met, 34 per cent use the sites to make new friends (ibid., 2007a: 32), 4 per cent of mobile-owning children from the age of 12–17 have sent provocative or nude images of themselves via SMS text (Lenhart, 2009: 5) and 13 per cent of teens have received threatening or aggressive email, instant message or text messages (Lenhart *et al.*, 2007b: 3). The Eurobarometer 2007 Survey also reported similar experiences by children in the age groups

9–10 and 12–14 (Eurobarometer, 2007). Online child safety governance has to address the child protection issues emerging from children as users/consumers and the risks generated by misuse of network infrastructure and communication technologies (Brenner, 2010). The online environment creates incentives for behaviour that we ordinarily would not encounter in the offline environment. Yar points to the exceptional nature of the "social interactional features of the cyberspace environment" which contributes to the growth of illegal activity and vulnerabilities (2006: 12). This is perhaps misconceived. At best, the online environment can be seen to raise intractable problems of policing and enforcing domestic laws and regulations (Brenner, 2010, 163–76). What perhaps distinguishes networked communications and information flows from their real space equivalents are the speed, scale and frequency with which deviant criminal activity can be perpetrated and the compliance issues they generate for national legal systems. However, it should be said that even though the risks are unexceptional, they are essentially invisible and their materialisation uncertain (Van Asselt *et al.*, 2009: 360–1). How we identify, assess and respond to risks is a perennial problem for designing effective risk-based regulation processes. The significance of the rhetoric of "safety" and its relationship with Beck's "risk society" is explored more fully below.

The logic of information flows and the individualisation of risks

Digital spaces are now seen as threats to children's safety and well-being. Network structures and information flows provide a new context where society becomes preoccupied with managing risks. Mobile phones and social networks are regarded as tools for victimising peers, chat rooms can now be misused by adults to solicit minors and P2P software programmes enable individuals to seek out illegal content stored on networked repositories with a global reach. Web 2.0 technologies are regarded by organised criminal gangs as enabling them to undertake their activities without detection by law enforcement (Tarissan *et al.*, 2009). Often, this can be done across transnational borders and without regulatory oversight (GAO, 2003). As noted previously, communication networks now create multiple opportunities for misuse and numerous access points through which children can be exposed to harm. Not only can a child be exploited through a number of access points (e.g. mobile phones, email, IM, virtual worlds, online games and social networking sites) but the abuse or exploitation of a child victim can also be relayed live to other observers for their sexual gratification or the impact can be significantly intensified by making the content or incident accessible to everyone with an Internet access (e.g. sexting and cyberbullying). It is this sheer complexity of the networks of information flows and the problems of managing risks and uncertainty that exacerbates the problems of policing and the difficulties faced in securing compliance with national laws and rules. Information flows are seen as contributing to the growing feeling that the networked society generates risks that cannot be easily managed and controlled. Some continue to view the characteristics of networks and information as *the* cause of social disorder and uncertainty "reminiscent of the wild, wild West" (Chisholm, 2006: 75) Policymakers have responded to the growing anxiety by adopting managerial strategies like identifying the "risk categories" as well as the activities that expose children to unacceptable risks to their safety and well-being. Accordingly, studies have been undertaken to help inform policymakers, law enforcement, parents and educators about the relationship between children's online activities and incidents encountered in these environments. Managing risk and uncertainty involves a process of generating surveys, studies, reports and research. The EU Kids Online Project is an apt example of one reflexive modernisation activity where empirical surveys and studies are regarded as an appropriate basis for promoting informed decision-making and formulation of policies (Table 2.5).

Even as a general overview of the nature of the online child safety governance challenge, this taxonomy provides us with a snapshot of Beck's risk society – risk, reflexive modernisation and individualisation of risks. It also illustrates a potential dilemma for governance strategy since a scientific appraisal of the risks is not readily possible as the likely materialisation of the harm is uncertain until a series of causal behaviours are engaged in. For example, faced with media and law enforcement reports of the threats posed by online sexual predators, policymakers take the view that the potential risk under conditions of uncertainty must be avoided by implementing rules and precautionary norms (e.g. privacy rules, filtering software, parental control rules and children being encouraged not to speak with

Table 2.5   Online child safety incidents

	Commercial	Aggressive	Sexual	Values
Content – *child as recipient*	Advertising, spam and sponsorship	Violence, hate, racist	Pornography, child sexual abuse and exploitation	Hate, biased or misleading advice
Contact – *child as participant*	Profiling, data mining	Victimisation by peers	Online sexual solicitation	Inappropriate lifestyle choices
Conduct – child as actor	Gambling, computer misuse, illegal downloading	Victimising peers	User generated sexual content	Participant in lifestyle communities (i.e. bulimia, self-harm and anorexia)

(Source: Adapted from EU Kids Online – Hasebrink *et al.*, 2009.

strangers). The globalisation of risk-based regulation is also evident in the reflexive processes in play in countries like Australia, Canada, the United States and Member States in the EU, who have also undertaken similar mapping exercises with the aim of grounding their responses in empirical work. The focus of child protection surveys is frequently directed at the relationship between children's access to the Internet and the likelihood of their increased exposure to online risks (Livingstone and Haddon, 2009b; AMF, 2009; Eurobarometer, 2006). In Canada a comprehensive study was conducted seeking to identify the attitudes, expectations and practices of children and young Canadians regarding their use of the Internet (Media Awareness, 2005). The study – *Young Canadians in a Wired World Phase II, Trends and Recommendations* – confirms the growing consensus amongst researchers and policymakers across the world that as the Internet and communication technologies become an integral part of children's lives, there will be an increase in their exposure and potential vulnerability to online safety incidents (2005: 5). The study also revealed that children (grades 8 and 9) encountered a number of sites with violent (28 per cent) or sexually inappropriate (32 per cent) content (2005: 17). Children, in this study, indicated that they did not actively search for websites with adult chat (91 per cent), only 16 per cent admitted searching for pornography, and boys were more likely than girls to seek out sites with violent or offensive content (2005: 18). These findings from Canada also correspond very much with those made by the Kaiser Family Foundation's *Generation M2* (Rideout *et al.*, 2010; OSTWG, 2010; ACMA, 2010a). In its studies of media consumption habits and trends amongst children and their families, the Australian Communications and Media Authority (ACMA) noted the close correspondence between media penetration in society and children's increased exposure to online safety risks (ACMA, 2010a). The findings also provide a context for thinking about the governance options and the nature of the measures to be adopted within the MSIG framework. A brief account of the three risks, which are mediated through networks and information flows will now be provided, and these are online sexual solicitation, illegal and inappropriate content and peer victimisation.

Online sexual solicitation

Web 2.0 technologies provide individuals with new avenues through which children can be targeted and lured into sexual activity without detection by parents or educators. Crucially, in online sexual solicitations, the offender aims to develop a foundation of trust with the child victim (CEOP, 2010a). Olsen observes that individuals targeting potential victims aim to identify

> three categories of characteristics that make them particularly vulnerable to a predator's lure: personality traits and emotional traits, behavioral patterns, and dysfunctional family dynamics. (Olson, 2007: 238)

Olsen is quick to add that the existence of these characteristics does not invariably lead to a meeting or abuse. The problems in establishing the identity of online participants and the ease with which some adults have used social engineering techniques to solicit minors for sexual activity have raised concerns about the security of these communication platforms for children. For example, in *R v Newman* (2010), the offender set up false identities in chat rooms accessed by young people with the aim of identifying prospective victims. In *R v Asplund* (2010), the offender had at his disposal a wide range of communication tools (e.g. mobile phones, SMS text messages and the Internet)

> to feed into and gratify his sexual titillation and fantasies with a long term view of having her submit to sexual activity with him...demonstrated by his use of the Internet to persuade her to send him photos of a highly intimate and sexual nature, by his access to resources to shower her with money and bombard her with communications, by his toying and manipulative Internet exchanges earlier referred to. (2010: paragraph 7)

Apart from the risk of children meeting their online contacts "face-to-face", it is also becoming apparent that a number of offenders use chat rooms and IM to engage in discussions with children about sexual matters as a way of self-gratification and grooming a child for non-contact sexual activity. These "hit and run" tactics have been particularly noticeable with the emergence of webcams. Online sexual solicitation can be broadly understood as the process by which a sender aims to procure a child to engage in sexual activity or other forms of sexual gratification. This can include flirtation as well as more explicit forms of sexual activity (McQuade *et al.*, 2008). Online sexual solicitation is one of the major parental concerns and source of anxiety and distress. In Australia, over 47 per cent of the parents in a survey expressed fears about their children talking to strangers (ACMA, 2009b: 75). In a recent study, it was pointed out that children received most online sexual solicitations from their peers or individuals from the age groups of 18 and 21 (ISTTF, 2008:14). The Child Exploitation and Online Protection Centre (CEOP) highlighted a rise in reports about grooming activity in online environments frequented by children (CEOP, 2009). The report notes that CEOP investigations increased from 20 per cent in 2006/7, 40 per cent in 2007/8 to 48 per cent in 2008/9 (CEOP, 2009: 8–12). It is also apparent, as the study conducted at the Crimes against Children's Research Centre points out, that one in five minors tend to be solicited online (Finkelhor *et al.*, 2000; Wolak *et al.*, 2006). There are a number of explanations for online solicitations of young children in particular. Adults, with an interest in young children can, for example, come into contact with children without an actual meeting in a physical environment. Social networking sites provide a range of facilities for gathering information (Kim-Kwang, 2009). Public directories on social networking sites contain a wealth of information, which are set out under various headings – groups, age, name, email, location and gender. Profile information, comment and dialog tools and Really Simple Syndication feeds, for example, provide offenders with mechanisms for monitoring their victims and gathering any new information uploaded by them. The task of identifying targets and gathering information about potential victims begins with perpetrators accessing directories on social networking sites and participating in chat rooms frequented by children (Kontostathis *et al.*, 2010). For example, depending on the privacy settings of the child and those on the child's network of friends, the acceptance of the offender as a friend on the social networking site will give the individual immediate access to the child's posts and profile pages. Most online sexual solicitations with children take place after an offender has gathered all the information about potential victims and assessed their amenability to being approached. The Provincial Court of Nova Scotia, in the trial of *R v Randall* (2006), was told that the accused logged into Internet chat rooms and scanned the profiles and communications before identifying his potential child victims. In *R v Gajjar* (2008), the offender used chat rooms on the Internet entitled "Family Sex" to engage in grooming activity. Online forums like these involve participants being favourably disposed towards sexually graphic communications. The offender in *Tector v R* (2008) used a pseudonym to send emails and text messages to persuade the victim to engage in sexual activity and even provided financial inducements. In *R v Dragos* (2010), the offender met the complainant on an Internet chat room called Habbo Hotel. This communication platform is designed to enable its users to discuss the sale of items of furniture for hotel rooms, and socialise with each other. The accused and the complainant used webcams to engage in non-contact sexual activity and communicated frequently through MSN. In all these instances, offenders tended to exploit the fact that electronic communications do not require face-to-face contact, and their belief that children were unlikely to disclose these interactions to parents or educators (Livingstone *et al.*, 2011). Webcams have also been used by individuals to record live images of children, which were subsequently stored, distributed or uploaded onto a website. In some cases, offenders have used images or conversations involving children they have been conversing with to coerce them into engaging in non-contact sexual activity, or arrange a face-to-face meeting. Malware have been used to allow individuals gain unauthorised access to a child's computer system, buddy lists, and webcams. On July 2010, a hacker broke into a child's computer, and gained remote access to the webcams of 150 girls (Deutsche Welle, 2008). Recently, a 25-year-old man coerced a 11-year-old girl to engage in acts of indecency in front of her webcam (Chong, 2010). He recorded these acts and threatened to release the images on the Internet unless she complied with his requests. According to the CEOP,

there is also a marked trend of the use of webcam streaming chat sites, enabling offenders to interact either through instant messages and/or webcam to share previously captured footage or live-time images of abuse of children in their care. (Selgren, 2010)

It is not always the case that adults seduce young adolescents (*R v Grout (Phillip)* (2011)). Some children lie about their ages or even pretend to be older than they actually are, so that they can engage in non-contact sexual activity with persons they meet online. Many children, it seems, are at ease with interacting with strangers online (Wolak *et al.*, 2008: 342–3). Wolak, Finkelhor and Mitchell point to the findings from a survey which show that young children also use the freedom and anonymity offered by Web 2.0 technologies to gain the necessary sexual experience and confidence, which can later be used by them to develop relationships in the offline environment (Wolak *et al.*, 2006). In a study by Finkelhor, Mitchell and Wolak, if was found that 7 per cent of the children interviewed engaged in sexual conversations with strangers in chat rooms (Finkelhor *et al.*, 2000). Some children have been known to engage in the practice of setting up 'jailbait webcams' where teenagers create profiles on websites, with links offering sex shows and photographs for financial reward. These accounts also suggest why children's online activities generate so much anxiety and concern notwithstanding the fact that for the majority of children who do not like unsolicited sexual attention simple measures can be adopted to deal with such situations (Wolak *et al.*, 2006). The task of making accurate risk assessments is also complicated by the fact that children's online interactions with strangers cannot be invariably depicted as harmful. In an important study funded by the European Commission, it was found that 30 per cent of their sample of Internet users formed a friendship with someone they had met online (Livingstone *et al.*, 2005a). Eight per cent of them had met the person face-to-face. The majority of these meetings were positive, and where face-to-face meetings did take place, the child concerned often took a friend or parent with them, or told someone where they were going in advance. In a report issued by the Internet Safety Technical Task Force (ISTTF), it was noted that non-technology-mediated sex crimes against children outweighed those perpetrated through the Internet (ISTTF, 2008: 10). These accounts of the risk-prone nature of children's online activities illustrate the difficulties faced by parents and educators in making a proper assessment about how best to manage threats posed by online sexual solicitation as the traditional visual and safety cues are not present in electronic interactions.

Illegal or inappropriate content

Children and young people now have increased opportunities to access illegal or inappropriate content (Ybarra, *et al.*, 2005; Table 2.6). Communication platforms provided by Smartphones, video game and PlayStation consoles (e.g. Nintendo Wii or Sony PlayStation) can now be used by children to access a wide range of content without parental oversight (European Commission,

Table 2.6 Children's exposure to online pornography

Per cent	Exposure
57	Had contact with online pornography
38	Viewed pornography unintentionally
54	Not bothered by pornography
16	Do not like encountering pornography
9	Sent porn by someone they knew
10	Deliberately searched for pornography

Source: Livingstone and Bovill, 2005.

2011a: 52, 57). We can categorise problematic content that children can access or be exposed to into those that are illegal (e.g. child abuse content) and those which are inappropriate or harmful (e.g. pro-anorexia, bulimia and dating websites). In many countries there are content classification schemes which define the subject matter that can be made available to a general audience and those which are illegal. Children's access to and use of the Internet can lead to potentially harmful or age-inappropriate content being accessed either deliberately or inadvertently. A number of websites hosting adult content do not provide effective age-verification controls – most websites providing such content only provide a notice requiring the visitor to verify that they are of an age where access to adult content is permissible. Search engine operators like Google or Yahoo provide tools which enable individuals to access adult material, images and videos. A number of websites also host user-generated content, which can be accessed for free, and do not have effective age-verification tools. The lack of effective age-verification controls is confirmed by surveys and reports (Livingstone *et al.*, 2005a; Ybarra *et al.*, 2005).

OfCom found that around 16 per cent of children aged 8 to 15 encountered inappropriate or violent content when using Web 2.0 technologies (2006: 45). A survey of children aged 9 to 10 and 12 to 14 across 29 countries found that children had either encountered violent or pornographic websites or harmful content (Hargrave, 2009: 8). This is a finding that is also mirrored in national reviews undertaken in countries like the United States and Australia (OSTWG, 2010: 14–16; ACMA, 2009b: 43). The studies did, however, indicate that children regarded encounters with problematic content as being of less concern than, for example, harms caused by malware and viruses. The 2008 Eurobarometer Survey revealed that over 65 per cent of parents feared that their children may be exposed to sexual or violent content or images of an explicit nature (Eurobarometer, 2008: 5). Children's exposure to inappropriate and harmful content is an important online child safety issue. Many children reportedly use the Internet to access inappropriate and harmful content like self-harm and suicide (Royal College of Psychiatrists, 2010: 52). What concerns educators and parents here is that whilst a number of websites provide children with invaluable assistance, there is some evidence of certain websites normalising the practice of self-harm and suicide (Whitlock *et al.*, 2006; Hargrave *et al.*, 2006). More worryingly, it has been reported that children are increasingly accessing information from online pro-eating disorder and self-harm communities (Fox *et al.*, 2005: 944–71). Self-harming behaviour, for example, is now regarded as a major public health problem (Hawton *et al.*, 2005: 891–4). The Royal College of Psychiatrists also reported that 4 in 1,000 people in the United Kingdom have harmed themselves (Royal College of Psychiatrists, 2010). Children as young as eight years old have been found to harm themselves and adolescent girls were more likely than boys to engage in the practice (Royal College of Psychiatrists, 2010: 31). One in five schoolchildren with a history of self-harming first discovered about self-harm from material they accessed online (Whitlock *et al.*, 2006). It also appears that without timely intervention those children who are most at risk or vulnerable are likely to accept the accuracy and reliability of the information presented to their detriment. There is also particular concern with regard to children's access to racist or xenophobic material on websites, since it is felt that consumption of such content could encourage prejudice, reinforce stereotypes and even incite bullying or other forms of peer victimisation (Ray *et al.*, 2001). In addition to these concerns other technological affordances like emails, IM and social networking sites now provide individuals with another medium for engaging in race- or gender-related abuse (Defeis, 1992; Blumenfeld *et al.*, 2010). The Byron Report advocated the use of education and regulatory mechanisms (e.g. codes of practice) to reduce the availability of harmful and offensive content (Byron, 2004: paragraph 4.34–43). Interestingly, the Report did not regard the requirement that web hosts remove material about harmful behaviours from their sites as a sustainable risk management response (ibid.: paragraph 4.33). One recurring view is that the public interest would not be served by blocking access to such content since "[b]anning such content risks driving vulnerable young people away to more obscure sites" (Byron, 2008: paragraphs 4.35–36) Even if the UK government did decide to make access to inappropriate content unavailable to children, these are likely to provoke objections from industry on the ground that the putative harms are more effectively addressed by educators and parents through the provision of relevant safety information and tools. In addition to this, it should be noted that technical solutions like filtering and blocking have undoubted limitations as a content regulatory mechanism. In a recent study funded under the SIP it was reported that many Internet filters did not adequately regulate the various forms of age-inappropriate or harmful content found on social networking sites, chat rooms and blogs (European Commission, 2011a).

Peer victimisation

There is general consensus that communication technologies now bring to the forefront increased opportunities that mobile phones and the Internet provide for victimisation (Lenhart, 2007). Bullying can, for example, take place through texts, emails, mobile phones or on social networking sites. Acts of coercion include the unauthorised distribution of texts and embarrassing images of children and film clips of victims being subjected to assaults, known as "happy slapping". Private information posted online have also been copied and distributed without the owner's consent, with the aim of causing distress. In a recent study undertaken in Iowa, United States, it was found that transgender bullying was quite common amongst young adolescents (Blumenfeld *et al.*, 2010). Blumenfeld and Cooper noted that lesbian, gay, bisexual and transgender individuals were increasingly subjected to victimisation by peers on social networking sites and other communication platforms (2010: 2–10). We should also add to this category of victims children who are disabled or who have particular learning difficulties (*TK v New York City Department of Education* (2011)). A three-year study in Australia noted an increase in peer victimisation (Cross, 2009). This study was commissioned by the Australian government amidst growing anxieties over the use of communication technologies to engage in "covert bullying" and the findings confirm growing concerns shared by policymakers in many countries about the scale of peer victimisation and its impact on victims and perpetrators (see Table 2.7).

In their studies on children's use of technologies Hinduja and Patchin suggest a close correspondence between increased consumption of Web 2.0 technologies and the rise in children's exposure to victimisation and, in a number of cases, participation in the deviant activity (see Tables 2.8 and 2.9).

These communication platforms are also venues where peer victimisation is encountered (Kowalski *et al.*, 2007; Patchin *et al.*, 2010a,b). Consequently,

Table 2.7 Web 2.0 technologies and peer victimisation

Email/IM	Social networks	Mobile phone	Virtual worlds
Forwarding secrets and private communication	Image defacing	Happy slapping	Targeting peers on the grounds of gender, race or religion
	Creating false profiles	Photographs	
	Forwarding private images/text		
	Listing "unpopular" peers		

Table 2.8   Children's risk-prone activities

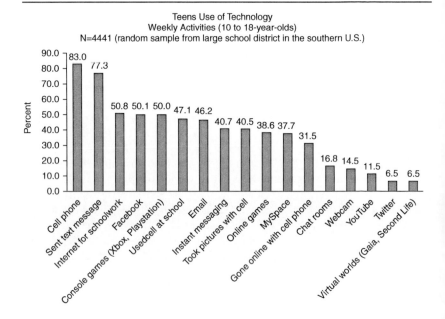

the misuse of technologies and departure from social or ethical norms to humiliate and cause maximum upset illustrates how such activities can escalate into child protection issues.

Framing the risk facing children is in itself a complex endeavour. For example, in *TK* (2010), the peer victimisation activities included the making of prank phone calls to the victim and drawings depicting the victim in a negative light. At the recent White House Conference on Bullying Prevention, over 40 per cent of the educators and support staff surveyed reported that bullying was a major problem in their schools (White House, 2011). Cyberbullying has been described as a type of conduct where

> someone repeatedly uses the Internet or a mobile phone to deliberately upset or embarrass somebody else. It is intended to harm others and can include sending mean or nasty words or pictures to someone over the Internet or by mobile phone. (ACMA, 2009c: 63)

Another view is that cyberbullying involves a

> repeated or sustained pattern of intentional cyber-attacks that causes distress and is directed against a specific student or group... [it can] also be a multi-faceted or multi-step campaign of humiliation or hostility that causes distress and is directed against a specific student or group. (AMF, 2009: 4)

Table 2.9 Web 2.0 Technologies and online child safety incidents

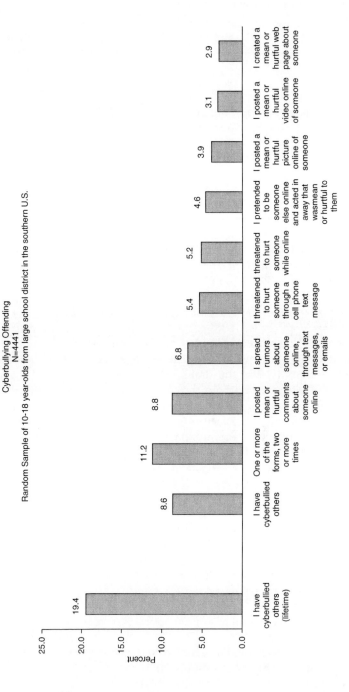

Cyberbullying Offending
N=4441
Random Sample of 10-18 year-olds from large school district in the southern U.S.

The absence of a settled meaning or understanding of the term makes it difficult to frame the problem, and more often than not can lead to safety measures and strategies that adopt a managerial approach to risk management – "delete offensive texts and emails", "do not upload information on websites" and "mobile phones should not be used during school hours". The rise in bullying, particularly through the use of Web 2.0 technologies, cannot be simply attributed to the existence of a legal and policy vacuum (Shariff, 2009) or to the fact that new technologies enable children to express their aggression (Hinduja *et al.*, 2009). In their study, Ybarra and Mitchell highlight the close relationship between online and offline bullying (Ybarra *et al.*, 2004). In some instances, it was found that those who were victims in the offline environment used the online environment to redress the power and social balance when inflicting distress on their perpetrators (Patchin *et al.*, 2006; Ybarra *et al.*, 2007). In one survey, 56 per cent of the online aggressors claimed to have been the subject of offline victimisation (Ybarra *et al.*, 2004). Interviews commissioned by ACMA reported that a child's exposure to peer victimisation incidents also showed a marked increase with the age of the child (ACMA, 2009c: 66).

Technology-mediated victimisation has three features that incentivise "an overt, intentional act of aggression towards another person online" (Ybarra *et al.*, 2004: 1038) or "wilful and repeated harm inflicted through the use of computers, cell phones, and other electronic devices" (Hinduja *et al.*, 2009: 5). These are the anonymity that the bully leverages to victimise an individual; the viral nature of the victimisation (i.e. many to one) and the lack of visibility in the consequences of the victimisation. Swearer highlights a number of risk factors that contribute to bullying and victimisation: individual risk factors (e.g. age, gender, socio-economic status, ethnicity and religion), peer-group risk factors (e.g. homophily and deviancy), school risk factors (e.g. educators' attitudes, school architecture, belonging, academic and social engagement) and family risk factors (e.g. violence in family, family upheavals) (Swearer *et al.*, 2010).

The media spotlight on peer victimisation has elevated bullying into public and political consciousness. Such is the gravity with which peer victimisation is viewed that the White House was moved to convene a Conference on Bullying Prevention. Interestingly, the First Lady's remark's illustrates the close interplay between heightened public anxiety, parents' individualisation of fears for their children's well-being and the media's definition of the problem:

> I want to thank all of you for joining us here today to discuss an issue of great concern to me and to Barack, not just as President and as First Lady, but as a mom and a dad. And that is the problem of bullying in our schools and in our communities...

As parents, this issue really hits home for us. As parents, it breaks our hearts to think that any child feels afraid every day in the classroom, or on the playground, or even online. It breaks our hearts to think about any parent losing a child to bullying, or just wondering whether their kids will be safe when they leave for school in the morning.

And as parents, Barack and I also know that sometimes, maybe even a lot of the time, it's really hard for parents to know what's going on in our kids' lives...

But parents aren't the only ones who have a responsibility. We all need to play a role – as teachers, coaches, as faith leaders, elected officials, and anyone who's involved in our children's lives. And that doesn't just mean working to change our kids' behavior and recognize and reward kids who are already doing the right thing. It means thinking about our own behavior as adults as well. (White House, 2011).

Many of the observations made by Beck resonate in this excerpted speech – heightened anxiety, risks generated by information flows, children viewed as being vulnerable to risks as well as being perpetrators of online safety incidents and the need for risk management strategies. This is not to say that efforts to combat peer victimisation are not being made (Olweus, 2007; Sampson, 2002; Mencap, 2007). The public health model, which regards targeted interventions and support, creating appropriate school culture of respect and civility, social skills training, monitoring and engagement with parents and the community as a governance strategy, is an important step towards creating a "whole-school/community" approach to bullying prevention (Chamberlain *et al.*, 2010).

Managing insecurity (anxiety) and reflexive modernisation

Risk is conspicuous even though Web 2.0 technologies and network publics appear on the surface to involve nothing more than participatory genres and cultures of self-presentation and identity experimentation. Questions about how we manage risks the way we do, the evidence informing the conclusions drawn from the relationship between technology and risks, the assumptions we make about children's use of media and the evolving role of parenting cultures are very much a part of living in the risk society (Beck, 1999). Buckingham is right when he alludes to children being regarded as natural subjects for regulatory oversight, since "assumptions about who these other people are – and, in this case, about what 'childhood' is, or should be" (2000: 104). The threat of technology-enabled crime has given rise to a growing demand for strategies for prevention and control, particularly in the area of online child exploitation. Mazzarella regards societal safety concerns borne out of interest in children's immersion in communication technologies as indicative of cultural attitudes towards children – a body of individuals requiring constant supervision and monitoring (2007: 46–7).

Two further observations need to be made with regard to the process of reflexive governance in the area of online child safety. First, risk-taking behaviour amongst children is conceptualised in negative terms whether it is in virtual worlds, social networking sites or network publics. It is readily assumed, for example, that children's exposure to potential (or perceived) contact and non-contact risks results from their willingness to disclose personal identifiable information online, their immaturity and lack of understanding about the nature of the risks. It is true that one of the consequences of being connected with communication networks is that everyone is potentially at risk, even though paradoxically, it is unlikely to be experienced by all individuals. Interestingly, children's online activities and use of Web 2.0 technologies are singled out and described as "risk-prone behaviours" (ITU, 2010b: 16). It is important to acknowledge that many children who are solicited online by adults do not arrange to meet them. Social networking sites, chat and IM platforms have tools to block and report unwanted contact. Recently, Facebook created a social abuse reporting mechanism for individuals to alert their "friends" about potential abusive or inappropriate activity. Ironically, rather than demonise activities and behaviours as "risk-prone", it should also be remembered that it is through the norms of sharing and engagement that a community of networked sociability can be leveraged to reinforce civility and respect. The integration of civic responsibility and appropriate behaviour norms through design solutions in effect allocates to children some of the responsibility for policing the networked community. In viewing all online activities as "risk-prone" or "risky" it has been suggested that we may attach little importance to the value of positive risk taking in promoting good decision-making skills, developing resilience and enhancing children's ability to respond to online incidents in a safe and responsible manner. One is also inclined to agree with Gill, when he suggests that curbing a child's ability to take reasonable risks may be counterproductive and have the unintended effect of leading them to engage in more dangerous and unsupervised activity (Gill, 2007: 15–16). Second, the culture of reflexive governance has also led to the institutionalisation of risk management. The State has an obvious role in allaying public fears and concerns, as suggested by the former Home Secretary David Blunkett:

> Public protection, particularly of children and the most vulnerable, is this Government's priority...But sexual crime, particularly against children, can tear apart the very fabric of our society. It destroys lives and communities and challenges our most basic values. (Home Office, 2002: 5)

In a House of Commons Select Committee hearing, the following observation was made about the technology and its implications for parents:

> However, anyone who regularly watches television or reads the press is likely to have become aware of growing public concern in recent months

at the Internet's dark side: the easy availability of hardcore pornography, which people may find offensive, the uploading by ordinary people of film of real fights, bullying or alleged rape, or the setting up of websites encouraging others to follow extreme diets, or self-harm, or even commit suicide. In particular, there is *increasing anxiety among parents about the use of social networking sites and chatrooms for grooming and sexual preda-tion*. (House of Commons, 2008: 7) (my emphasis)

As a broad statement of intent, these observations appear to overstate both the context and experiences of many children and consequently advocate the need for greater protection and oversight of children's online activities. Management of theoretical risks rather than those encountered by children becomes the focal point of a precautionary approach to child safety govern-ance. Crucially, the difficulties in assessing the scale of the risks, the use of risk-based regulation to require shifts in behaviour of all stakeholders (in-cluding children) and the trade-offs involved also illustrate the challenges and potential objections that may be encountered under the MSIG model of institutional design and governance (Hood *et al.*, 2001: 181–4).

Children's risk-prone activities, individualisation of risks and moral panics

Safeguarding children in the online environment can be viewed as mobilis-ing cultural attitudes towards children and risks – the individualisation of risks leads to risk management techniques focusing on perceived and actual threats (Giddens, 1991: 198). Policymaking forums at national, regional and supranational levels now adopt risk-based regulatory strategies, which en-gage industry, experts and other stakeholders in identifying and assessing the risks faced by children. Holmes has questioned the imbalance in online child safety debates (Holmes, 2007). The Byron Report is singled out for magnifying the risks faced by children in the online environment rather than emphasising good online behaviour and appropriate computer use practices (Holmes, 2009: 1175). Risk discourse manifests itself in a number of ways in child protection policymaking. McAlinden, for example, high-lights how media construction of sex offenders contributed to legislative responses to regulating sex offenders (2007: 11). Gerbner articulated similar discourses about children's well-being and safety being compromised by their exposure to television (Gerbner *et al.*, 1976). It has been suggested that anxieties surrounding children are also magnified by the disproportionate emphasis placed by both the media and policymakers on the threat land-scape. A "moral panic", according to Stanley Cohen, is when a

condition, episode, person or group of persons emerges to become defined as a threat to societal values and interests; its nature is presented in a styl-ized and stereotypical fashion by the mass media; the moral barricades are manned by editors, bishops, politicians and other right-thinking people. (1972: 1)

The concerns raised by the Attorney General's press release (noted at the start of Chapter 1) could be regarded as addressing a "condition", "episode" and a "group of persons" which pose threats to children's safety and well-being. Online service providers, parents and educators, according to the definition of a "moral panic", would seem now to be the digital equivalent of "bishops" and "right-thinking" individuals. The media reporting could also be seen as one example of risks facing children being presented in a "stylized and stereotypical fashion" (Ungar, 2001; Garland, 2008). The law enforcement response in relation to the presence of online sexual predators and potential threats to children is depicted as legitimating the elevation of safeguarding children as a social and moral obligation on all adults and businesses in society. The risk-based regulation model extends to corporate stakeholders – social networking sites and mobile phone providers now become the focal points for allocating blame and responsibility (Critcher, 2008). The mischaracterisation of the precautionary principle will only serve to deflect "from the truth and thus simply makes it more difficult to figure out what we should do to effectively address the situation" (Ohler, 2010: 144). The European Commission was clear in its Communication that

> [t]he precautionary principle, which is essentially used by decision-makers in the management of risk, should not be confused with the element of caution that scientists apply in their assessment of scientific data. (European Commission, 2010: 3)

Determining what is a proportionate policy response continues to prove to be an ongoing challenge since the construction of risks and their alignment with child abuse and victimisation evoke strong emotive reactions (Ostertag, 2010). Increased regulatory interventions tend to fuel rather than allay concerns. This is hardly surprising since

> the government in many ways reinforces adult perceptions of risk to children by reacting to public and media pressure rather than responding to evidence. This can mean that policies that reflect and reproduce risk anxiety rather than reflecting a proper, informed evaluation or appraisal of the real dangers facing children. (Madge *et al.*, 2007: 22)

Public anxiety and concerns leading to moral panics pose considerable problems for policymakers (Goode, *et al.*, 1994). McAlinden regards the cycle of moral panic as reconstructing social reality, resulting in perceived risks being transformed into a discourse about a society "full of sexual predators" (2007: 11). The process of "constructing a social problem" has a more immediate relevance – it leads to a cycle of, what Beck regards as, heightened anxiety and public expectation that policymakers respond to the critical tensions raised by children's exposure to Web 2.0 technologies (Hawkins *et al.*,

1983). Taking the MySpace incident, which opened the discussion in the book as an example, very little weight or importance was attached by the Attorney General to the practical question of whether the online services provider had taken appropriate and reasonable measures in enhancing the safety of its products and services. Without MySpace's due diligence protocols, 90,000 registered sex offenders would not have been identified in the first place. The Sentinel SAFE software, which is funded and developed by MySpace, cross-references the information of its 130 million users with the national database of known registered sex offenders. By focusing on the uncertainty generated by the presence of the registered sex offenders, risk management becomes inseparable from managing uncertainty – consequently, it seems that in the absence of absolute proof that uncertain risks are eradicated, social networking sites are to be viewed as unsafe for children (Ungar, 2001: 273). The press release also contributes to increased preoccupation with managing uncertainty, as it appears to imply the existence of an ideal or appropriate risk management response. A recent illustration of the uncertain boundaries between moral panics and legitimate risk management governance can be seen in the claim made by CEOP to have made the online environment safer, following the adoption by social networking sites and a number of online service providers and ISPs of the ClickCEOP reporting button (CEOP, 2009: 15). Without overstating the obvious, if this claim holds true, it is difficult to see why the same could not be said for the efforts made by MySpace or Facebook in adopting the proactive measures that they have. Accordingly, as risk is pervasive in society, and is accentuated by networks and information flows

> fear of crime is a particularly apt discourse within the modernist quest for order since the risks it signifies, unlike other late modern risks, are *knowable, decisionable, (actionable)*, and potentially *controllable*. In an age of uncertainty, discourses that appear to promise a resolution to ambivalence by producing identifiable victims and blameable villains are likely to figure prominently in the State's ceaseless attempts to impose social order. (Holloway *et al.*, 1997: 265)

As Fortin points out, policymakers struggle to find an appropriate balance when designing systems to manage complex and intractable issues (Fortin, 2010: 586–7, 590–1). By way of conclusion to this chapter, it may be useful to assess how the crossover between moral panics, risks and governance takes shape in evolving parental cultures.

Evolving parental cultures in a risk-averse society

For many parents and educators, the Internet and mobile technology are seen as increasing children's vulnerability and exposure to inappropriate content, sexual exploitation and peer victimisation (OfCom, 2006; Table

2.10). The findings from the Eurobarometer Survey, noted below, can be used to illustrate Beck's central ideas about living in the risk society, in particular for evolving parental cultures (Eurobarometer, 2008).

Risk anxiety is particularly noticeable in relation to online sexual solicitation (60 per cent) and exposure to sexual and violent content (65 per cent), but does not appear to be particularly high in relation to peer victimisation (54 per cent) or exposure to age-inappropriate or harmful content (55 per cent). Parents anxieties about children being sexually victimised or exposed to sexually explicit content is not new – it should also be noted that it is not entirely clear whether the Internet accentuates these anxieties. Another interesting finding relates to the number of parents who indicated that they were not really worried about online sexual solicitation (36 per cent), exposure to sexual and violent content (31 per cent) or exposure to age-inappropriate or harmful content (41 per cent). It seems that parental anxieties were much higher in cases where they did not use the Internet themselves, in contrast to those who did use the Internet (2008: 30). Additionally, where low scores were highlighted, it is unclear from the survey whether

Table 2.10   Parents' perspectives of online child safety incidents

Risks	Very much worried	Rather Worried	Rather not Worried	Rather not worried at all	Do not know/not applicable
Might see sexually/ violently explicit images on the Internet	45	20	14	17	4
Victim of online grooming	46	14	13	23	5
Access to self-harm, suicide, anorexia content	39	16	15	26	5
Bullying	37	17	18	23	5
Might see sexually/ violently explicit images via the mobile phone	37	14	13	26	11
Mobile phone bullying	34	15	14	25	11
Might give out personal/private information online	26	21	24	25	4

Source: Flash Eurobarometer, 2008.

Table 2.11 Parents' strategies regarding children's use of the Internet

Parental mediation	Dialogue about online use (per cent)	Remain in vicinity when computer used (per cent)	Co-surfing (per cent)	Check the computer later to see which sites child visited (per cent)	Check whether your child has a profile on a social net-working site (per cent)	Check the messages in your child's email account/IM service (per cent)
Parents' Internet use						
Non-users	60	44	28	24	17	18
Occasional users	75	65	40	44	29	26
Frequent users	76	60	36	44	31	24

Source: Flash Barometer, 2008: 39.

parents were in effect underestimating the realities of children's experiences (Livingstone *et al.*, 2011; Table 2.11).

Whilst parents adopt different safety enhancing strategies, the findings show that greater control tends to be exercised over the child's Internet use – these findings can be interpretated in one of two ways. First, parents with greater ICT competence and knowledge of the safety issues appear to engage more fully with a child's online activities. Second, the lack of supervision could be attributable to a number of factors (e.g. level of ICT competence, limited awareness of the risks or trust in children's online activities). The findings from the Flash Barometer Survey also correspond with a similar study undertaken by ACMA in 2010:

> Parents of 8 to 11 year olds reported that they became increasingly con-
> cerned about cybersafety issues because their children were now at an
> age where being online was an integral part of their school education and
> their social life. (ACMA, 2010b: 7)

Another way of interpreting the Flash Eurobarometer findings is to view the survey results as illustrations of the way the logic of information flows contributes to the convergence of risk anxiety, constructions of childhood and parenting cultures. Youn has noted a number of mediatory strategies adopted by parents when socialising their children to the risks surround-ing Internet activity (2008: 362–88). Parents, for example, view their role in establishing rules on Internet use at home as an integral aspect of their social and moral responsibilities towards children. Those who have a better understanding of the scale and extent of the risks may tend to supervise and monitor children actively. Parents with younger children may be more protective and consequently co-surf or check on their child's online activ-ities (Mesch, 2009). McCarty remarks that as parents acquire information of their child's perceived online risky behaviours, it may also lead to more active parental oversight (McCarty *et al.*, 2011: 169–74).

The characterisation of children's lives as being more risky than those of adults has also resulted in a discernible shift in the way parents view the responses expected from them. This is a view expressed by Knaak, who has argued that the ideology of risk has contributed to evolving social norms that surround the role of parents in managing risks encountered by children at home, school and elsewhere (Knaak, 2009). It is, for example, noticeable that many parents justify purchasing mobile phones for their children on the grounds of ensuring the child's safety and allaying parental anxieties (Haddon, 2002: 118). The move away from the "bedroom" culture (e.g. chil-dren using computers in the privacy of their bedrooms) is also indicative of the evolving parental views that children's exposure to risks can only be minimised in spaces where they can be monitored (Haddon, 2002). Knaak makes an interesting observation, namely, that responsible parenting is now viewed very much through the lens of institutional and regulatory processes for managing risks (Knaak, 2009). There is also a noticeable trend in the way anxieties about managing risks also lead to greater intervention by industry and government in creating a safer environment for children (ITU, 2008a, 2009d,e). Strategies to promote trust and confidence continue to be merged with discourses on empowerment and responsible parenting. Parents are not regarded as passive actors, as risk management become institutionalised; there is an expectation that they be seen to take an active part in the daily online and offline lives of their children. These developments can at a very abstract or theorised level be seen as impressing on adults in society that a child's well-being and safety is best assured within an institutional framework of defined rules on monitoring computer use and instilling risk-averse behaviour (Hier, 2003). Networks and information flows have led to a gradual weakening in parental authority and control over children (Lamborn *et al.*, 1993). In some cases, as Web 2.0 technologies accelerate the "de-traditionalisation" of the social paradigm, parents now seek to bolster their trust by turning to their own experiences, media accounts of threat levels and assessments made by experts and institutions (Hier, 2003). For example, ACMA, like many regional and national institutions, continues to assist parents in discharging their ethical and social obligations by raising their awareness of online safety issues (ACMA, 2010b: 1). This view of the role of institutions in shaping parenting cultures can be regarded as another example of living a risk society where

> the parent is construed as unable to risk-manage effectively without professional "support". Cultural norms...thus construct the "good/responsible mother" as the mother who is alert to the manifold risks posed to her child(ren) by contemporary society, and considers it her job to manage these risks through reference to expert opinion. (Lee, 2008: 469)

It is also an illustration of how the patriarchal framework within society continues to negotiate the disruptive tendencies of Web 2.0 technologies.

Conclusions

One reason that "online child safety" continues to dominate policymaking is that it has rhetorical purchase for a number of child welfare and political entities. The claims that reporting mechanisms have saved a number of children does not address some of the crucial normative issues at stake when risks are "institutionalised" and filtering and blocking are seen as value free. It is therefore not surprising that appeals to policymakers, parents, educators and law enforcement that the fears and anxiety should be kept in perspective continue to go unheeded. The main focus of this chapter has been directed at the interplay between design, convergence and risks and its significance for the policy choices governments, regulators, and industry have to grapple with. This is a considerable challenge made all the more complicated by the fact that our preoccupation with online sexual predatory activity, exposure to illegal or harmful content and peer victimisation cannot be easily disentangled from societal constructions of childhood and discourse on risks and safety. The chapter has provided some examples and reasons why this might be the case. Whilst it is true that childhood is politicised and constructions of the "victim" child continue to define much of how we think about societal obligations to children, this chapter has identified an equally important dimension – how increased risk consciousness can be influential in shaping institutional and parental responses towards children's safety and well-being. It is important to recognise how such constructions of risks can shape the way safety responses like monitoring, surveillance and restrictions on children's access to and use of Web 2.0 technologies become operative norms in the networked society. Beck's insights and of those who have examined the impact of "risk consciousness" on parenting cultures reveal some of the governance implications arising from the discourse on risk and its significance for childhood in the networked society. We need to keep these considerations in mind since the architecture and the design principles that led to the exponential growth of the Internet continue to provide the critical infrastructure for economic and social activity (OECD, 2010a: 38; Schewick, 2010: 387). As policymakers aim to respond to the governance challenges, we need to be equally mindful that these developments, even in the domain of the criminal law, are

> set against the backdrop of a heightened sense of risk consciousness, "the new etiquette" of caution, fear and danger has distanced itself from judgments about what is morally proper or acceptable, becoming transposed into discourses of safety, security and communal living...To put this succinctly, as anxieties endemic to the risk society converge with anxieties contained at the level of community, we should expect a proliferation of moral panics as an ordering practice in late modernity. (Hier, 2003: 19)

3
Online Sexual Grooming of Children, Obscene Content and Peer Victimisation: Legal and Evidentiary Issues

Overview

As traditional methods for harming and abusing children become increasingly mediated through Web 2.0 technologies, a new dimension emerges for online child safety governance. Convergence has now made possible new avenues through which harms can be perpetrated against children. Difficult policy issues still have to be confronted as policymakers and regulators grapple with the dilemma of using the criminal law, in an environment where enforcement, rather than the application of its substantive rules, is proving to be a problem (Luüders *et al.*, 2009). Additionally, the ramifications of an expanding child protection agenda for civil liberties and innovation are still uncertain (Lindsay *et al.*, 2008). Policymakers and law enforcement are also having to deal with the issue of whether the criminal law should be used in cases where children become the offenders – sexual solicitation of other minors, hacking into social network profiles, posting hateful messages or defacing websites and distributing self-generated nude images of themselves. Is the criminal law outdated and unresponsive, or does living in a risk society require policymakers to reassess how we approach the strategies for extending legal standards and rules to an increasingly connected and "always-on" society? Indeed, it is a particularly relevant question to ask when reflecting on how the criminal law addresses these tensions either through direct State intervention or indirectly through the MSIG framework. These matters provide the background to the chapter, which is the legal and evidentiary issues emerging from the use of the criminal law in managing risks in three areas of online child safety governance: online sexual grooming, exposure to obscene content (with particular emphasis on child pornography) and peer victimisation. I integrate into the analysis an account of the key substantive criminal law rules to highlight its role and shortcomings when addressing the regulatory challenges in this area of child protection policymaking. Finally, some caveats may be necessary with regard to the discussion that follows. This chapter does not rehearse or critique the reports or scholarly works undertaken by researchers in this field (Akdeniz, 2008; Shariff, 2009; Brenner, 2010; Kerr, 2009). Neither does this chapter review the role of criminal law in virtual worlds (Lastowka, 2010). Even though these and other works provide some useful insights on the challenges posed by Web 2.0 technologies to the criminal law, the task undertaken in this chapter is deliberately narrowed to a consideration of three specific forms of online child safety incidents/risk-prone activities. The aim of the discussion is to reflect the nuances of online child safety governance with regard to the standards and principles the criminal law aims to uphold and, more specifically, examine the extent to which Web 2.0 technologies can be said to undermine its ability to promote certainty, order, trust and confidence. The governance challenge for law and its ability to secure compliance with its standards and principles lies at the core of the evolving MSIG framework aimed at confronting parental anxieties resulting from the vulnerabilities children face in an environment of de-centralised networks and information flows. Secondly, the coverage of these areas will be conducted against the background of the national legal system in England and Wales. Where appropriate, references will be made to relevant legislation, case law and materials from Australia, the United States and Canada, noting that some caution should be exercised when making comparisons between the approaches in these jurisdictions, given that governments ground their legal and policy responses on their "legal traditions, approaches, techniques (e.g. direct regulation vs. self- or co-regulation), and law enforcement practices" (Gasser, *et al.*, 2010: 10). The differences in legal traditions and policy responses do not detract from the tasks undertaken in this chapter. The implications of these rules for evidentiary investigations and online intermediary liability will also be identified and explained.

Preliminary observations

As many commentators have pointed out, the criminal law is one means through which the State establishes rules and standards of conduct expected from its citizens. The role of the State in defining the types of conduct and harms where penal sanctions are justified has a public interest dimension (Muncie, 2001). Beck's works on living in the risk society also remind us that the criminal law is not immune to the assumptions made about who, when and how legal and moral obligations are imposed on individuals. Even self-help is seen as being consistent with the normative foundations of the criminal law (Gardner, 1996: 116–17). With regard to child protection, however, there have long been tensions regarding the way the criminal law targets particular harms, conduct and interests but leaves scope for individuals to assume responsibility for their own actions (Lacey, 2007: 251). Whilst the criminal law has been unequivocal in its prohibition of serious forms of commercial sexual exploitation, the evolution of this branch of public law also illustrates that social and ethical conceptions of responsibility, autonomy and risks continue to present courts and policymakers with difficult choices regarding the boundaries of criminal responsibility and culpability. These tensions also lie at the core of child protection policymaking emerging from technology-mediated harms (e.g. peer victimisation), identifying strategies for regulating the broadcasting and online services industry and assessing the role of the law in securing compliance with its standards and rules. From a policy perspective, the legal standards provided by the criminal law provide a principled framework through which the duties, obligations and social norms for maintaining public order in society can be identified. It does this by defining the types of prohibited conduct and the penalties accompanying violations of its standards and obligations (Goold *et al.*, 2007). Ashworth identifies one of the central preoccupations of the criminal law as being to "prohibit behaviour that represents a serious wrong against an individual or against some fundamental social value or institution" (Ashworth, 2004: 1). These observations are also very much in line with the standards and principles in the UNCRC, in particular Articles 19, 34 and 37. The criminal law is one instrument through which children can be safeguarded from all forms of violence and exploitation (Articles 19 and 34) and "inhuman or degrading treatment" (Article 37). Securing compliance with the law is made more complex when we recall that the traditional model of law enforcement relies on there being a nexus between the criminal act and the territorial space (Brenner, 2004). Crimes which are mediated through technology tend to be categorised in any one of three ways:

(i) Offences against the confidentiality, integrity and availability of computer data and systems;
(ii) Computer-related offences; and
(iii) Content-related offences.

Online sexual solicitation or grooming, for instance, is an example of a "computer-related offence", whilst distribution of illegal material (e.g. child pornography) would clearly give rise to a "content-related offence". Hacking into a child's user account with a social networking site and altering data would be an example of an act which is held to impair the integrity of the computer system. As highlighted previously, the *EU Kids Online project* indicated that as children's exposure to the Internet increased, it also resulted in an increase in their exposure to some specific online safety incidents – inadvertently viewing harmful or inappropriate content, becoming victims of online harassment, intimidation and bullying and being solicited by strangers for sexual activity (Hasebrink *et al.*, 2009). Though rare, children have also been known to meet online contacts for sexual activity.

When contemplating the role of the criminal law in enhancing the safety of children, it may be important to also bear in mind the significance of

Table 3.1   Relationship between children's risk-prone activities and online child safety incidents

Risk-prone activities	Online safety incidents
User-generated content (profile, text and photos)	Online sexual solicitation Sexting Bullying
Communications (email, IM, chat rooms, online forums)	Illegal and harmful content Sexual solicitation Bullying Harassment
Online gaming	Harassment Sexual solicitation
Social networking sites	Contact risks Conduct risks Conduct risks

Source: Eurobarometer Survey, 2007.

the distinction between their risk-prone activities and risky activities (Table 3.1). The former is concerned with children's engagement with technological affordances that expose them to online incidents and risks, whilst the latter is concerned with children's risky behaviours as participants or perpetrators (ITU, 2010b: 16–20; Livingstone *et al.*, 2009b). As an example, a recent survey highlighted that teenagers (13- to 17-year-olds) posted personal information, or engaged in communications with strangers, assuming that they were invulnerable (Cox Communications, 2010: 9). The *Eurobarometer 2007* and *EU Kids Online II 2011* surveys also illustrate the correspondence between children's online activities and their exposure to online safety incidents and experiences (Eurobarometer, 2007; Livingstone *et al.*, 2011). It should, however, be borne in mind that such distinctions can be used to characterise any activity undertaken by a child in both the offline and online environments.

Online child safety governance: Key principles of the criminal law

Before considering the extent to which the principles and standards enshrined in the UNCRC are reflected in existing criminal laws, four key points should be borne in mind. First, it is a fundamental principle of the criminal justice system that prosecution provide relevant and admissible evidence showing that the offender committed the offence for which he is being charged, beyond all reasonable doubt. Second, it follows from this that before a defendant can be charged with a crime, the conduct must be proven to be one, which is described by the law as constituting an offence. A failure on the part of prosecution to prove the existence of any one of the elements of the offence to the requisite standard of proof will lead to the offender being acquitted. Indeed, the requirement for the prosecution to establish each element of the offence will circumscribe the types of incidents when the law is unlikely to intervene. One can infer that this self-imposed constraint on the State's penal authority is consistent with the public policy objective that individuals in society also assume some responsibility for their well-being. The much publicised prosecution of *US v Lori Drew* (2009) is one example of the complex balances maintained by the criminal law between State intervention and individual self-help. The facts can be briefly recounted. The accused was an adult who set up an account in MySpace and assumed the fictional identity of a 16-year-old under the name of "Josh Evans". A photograph of a boy was posted on this site to provide credence to the identity assumed. The accused used the pseudonym whilst engaging in conversations with Megan. They began to flirt with each other. Sometime later, "Josh" informed Megan that he was moving away, and a week later said that "the world would be a better place without her in it" (2009: 452). Megan committed suicide after reading this message. The tragic death of Megan attracted great media attention and public outrage over the conduct of the accused. The relevant state law provides that for an accused to be found liable for the tort of intentional infliction of emotional distress the following elements must be established: the defendant is shown to have acted with intent or was reckless; the conduct must be regarded as extreme or outrageous; the conduct must be the cause of extreme emotional distress. It is not entirely unexpected that during the first trial, the jury was unable to agree as to whether the accused had the requisite mental state of mind, namely, to inflict emotional distress either intentionally or by being reckless as to the consequence. An attempt was then made to charge the accused for a lesser offence of computer misuse. Under the provisions of § 1030 of the Computer Fraud and Abuse Act, it is an offence to access a computer without authorisation, or the conduct is regarded as exceeding authorisation and obtaining information from a computer if carried out in furtherance of a crime or tortuous act. This attempt proved unsuccessful. The court cited with approval, dicta in *Kolender v Lawson*:

> The void-for-vagueness doctrine requires that a penal statute define the criminal offense with sufficient definiteness that ordinary people can understand what conduct is prohibited and in a manner that does not encourage arbitrary and discriminatory enforcement. (2009: paragraph 11)

The court concluded that the accused could not be regarded as having committed a crime on the grounds of violating a website's terms of reference alone; to do this, it was observed by the court, would have amounted to an unwarranted extension of the scope of the Act and would criminalise many users, including Megan, who had herself used a false age to register an account on the site. One reading of this case is that the court adopts a highly juridical and technical approach to the issues raised. Another view is that the decision illustrates the balance the criminal law sometimes appears to make between protection and self-help principles; the ruling in this case indicates that beneath the linear and formalistic rules, the criminal law has never been entirely comfortable with intervening in situations where the obligations to be assumed by individuals are not capable of being defined clearly or where there is an expectation that individuals assume some responsibility for the actions they take (Morse, 1999: 267–70). Third, it is an incontrovertible principle that the person charged is innocent until proven to be guilty of the offence for which he is being charged (*R v G Lighting* (2009); *R v Gibson* (2009); *R v Pearson* (2009)). Consequently, prosecution need to provide relevant and admissible evidence, which demonstrates beyond reasonable doubt that the accused engaged in the crime for which he has been charged. The accused can effectively say nothing and require prosecution to prove the allegations against him. This was the case in *R v Ashby* where the accused refused to admit to being in possession of indecent images of children on his laptop (2009). The accused sold a laptop computer to an individual. Some time after having purchased the laptop, the individual started experiencing difficulties with the machine and brought it to a shop for repairs. During the course of the repair work, a technician inadvertently came across a file containing indecent images of children on the laptop. The police were alerted, and the investigations which followed eventually led to the accused being traced and charged with possession of child pornography. During the interview, the accused denied any knowledge of being in possession of indecent images contained on the laptop, and refused to answer any of the questions posed to him. The accused was successfully prosecuted when evidence was subsequently produced which indicated his guilt for the offence charged. Fourth, unlike the civil law, in criminal prosecutions, the offences under consideration in this book require the accused to possess the requisite state of mind in respect of the elements of the offence for which he is being charged. The type of mental element which leads to culpability will depend on the construction of the criminal offence. The mental element may include "intent", "recklessly", "wilfully", "maliciously", or "reasonable belief" (Feinberg, 1987: 31). In judicial proceedings, the meanings to be attached to a particular mental element will depend on the applicable judicial precedent to the specific facts before the court (Feinberg, 2003: 3–7).

In the next section, an account will be provided of the role of the criminal law in dealing with contact, content and conduct risks, the substantive elements of those offences and the significance of the allocation of the risks for the way society and individuals are expected to assume responsibility in managing them.

Online sexual solicitation

Virtual worlds, social networking sites, mobile phones and chat rooms provide new avenues through which children can be exposed to individuals seeking to exploit them for sexual activity (Jewkes, 2010). The public policy concerns informing the enactment of laws criminalising online sexual exploitation and abuse of children can be gleaned from the observations made in the following House of Representatives report:

> With the advent of ever-growing computer technology, law enforcement officials are discovering that criminals roam the Internet just as they roam the streets. While parents strive to warn their children about the dangers outside of the home, they are often unaware of the dangers within – on the World Wide Web. "Cyber-predators" often "cruise" the Internet in search of lonely, rebellious or trusting young people. (House of Representatives, 1998: 680)

These fears are rooted in the fact that de-personalised communications increase children's exposure to online safety incidents like online sexual solicitation. The absence of face-to-face contact enables individuals to create *false personas* or provide misleading information about themselves and their interests with the aim of seducing children. As previously noted, social networking sites like Facebook, MySpace and Bebo make available technological affordances, which can be used for both legal and illegal purposes. Article 23 CPC Convention makes it clear that online sexual solicitation is a violation of the child's rights to be protected from such abuse. It provides a benchmark for legislation in many countries. Article 6 of the Proposed Directive requires Member States to enact legislation criminalising the use by an adult of ICT to solicit a child who has not attained the age of sexual consent under national law, for the purpose of engaging in sexual activity (European Commission, 2010e). The legislative changes made to the Sexual Offences Act (SOA) 2003 in England and Wales (and similar reforms for Scotland and Northern Ireland) anticipate many of the proposed recommendations in the Proposed Directive. More specifically, Article 6 of the Proposed Directive envisages the creation of a new offence of solicitation of children for sexual offences. It is targeted at an adult's misuse of the Internet and other communication technologies like mobile phones, IM and email to solicit minors. Unlike Section 15 of the SOA 2003, the Proposed Directive regards a single communication undertaken with the goal of engaging in sexual activity with a child as being sufficient to give rise to criminal liability (European Commission, 2010e: Articles 7 and 5(6)). The public policy issues raised by children's exposure to online sexual solicitation have been mirrored by parallel legislative activity in many jurisdictions: Provision (2) in Article 205 of the Criminal Code (the Czech Republic), Article 240a of the Penal Code (the Netherlands), Article 227–24, of the Penal Code (France) (Davidson *et al.*, 2011). Countries like Singapore and New Zealand have also amended their laws to reflect the threats posed to children by adults using ICTs (e.g. Section 376E of Penal Code (Singapore), Section 131B of the Crimes Amendment Act 2005 No. 41, Public Act). It is worth noting in passing that signatories to the CPC Convention also undertake to enact "necessary legislative or other measures" to criminalise solicitation of minors for sexual purposes (Article 23).

Before looking at three specific legislative attempts which criminalise online sexual solicitation, a brief account of attempts to construct the nature of sexual grooming may be helpful in understanding their relevance for governance strategies, particularly for the deterrent role of the criminal law.

Sexual grooming laws not only delineate the standards of behaviour expected from individuals towards children but its provisions also identify the types of conduct, which if entered into will give rise to criminal liability. This latter aspect is important, since the clearer the prohibited conduct, the easier it is for law enforcement to investigate and prosecute an offender of the relevant crime. Davidson's definition of sexual grooming aims to capture the dynamics of the offending characteristics by describing the criminal activity in terms of

> a process of socialisation during which an offender seeks to interact with the victim (and sometimes the victim's family), to share their hobbies and interests and to become a part of their life, in order to prepare them for abuse. (Davidson *et al.*, 2011: 4)

O'Connell, on the other hand views, the act of sexual grooming as comprising

> a course of conduct enacted by a suspected paedophile, which would give a reasonable person cause for concern that any meeting with a child arising from the conduct would be for unlawful purposes. (O'Connell, 2003)

Like Davidson and O'Connell, Gillespie views sexual grooming as a relational activity involving a child who

> is befriended by a would-be abuser in an attempt to gain the child's confidence and trust, enabling them to get the child to acquiesce to abusive activity. It is frequently a pre-requisite for an abuser to gain access to a child. (Gillespie, 2002: 411)

Finally, in a recent review of sexual grooming literature it has been pointed out that the above definitions do not capture the way a number of individuals engaged in sexual grooming direct their attention towards parties other than the child (Craven *et al.*, 2006). Sexual grooming is regarded as embracing a wider range of deceptive conduct, which include "self-groom-ing", "grooming the environment and significant others" and "grooming the child" (Craven *et al.*, 2006). Sample studies have shown the tendency of some offenders to "self-groom" themselves and thereby justify the sexual solicitation and abuse of children (Howitt *et al.*, 2007: 469–86). Whilst there are doubts about the weight to be accorded to offenders' accounts of deci-sions to "groom" or make contact with children, it does highlight that some individuals appear to be motivated solely by the need to gratify their fanta-sies rather than use the online communications as a prelude to an eventual meeting (Quayle *et al.*, 2003: 93–106). This last aspect raises some inter-esting issues about the doctrinal, investigatory and prosecution challenges faced when apprehending individuals for engaging in voyeuristic conduct for sexual gratification purposes (Feinberg, 2003: 137; Section 8 of the SOA 2003; *R v Grout (Phillip)*). The question regarding the acts which constitute, for example, "an intention to incite" a child aged 13 to engage in sexual activity via a webcam can be problematic. The accused in *R v Grout (Phillip)* engaged in a webcam conversation with a child, and during the interaction asked her to reveal her bra and then subsequently suggested that she also take off her clothing. The child refused to comply with the last request. It is clear from this account why Lord Justice Aikens did not feel that the act of revealing a bra strap constituted a "sexual activity" and justified charging the accused (paragraphs 43–7). Can or should the criminal law penalise such individuals by the mere fact that the revelation of a bra strap would consti-tute a form of sexual gratification (Feinberg, 2003: 23)? Sexual grooming as a process of deviant criminal behaviour comprises a number of character-istics which pose complicated normative issues-deception, gaining the co-operation or trust of the child or adults who have responsibility for the child and de-sensitisation. None of this would appear to be readily apparent when we depict sexual grooming as simply involving a "process by which a person prepares a child, significant adults and the environment for the abuse of this child" (Craven *et al.*, 2006: 297). This description does serve the pur-pose of at least highlighting acts, which include inciting a child to engage in sexual activity as a prelude to a face-to-face meeting. This move away from "offender" characteristics to the dynamic process of victim identification and the strategies adopted by perpetrators in de-sensitising children is par-ticularly instructive in helping us come to terms with the complex dimen-sions of the grooming process. Attempts have also been made to model the cycle of victimisation that distinguishes sexual grooming from other types of interaction between adults and children. The "precondition model" developed by Finkelhor identifies four steps in the cycle leading to abuse: a motivated perpetrator, overcoming the inhibitions through rationalisation and justification, overcoming the external constraints or barriers to gain access to the child and, finally, reducing the child's resistance to engaging in sexual activity (Finkelhor, 1984; *cf.* Howells, 1995: 201–14). Brackenridge, on the other hand, proposes a three-step process describing sexual exploitation generally (see Table 3.2).

Ward, Louden, Hudson and Marshall provide an elaborate nine-step model, which aims to establish a causal link between the perpetrator's psychological and social profile, the conditions for planning and access, the priming of the victim culminating in the sexual abuse which leads to a grounded insight into the process of grooming (Ward *et al.*, 1995). It is fair to say that these models vary in terms of emphasis but they do offer an insight into the spectrum of activities that begin with the factors motivating the entry into a trust relationship by the perpetrator with the targeted victim before steps are taken in preparing a child for sexual self-gratification. We can use the framework provided by O'Connell in teasing out the issues to be grappled with by the law. O'Connell's six-step grooming cycle illustrates how this process evolves from the initial contact to the eventual sexual activity (O'Connell, 2003; Table 3.3).

Three particular observations could be made with regard to the significance of the process of grooming for the way the criminal law frames the relevant legal and evidentiary issues. First, since online sexual grooming involves a process where the progress from each stage to the next is not easy to discern, conduct must be shown to clearly engage the substantive law. It is important to keep this in mind when ascertaining whether the criminal law is wanting in its ability "to protect children" (Gillespie, 2002: 411). As O'Connell (2003) and, more recently, Bryce note:

> The friendship and relationship forming stages are similar to those of the development of other online friendships, and involve the offender

Table 3.2   Brackenridge's three-step cycle of child abuse

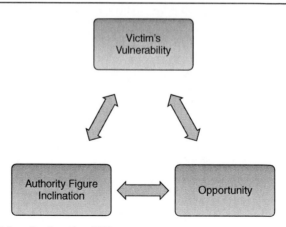

Source: Adapted from Brackenridge, 2002.

Table 3.3 O'Connell's six-step grooming cycle

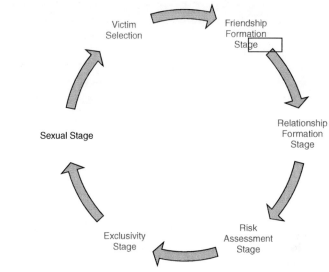

Source: O'Connell, 2003.

approaching and befriending the young person, and encouraging them to discuss their life in order to initiate friendship. (Bryce, 2010: 330)

Second, it does not always follow that the "victim selection" stage will progress to a "relationship formation" or actual "sexual" stage. One reason why that might happen is that the offender may have already obtained his sexual gratification at this stage (Attorney General's Reference (No. 28 of 2010) (2010)). Alternatively, it could also be that the offender may have decided that the risks of detection outweigh the gratification derived or the child may have taken steps to block all unwanted contact. Third, the time lapse between each stage may vary depending on a number of variables – motivations of the offender, opportunity and location of the victim and offender. Consequently, we may have to accept the observation of the Court of Appeal in *PDA v R* (2008) that grooming "is not a term of art but connotes something along the lines of steps taken by the offender to persuade, or prepare, or encourage, the object of sexual attention to participate in sexual activity" (2008: paragraph 8). More generally, both offline and online grooming of children are not linear socialisation processes that come within a pre-determined time frame, and which can add to the complications in detecting or investigating sexual grooming activity (Mitchell *et al.*, 2007c). Whilst the criminal law defines the substantive elements of the offence which justifies legal intervention, O'Connell's identification of the "risk assessment" stage has another significance, namely, that it alerts vigilant parents/law enforcement to the possibility of other motivations held by the person communicating with the child in the online environment and enables early intervention (i.e. "where is your computer", "let us keep this secret to ourselves", "can we talk privately" and "I hope your parents don't mind you spending so much time on the computer"). Whilst the earlier stages in the six-step cycle aim to develop a level of trust, the progression in the communications can be seen as providing important cues that a more intimate and sexual aspect to the relationship is likely to emerge. Finally, these depictions of the cycle of victimisation can be used to develop preventative intervention measures and programmes as envisaged by Article 20 of the Proposed Directive.

United Kingdom: Section 15 of the SOA 2003

Section 15 of the SOA 2003 (as amended by the Criminal Justice and Immigration Act 2008, Section 73(a)) can be seen as a legitimate governance response aimed at enhancing the safety of children in both the online and offline environment. The rationale underpinning this prudential legislation is to ensure that a child who has been rendered vulnerable is not subsequently harmed by an actual meeting with the offender or in a non-contact situation encouraged to engage in sexually inappropriate conduct which may go undetected by parents or not reported owing to the child's embarrassment or shame. It should be noted that unlike the provision in the Proposed Directive, the offence could be committed through the use of electronic and non-electronic communication technologies. Section 15 is an inchoate offence. Attempts to rely on rules on incitement or even conspiracy run the risk of promoting greater controversy and debates on when a child can be deemed to be competent to provide consent in respect of sexual activity with adults (*cf.* Gillespie, 2002). For the purposes of the SOA 2003, the law on sexual grooming applies to adults who engage in sexual solicitation of children aged below 16. There must be communications with the minor on at least two occasions which lead to an actual meeting or result in the offender (A) travelling with the intention of engaging in sexual activity. The section also provides A with a defence; reasonable belief that the child is 16 years old or above. It should be borne in mind that the legal age for consenting to sexual activity varies according to the jurisdiction and the type of child sexual abuse and exploitation crimes charged. For example, the age of consent to sexual activity in England and Wales is 16, but exploitative activity like child pornography is 18. In Spain the age of consent is 14, and in Philippines it is 19. In Australia most jurisdictions stipulate the age of consent as 16, but South Australia and Tasmania have a higher threshold of 17 (Griffith *et al.*, 2007: 30). In the United States, the age limit of 18 years applies to both online sexual solicitation and child pornography. The

UNCRC and the CPC Convention recommend that the threshold be raised to 18 years of age, so that all children are provided with the maximum legal protection possible.

Whilst adults and society may have a view about children communicating with strangers, particularly in an online environment, the law's response is more measured. When the question whether the criminal law is violated is posed, the sexual grooming activity is formalised in the following manner: is the individual an adult? Is B a child aged 16 years old or above? Have there been at least two communications? Has A met B, or arranged to meet B or travels with the intention of meeting B, which if done would amount to a "sexual offence"? Is there cause for A to have believed that B was 16 years old? Such is the seriousness with which sexual grooming is viewed that an individual convicted under the offence can face imprisonment of at least 10 years. Prosecutions for grooming have generally been successful, and many of the cases heard on appeal are to do with sentencing, which is not the focus in this chapter.

In cases where offenders have been convicted, prosecution have been able to discharge their legal and evidentiary burdens: the existence of a series of communications between the offender and the victim (i.e. email and text messages), the offender knew that he was dealing with a minor, there was incriminating evidence of an intention to commit a sexual act with the child and the offender has either met the child or travels with the intention of meeting the child with the object of engaging in sexual activity. In *R v Luis Cotilla* (2009), the offender contacted an individual ("Charlotte 12") in a chat room entitled "No Adults". He initiated contact with Charlotte 12 via an IM facility. The conversations initiated by the offender assumed sexual overtones, during which time he expressed his intention to have sex with Charlotte 12 and proceeded to describe the intended activity in graphic detail. A meeting was subsequently arranged and the offender was arrested when he turned up at the pre-arranged venue. In *R v CB* (2010), the offender contacted one of the girls on the social networking site Facebook. He sent her a message requesting her to become his "friend". The girl added his name to her site. The offender's profile indicated his date of birth as 14 December 1992. They communicated with each other via the IM facility on Facebook and the conversations eventually turned to sexual matters. The girl showed the offender's messages to her classmate and they both entered into conversations with the offender on Facebook. The offender met with the girls at a pre-arranged venue. No sexual activity was, however, engaged in during this and at another pre-arranged meeting. These matters came to light when the girl complained to her mother, who then alerted the police. The offender was convicted under Section 15(1) of the SOA 2003. The fact that no sexual activity occurred was held not to be a defence to conviction under this section. The case of *R v Mohammad* (2006), even though not strictly an online sexual grooming incident, serves to illustrate the pre-emptive value of Section 15. The offender in this case was a security guard on a building site. Local schoolgirls regularly hung around this site, and it transpires that some of them approached the offender and engaged him in conversations. During one of these meetings, the offender was introduced to the complainant, aged 13. Both the offender and the complainant developed a friendship and they subsequently exchanged telephone numbers. Over a three-month period, the relationship between the offender and the complainant progressed to an intimate level. At the trial of the offender, no evidence was produced of sexual activity having taken place between the complainant and the offender. The offender was, nevertheless, convicted for abduction and the offence of meeting with a child following sexual grooming. Following an appeal on the sentence handed down by the trial judge the Court found no reason to disagree with the decision that the accused was guilty under Section 15 of the SOA 2003. It is particularly interesting to note that the court held the intervention by law enforcement to be timely as the girl (who was in foster care) was deemed to be vulnerable to being socialised into accepting that sexual activity with the offender was a natural part of their friendship (2006: paragraph 13). It should also be made clear that even though the process of sexual grooming may not be advanced sufficiently to warrant a Section 15 prosecution, it does not preclude law enforcement from charging the individual with other sexual offences against minors if appropriate. For example, a perpetrator could be prosecuted for non-contact offences like causing a child to watch a sexual act, inciting the child to engage in sexual activity or engaging in a sexual activity in the presence of a child. *R v H* (2010) is an apt illustration of the alternative charges that may be made against an offender suspected of grooming a child for sexual activity. The perpetrator, in the course of grooming a child, committed a series of sexual offences, namely, those of engaging in sexually obscene behaviour, causing or initiating a child to engage in sexual activity contrary to Section 10(1) of the SOA 2003 and having indecent photos of a child contrary to Section 1(1) of the Protection of Children Act (PCA) 1978. The defendant's *modus operandi* was to wait in a car parked close to a phone booth. When girls aged 12 to 15 passed by, he rang the phone from his mobile. On occasions when the girls did answer the phone, he engaged in conversations and obtained their mobile phone numbers. He offered the girls payment and gifts when they responded to his sexual requests.

The criminal law does not absolve an adult from adhering to its standards even when the suggestion to engage in sexual activity is initiated by the child. A case that highlights the standards of behaviour expected from adults is *R v Walker* (2007). The accused worked in a public library, and entered into conversations with four girls at the venue. The girls were below the age of 16 years. As their friendships developed, the girls initiated a meeting with the accused at his flat. On one occasion at the flat, the accused was invited to kiss one of the girls, and the invitation was accepted. The accused then proceeded to kiss the other girls and as the evening progressed, the parties engaged in several overt sexual activities. The accused was convicted not only of meeting a child consequent to sexual grooming (Section 15 of the SOA 2003), but also for the offences of causing or inciting a child to engage in sexual activity (Section 10 of the SOA 2003); engaging in sexual activity in the presence of a child (Section 11 of the SOA 2003) and sexual activity with a child (Section 9 of the SOA 2003).

How does the online environment affect the standard setting role of the criminal law, particularly where the interactions between the parties are mediated through ICTs and affordances? This is a relevant question with regard to the application of the law where the parties, as a general rule, do not have face-to-face interactions. For example, an adult may pretend to be a minor and register false details on a social networking site to gain access to children within this age group. Some children may be unaware of these risks or may themselves deliberately conceal their ages with the aim of making contact with adults. *R v Costi* (2006) illustrates the protective role of Section 15(1) of the SOA 2003 in the online context. The offender in this case engaged in a conversation with a girl, aged 14, in an Internet chat room. He told her that he was aged 20 years, and the complainant informed him that she was aged 12. At the offender's request, the complainant exposed herself on her webcam and masturbated herself. Following these activities, the offender arranged to meet up with the girl and sent his photograph to her. He did not turn up for the pre-arranged meeting. The girl informed her mother, who in turn contacted the police. The offender was charged and convicted on one count of causing or inciting a female child under 16 to engage in sexual activity (Section 10 of the SOA 2003) in addition to Section 15(1) of the SOA 2003. Clearly, the interactions, the extent of the non-contact sexual activity and the plan to meet the child at a pre-arranged venue were deemed to be sufficient for the court to hold that the grooming offence had been committed. Some may argue that the offence is not widely constructed, and consequently recourse should be had to Sections 14 or 62 of the SOA 2003. Section 14 of the SOA 2003 provides that a person is guilty of the offence of arranging or facilitating the commission of a child sex offence, but only if two conditions are met:

(i) he intentionally arranges or facilitates something that he intends to do, and
(ii) doing it will involve the commission of an offence under any of Sections 9 to 13.

In addition to Section 14, Section 62 of the SOA 2003 provides that an offender can be prosecuted if he does an act which is regarded as being more than merely preparatory to the commission of the offences under Part 1 of the legislation (Section 1 of the Criminal Attempts Act 1981 and *R v Jones* (2007)). On this line of reasoning, an appropriate charge of attempting to commit a Section 15 offence could be considered if the accused had communicated to the child details of the meeting place (*Shivpuri*). Two points should be noted by way of response to these claims. First, Section 15 of the SOA 2003 creates an inchoate offence and permits intervention even in cases where the accused does not carry out the intention to arrange or facilitate the carrying out of relevant child sex offences. Should an individual terminate the relationship at step 3 (i.e. O'Connell's cycle of victimisation) it appears that Section 15 of the SOA 2003 would have fulfilled its deterrent role. Second, Section 62 of the SOA 2003 may appear to be an attractive proposition, until we recognise that the early intervention permitted by Section 15 is concerned with attempts to engage in some form of sexual activity with a child. To suggest otherwise would be tantamount to holding that one can be prosecuted for attempting to commit an inchoate offence – whatever that might entail. A more immediate and relevant concern is whether the absence of knowledge that the accused knew he was interacting with a minor is relevant for the purposes of the legislation. It is an issue that has been addressed by courts in a number of jurisdictions. As a general rule, in the offline world there is no real difficulty in determining the circumstances when an adult should be put on notice – wilful blindness is not a basis for running the defence of reasonable belief that the child was 16 years old or above. The question of whether the offender entertained a reasonable belief that a child was 16 years of age or older is a question of fact and is a matter for the jury. Some indication as to how such online interactions can be brought within the ambit of the SOA 2003 can be inferred from the *Attorney General's Reference (No. 29 of 2008) R v D* (2008). The complainant met the offender (aged 19) in an Internet chat room. The complainant stated her age on her chat room profile as 20, even though she was only aged 11. The offender believed the complainant to be 20 years old. As their online relationship progressed, sexually explicit messages were exchanged, and at the request of the offender, the complainant sent him a nude photograph of herself. Some time later, the complainant revealed her true age to the offender. Despite the disclosure of this fact, the offender continued to communicate with the minor. They subsequently met but did not engage in penetrative sex. The complainant later informed her parents about the offender, and the police were subsequently alerted. The offender was arrested and charged with various offences under the SOA 2003. The court accepted evidence showing that the complainant was complicit in the online interactions and meetings. The court, however, held that an adult was put on notice of potential criminal liability as soon as he was made aware that the individual he was dealing with was a minor:

> The basic problem in this case is that the law exists, not only to protect children from the baleful, damaging influence of adults with a sexual

interest in children, but also because the law acknowledges the reality that some children, even children as young as 11 years of age, need protection from themselves. (2008: paragraph 35)

It may be useful to briefly examine the parallels between Section 15 of the SOA 2003 and similar substantive provisions in jurisdictions like the United States, Canada and Australia.

The United States: 18 USCA § 2422

The relevant anti-sexual grooming Federal Law can be found in 18 USCA § 2422. For example, under § 2422 (a) a person who "knowingly persuades, induces, entices, or coerces any individual who has not attained the age of 18 years, to engage in prostitution or any sexual activity" will be prosecuted. When prosecuting an offender for the offence under § 2422 (b) it must be shown that the individual has used a communication tool and has "knowingly" persuaded, induced, enticed or coerced an individual below the age of 18 to engage in sexual activity or prostitution. The section does not prescribe the presence of two communications and like the Proposed Directive (Article 6) requires evidence indicating some form of communication which indicates enticement, inducement, persuasion or coercion. Additionally, the protection is afforded to all children below the age of 18 years.

There are two issues raised by the anti-grooming provision that could be explored here: is there a need for the accused to entice a "real child" and what is the scope of the "reasonable belief" defence? Some answers to the issues were provided in *US v D'Amelio* (2009). The offender engaged in an online conversation with a child ("MaryinNYC1991") in an America Online (AOL) chat room. Mary's online personal profile indicated that she was 12 years old. The perpetrator engaged in a wide range of sexual discussions both online and over the telephone, and he subsequently met with Mary (a female police officer). The offender was charged and successfully prosecuted under § 2422 for enticing a minor. The Court held that the online and offline communications represented a "single course of conduct – one designed, under the Government's theory of the case, to gain the trust of a child and convince her to meet the defendant in person, so he could lure her into a secluded place for the purpose of engaging in sexual conduct" (Id. 243). The Court ruled that the absence of an actual victim was not fatal to a conviction if evidence produced showed that the offender believed he was enticing a minor to engage in criminal sexual activity and took preparatory steps to induce a minor to engage in sexual activity. Another example of how the criminal law can be used to deter individuals from engaging in such forms of sexual exploitation activity is *US v Cote* (2007). The offender in this case entered a chat room named "# O!!!!!!!!! younggirlsex". The chat room was set up as a fantasy forum for young girls and those who loved them. Whilst in the chat room, the offender met "lil'mary" (Mary) and he managed to persuade her to enter into a private conversation in a separate chat room. Mary described herself as "14f chgo" (14-year-old female from Chicago). Cote sent Mary a photograph of himself. Mary replied to his email and sent a picture of a young blonde on a bicycle. They then engaged in a series of conversations of a sexual and graphic character. Eventually, the conversation turned to organising a face-to-face meeting in Chicago. The accused was charged and convicted under § 2422 (b) as he was deemed to have satisfied all the elements of the offence including that concerning his knowledge of the age of the victim. The attempt to rely on the defence of mistaken belief (since he was actually dealing with a police officer) was rejected. The Court held that § 2422 created an inchoate offence, and consequently, the only legal issue to be addressed was whether the "defendant specifically intend to induce, entice or coerce a minor" (2007: 687). Two observations can be made. First, the court made it clear that the inchoate offence did not require an actual child to have been solicited – for a crime to be committed under the section, prosecution had to adduce evidence showing that the accused, in doing what he did, believed that he was dealing with a minor. Second, an accused will be deemed to have "knowingly" induced or enticed a minor if his actions were founded on knowledge and awareness of the consequences of his conduct, and that the outcome was not the result of mistake or accident. This last aspect was addressed in *US v Myers* (2009). The accused entered an Internet chat room and met a user ("stephanieboyd1994") who described herself as a 14-year-old female. During one of the chat room conversations an oversight led to stephanieboyd1994's screen name being changed to "Kim Wilson". The accused appeared not to have noticed the change and continued to engage with Kim Wilson as he had with stephanieboyd1994. The following is an extract of the conversation between the two parties after the inadvertent change in the screename:

Todd Myers:	So I can come down like next Tuesday if you wanna see me
Kim Wilson:	k
Kim Wilson:	What time?
Todd Myers:	Well is there anyway you can be home alone all day?
Kim Wilson:	I can skip [school] if your 4 real
Todd Myers:	Yes I am
Todd Myers:	Will u be home all day alone?
Kim Wilson:	Can be

The conversation then turned to graphic accounts of the anticipated sexual encounter, during which time Kim's (and not stephanieboyd1994's) age was introduced. The following day the offender travelled to meet Kim at the pre-arranged destination. Whilst on the way to the venue he sent a series of texts to Kim. The offender was arrested at the pre-arranged venue and was found with condoms and a digital camera. During the trial the offender claimed that at all times he knew that the person he was chatting with in the chat room was not a minor. The Court had to address two issues at the trial – entrapment and the offence of knowingly enticing a minor for sexual activity. We will focus on the latter issue for the purposes of the present discussion. The Court held that from a review of the chat logs there was very little suggestion that the offender was disinclined to engage in sexual activity with a minor had the opportunity presented itself. Particular reference was made to the fact that the offender met Stephanie in a romance chat room, that he was aware a minor was involved and that he was disposed to engaging in sexually explicit conversations. Notwithstanding that the second chat conversation was with an individual using the pseudonym – Kim, rather than stephanieboyd1994 – the offender was found to have initiated the discussions about engaging in sexual activity and was the person who initiated the discussion regarding a face-to-face meeting, despite being informed that Kim was a minor. When viewed together with a four-minute video sent to Kim, and of himself engaging in acts of sexual self-gratification, the Court concluded that a reasonable jury would have found that there was an attempt to entice a minor to engage in sexual activity.

Australia: Various territorial competences

Another jurisdiction where the criminal laws have been instrumental in dealing with online sexual solicitation is Australia. It is worth pointing out that in Australia, the Commonwealth, States and Territories assume responsibility for child sexual abuse and exploitation at varying levels of involvement. As a general rule, in relation to child sexual abuse and exploitation issues, States and Territories assume a direct role in dealing with incidents at a domestic level. The Commonwealth's responsibility covers the offences that take place across all Australian jurisdictions and beyond. An individual can be effectively charged for grooming or grooming-related offences under Commonwealth, State and Territory legislation (Griffith *et al.*, 2007: 36; Kim-Kwang, 2009: 50–1). The use by law enforcement of sting operations is a good example of securing compliance with appropriate standards of behaviour towards children in the online environment. Like the case in *Myers* (discussed previously), in *R v Gedling* (2007) the offender attempted to argue that prosecution was under a legal and evidentiary burden to prove beyond reasonable doubt that he knew that the person he was communicating with was a "child" or that he did not have an honest and reasonable belief and, consequently, that he communicated with the intent to procure a child to engage in, or submit to, sexual activity contrary to Section 63B(3)(a) of the Criminal Law Consolidation Act 1935. This attempt by the defence to redefine the substantive elements of the offence was rejected by the Court. Judge Millsteed stated unequivocally that the substantive elements of the offence did not include disproving the offender's honest and reasonable belief, nor the requirement of proving that the offender knowingly procured a real "child" below the legal age of consent to engage in or submit to sexual activity. He suggested that the imposition of these substantive requirements on prosecution "would undermine Parliament's intention to protect children from sexual exploitation through the Internet and other mediums of communication" (paragraph 53).

Section 218A of the Criminal Code 1899

Section 218A(1) creates two specific offences. First, the use by an adult of electronic communications with the intent to procure a person *under the age of 16 years*, or a person the adult *believes is under the age of 16 years*, to engage in a sexual act, either in Queensland or elsewhere. A child is regarded as being procured when a person is knowingly enticed or recruited for the purposes of sexual exploitation (section 218A(1)). Non-contact sexual acts are sufficient to trigger the relevant section. Section 218A(9) provides the offender with a defence to a charge under this provision if evidence shows that he believed on reasonable grounds that the person was at least 16 years old. Section 218A(8) creates a rebuttable presumption where evidence is provided

> that the person was represented to the adult as being under the age of 16 years, or 12 years, as the case may be, is, in the absence of evidence to the contrary, proof that the adult believed the person was under that age.

It is critical, however, for the offence under Section 218A(1) that prosecution discharges its legal and evidentiary burdens with regard to the age of the person. It is not open to a judge to direct a jury on the basis of the rebuttable presumption under Section 218A(8), thereby absolving prosecution from establishing that the offender intended to procure a person whom he believed to be below 16 years of age. This point was further elaborated by the Supreme Court of Queensland in *R v Shetty* when it stated that "s 218A(8) does not alter the position that the jury must be satisfied that the accused had the belief essential to establish a contravention of s 218A(1)" (2005: paragraph 26).

The Crimes Act 1990 (ACT)

The communications which are deemed to constitute violations of the criminal law include those which aim to procure or incite the child to engage in sexual activity (Section 66), acts which are preparatory to the offender engaging in sexual activity with the child and depravation or corruption of the child through exposure to indecent or illegal material. For example, Section 66(1) of the Crimes Act 1990 (ACT) criminalises the use of the Internet and interactive technologies like email, chat rooms, SMS messages and audio-visual web streaming technology to "suggest to a young person that the young person commit or take part in, or watch someone else committing or taking part in, an act of a sexual nature". The rationale for criminalising this type of conduct, as observed previously, is aimed at assisting law enforcement in preventing the child from being groomed for actual abuse or exploitation. Unlike Section 15 of the SOA 2003 this provision does not stipulate the number of communications that should have been entered into before the criminal law intervenes. Additionally, the use of the word "suggest" appears to provide law enforcement with the flexibility in drawing on a range of communications, which extend the scope of the conduct prohibited by the criminal law. Liability can arise as soon as the prohibited communication is made to a minor below the age of 16 years. The consent of the minor to the suggestion or the agreement to receiving the material either directly or by accessing from a separate source is not a defence (Section 66(4)).

In New South Wales, for example, Section 66EB creates offences of procuring and grooming a child for unlawful sexual activity. "Grooming" is deemed to take place as soon as an adult "engages in any conduct that exposes a child to indecent material or provides a child with an intoxicating substance, and (b) who does so with the intention of making it easier to procure the child for unlawful sexual activity with that or any other person" (Section 66EB(3)). In *R v Asplund, Kenneth* (2010), the offender used an Internet chat room to initiate a sexual encounter with a 14-year-old girl whose online profile was "Aussie Girl". The District Court held that the graphic sexual conversations and the exchange of indecent material (both suggestive and explicit) through mobile phone and SMS/multimedia was evidence of "his fantasies of sexual activity with Aussie Girl, morphed into an intention to have sexual intercourse with her in one or more of the forms that that term is used in the Crimes Act 1900" (paragraph 12).

The Commonwealth Criminal Code 1995

The Commonwealth Criminal Code 1995 provides another example of the role of the criminal law in enabling law enforcement to intervene at the earliest possible opportunity when steps are taken to engage a child in sexual activity. Section 474.25 specifically states that the use of a carriage service to "groom" a minor below 16 years of age is a criminal offence. The substantive elements of the offence are the use by the sender (18 years of age) of a carriage service to transmit a communication to the person; communication sent with the intention of making it easier to procure the person to engage in sexual activity with the sender and the individual being someone who is, or *who the sender believes to be*, under 16 years of age. Procurement can take place where an individual embarks on a course of conduct to entice or recruit a minor for the purposes of sexual activity. Section 474.25A also creates the offence of using a carriage service to transmit indecent communication to person under 16 years of age or who the sender believes to be under 16 years of age. An "indecent" communication is to be determined by reference to the standards of ordinary people. The section also applies where the child engages in sexual activity with other persons as a consequence of the encounter with the offender. In relation to both offences under the section, there is a general defence available to the offender; to avoid a criminal prosecution, the offender must offer evidence showing that the presence of the child was inadvertent and that there was no intention to "derive gratification from the presence of the child during that activity" (Section 474.25A (4)). The offender can avoid the charge if he shows that he believed that the child was not under the age of 16 years. The offence of grooming seems to be worded in a way that makes prosecution relatively easier. The Explanatory Memorandum, for example, states that Sections 474.26–9 aim to deal with preparatory steps undertaken by adults to exploit children for their sexual gratification (Table 3.4).

Canada: Criminal Code, RSC 1985, c. C-46

Finally, policymakers in Canada have also enacted legislation criminalising online sexual solicitation of minors. "Luring a child" is a criminal offence and the relevant law is contained in Section 172.1 of the Criminal Code, RSC 1985. Unlike the United Kingdom, the age threshold in Canada for consenting to sexual activity is 18 years. There are three age-related offences under Section 172.1. First, a person is deemed to have committed an offence if a computer system is used to communicate with a minor who is or who the accused believes is under the age of 18 years old, for the purpose of engaging, enticing or procuring sexual activity with that minor. Second, where the person is under the age of 16, the use of the

---

Table 3.4   Prosecutions and charges in Australia

Before 2007, there were 130 prosecutions for online procuring, grooming and exposure offences in Australia.

Between 2008 and 2009, there were

- two Summary (Charges) and 18 Indictable (Charges) under Section 474.26 Criminal Code 1995 (Cth) – Using a carriage service to procure persons under 16 years of age and

- five Summary (Charges) and 15 Indictable (Charges) under Section 474.27 Criminal Code 1995 (Cth) – Using a carriage service to "groom" persons under 16 years of age (CDPP 2010).

Over 150 people were reportedly charged in the financial year 2008–09 with online child sex exploitation offences (AFP, 2010, Millar, 2010), and the Commonwealth Director of Public Prosecutions also reported prosecuting an increasing number of offences involving the online exploitation of children in the financial year 2008–09 (CDPP, 2010).

Source: Tomison *et al.*, 2010: 5.

communication system to facilitate the commission of acts of indecency like exposure to a person of that age, committing an act of bestiality or inciting a person of that age to engage in that act, or abducting a person of that age, will result in an offence under this section. Finally, where the minor is below the age of 14 years, the use of the communication system for the specific purpose of facilitating the commission of a specified secondary offence – that is, abduction or one of the sexual offences mentioned in Section 172.1(1)(c) with respect to that person (e.g. invitation to sexual touching under Section 152), is deemed to be an offence. In *R v Legare* (2009) the accused was charged and prosecuted for luring a minor under Section 172.1(1)(c). The offender in this case communicated with the complainant in a private online chat room on two occasions. The complainant was 12 years old at the time of the online interactions. The conversations were of a sexual nature, with both parties expressing their desire to engage in sexual activity with each other. The parties did not reveal their true ages during these conversations. The accused claimed that he was 17 years old, whilst the complainant said she was 13 years of age. They continued to have conversations of a sexual nature and the complainant gave the accused her phone number. The accused in turn gave her details of his home address. During a telephone conversation he expressed his wish to perform oral sex on her. There was no actual meeting between the complainant and the offender. When the accused was prosecuted for luring, two arguments were put forward as defence – first, that there had been no arrangement made to meet the child; and, second, that there had been no intention to lure the child as set out in Section 172.1(1)(c). The accused maintained that his sole intention and purpose at all times was to only "talk dirty". The trial judge accepted these arguments. Mr Justice Agrios went so far as to admonish prosecution's attempt in arguing that the conversations entered into by the accused was in itself evidence of an inchoate offence being committed; accordingly he regarded the communications as nothing more than a form of "intimate communication [and that] ... some individuals never intend to meet the children, but rather intend only to 'talk dirty', so to speak. The wording of the legislation is clear: the communication must be 'for the purpose of facilitating the commission of an offence' " (*R v Legare* (2006) paragraph 11). This line of reasoning appears to distinguish between conduct attracting legal censure and those which can be viewed as nothing more than what some in society might characterise as morally reprehensible conduct. In construing the provisions of Section 172.1(1) (c) as he did, Mr Justice Agrios was also making it clear that the formal mechanisms of the criminal law could not be used to penalise conduct not expressly prohibited. The court held that it was disingenuous for the prosecution to suggest that the building of the trust relationship was capable by itself from being regarded as evidence of a crime being committed. On appeal to the Alberta Court of Appeal, this part of the court's ruling was reversed. The Court of

Appeal characterised Mr Justice Agrios's reasoning as being influenced by his view that the legislation required luring to have actually taken place (*R v Legare* (2008)). According to the Court of Appeal, such a construction of Section 172.1(1)(c) was overly narrow and overlooked the mischief that the Legislature had intended to address. The Court of Appeal concluded that it was sufficient if the communications were of a nature designed to gain the acquiescence of the child to engage in the secondary conduct set out in Section 152. This characterisation of the anti-sexual grooming provision appears to attach much greater weight to the risks posed to children from adults contacting them online, the sexual nature of the conversations and the real possibility that sexual activity might have taken place had the opportunity presented itself:

> The communication involved sexual dialogue about sexual activity involving them. A trier of fact might find that there was a process of seductive sexualization and exploitation of the child in the communication which would facilitate the commission of an offence under s.151 or s. 152 with respect to that child and that such facilitation was the respondent's purpose. It is to be borne in mind that the offence under s. 151 or s. 152 was not particularized in this count. A trier of fact might infer that the purpose of the respondent was to facilitate an offence under s. 152 which could occur over the Internet. ((2008) paragraph 66)

Indeed, the Court of Appeal seems to regard the "relationship", "risk assessment" and "sexual" stages as indivisible. Following an appeal by the accused, the Supreme Court of Canada agreed with the decision by the Alberta Court of Appeal (*R v Legare* (2009)). The unanimous view of the Supreme Court was that the communications between the offender and the victim came within the conduct prohibited by Section 172.1(1)(c) since

> in this context, "facilitating" includes helping to bring about and making easier or more probable – for example, by "luring" or "grooming" young persons to commit or participate in the prohibited conduct; by reducing their inhibitions; or by prurient discourse that exploits a young person's curiosity, immaturity or precocious sexuality. (2009: paragraph 28)

The case of *R v RJS* (2010) offers an illustration of the court's response when faced with arguments that the accused was merely engaging in role play or that the person was an adult, not a minor. The latter is an argument often raised by an accused when charged following a sting operation, which was the case here. The accused engaged in sexual conversations with a police officer who assumed the fictional identity of a 13-year-old child. The observations of the Court make clear the respective legal and evidentiary burdens assumed by the prosecution and defence:

If I believe the evidence of the accused that he did not believe he was online with a minor having these sexually explicit conversations that included an invitation to touching, I must acquit the accused. That is not the case. I do not accept the evidence of the accused. (2010: paragraph 58)

It is always open for the defence to suggest reasonable belief or, as is the case here, that the accused did not believe that he was dealing with a child. It is, however, a question of fact, whether in the light of the evidence presented that this is an inference which can be legitimately drawn. The approach adopted in *Legare* and *RJS* illustrates the courts' awareness of the way adults use online communication tools to express their sexual preferences and even re-enact their fantasies. However, in both these cases, the courts also seem to be indicating that adults need to demonstrate that additional steps have been taken to verify that they were not interacting with minors. The imposition of these legal obligations correspond with the recognition that the criminal law has as one of its goals the protection of

young girls against their own immature sexual experimentation and to punish much older men who take advantage of them. (*R v Mansfield* (2005) paragraph 19)

Before concluding the discussion on online sexual solicitation, reference should also be made to Section 123 of the SOA 2003. An application can be made by the police to the magistrates for a "Risk of Sexual Harm Order" (RSHO), if there is evidence that an individual has on at least two occasions communicated with a child, where sexual matters formed part of the exchange. Before an order can be granted, the magistrates must be presented with evidence showing that the alleged communications did in fact take place and that the grant of the order against the offender is necessary for the purpose of protecting children generally or any child from harm. This order significantly broadens the scope of the child protection objective of the SOA 2003. As part of the application, an assessment has to be made of the risk an offender is likely to pose to children generally other than the immediate child concerned. Given the expansive nature of the order and the discretion vested in magistrates, the legislators have imposed some limitations on the circumstances when Section 123 applications could be made. For example, the police must demonstrate that the child concerned was under the age of 16 and that the communication was of a sexual nature. A communication is sexual if it refers to sexual activity or if a reasonable person would regard the description or image sent as being of a sexual nature (Section 124(6)). One difficulty that may arise in obtaining an RSHO under Section 123 stems from the references in Section 124(6) and (7) to the exclusion of the motives of the individual sending an image or communication that relates to sexual activity. The requirement of an objective assessment does not correspond, for example, with the models of sexual grooming activity; the latter gives weight to both context and motive as being an integral aspect of assessing the criminality of the communications between the offender and the object of his sexual gratification. Surely, the process of reducing the child's inhibitions to sexual activity does not necessarily have to begin with explicit descriptions of sexual acts or images of pornographic activity. We can, for example, imagine an instance where an online sexual predator engages in innocuous communications with a child based on information uploaded on the social network account.

Obscene content and child pornography

Search engines, IM, emails, social networking sites and mobile phones now provide children with potentially unrestricted access to adult pornography, age-inappropriate content like violent online games and literature. Access to illegal or harmful content is regarded as accelerating the sexualisation of children (Papadopoulos, 2010). Premature sexualisation is felt to increase children's susceptibility to self-victimisation (e.g. sexting) or increase children's exposure to violence (or pressure to conform with sexual stereotypes), sexual grooming and have long-term developmental and psychological consequences (Sacco, 2010). The ready availability of all forms of sexual and age-inappropriate content can also desensitise children to the harmful aspects of such material and create addictive behaviours (Quayle, 2010, 2011). Bryant suggests that increased exposure can also lead to shaping and transforming children's attitudes towards sexual activity, intimacy and sexual violence in society (Bryant, 2009: 3–8). Policymakers are also rightly concerned that children are now using Web 2.0 technologies to manipulate adult pornographic images to victimise peers, or using these tools to engage in invasions of privacy or to distribute images taken in locker rooms and other venues without regard to the privacy or sensitivities of these individuals (Powell, 2009). In 2009 the software security provider Symantec reported that the words "sex" and "porn" were the most searched words by minors, particularly amongst younger children (Norton Online Family, 2009). Content which is deemed to be inappropriate or potentially harmful to children is regulated by the ICT industry or broadcasting and entertainment industries. In the United Kingdom, such issues are addressed by bodies like the OfCom Content Board (Section 12(1) of the Communications Act 2003), the Independent Mobile Classification Body, the British Broadcasting Corporation (BBC), the British Board of Film Classification (BBFC) and the Authority for Television on Demand. Criminal sanctions are applicable to illegal content like child abuse images, adult content that violates the obscenity laws, racist materials and terrorism content (*R v Sheppard and Whittle* (2010) and racially inflammatory content posted online. The Internet Watch Foundation (IWF) 2010 report also found that child abuse images were depicting children of very young ages and the violence increasing in severity (IWF, 2010b).

There are a number of rationales informing the role of the criminal law in this area of child protection. These include the need to protect children from being exploited by those engaged in the Commercial Sexual Exploitation of Children (CSEC) industry, the adverse effects on children from inadvertent exposure and the threats posed to children by the creation and distribution of child abuse content. It is, however, unclear whether there is a relationship between possession of child pornography and actual abuse of children (Quayle, 2010). In *R v Sharpe* (2001) the Court held that

> possession of child pornography increases the risk of child abuse. It introduces risk, moreover, that cannot be entirely targeted by laws prohibiting the manufacture, publication and distribution of child pornography... Only by extending the law to private possession can these harms be squarely attacked. (2001: paragraph 94)

In some instances, individuals distort the seriousness of the exploitation by viewing the creation of child abuse images as an acceptable form of behaviour. In *R v Grant* (2009) the offender sought to justify the nude photos showing the sexual organs of his four-year-old foster child as ""cute" behaviour of a child playing freely" (paragraph 15). Content management strategies in terms of reducing the ready availability and supply of illegal content as well as ensuring that children do not access inappropriate content have become a priority for policymakers (Livingstone *et al.* 2011; ACMA, 2009d). Increased broadband access and the ready availability of online sexual content have made policing and enforcing the laws on obscenity (and pornography) a logistical challenge. Optenet, a global IT security company, found that pornographic content constituted 37 per cent of the overall online content on websites (Optenet, 2010). It appears from this study that the volume and range of content as well as the platforms for accessing such content have been steadily rising. Adult content on the Internet was deemed to have increased by 17 per cent in the first quarter of 2010, when compared with the same time period in 2009. The Director of the Child Protection Projects at Optenet remarked on the way children's increasing use of the Internet for games, entertainment and online interaction also contributes to their potential exposure to age-inappropriate and harmful content. It was noted that there was a "growing trend for online role-playing games to encourage negative behavior, by rewarding violent and brutal activities within the online games" (Optenet, 2010).

One of the consequences of the end-to-end principle is that content control through filtering software operates at either the server or the user level. Consequently, where the harmful or violent content is not classified or not covered by the "block list", these can be accessed through numerous communication platforms and devices. There are a number of legislative rules governing the management of content deemed to pose risks to the safety and well-being of children. We will briefly identify and explain some of the most common obligations imposed by the law in respect of illegal and adult content deemed to be obscene (in so far as they are relevant to online child safety governance).

Obscene Publications Act 1959 and 1964

One example of the standard setting role of law in relation to content management has been the imposition of legal obligations on individuals and industry to avoid publishing and distributing content contrary to the provisions of the Obscene Publications Act (OPA) 1959 and 1964. The strategy here is a simple one – access to such content can be reduced if the law can be used to deter individuals from engaging in the prohibited activity. It should, however, be pointed out that digital content cannot be "reduced" in the sense that electronic data by nature is a permanent record, which can be stored, manipulated, reproduced and disseminated across networks. Consequently, the criminal law not only attempts to deter individuals from creating new illegal content but it also attempts to prohibit individuals from accessing, distributing and possessing existing content. In the remainder of this section, we will consider the principal issues raised by the role of the law in minimising children's likely exposure to illegal content.

Possession of obscene content is not a criminal offence, only its publication, supply, distribution and importation would be caught by the Act (Section 2 of the OPA). The fact that obscene content is now accessed via the Internet or mobile communication technologies does not prevent the application of the OPA. The passing of the Criminal Justice and Public Order Act 1994, Section 168(1) and Schedule 9, now subjects online content to the OPA. Digital images stored on a computer, which can either be accessed through subscription or be freely available on networks, are also covered by the Act (*R v Sheppard and Whittle* (2010)). The type of media that will constitute an "article" for the purposes of the OPA will include any media, which contains or embodies matter that can be read or viewed as sounds or film (Section 1(2)). Compact discs, memory sticks and videocassettes would also be regarded as an "article" for the purposes of Section 1(2) (*A-G's Reference (No. 5 of 1980)* (1980), *R v Fellows, R v Arnold* (1997)). Every act of downloading the content will constitute an act of publication (*R v Waddon* (2000). The use of "thumbnail" images or text on websites is regarded as an act of publication. In *R v Perrin* (2002), Kennedy LJ stated that publication means "the making available of preview material to any viewer who may chose to access it" (paragraph 22). In *Perrin*, the accused published an obscene article on a web page. This web page also had a trailer, which provided a preview of its contents. The fact that the obscene content is only available on a subscription basis is unlikely to be analogised as a form of "private possession".

Ownership, possession or control of obscene content with the aim of making a gain from its subsequent distribution would also amount to a violation of the criminal law (*R v Levy* (2004)). The criminal law also continues to play an important role in ensuring that those who are in the business of publishing or distributing material contrary to the provisions of the OPA 1959 are prosecuted. Recently, in *R v John Snowden* (2009), the accused was prosecuted and convicted under Section 1(2) of the OPA. The police seized DVD copying computer equipment and 2,840 pornographic DVDs involving a range of obscene content (e.g. animals, urination and coprophilia). These materials were found to be in his possession with a view to "publication for gain" (Section 2(1) of the OPA). In the digital environment, an electronic transmission of obscene articles will now constitute an act of publication. The fact that an individual has not seen or accessed the content will not prevent it from being regarded as a form of publication. The legal prohibition of publishing obscene content is undoubtedly a curb on the rights to an individual's freedom of expression. Article 10 of the European Convention on Human Rights (ECHR) provides that the right to freedom of expression shall include the "freedom to hold opinions and to receive and impart information and ideas without interference by public authority and regardless of frontiers". However, Article 10(2) also recognises that curbs on this freedom may be necessary in a democratic society "for the prevention of disorder or crime, for the protection of health or morals, protection of the reputation or rights of other". In *Handyside v UK* (1976), it was held that the OPA was not incompatible with Article 10(1) as the protection of morals in a democratic society was a legitimate aim under Article 10(2).

The final issue to be addressed is the legal characterisation of the content that is deemed to be obscene. The OPA does not provide a statutory definition regarding the type of content that will be regarded as obscene. This is ultimately left to the jury to determine. The law, however, provides a benchmark by requiring individuals and industry to take into account the effect of the publication on the audience likely to be exposed to the content. Unlike the offence of sexual solicitation, which focuses on the conduct to be sanctioned, the OPA focuses on the effect of the publication on persons likely to read or access the content. More specifically, the law will regard content as being "obscene" if its publication will tend to deprave and corrupt persons who are likely, having regard to all relevant circumstances, to read, see or hear the matter contained or embodied in it (Section 1(1) of the OPA). One construction of this term is that the content must be of a character which will tend "to deprave and corrupt those whose minds are open to ... immoral influences, and into whose hands a publication of this sort may fall" (per Cockburn J in *R v Hicklin* (1868): 371). Notwithstanding the relativity of the term "obscene" it is generally accepted that content which is likely to encourage children to commit sexual offences or is likely to deprave or corrupt would be covered by the legislation (e.g. simulating rape, graphic mutilation and sadomasochism). Lord Reid observed in *Knuller (Publishing, Printing and Promotions) Ltd v DPP* (1973) that the words "deprave" and "corrupt" could be viewed as synonymous and should not be construed narrowly to mean sexual or moral depravation (at 456). In *John Calder (Publications) Ltd v Powell* (1965) it was held that the definition of "obscenity" was not limited to publications on sex. This case involved the publication of a book recounting the life (or a fictitious one) of a drug addict in New York. Lord Parker CJ agreed with the decision reached by the Justices, namely, that the contents of the book had a tendency to deprave and corrupt and that its negative aspects were outweighed by its possible merits. In *R v Calder & Boyars Ltd* (1969), the Court of Appeal was faced with the prospect of adjudicating on the issue of whether a book intended to provoke shock and disgust contravened Section 2(1) of the OPA. The Court of Appeal was of the view that in any jury direction it was not appropriate for a judge to describe obscene content in terms of making "a person behave badly or worse than he otherwise would have done, or to blur his perception of the difference between good and bad" (ibid: 168). Lord Wilberforce indicated in *DPP v Whyte* (1972) that the OPA was not concerned with addressing the effect of the publication taken as a whole on those who are wholly innocent but also those who are less innocent and likely to become addicted to the content (paragraph 863B). The ensuing uncertainty regarding the nature and scope of "obscene content" perhaps explains why there have been very few successful prosecutions under the OPA (*R v Anderson* (1972)). The inherent ambiguity of the phrase also creates problems for parents and educators since the criminal law does not prohibit individuals accessing inappropriate or potentially harmful content, which is not obscene.

Protection of Children Act 1978

Apart from establishing standards governing the creation and distribution of obscene content, the law takes a more forceful approach with regard to indecent content comprising minors (Table 3.5). The principal legal instrument in England and Wales governing such forms of content is the PCA 1978. The UK law does not, however, provide a statutory definition of "child pornography". It may very well be that in the future judges may be inclined to adopt a canon of construction that adheres to its Treaty commitments and the measures under the Proposed Directive. Article 2(b) of the Proposed Directive expands the scope of "child pornography" in some notable respects. First, child pornography content comprises any material that visually "depicts" a child in the act of engaging in real or simulated sexually explicit conduct. Article 2 does not draw a distinction between a "real", "pseudo" or "virtual" child. Under the Framework Decision 2004/68, child pornography was defined narrowly in terms of a "real child" or "realistic images of a non-existent child". The clarification of the type of content that would now be considered to be child pornography should promote greater consistency in the application and enforcement of national laws in this area. In passing, it could be suggested that the phrase "sexually explicit conduct" can be understood along the lines defined under the US Federal Law 18 USC § 2256, to include not only any sex act but also lascivious exhibition of the genitals or pubic area of any person. Whether a particular image or description would be regarded as such is a matter for the trier of fact. In *US v Dost* (1986) it was observed that six factors could be used to determine whether the exhibition of the genitals or pubic area was "lascivious": (1) whether the focal point of the picture is on the minor's genitals or pubic area; (2) whether the setting of the picture is sexually suggestive; (3) whether the minor is depicted in unnatural poses or inappropriate attire considering the minor's age; (4) whether the minor is fully or partially clothed or is nude; (5) whether the picture suggests sexual coyness or a willingness to engage in sexual activity; and (6) whether the image is intended to elicit a sexual response in the viewer ((1986) 828, 832).

Second, content will be regarded as child pornography even if the person depicted is not a child. The content will be deemed to be illegal if the person concerned is engaged in real or simulated sexually explicit conduct, or if the sexual organs of the person appearing to be a child is depicted for primarily sexual purposes. Finally, the Proposed Directive also covers content created through software tools or technologies, which

Table 3.5 Sample definitions of child pornography in international instruments

---

Council of Europe Convention on the Protection of Children against Sexual Exploitation and Sexual Abuse

Article 20(2) "For the purpose of the present article, the term "child pornography" shall mean any material that visually depicts a child engaged in real or simulated sexually explicit conduct or any depiction of a child's sexual organs for primarily sexual purposes."

Cybercrime Convention

Article 9(2) "For the purpose of paragraph 1 above, the term "child pornography" shall include pornographic material that visually depicts:

  a. a minor engaged in sexually explicit conduct;

  b. a person appearing to be a minor engaged in sexually explicit conduct;

  c. realistic images representing a minor engaged in sexually explicit conduct."

Optional Protocol to the CRC on the sale of children, child prostitution and child pornography

Article 2(c) "(c) Child pornography means any representation, by whatever means, of a child engaged in real or simulated explicit sexual activities or any representation of the sexual parts of a child for primarily sexual purposes."

---

depicts "realistic images of a child engaged in sexually explicit conduct or realistic images of the sexual organs of a child, regardless of the actual existence of such child, for primarily sexual purposes". The governance challenges in policing and enforcing legal standards and norms are considerable. The US House of Representatives report indicated that the commercial sexual exploitation industry is a multi-billion industry (House of Representatives, 1998: 1–2).

Section 1 of the PCA focuses on an "indecent photograph" of a child. Under the section, it is an offence to possess an indecent photograph of a person under 18, whether or not they look older than they actually are. Section 45(2) of the SOA 2003 amends Section 7(6) of the PCA 1978, which now defines a "child" as a person below the age of 18. These changes have been introduced to reflect the government's commitment to its various international obligations, including those under the UNCRC and the European Framework Decision. Before the amendment, the relevant age was 16. The question whether the child is below the age of 18 years is one of fact and will require an objective assessment of the image deemed to be illegal (*R v Land* (1998)). With regard to the practice of "sexting" (see later), Section 1A of the PCA states that the making or possession of a photograph of a child over 16 is not an offence if at the time of the charge the accused and the child were either married or cohabiting. Recent amendments to the legislation also reflect the role of the criminal law in keeping abreast of emerging trends in the supply of and demand for extreme pornography. The UK government, for example, made amendments to the principal provisions dealing with this category of content in Section 1 of the PCA 1978 and Section 160 of the Criminal Justice Act (CJA) 1988. Whilst it reasonably clear that the law criminalises activities like the creation, possession and distribution of indecent images of real children being sexually exploited, advances in technology and software tools have also led to a proliferation of computer-generated images which depict children in the act of being sexually abused. In a number of instances, graphics software have been used to copy photographs of women and men from the adult entertainment industry and these in turn have been manipulated so that the images appear to depict to a viewer minors engaged in sexual activity. It could be argued that as these are images of adults, the standards under child protection legislation should not be applied in this context, as images of real children are not used. As we can see from both Article 2 of the Proposed Directive and Section 1 of the PCA, such an argument will not be available as a defence to the charge under the legislation. It is true that one of the justifications traditionally offered in criminalising the production and possession of indecent images of children is the harm perpetrated on the children during the creation of the images and the subsequent trauma inflicted on them as they either live with the knowledge of the abuse or regard sexual exploitation as a normal part of childhood. The so-called "tarts and vicars" defence, will similarly be unavailable, following the amendments introduced by Section 160(4) of the CJA 1988, which addresses child sexual exploitative activities involving "pseudo-photographs" of a child. "Pseudo-photograph" for the purposes of the legislation will include images, whether made by computer graphics or otherwise howsoever, which appear to be a photograph (Gillespie, 2010). The extension of legal standards to cover "pseudo-photographs" would seem to be consistent with the protective role of the criminal law. As the preamble to the PCA 1978 makes apparent, the aim of child protection legislation is to prevent the exploitation of children by making indecent photographs of them; and to deter and penalise those engaged in the distribution, showing and advertisement of such indecent photographs. In *R v Harrison* (2007), Cranston J remarked that the policy behind the Act was clear, namely, to reduce or eliminate demand for the type of content which contributed to normalising the exploitation and degradation of children. A "pseudo-photograph" will be regarded as one form of normalising the commercial sexual degradation of children "if the impression conveyed by a pseudo-photograph is that the person shown is a child". It is the dominant impression conveyed that is the key to determining whether the pseudo-photograph is one, which comes within the scope of the PCA 1978. The fact that some of the physical characteristics of the child in the pseudo-photograph are those of an adult will not prevent the photograph from contravening Section 7(8) of the PCA 1978. What is covered under the term "pseudo-photograph" can be problematic, particularly where the child's age in the fictional depiction creates only an impression but not a dominant one. Except in the clearest of cases where the fictional depiction is one of pre-pubescent children, it is difficult to see law enforcement using these new legislative reforms to full effect. Once it has been determined that the photograph is an indecent image of a child covered by the 1978 Act, the exploitative activities which are criminalised include publication, distribution, taking and possession with a view to distributing such content.

Elements of the offence

Prosecution has the legal and evidentiary burden in respect of the following elements for each type of offence:

a. The defendant deliberately and/or knowingly either made, took, or permitted to be taken, distributed or showed indecent photographs or pseudo-photographs, or possessed them with a view to their being distributed or shown, published or caused to be published an advertisement for indecent photographs.
b. The photograph or pseudo-photograph was indecent.
c. The photograph or pseudo-photograph was that of a child below the age of 18.

A "photograph" will now include films, or a copy of a photograph or film, computer data and any form of video recording. In *R v Fellows* (2007), the Court of Appeal adopted a purposive construction to the 1978 Act when it held that a "photograph" would include images or data stored on a computer disc. Following the amendment introduced by Section 84 of the Criminal Justice and Public Order Act 1994 the definition of photograph will include "data stored on a computer disc or by other electronic means which is capable of conversion into a photograph". The question whether the photograph is indecent, as noted above, is a matter for the jury (*R v Owen* (1988), *R v Graham-Kerr (John)* (1988)). The latter case illustrates the difficulties some judges have previously encountered when directing juries on this issue. The accused was charged with taking indecent photographs of a minor contrary to Section 1(1)(a) of the PCA 1978. The facts leading to the charge can be briefly recounted. The public baths, which provided the setting for the incident, was used by a naturist organisation for a private event not open to the public. The accused at some stage during this event approached the parents of the complainant, informing them that he was a swimming instructor and offered to teach the child to swim. The parents consented to this. There was no ill motive or impropriety, and nothing untoward took place during the swimming instruction. The organisers of this event also had in place an official photographer for those who wished to have their photos taken. The accused obtained the parents' permission to have a photograph taken by the official photographer, and some were indeed taken. However, without obtaining separate consent from the parents, the accused proceeded to take some frontal and rear photographs of the child. One question that emerged before the trial was whether the circumstances leading to the taking of the photograph were relevant and hence admissible evidence. The trial judge ruled that these factors were indeed relevant and therefore admissible, including the motive of the accused when taking the photos. Following this ruling, evidence based on the accused's answers to the police during interview regarding his motives when taking the photograph of the children were admitted and more specifically the following exchange was recounted in court:

> ' "Q. Do you find (the boy) particularly attractive? A. Yes." A little later: "Q. Do you receive or enjoy sexual gratification by taking or looking at such photographs? A. Yes." ' (1988: 1000)

The accused was convicted and appealed. Stocker LJ cited with approval the decision of the Court in *R v Stamford (John David)* (1972) when ruling that the trial judge's admission of extrinsic evidence was erroneous. The Court of Appeal stated that the question whether the photograph was indecent had to be determined objectively, and could not include a consideration of whether "right-thinking people would regard as indecent, the motivation of the original taker" (1988: 1104). In *R v O'Carroll* (2003) it was stressed that the image had to be looked at objectively when determining whether it was in fact indecent. It should not be based on the subjective opinions of the jury (*R v Stephen Neal* (2011)). Furthermore, in *R v Oliver and Others* (2002) the Court of Appeal noted that "neither nakedness in a legitimate setting, nor the surreptitious procuring of an image, gives rise, of itself, to a pornographic image" (paragraph 10). This would appear to be the current position of UK law (*R v Murray (Arthur Alan)* (2004)). Finally, in *R v Nicklass (Karl Christopher)* (2006), it was made clear that the test of indecency should not be equated with "standards of modesty and privacy" (paragraph 12).

The issue of when an individual is deemed to be "making" an indecent image has been the subject of judicial deliberations. One view is that the requirement of "making" an indecent image is satisfied if the individual is deemed to have produced or brings a photograph into existence. The prohibited conduct will also extend to individuals who develop negatives. In *R v Bowden* (2000) the Court of Appeal held that in view of the policy behind the law, downloading an image from the Internet would also constitute the act of "making" an image. The accused in this case was a teacher, who was charged with downloading indecent images of children from the Internet. These images were stored on a computer disc and printed out on paper. The Court of Appeal observed that

> the words "to make" must be given their natural and ordinary meaning. In this context this is "to cause to exist; to produce by action, to bring about" (Oxford English Dictionary). As a matter of construction such a meaning applies not only to original photographs but, by virtue of Section 7, also to negatives, copies of photographs and data stored on computer disk. (2000: 444)

This approach can be justified on the grounds that the criminal law aims to enforce its child protection goals by seeking to deter individuals from fuelling the market for supply and consumption of indecent photographs of children or printing them. Additionally, the opening of an attachment in an email containing a child's photograph would be construed as "making" for the purposes of the Act (*R v Smith, R v Jayson* (2002)). In the joined appeals of *R v Smith and R v Jayson* (2000) the Court of Appeal elaborated on the scope of the offence of "making" an indecent image of a child. In this case, evidence was produced showing that the accused browsed a number of child pornography websites, and in the process downloaded images from the browser, which enabled these to be viewed on the computer screen. The Court of Appeal held that a deliberate act of accessing content constituted a "making" of these images (2000: paragraph 33). The issue of what constitutes "possession" in respect of materials downloaded from websites and stored on a computer may raise doubts as to the scope of the type of conduct, which can be sanctioned by the law. When determining whether an individual can be held liable for being in possession of illegal child abuse material, the law requires prosecution to prove that the accused was in control or in custody of the relevant content (*R v Porter* (2006)). It is not open to a court, however, to invite a jury to draw an adverse inference by the mere fact that the accused was in possession of a computer which contained the prohibited image (*R v James McNamara* (1988)). Evidence must be produced, for example, which shows that the accused was aware of the existence of the illegal images on his computer (*Atkins v DPP, Goodland v DPP* (2000)). As the Court of Appeal (Criminal Division) stated in *R v Ping Chen Cheung* (2009), it is incumbent on prosecution to show not only the fact that the accused was in physical possession or control of the computer which had the offending item but that he had knowledge of the existence of the indecent images of children on the machine. The question of what constitutes relevant culpable knowledge was considered in *Atkins v DPP* (2000), where the accused was charged, amongst others, with the offence of being in "possession" of child pornography. The accused had saved indecent child abuse images from sites that he had visited onto a directory in his computer. The computer programme automatically saved images from other websites the accused had visited in the temporary Internet cache. An important feature of online browsing is that the browser automatically stores the information in a temporary cache of recently viewed documents. When an individual wishes to revisit the site, the browser accesses the information in the temporary cache to speed up the connection to the website. This document folder is only emptied when it becomes full. The accused was charged for possession of these contents under the PCA 1978. Law enforcement retrieved the illegal content through a forensic process and submitted these as incriminating evidence. One question addressed by the High Court on an appeal was whether the images retrieved through the forensic process could be regarded as evidence of the accused being in possession of indecent images of children. The defence argued that to hold the accused liable for possession would be tantamount to regarding constructive notice of the functioning of the computer's temporary Internet cache (i.e. automatically storing the indecent images from the websites he visited) as being sufficient to ground criminal liability. Consequently, it was suggested that without direct knowledge, the accused should not be found liable for possessing indecent child abuse images at the time of the charge. The High Court appears to have accepted this argument – the offence of possession cannot be committed if an accused has no knowledge of the temporary cache storing these images. It seems from this ruling that visiting websites which contain child abuse images would not be sufficient for a charge of possession under the Act. If the lack of awareness regarding the availability of the images being accessed from the temporary folder could prove decisive, the same could not be said, however, with regard to being in possession of child sexual abuse material received as an attachment via email. In *R v Smith and R v Jayson* (2002), the first accused's "inbox" contained an email with attachments containing indecent photographs of children. The accused argued that the email containing the attachment was unsolicited and that his viewing of the contents was inadvertent. Prosecution disputed this claim and offered supporting circumstantial evidence disclosing an email exchange between the first accused and an unidentified email correspondent where indecent images were being solicited. The court held that the first accused was correctly charged and convicted under the offence of making an indecent image of a child, contrary to Section 1(1)(a) of the 1978 Act, or being in possession of the indecent image contrary to Section 160(1) of the 1988 Act, as he was deemed to have known the likely content in the attachment to the email (2002: paragraph 20). *R v Harrison* (2007) raises an interesting issue relating to the circumstances when an accused can be held to be in possession of indecent images of children. The accused was convicted of possessing indecent photographs of a child below the age of 16. The appellant admitted that he visited pornographic websites and was aware that these sites contained "pop ups" of illegal images. He, however, claimed that he was not aware that the images from the "pop ups" would be stored on his computer's hard drive. The Court of Appeal did not accept this line of argument nor the evidence adduced in support his claim. Interestingly, it seems that the offence of possession will be committed if evidence is offered, which shows that the accused knew about the automatic "pop up" activity when accessing the pornographic website and was aware that by accessing these sites there was a likelihood that these images would be stored on the computer. One final issue remains to be considered: can an accused be convicted for possession of indecent child abuse content stored in the "recycle bin", when these are deleted prior to being charged under the PCA? One view is that the deletion of the files prevents the accused from being able to access the content and therefore should not be found guilty for being in possession of the indecent images of children. A competing argument offered is that the deletion of the files should not make a significant difference to a successful prosecution if the illegal content can still be accessed from the hard drive albeit by someone using sophisticated retrieving technology. These arguments formed the basis of the issues addressed in *R v Porter* (2006). The accused was charged with a number of counts of possessing indecent images of children, and, rather curiously, with possession of material that had been deleted on the day the computer was seized by law enforcement. The Court of Appeal's ruling suggests that such issues can be addressed by providing answers to three questions. The first question that has to be determined is whether the accused has physical possession in the sense of having custody and control over the contents. Second, if the answer to this question is that he has no control, because these have been deleted and emptied from the recycle bin, the accused will not be regarded as being in possession of illegal content. Third, if, the content is within his control, and he can reproduce these images on his screen, reproduce a copy or distribute the content that will be regarded as evidence of possession. The question whether the accused is deemed to be in possession of illegal content is a question of fact and ultimately one which the jury is competent to determine. When addressing this matter, it is open to a jury to take into account all these factors including the specific knowledge and expertise of the accused. It should be noted that it is incumbent on prosecution to discharge its legal and evidentiary burdens. In *R v Rowe* (2008) the Court of Appeal overturned the conviction of an accused for being in possession of deleted indecent images of children from his computer. The police seized 20 floppy discs from the appellant's bedroom. Eight of these discs contained a large number of deleted files containing such images. The other discs contained movie files and child abuse images. Files deleted from a floppy disc continue to occupy the storage space until they are replaced by subsequent use. The accused argued that the prosecution had failed to discharge its evidentiary burden of proving that he knowingly possessed deleted indecent images of a child contrary to Section 160(1) of the CJA 1988. The Court of Appeal held that for an accused to be liable for possession of these images, knowledge or even the lack of it was relevant to criminal liability under the legislation. As these issues and their significance to the question of knowledge were not brought to the attention of the jury, the earlier convictions for these offences were quashed. In *R v Collier* (2004) it was made clear that on a charge for possessing an indecent photograph of a child, contrary to Section 160 of the CJA 1988, an accused should not be prevented from putting before the jury his defence that he had not seen the indecent photograph of a child, nor had he any reason to suspect that the content was an indecent photograph of a child.

These cases illustrate judicial awareness of the process by which indecent images, sound and text can now be created, accessed and possessed via Web 2.0 technologies. We should, however, note by way of conclusion to this part of the analysis the three defences to charges brought under Section 160(1). Where a person is charged with the offence of possession, it shall be a defence for him to prove (Section 160(2)):

(a) that he had a legitimate reason for having the photograph [or pseudo-photograph] in his possession; or
(b) that he had not himself seen the photograph [or pseudo-photograph] and did not know, nor had any cause to suspect, it to be indecent; or
(c) that the photograph [or pseudo-photograph] was sent to him without any prior request made by him or on his behalf and that he did not keep it for an unreasonable time.

For example, the "legitimate reason" defence could be relied upon in a case where a police officer responsible for the investigation of child pornography is required as part of the evidence gathering process to assume possession of the illegal photograph or pseudo-photograph. This defence may also extend to organisations like the IWF, which may, in the process of managing and operating hotline services combating the creation and distribution of images of child abuse, come into possession of such content.[1] It is, however, not open to an individual to access or download illegal child abuse images on the grounds of pursuing general research. In *Atkins v DPP* (2000), Simon Brown LJ stated that what constitutes a "legitimate reason" is ultimately a question of fact depending on the legitimacy of the research and

> whether the defendant is essentially a person of unhealthy interests in possession of indecent photographs in the pretence of undertaking research, or by contrast a genuine researcher with no alternative but to have this sort of unpleasant material in his possession. (2000: 257)

As the Court of Appeal in *R v Porter* (2006) observed, it would be surprising if Parliament intended to subject an individual to the strictures of the criminal law if after receiving an unsolicited image of child abuse content as an attachment in an email, the individual inadvertently views the content and deletes it without taking any further measures to ensure its complete removal (paragraph 18).

It is worth mentioning briefly three other developments which will continue to ensure that the child protection objectives under the OPA and the PCA 1978 keep pace with developments in technology.

Tracings

The first development concerns the application of the 1978 Act to tracings or drawings. It will have been noted that the focus of the 1978 Act has long been on "photographs". Section 69 of the Criminal Justice and Immigration Act 2008 now extends the definition of photographs to include a tracing or other image, whether made by electronic or other means. The tracing must be one which is derived from the whole or part of a photograph or pseudo-photograph (or a combination of either or both). Data stored on a computer disc or by other electronic means which is capable of being converted into a tracing is also covered. Software tools now enable individuals to create and manipulate high-resolution and three-dimensional drawings of fictitious or virtual images of pre-pubescent girls and boys. The most common type of activity that leads to the offence being committed is one where an individual traces an outline of a photograph onto a tracing paper, and the tracing is then transferred onto a real piece of paper, with the drawing being coloured. There has been some uncertainty regarding the issue of whether tracing and its derivatives which also involved the creation of morphed images comprising features from children and adults could be regarded as a "photograph" under the PCA 1978. When charging a person for this offence, it is incumbent on prosecution to show that there is a nexus between the image and the photograph or pseudo-photograph involving a child. Additionally, it must be shown that the image is a tracing. Under the current legislation, it would appear that freehand drawings are excluded. An individual can, however, raise the defence that he did not know that the image downloaded was a "tracing".

Prohibited images of children

With the coming into force of Section 62 of the Coroners and Justice Act 2009 on 6 April 2010, possession of prohibited images of children will amount to a criminal offence, irrespective of how the images are created. The following elements constitute the offence under Section 62:

a. the person must be in possession of a prohibited image of a child.
b. the image must be pornographic. An image is "pornographic" if it is of such a nature that it must reasonably be assumed to have been produced solely or principally for the purpose of sexual arousal. Whether the image is pornographic is a question of fact, and consequently a matter for the jury to determine. Legitimate works of art, literature or science would seem to be excluded.
c. the image is prohibited. The category of images include those which focus solely or principally on a child's genitals or anal region, or portrays the engagement of sexual activity either with or in the presence of a child

and

d. is grossly offensive, disgusting or otherwise of an obscene character.

This section creates a discrete offence from those prohibited images and content already covered by the OPA and the PCA 1978. Section 65(2), which is the definitional provision, states that an "image" includes

(a) a moving or still image (produced by any means), or
(b) data (stored by any means) which is capable of conversion into an image within paragraph (a).

For the purposes of Section 62 an image does not include an indecent photograph, or indecent pseudo-photograph, of a child. References to an image of a person and an image of a child include references to an image of an imaginary person and imaginary child, respectively.

Extreme pornography

The Criminal Justice and Immigration Act 2008 makes two important inroads into the growing use of the Internet to disseminate extreme forms of pornography (Murray, 2009). First, Section 63 identifies specific types of pornographic material, which are now to be regulated by the criminal law. Second, Section 71 amends the OPA 1959 by increasing the maximum penalty for offences under that Act from three to five years' imprisonment (Ministry of Justice, 2009). The original proposals to regulate the possession of extreme pornographic material was in part influenced by the proliferation of material like necrophilia, bestiality and violence which even though were hosted abroad were found to be accessed and distributed within the United Kingdom via the Internet. The publication and distribution of such content was in many ways rendering the regulatory mechanisms put in place under the OPA 1959 redundant (McGlynn *et al.*, 2007, 2009a). Consequently, re-form of the 1959 Act was seen as being long overdue, and the amendments introduced by the 2009 Act will serve to ensure that possession of extreme pornography is now a prohibited act (Henry *et al.*, 2010). When prosecuting an individual for this possession offence, the following three elements must be shown to be present:

a. image is pornographic;
b. image is grossly offensive, disgusting, or otherwise of an obscene char-acter; and
c. image portrays in an explicit and realistic way, at least one of a number of acts (e.g. depictions of hanging, suffocation, mutilation of breasts or genitals or an act involving sexual interference with a human corpse).

Some prosecutions have been already been made under this Act. In *R v Derek Arnold Wakeling* (2010) the accused was convicted for being in possession of extreme pornography, which included material involving bestiality within Levels 4 and 5 of the Oliver guidelines. In *R v Thomas John C* (2010) the accused was prosecuted for possessing extreme pornography. The materials found in his possession included movies involving adults, horses and dogs engaging in various forms of sexual activity. In the Australian case of *R v Gent* (2005) an accused was convicted under its child pornography legis-lation for importing material which included children being subjected to sadomasochistic penetration. This form of child abuse content would also be covered by this new piece of legislation.

From a sentencing perspective, the Court of Appeal in *R v Oliver and Others* (2002) expressed the view that it was desirable to indicate whether the photographs downloaded by the offender were photographs or pseu-do-photos. Possession and downloading of computer-generated pseudo-photographs and the making of such images are regarded as being of a lower level of seriousness than, for example, those cases involving the pos-session or making of photographic images of real children. The range of indecent images of children circulating on the Internet undoubtedly cre-ate legal and practical difficulties in assessing whether the criminal law is violated. The Combating Paedophile Information Networks in Europe

(COPINE) project developed a classification system which helps rate the various types of child pornography content. The COPINE Scale has ten levels, with each level depicting images of a child in varying degrees of sexuality. The premise in the taxonomy rating system is that differentiating child pornography from other forms of sexualised images of the child cannot be understood through legal definitions or judicial deliberations. When reviewing the images of child abuse material under the COPINE project, the team of researchers attempted to understand the nature of such content, the motivations leading to their creation, collection and distribution by individuals. To put it another way, the COPINE project team concentrated on the particular sexual characteristics and features that made them attractive to adults with a sexual interest in children. There is general acceptance that an understanding of the psychological factors leading to the consumption of particular forms of child abuse content over others can assist regulatory and therapeutic strategies (Lanning, 1992; Kincaid, 1998; McCabe, 2000). Consequently, the COPINE Scale aims to bridge the content with the particular needs and expectations of adults who collect the material (Quayle, 2010: 354–8). As Taylor, Holland and Quayle note, an overemphasis on legal categorisations tends to "deflect attention away from a more discriminating analysis of the photographs themselves, and the relationship between the child, the photographer, the photograph and the user (2001: 97; Table 3.6).

This typology has not been fully accommodated by the legal system. This is understandable, given the premise informing the COPINE rating scale. When classifying pornographic material, prosecution use the "Oliver scale", from *R v Oliver and Others* (2002). The five-point classification is derived from the proposals made by the Sentencing Advisory Panel, which now advises the Sentencing Guidelines Council. According to the guidelines, for example, an accused involved in the making of or trading or distributing of material at Levels 1 to 3 will attract a two-year custodial sentence, with sentence ranging from one to four years (Table 3.7). The Oliver scale was developed to reduce any potential legal uncertainties or disputes regarding the images that would now be the subject criminal law sanctions.

Other jurisdictions

We may briefly consider some of the case law and prosecutions in other jurisdictions, which also highlight the similarity of the policy responses and the standard setting function of their criminal laws.

United States

The approach to regulating content deemed to be illegal or harmful is complicated by the fact that the First Amendment regards free speech as the

Table 3.6 Taylor and Quayle's taxonomy of child images

1	Indicative	Non-erotic and non-sexualised pictures showing children in their underwear, swimming costumes from either commercial sources or family albums. Pictures of children playing in normal settings, in which the context or organisation of pictures by the collector indicates inappropriateness.
2	Nudist	Pictures of naked or semi-naked children in appropriate nudist settings, and from legitimate sources.
3	Erotica	Surreptitiously taken photographs of children in play areas or other safe environments showing either underwear or varying degrees of nakedness.
4	Posing	Deliberately posed pictures of children fully clothed, partially clothed or naked (where the amount, context and organisation suggest sexual interest).
5	Erotic posing	Deliberately posed pictures of fully, partially clothed or naked children in sexualised or provocative poses.
6	Explicit erotic Posing	Pictures emphasising genital areas, where the child is naked, partially clothed or fully clothed.
7	Explicit sexual activity	Pictures that depict touching, mutual and self-masturbation, oral sex and intercourse by a child, not involving an adult.
8	Assault	Pictures of children being subject to a sexual assault, involving digital touching, involving an adult.
9	Gross assault	Grossly obscene pictures of sexual assault, involving penetrative sex, masturbation or oral sex, involving an adult.
10	Sadistic/bestiality	a. Pictures showing a child being tied, bound, beaten, whipped or otherwise subject to something that implies pain. b. Pictures where an animal is involved in some form of sexual behaviour with a child.

Source: Taylor, 2001.

presumptive rule. Attempts to enact statutes aimed at regulating content deemed to be illegal or harmful to children must not overreach the rights available to all citizens (*Reno v ACLU* (1997); *Ginsberg v New York* (1968)) The First Amendment, however, does not protect obscene speech that is deemed to offend fundamental notions of decency. "Obscene material" was described as material "which deals with sex in a manner appealing to prurient interest" ((1957) 476, 487) In *Miller v California* (1973) Mr Chief

Table 3.7   The Oliver guidelines

R v Oliver (2002) All ER (D) 320 (Nov) on the descriptions of different levels of indecent activity derived from the COPINE programme description of instruments.	Sentencing Panel Characterisation of the COPINE Scale
Level 1 indicated images depicting erotic posing with no sexual activity.	Levels 2–6 *Levels 2 and 3 doubted by Rose LJ (para. 10)
Level 2 indicated sexual activity between children or solo child masturbation.	Level 7
Level 3 indicated non-penetrative sex between adults and children.	Level 8
Level 4 indicated penetrative sexual activity between adults and children.	Level 9
Level 5 indicated sadism or bestiality.	Level 10

Justice Burger set out some basic guidelines for the trier of fact, when determining the standard of review:

(a) whether "the average person, applying contemporary community standards" would find that the work, taken as a whole, appeals to the prurient interest; (b) whether the work depicts or describes, in a patently offensive way, sexual conduct specifically defined by the applicable state law; and (c) whether the work, taken as a whole, lacks serious literary, artistic, political, or scientific value. (413 US 15, 24)

With regard to child pornography, the relevant Federal Law brings within its scope all visual depictions of a minor engaging in sexually explicit conduct (18 USC § 2256 (2008)). These depictions include all forms of media used to represent the prohibited image (e.g. photograph, video, computer-generated image or picture). Obscene visual representations of the sexual abuse of children do not obtain First Amendment protections. In *Roth v United States* (1957) it was held that the free flow of information, which is based on the liberal ideal of promoting exchange of ideas and individual autonomy, could be circumscribed where the material was found to be obscene, lewd, lascivious or filthy. That said, the three guidelines provided in *Miller v California* (1973) also make clear that appropriately drafted content regulation would not infringe the free speech rights of its citizens. For example, following the decision of the Supreme Court in the United States in *New York v Ferber* (1982) it was observed that the law criminalising pornographic depictions of real children below the age of 16 did not contravene the First Amendment speech protections guaranteed by the Constitution.

In reaching this conclusion, the Supreme Court reflected the growing public unease over the way children's physical and emotional well-being were potentially being compromised by those who sought to exploit them for sexual purposes. Justice White also emphasised the need to clearly define the conduct to be prohibited, so that individuals understood that the law only criminalised those "works that visually depict sexual conduct by children below a specified age" (458 US 747, 763). These constraints on First Amendment were seen as both justified and necessary since

> the distribution of photographs and films depicting sexual activity by juveniles is intrinsically related to the sexual abuse of children in at least two ways. First, the materials produced are a permanent record of the children's participation and the harm to the child is exacerbated by their circulation. Second, the distribution network for child pornography must be closed if the production of material which requires the sexual exploitation of children is to be effectively controlled. (458 US 747, 759)

This approach to combating the problem of child pornography is also very much apparent in the decision reached in *Osborne v Ohio* (1990). The Supreme Court had to determine if a curb on the individual's expectation of private possession of child pornography was an infringement of his First Amendment rights. It was held that if the problem posed by child pornography to the well-being of children was to be addressed, there was not only a need to disrupt the creation and distribution markets but laws were also needed to deter individuals from gaining possession of such material in the first instance. That said, the Courts have also been mindful that legislative attempts to curb child pornography should not unjustifiably curb free speech entitlements under the constitution. One example of legislative overreaching was the Child Pornography Prevention Act (CPPA) of 1996. In *Free Speech Coalition v Reno* (1997) the extension of the definition of "child pornography" under the 1996 Act to cover images of fictional and morphed images of minors were seen as overbroad and unconstitutional. In *Ashcroft v Free Speech Coalition* (2002) Justice Kennedy, whilst accepting the legitimate role of the State in criminalising child pornography, did not regard its powers as extending to the prohibition of depictions of children, which included computer-generated images. To do so, it was argued, would bring within the remit of child protection laws a "[r]enaissance painting depicting a scene from classical mythology, a 'picture' that "appears to be, of a minor engaging in sexually explicit conduct". (535 US 234, 241). Child protection legislation regulating child pornography should not, it appears, criminalise youthful-looking adults seeking to engage in their lawful activities. It was also felt that computer-generated images of children in themselves did not constitute the type of images that attracted criminal sanctions since these "images do not involve, let alone harm, any children in the production process" (ibid., 241). Additionally, in *Free Speech Coalition*, the criminalisation of material that had been pandered as child pornography, regardless of whether it was the case in fact, was deemed to be overbroad. In view of the ruling as to the unconstitutional elements of the CPPA, the Prosecutorial Remedies and Other Tools to end the Exploitation of Children Today (PROTECT) Act in 2003 was passed to remedy these deficiencies. The PROTECT Act in 2003 can be viewed as the most recent legislative attempt to overcome some of the problems faced by law enforcement in prosecuting cases on child pornography, in particular, where computer technology is used to create child sexual abuse images that also disguised real images of abused children. It appears that prior to the enactment of the PROTECT Act 2003 prosecutions were not brought in a number of cases owing to the difficulties faced by law enforcement in producing evidence that the visual images depicted were those of real rather than fictional children. Under the PROTECT Act 2003, any person who

> knowingly...advertises, promotes, distributes, or solicits...any material or purported material in a manner that reflects the belief, or that is intended to cause another to believe, that the material or purported material is, or contains – (i) an obscene visual depiction of a minor engaging in sexually explicit conduct; or (ii) a visual depiction of an actual minor engaging in sexually explicit conduct. (18 USC § 2252(a)(3)(B))

In *US v Williams* (2008), the Supreme Court pronounced that the provisions criminalising the possession and distribution of material pandered as child pornography did not encroach into the First Amendment protections. Even though there was a majority decision in favour of this finding, the dissenting opinion of Justice Souter, with whom Justice Ginsburg agreed, does suggest that the boundaries between protected and unprotected speech will continue to dominate much of the debate that surrounds the subject of virtual child pornography (553 US 285, 323–5).

However, obscene content involving children is covered by the criminal law. In *US v Whorley* (2008) the accused was charged with knowing, sending and receipt of 20 obscene emails and downloading of obscene Japanese anime cartoons contrary to 18 USC § 1462. The emails described in graphic detail a range of sexual activities between children and adults including incest and sexual abuse. The 20 cartoons depicted pre-pubescent children engaged in explicit sexual activity with adults. Following his conviction the accused argued that § 1462 was unconstitutional on the grounds of being vague, that possession of obscene content was protected, that § 1462 did not apply to text communications and that § 1466A(a)(1) was unconstitutional and could not apply to cartoons. The Court, however, observed that the right to mere possession of obscene content within the privacy of one's home did not extend to an expectation of a right to receive, transport or distribute such content on interstate commerce. Accordingly, 18 USC § 1462 regulates and prohibits the use of interstate commerce to move, send or receive obscene content. § 1462(a) covers any obscene, lewd, lascivious, or filthy book, pamphlet, picture, motion picture film, paper, letter, writing, print, or other matter of indecent character. Both the text and the cartoons were held to be within the scope of the formulation of "obscenity" by the Supreme Court in *Miller v California* (1973).

The criminal law now prohibits the creation and distribution of extreme forms of child abuse images, which are obscene and indecent, regardless of whether they are real or fictional. In the United States, a comic book collector was charged and convicted for importing and possessing Japanese manga books, which contained illustrations of child sex abuse and bestiality (Kravets, 2009).

Australia

There have been a number of legislative enactments in Australia and decisions reached by the courts in the States/Territories with regard to this aspect of child protection policymaking. At the Commonwealth level, content regulation is overseen, for example, by classification restrictions and child pornography legislation (Griffiths *et al.*, 2007: 31–4). ACMA administers the rules and laws relating to radio, television and Internet content. The Broadcasting Services Act 1992, for example, sets out the licence conditions for the broadcasting industry. A series of mandatory programme standards for children (Children's Television Standards 2009, Broadcasting Services (Australian Content) Standard 2005) and industry codes of practice ensure that age-appropriate content are clearly designated as such. In 2007, ACMA formulated a set of age-restricted content rules (commercial MA15+ content and R18+ content) either hosted in Australia or provided from Australia (Lindsay *et al.*, 2008). These rules are set out in the Restricted Access System Declaration of 2007. The rules apply to content service providers who make their content available via a carriage service (i.e. Internet, mobile phones and SMS services).

With regard to child pornography legislation, the issues faced by policymakers and law enforcement mirror many of those we have already discussed. Possession, distribution and creation of child pornography content are activities that give rise to criminal prosecutions. Additionally, the legislation also addresses evolving forms of child abuse material and consumption practices that are facilitated by the Internet. As with the rulings and enactments we have considered above, issues regarding the definition of the "child" and the substantive elements of the offence of engaging in child pornography are equally pertinent to the matters addressed in Australia. There are some issues worth highlighting. Given the number of jurisdictions in Australia, the definition of a "child" for the purposes of child pornography legislation varies. New South Wales, Queensland, South Australia and Western Australia regard 16 years as the age threshold. The Australian

Capital Territories, Northern Territories, Victoria and Tasmania adopt the higher age threshold (i.e. 18 years) as recommended by the Optional Protocol. Clearly, policymakers and law enforcement will have to take into account these age differences when individuals are found to have accessed or downloaded content from jurisdictions where the age threshold is lower. The presumption of legality/illegality is something that will become an issue as law enforcement aims to curb the prevalence of child pornography content accessed over the Internet. The definition of child pornography is also widely constructed. The Commonwealth Criminal Code, for example, sets the age threshold of a child for the purposes of child pornography at 18 years and "child pornography material" is defined as material that depicts, describes such a person who is or appears to be under 18 years old or a representation of the person engaged in or appears to be engaged in a sexual pose or sexual activity (Section 473.1 (a)(b)). The material must have as its dominant characteristic the depiction for a sexual purpose: (i) a sexual organ or the anal region of a person who is, or appears to be, under 18 years of age; or (ii) a representation of such a sexual organ or anal region; or (iii) the breasts, or a representation of the breasts, of a female person who is, or appears to be, under 18 years of age; in a way that reasonable persons would regard as being, in all the circumstances, offensive (Section 473.1(b). The use of the words, "representation", "description" and "depiction" is also indicative of the potential reach of the legislation, namely, in covering audio, text and visual representations of child pornography content (Griffith *et al.*, 2008: 24–5). Another piece of legislation that adopts an expansive definition of child pornography content is the Crimes Act 1900. Section 91FA of the Crimes Act 1900 (New South Wales Consolidated Acts) regards a "child" as a person under the age of 16 years and "child abuse material" comprises material that "depicts" or "describes" in a way that reasonable persons regard as being offensive (Section 91 FB). The legislation also covers three categories of material, including those which depict or describe a person (who is or appears to be or implied to be a child) "as a victim of torture, cruelty or physical abuse", "engaged in a sexual pose or sexual activity (whether or not in the presence of other persons)", or the private genitalia of a person who is or appears to be a child. Material which has been manipulated so as to make the person "appear" to be a child will also be construed as child abuse material. Pseudo-child abuse photographs, virtual child pornography and digital manipulations of "adult pornography" which create the appearance of the child will now be covered by this enactment. The Act provides for limited defences, which absolve the individual of liability for innocent production, dissemination or possession (Section 91HA). The absence of any mention of accessing illegal content would seem to be an obvious oversight, in view of the fact that criminalising access will also make inroads to the creation and distribution of child abuse content. In *Gibson v Evans* (2008) the offender was charged with the offence of being in possession of child pornography content under Section 91H(3) of the Crimes Act 1900. The issue before the court was whether access to child abuse content via a hyperlink, as opposed to such images being saved on the computer, could be deemed to be possession. The court held that the intentional act of accessing websites containing child pornography was an act of possession "within the meaning of s 91H(3) if they happen to be displayed, although it might be fleeting" (2008: paragraph 7).

The test for determining whether the material is a form of "child abuse material" is that of the "community" standard, namely:

(2) whether reasonable persons would regard particular material as being, in all the circumstances, offensive, include:
  (a) the standards of morality, decency and propriety generally accepted by reasonable adults, and
  (b) the literary, artistic or educational merit (if any) of the material, and
  (c) the journalistic merit (if any) of the material, being the merit of the material as a record or report of a matter of public interest, and
  (d) the general character of the material (including whether it is of a medical, legal or scientific character) (Windeyer, J. in *Crowe v Graham* (1969) 121 CLR 375).

Finally, Section 62 (of the Criminal Law Consolidation Act 1935) includes another set of materials within the scope of child pornography:

(a) that
  (i) describes or depicts a child engaging in sexual activity; or
  (ii) consists of, or contains, the image of a child or bodily parts of a child (or what appears to be the image of a child or bodily parts of a child) or in the production of which a child has been or appears to have been involved; and
(b) that is intended or apparently intended –
  (i) to excite or gratify sexual interest; or
  (ii) to excite or gratify a sadistic or other perverted interest in violence or cruelty.

Obviously, whether content can be said to "excite or gratify sexual interest" is a question of fact and one which involves an objective assessment being made by the jury. It would appear to bring in a wide range of erotica content under Level 1 of the Oliver scale, which arguably could be created to pander to particular audiences (see *US v Knox* (1991)). The focus appears to be not so much on whether the child consciously aims to excite or gratify sexual interest but given the context of the legislation which applies "to the conduct of children, lasciviousness is not a characteristic of the child photographed but of the exhibition which the photographer sets up for an audience that consists of himself ... [and like-minded individuals]" (*US v Wiegand* (1987) 1239, 1244).

Generally, these legislative enactments, notwithstanding the different age groups and use of differing terminology (i.e. child abuse, child pornography), will undoubtedly enhance the ability of law enforcement to prosecute offenders engaged in the creation and distribution of extreme child pornography, particularly those aimed at exciting or gratifying sadistic or violent interests. The law in this area is still evolving and some definitional and jurisdictional issues will have to be addressed (e.g. the varying age groups of the "child", "excite or gratify sexual interest", the current status of "sexting" and the appropriateness of criminalising unauthorised distribution of "up-skirt" images via mobile phones and the Internet). It is unclear whether child pornography laws are the appropriate medium for addressing children's inappropriate use of Web 2.0 technologies (see later discussion). Griffiths and Simon leave open this issue in the light of the ruling in *DPP v Drummond* (2008) which treats covert "up-skirt" filming of a minor's underwear and related areas as a form of child pornography, rather than an invasion of an individual's privacy (Griffiths and Simon, 2008: 16). The magistrate in this case regarded the particular image as being contrary to the community standards of decency, and seems to have attached particular weight to the motive and surreptitious nature of the offender's conduct ((2008) paragraphs 20–30).

Finally, the potential for using the criminal law to prohibit the use of computer graphic software to create child abuse images and indecent drawings of children has recently been the subject of legal proceedings in Australia. *McEwen v Simmons* (2008) provides another illustration of the amenability of the criminal law to addressing the challenges posed by new technologies. The accused was charged with offences of possessing child pornography contrary to Section 91H(3) of the Crimes Act 1900 (NSW) and with using his computer to access child pornography material contrary to Section 474.19(1)(a)(i) of the Criminal Code Act 1995 (Cth) (the Code). The material subject of the offences comprised fictional cartoon characters from the televised animated series *The Simpsons*. The accused accessed content on a website which depicted the adult and child characters from the television series engaging in various sexual acts, with their genitalia being clearly identified before downloading selected images onto his computer. The principal issue addressed by the court was whether a fictional cartoon character could be deemed to be a person, and, more significantly, a "child" for the purposes of the "possession" and access offences. The court acknowledged that there was a distinction between acts undertaken by an actual human being and those depicted by a fictional or imaginary person. Counsel for the accused attempted to suggest that no offence could be committed where the subjects of the work were fictional cartoon characters. To hold otherwise, it was suggested, would be tantamount to regarding depiction of violence in video games and comics as harms perpetrated against real individuals (paragraph 5). The court rejected the use of these analogies and was particularly scathing of the defence which attempted

> to suggest that the distinction [between actual and imaginary depiction] is merely one of degree. This is quite wrong. Such an approach would trivialise pornography that utilised real children and make far too culpable the possession of representations that did not. Of course, the use of the imaginary material to groom children would make its possession more serious. (Ibid.)

The court held that fictional drawings of persons could be regarded as child pornography, even though they were not realistic representations of human beings. It was sufficient, in the court's view, that the fictional representation was that of a human being and was recognised as such. The fact that no specific human being was depicted, it would seem to follow from this reasoning, may not be relied upon as a defence to prosecution for child pornography. This approach obviously stands in marked contrast to the observation in *Ashcroft v Free Speech Coalition*:

> The Government submits further that virtual child pornography whets the appetites of pedophiles and encourages them to engage in illegal conduct. This rationale cannot sustain the provision in question. The mere tendency of speech to encourage unlawful acts is not a sufficient reason for banning it. The government "cannot constitutionally premise legislation on the desirability of controlling a person's private thoughts". (535 US 234, 253 (2002))

Canada

The position in Canada with regard to prosecuting individuals for making, possessing and distributing illegal child abuse images is not dissimilar to the regulatory responses we have already discussed. The leading case of *R v Sharpe* (2001) characterised the juridical question facing the Supreme Court as one of whether criminalisation of the possession of child pornography was consistent with the constitutional right of Canadians to free expression. In framing the subject of child pornography in these terms, the court attempted to address, at least, the then perception of a conflict between the rights to free expression and the right of children to be protected from harm. The accused was charged with one count of illegal possession under Section 163.1(4) of the Criminal Code, RSC 1985, c. C-46, and another count of possession for the purposes of distribution or sale under s. 163.1(3) of the Criminal Code. In the lower court, Mr Justice Shaw ruled that Section 163.1(4) was unconstitutional on the basis that it unjustifiably intruded into the privacy of an individual ((1999) paragraphs 49–50). The Court of Appeal (1999) on a narrow majority of 2 to 1 upheld the trial judge's conclusion. In reaching this conclusion, the Court of Appeal seems to have attached particular prominence to what it regarded as mere possession of child pornography for private purposes (which should not be criminalised) and other activity like making and distributing such content (which should be criminalised). One could legitimately query whether such a distinction is defensible; the market for child pornography is defined very much by suppliers and distributors meeting the needs of its audience of consumers who seek access to such content in both private and public domains. Not surprisingly, the Supreme Court (2001) held that the right to free expression was not absolute and could be qualified in order to protect the underlying values served by prohibiting the possession of child pornography. The propositions at stake were neatly encapsulated in the following dicta:

> Just as no one denies the importance of free expression, so no one denies that child pornography involves the exploitation of children. The links between possession of child pornography and harm to children are arguably more attenuated than are the links between the manufacture and distribution of child pornography and harm to children. However, possession of child pornography contributes to the market for child pornography, a market which in turn drives production involving the exploitation of children. Possession of child pornography may facilitate the seduction and grooming of victims and may break down inhibitions or incite potential offences. Some of these links are disputed and must be considered in greater detail in the course of the s. 1 justification analysis. The point at this stage is simply to describe the concerns that, according to the government, justify limiting free expression by banning the possession of child pornography. ((2001) paragraph 28)

By setting out the public interest issues at stake both for and against the prohibition of child abuse content, the Supreme Court was at pains to avoid the overreaching of child pornography legislation into those private spheres where individuals may keep a diary recounting their sexual fantasies and encounters (ibid., paragraph 59). This ruling reflects, as in the United States, the continued tensions between free speech and child protection laws (McGlynn *et al.*, 2009b). It also indicates that civil libertarian claims of the provenance of free speech should not be overstated and instead should take into account the concerns of the criminal law in addressing five harms to children resulting from possession of child pornography:

(1) child pornography promotes cognitive distortions; (2) it fuels fantasies that incite offenders; (3) prohibiting its possession assists law enforce-

ment efforts to reduce the production, distribution and use that result in direct harm to children; (4) it is used for grooming and seducing victims; and (5) some child pornography is produced using real children. (Ibid.: paragraph 86)

It is perhaps fair to say that since the ruling in *R v Sharpe* (2001), the legal basis upon which individuals are made liable for "possession" of child pornography appear to be reasonably well settled (*R v LM* (2008); *R v Morelli* (2010)). There are some refinements which should be noted by way of completeness. For example, in *R v RD* (2010) the Court of Appeal for British Columbia stated that the law regarding possession of child pornography did not apply to images viewed on the computer screen. It concluded that if an accused was to be found liable for accessing child pornography content, something more than the fact of it being saved automatically by the computer onto its hard drive was required (paragraphs 32–8). Canada's Criminal Code contains a series of provisions criminalising the creation, publication, transmission, possession, and accessing of child abuse content (Section 163.1 of the Criminal Code). Canada's Bill C-2, an Act to amend the Criminal Code (protection of children and other vulnerable persons), and the Canada Evidence Act reflect the Government's continuing commitment towards strengthening the protection of children from violence and sexual abuse. The Government established a National Strategy to Protection from Sexual Exploitation on the Internet. The National Child Exploitation Coordination Centre (NCECC), which is part of the Canadian Police Centre for Missing and Exploited Children (CPCMEC), is the law enforcement arm of the National Strategy. The Centre was set up in response to growing parental and public concerns raised by children's access to and use of Web 2.0 technologies. Bill C-2 is one governance response to enhancing the safety of children in the online environment. The preamble notes that this enactment reflects Canada's commitment to the standards and principles under the UNCRC, and in particular its obligation to protect children from all forms of sexual exploitation and sexual abuse, following its ratification of the Optional Protocol. Bill C-2 also resolves some of the issues raised by *Sharpe* (2001), namely, the types of material that can now be characterised as "child pornography" (s163.1); these can now include

(c) any written material whose dominant characteristic is the description, for a sexual purpose, of sexual activity with a person under the age of 18 years that would be an offence under this Act; or

(d) any audio recording that has as its dominant characteristic the description, presentation or representation, for a sexual purpose, of sexual activity with a person under the age of 18 years that would be an offence under this Act.

There is now no requirement for written content to counsel or advocate sexual activity. Courts can also take into account aggravating factors when sentencing offenders (e.g. child abuse content created for commercial and sexual exploitation) (Section 163.1(4.3)). Additionally, the defence of "artistic merit or an educational, scientific or medical purpose" is now replaced with a more limited defence, namely, "legitimate purpose related to the administration of justice or to science, medicine, education or art; and does not pose an undue risk of harm to persons under the age of eighteen years" (Section 163.1(6)). Consequently, the replacement of the "artistic merit" defence with that of the offender having a "legitimate purpose" imposes an objective two-step test. Finally, the amendments also keep abreast of the misuse of Web 2.0 technologies, and criminalise acts like those of the offender in *DPP v Drummond* (Section 162(1)). The prohibited acts are not only limited to the "surreptitious" observation in circumstances giving rise to a reasonable expectation of privacy, in any one of three situations identified but also to the knowing distribution of such material or possession of material knowingly obtained in violation of Section 162(1) (Section 162(4)). There is a defence of "public good" against prosecution under Section 162 (Sections 162(6) and (7)). Bill C-2 also makes it easier for child victims to assist in the investigation and prosecution of individuals for child pornography offences. It remains to be seen whether the Charter of Rights and Freedoms may be relied upon at some stage in the future to challenge the constitutionality of the "legitimate interest" defence and the inclusion of "fictional" depictions of children within the definition of child pornography. It could be said that given the pernicious nature of child pornography, it may be constitutionally acceptable to require individuals to prove that they have a legitimate interest and that the works show a "public good". Fundamentalists may take a different view, but it completely ignores the growing need for a balance to be struck between speech and protection concerns.

One final observation should be made with regard to the applicability of the rules on the distribution and possession of child pornography when these are undertaken via P2P file software downloaded onto the computer. There have been a number of successful prosecutions, particularly in the United Kingdom, the United States and Australia, which show that child pornography laws extend to the misuse of P2P technologies for accessing and distributing illegal content. In *R v Gary Palmer* (2009) the accused was prosecuted for a range of offences under the PCA including counts on distributing 856 indecent photographs and in receipt of 712 such images whilst using the file-sharing site LimeWire. The decision of the Supreme Court of Queensland in *R v Carson* (2008) provides another illustration of the way existing provisions in child pornography legislation could be used to regulate the use of P2P file-sharing software for distributing illegal child abuse content. The accused was charged with two counts of possession of 11,816 child exploitation files downloaded from the LimeWire file-sharing software and distribution of 2,483 child exploitation files stored on his computer's "shared folder" which were available for downloading by other LimeWire users. It was contended that the offender did not "actively" send any files to others, that he did not engage in any commercial exchange of files and that there was no evidence that anyone had actually accessed the files on his folder. The critical point emphasised by the Court was that in doing what he did, the accused had facilitated the ability of other users of file-sharing software to gain access to a large repository of child exploitation material from his computer. The Court demonstrated a good understanding of the file-sharing software, and in particular its awareness of the way P2P file-sharing programmes can be misused by individuals to make illegal content available to persons with prurient interests:

> The applicant's submissions overlook the reality of modern day information dissemination ... Indeed on one level, the distribution of material through a file sharing program such as LimeWire may be seen as particularly pernicious because it provides ready world-wide access within a system designed to facilitate proliferation of the material, while offering a degree of anonymity to the distributor. (paragraph 36)

Sexting: Child pornography?

Finally, one child protection issue that has emerged in recent times concerns the practice amongst some children and young adolescents in taking sexually explicit photographs of themselves. Even though there is no one definition of "sexting", the National Campaign to Prevent Teen & Unplanned Pregnancy (National Center for Missing and Exploited Children (NCMEC)) offers an acceptable description, which is regarded as involving the practice of

> youth writing sexually explicit messages, taking sexually explicit photos of themselves or others in their peer group, and transmitting those photos and/or messages to their peers. (NCMEC, 2009)

This practice is part of a broader trend of individuals, more particularly adolescents, using the Internet and social media to express their identities and status amongst their peers. Whilst the practice of children taking semi-nude or provocative photographs in itself, for example, through the use a Polaroid camera is not new, the convergence between the self-presentation culture and mobile technologies (e.g. mobile phones) has contributed to the media and policy focus on sexting (Lenhart, 2009; Senft, 2008). The Proposed Directive leaves Member States with the flexibility in the way its criminal laws are used to address consensual activities of this nature between minors (European Commission, 2010e, recital 7). Under US Federal

Law, no distinction is made by 18 USC § 2256(8) between child pornography content generated by minors and adults. It is generally accepted that an adult who persuades or induces a minor to take sexually explicit photographs should be prosecuted under the sexual offences legislation. Failure by prosecution to establish the substantive elements of the offence can be fatal, as seen in the case of *US v Broxmeyer* (2010). The accused was a 36-year-old field hockey coach, and was convicted of two counts of producing child pornography, contrary to 18 USC § 2251(a), and possession of child pornography under 18 USC § 2252A(a)(5)(B). Under Federal law, § 2251(a), prosecution has to prove beyond reasonable doubt the following elements of the offence for producing child pornography: (a) the victim was below the age of 18 years old; (b) the defendant persuaded, used, induced or enticed the minor to take part in sexually explicit conduct for the purpose of producing a visual depiction of that conduct; and (c) the visual depiction was produced using materials that been transported in interstate or foreign commerce. The accused was convicted in the District Court for the Northern District of New York on production of child pornography. On appeal, he challenged successfully the legal basis of his conviction with regard to the sufficiency of evidence provided by prosecution under § 2251 (b). The Court of Appeal stressed that if the conviction for production of child pornography was to be upheld, evidence had to be produced by prosecution proving a causal link between the acts of the accused and the decision by the minor to take the two sexually explicit photographs of herself. The Court found there was no evidence that the accused in fact "induced" the minor to take the sexually explicit photographs. It is clear, however, that had the accused in fact solicited or persuaded the minor to send him nude images of herself, the offence would have been committed.

With regard to the practice of sexting between minors, there is some degree of ambivalence regarding the appropriateness of using child pornography laws to prosecute children. A study carried out by *Girlfriend* magazine showed that 40 per cent of the 588 Australian teenage girls that participated in the study had been asked to take semi-nude or sexually explicit images of their bodies (Battersby, 2008). In the United States, a study involving 653 teenagers found that 20 per cent had engaged in sexting (National Campaign, 2008). In the United Kingdom, a recent survey amongst young adolescents showed that 40 per cent of the respondents indicated that they knew friends who engaged in sexting (Phippen, 2009). Twenty-seven per cent of the respondents indicated that sexting was a common practice amongst their peer group. Over 56 per cent of the respondents observed that in a number of instances the images and videos were distributed beyond the immediate recipient without the express consent of the parties concerned. Sexting raises undoubted governance issues since electronic images or information can be disseminated to a wide audience, be manipulated and even used to harass, intimidate or bully the person whose image is on the photograph. According to the NCMEC, the practice implicates a number of individuals: the person whose image is displayed in the photograph, the person who takes the photograph, the persons who distribute the photographs and, finally, the persons who receive and distribute the photographs. It is worth recalling that by uploading photographs onto a social networking site or taking pictures on a webcam or mobile phone, permanent electronic records are made of the images and that these can be easily distributed across the Internet and other communication tools like emails, mobile phones and sites like YouTube.

In the United Kingdom, the various participants in the sexting chain can be prosecuted if the images satisfy the substantive elements of the OPA and the PCA legislation. For example, the question of whether a visual image taken by a minor is indecent will be determined by reference to the jury's determination of whether the photograph offends "currently accepted standards of decency; and indecency must always be judged in the light of time, place and circumstances" (*R v Flynn* (2010) paragraph 30). Technically, the practice of sexting will automatically trigger the *actus reus* of the following elements of the PCA 1978 – making, distribution and possession offences. There is also the question whether the content of the photographs will meet the threshold stipulated by the provisions in the PCA 1978 and, finally, whether the discretion should be exercised for or against prosecuting the young individuals.

The appropriateness of using child pornography legislation to curb sexting has been the subject of judicial comment in *Miller v Mitchell* (2008). The context for this legal action is particularly significant. In 2008, the District Attorney of Wyoming County in Pennsylvania was presented with evidence of three teenagers engaging in sexting. Officials in the Tunkhannock, Pennsylvania School District, discovered a number of male students trading in allegedly sexually explicit images of a number of teenage girls over their mobile phones. It is not entirely clear what decisions were taken in respect of the individuals found to have made these images. Students in Tunkhannock High School were, however, informed that those found in possession of inappropriate images of minors could be prosecuted under State law for possession or distribution of child pornography, or for offences relating to the criminal use of a communication facility for such activity. A group of students whose images were found on their mobile phones were presented with two options: (1) participate in an education programme or (2) face criminal prosecutions. Some of the photographs deemed to be child pornography included girls shown from waist up wearing white opaque bras, a girl posing provocatively in a bathing suit and finally a photograph of a girl wrapped in a white, opaque towel, just below her breasts, appearing to have just had a shower. The parents instituted a § 1983 action against the District Attorney, alleging no probable cause and that the threats of potential charges contravened the minor's First Amendment rights. James

Munley J. granted the order for a preliminary injunction. The rejection of the District Attorney's subsequent appeal to the Court of Appeal has been regarded as illustrating the inappropriateness of prosecuting minors under child pornography laws (Pavia, 2011). Concerns have been expressed in Australia regarding the use of child pornography laws to prosecuting minors engaged in sexting, in view of the proposed reforms to the Crimes Legislation Amendment (Sexual Offences against Children) Bill 2010 (paragraphs 3.32–6).[2] Section 474.27A, which is the relevant provision of the Bill, requires the following elements to be satisfied: (1) a carriage service has been used to transmit a communication between the sender and a recipient; (2) the communication includes material that is indecent; (3) the recipient is someone who is or who the sender believes to be below the age of 16 years; and (4) the sender is at least 18 years of age. Sexting, however, raises an important public policy issue, namely, whether the criminal law is an appropriate mechanism for deterring the practice as between young adolescents. It could be argued that the criminal law should not be extended to this practice, since sexting involves voluntary acts of children grappling with their identities and sexuality (Sacco, 2010). It is, however, worth noting an important point highlighted by the Senate Legal and Constitutional Affairs Legislation Committee, when it observed that[3]

> while the committee acknowledges that the practice [of sexting] may be undesirable, it agrees with arguments that young people engaged in such behaviour should not be exposed to the grave consequences and stigma that attach to allegations of, and convictions for, child sexual offences. (paragraph 3.55)

It is a view that is mirrored in the guidance issued by the Crown Prosecution Service (CPS) to prosecutors when deciding whether the public interest is best served by instigating criminal prosecutions against young adults engaged in such forms of behaviour. Accordingly, with regard to photographs, which are deemed to be "indecent" images of minors, the PCA 1978 provides a limited defence in relation to an image which relates to a child aged 16 or 17 years – where the parties were married or lived together in an enduring loving relationship the production and exchange of images between them would not constitute a violation of the criminal law. Clearly, in the type of sexting practices reported by the media or surveys as taking place between minors, these exceptions are unlikely to be relevant. That said, it is not always the case that prosecution will invariably follow from the making, distribution or possession of images which may technically be within the scope of the child pornography legislation. For example, Section 474.27A or Section 1 of the 1978 Act could be construed more narrowly; the prosecutorial discretion would not be exercised in favour of using the criminal law to intervene where the particular user-generated sexual content is shown not to have been produced by coercion or exploitation. There is a plausible argument for holding that sexually explicit images exchanged between consenting young adults should not be criminalised – notwithstanding our view of the moral soundness or appropriateness of such conduct. There is, however, another aspect to the governance issues raised by the practice of sexting, particularly where user-generated images of children are distributed or published to third parties, as a form of "sexy" communications via mobile phones or posted on profile pages on social networking sites. Legislation dealing with child pornography and indecent photographs containing pictures of minors were drafted to protect children and those less than mature from being sexually or commercially exploited by adults, and also to protect children from the reputational harm that could result as a direct consequence of their actions (Sacco, 2010). Clearly, if the images taken by children come within the type of prohibited conduct and are subsequently uploaded onto websites or distributed among peers there may be a case for saying that the public interest is served in bringing prosecutions. This is a dilemma that is unlikely to be readily resolved by the criminal law, as the following observation from Lord Falconer in the debates in Parliament makes clear:

> Our overriding concern is to protect children, not to punish them unnecessarily ... Where sexual relationships between minors are not abusive, prosecuting either or both children is highly unlikely to be in the public interest; nor would it be in the best interests of the children involved. (Hansard, 2003: column 1176)

This is true but it may, however, be recalled that in *New York v Ferber* (1982) the Supreme Court was at pains to stress the compelling reasons justifying the restriction on First Amendment rights, namely, the safeguarding of the physical, psychological and emotional well-being of the child. Sexting could be seen as being "intrinsically related to the sexual abuse of children" in the sense of perpetuating a culture of self-victimisation and commodification of children as objects of sexual interest (458 US 747, 758). In *AH v State* (2007) it was held that the State did have a compelling interest in regulating the practice of sexting. The 16-year-old in this case emailed nude photographs of herself to her 17-year-old boyfriend. Wolf J noted that

> prosecuting the child under the statute in question is the least intrusive means of furthering the State's compelling interest. Not prosecuting the child would do nothing to further the State's interest. Prosecution enables the State to prevent future illegal, exploitative acts by supervising and providing any necessary counseling to the child. (2007: 236)

In *State v ARS* (1996) the District Court of Appeal of Florida for the First District held that there was a compelling interest in State intervention even in a minor–minor situation, to protect the "minor from the sexual activity itself for reasons of health and quality of life" (1996: 1387). At the core of the controversy surrounding the practice of sexting is the extent to which the State and/or parents can or should intervene in children's expectations of their right or freedom to express their identities and autonomy (*In re Gault*, 387 US 1, 17). Whilst it is uncontroversial that parents or the State should intervene in cases of child abuse or where there are risks of exposure to illegal content, it is less than clear whether regulating the practice of sexting *per se* offends a child's rights to privacy and freedom of expression (*Tinker v Des Moines Independent Community School District* (1968); *Roper v Williams* (2005)). It is not surprising that in view of the difficult moral, social and legal issues raised by the practice of sexting that a balanced governance response has been advocated. Sexting, it is suggested, should not be seen purely as a law enforcement problem. The Federal Trade Commission (FTC), in accordance with its governance remit under the Broadband Data Improvement Act of 2008, has directed its efforts in raising the awareness of parents and educators so that these adults could mediate the activities of children (FTC, 2010a). Children need to be made fully aware of the reputational harms and legal ramifications of the practice; the transmission of texts and images of provocative or sexually explicit nature may result in their violation of pornography and obscenity laws, in addition to exposing them to peer victimisation (*Logan v Sycamore Community School Bd. of Education* (2011)). Jessica Logan committed suicide after nude pictures of her (from the neck down) were distributed amongst students. A timely response is also needed, as there are long-term developmental, social and career implications that accompany convictions under child pornography laws – imprisonment and requirements to register under the sex offender rules (Lenhart, 2009: 10). A number of legislatures have been at the forefront of revising existing laws or introducing new laws to deal with the practice of sexting. In 2011, at least 18 states in the United States have directed their efforts towards enacting a legislative framework which requires district education boards and schools to implement online child safety policies aimed at educating young children about the risks of sending images of minors engaged in lewd or sexually explicit activity, and also reminding children and their parents of the consequences of violating school policies prohibiting sexting. The Pennsylvania General Assembly, for example, has proposed a House Bill 2189 which amends its criminal code to deal with the offence of dissemination of prohibited materials by minors through the use of mobile phones and other communication technologies. The South Carolina General Assembly has introduced a Bill creating an offence of sexting. Children between the ages of 12 and 18 years who transmit to another minor a visual or other content depicting himself or another in a state of sexual activity or sexually explicit nudity will be subject to a fine and will be required to undergo an educational programme. Completion of the programme and payment of the fine will lead to the misdemeanour being expunged from the individual's record.

Peer victimisation: Bullying, harassment and stalking

Peer victimisation is a major online child safety issue in most countries. Internet, mobile phones and social media can now be used to bully, harass and stalk victims (Chamberlain *et al.*, 2010). The standard setting role of the criminal law with regard to protecting children from all forms of peer victimisation corresponds with the United Kingdom's international obligations under a number of conventions and instruments. For example, Article 3 of the ECHR (which have been enacted into the UK Law by virtue of the Human Rights Act 1988) provides that no one should be subject to "inhuman or degrading treatment". Article 28(2) of the UNCRC requires States to "take all appropriate measures to ensure that school discipline is administered in a manner consistent with the child's human dignity and in conformity with the present Convention". Articles 37 and 19 of the UNCRC elaborate the extent of the State's and by proxy the School's responsibility. Many of the laws which cover bullying, assaults, harassment and stalking can be used to address the safety and security concerns raised by technology-mediated victimisation. Most countries have in place legislation that requires schools to implement measures which create a safe environment for pupils (House of Commons, 2011; DCSF, 2008). For example, Section 61 of the School Standards and Framework Act 1998 requires schools to ensure that measures are in place to prevent all forms of bullying among pupils. The Act also requires each governing body to review its policy on bullying annually. Schools also owe a duty of care towards pupils (175 of the Education Act 2002 and Education and Inspections Act 2006 (EIA, 2006)). A failure to discharge the obligation to take reasonable safety and security measures towards protecting pupils can lead to schools and Local Educational Authorities being subjected to actions for breach of statutory duty or the common law tort of negligence. Educators can also utilise their powers under the 2006 Education Act to discipline pupils who engage in peer victimisation both off and on school premises (DCSF, 2008). Significantly, the liability of schools is subjected to the test of whether reasonable steps have been taken to provide pupils with a safe and secure environment (*Cox v State of New South Wales* (2007)). The imposition of the standard of reasonableness makes it clear that the duty does not extend to eliminating all forms of risks and harms to pupils (*Geyer v Downs* (1977)). In *Bradford-Smart v West Sussex County Council* Judge LJ giving the judgment of the Court of Appeal made this observation:

Any school has to have sensible disciplinary policies and procedures if it is to function properly as a school at all...But in order to hold the school liable towards a particular pupil, the question is always whether the school was in breach of its duty of care towards that pupil and whether that breach caused the particular harm which was suffered. (2002: paragraph 38)

As observed previously, bullying and other forms of victimisation in the on-line environment can manifest itself in physical, emotional and psychological effects on the victim (Office of the Children's Commissioner, 2006). Where online victimisation is different from non-electronic forms of bullying is the speed, scale and devastating effects on victims targeted by peers. During the last few years there have been increasing media reports of the rise in peer victimisation through the use of new communication technologies. Technology-mediated victimisation can be relentless and the consequences fatal. Growing concerns about the impact of cyberbullying on children's safety and well-being has led to calls for the New South Wales administration to respond swiftly (Jones, 2009). The 2008 Eurobarometer Survey highlighted the scale of parental concerns about electronically mediated victimisation; 54 per cent of European parents expressed concerns about their children being bullied online (Eurobarometer, 2008). As cases like *Lori Drew* (2009) make clear, unless the acts of victimisation come within the existing categories of crimes no criminal prosecution will be possible. Any redress for the harms suffered will require the individual to pursue the claims under the civil law (*Cox v State of New South Wales; TK; Logan*). In the remainder of this Section I identify some responses of the criminal law in addressing the risks posed by peer victimisation, namely, the Offences against the Persons Act 1861, the Malicious Communications Act (MCA) 1988, Section 127 of the Communications Act 2003 and the Protection from Harassment Act 1997. The discussion concludes with a brief examination of the significance of the alternative strategies for the MSIG model.

Offences against the Person Act 1861

The protection afforded to an individual with regard to his physical bodily integrity has been an established principle under the common law and Article 8 of the ECHR (Table 3.8). Unauthorised disclosures of private information and acts which interfere with the individual's safety and well-being are examples of infringements to the right to respect for private life and correspondence.

Clearly, where online peer victimisation extends to offline physical attacks or sexual violence, the law has mechanisms for addressing the harm suffered by an individual. Common law assault is a term used to describe those acts which cause an individual to apprehend imminent unlawful contact. For a common law offence to be committed, two requirements must be met. First, the accused must cause the victim to apprehend imminent

Table 3.8   Article 8 of the ECHR

Article 8
1. Everyone has the right to respect for his private and family life, his home and his correspondence. 2. There shall be no interference by a public authority with the exercise of this right except such as is in accordance with the law and is necessary in a democratic society in the interests of national security, public safety or the economic well-being of the country, for the prevention of disorder or crime, for the protection of health or morals, or for the protection of the rights and freedoms of others.

and unlawful force. Second, the accused must be shown to have intended or be regarded as being reckless to the consequence of the act (*Savage and Parmenter* (1992)). A text threatening violence when a student is making his way to school could be seen as an example of an "imminent" threat. The fact that the threat does not materialise is not relevant (*Longdon v DPP* (1976)). In addition to the common law offence of assault, individuals have also been charged with the offence of battery (*Fagan v MPC* (1976); *Collins v Wilcock* (1984)). The Offences against the Person Act (OAPA) 1861 envisages that any act or omission which results in a person being put in fear of his or her bodily integrity can be liable for an assault. An individual on summary conviction for an assault occasioning actual bodily harm can be imprisoned for a term not exceeding six months (Section 39 of the CJA 1988). Under Section 47 of the 1861 Act, an individual can be convicted for any assault occasioning actual bodily harm. There are two requirements to this statutory offence, which on indictment can result in a five-year imprisonment term. First, the accused must be shown by his actions (or omissions) to have caused actual bodily harm to the victim. Second, it must be shown that the accused intended or was reckless as to the assault or battery (*R v Ireland, R v Burstow* (1998)). In *R v Donovan* (1934) "actual bodily harm" was regarded as comprising any harm or injury calculated to interfere with the health or comfort of the victim. There are limits to the potential liability of schools in this respect. In *Webster v Ridgeway Foundation School* (2010) the perpetrators of an assault on a pupil by his peers and non-pupils on school premises were prosecuted under Section 18 of the OAPA. The victim in this case suffered a brutal attack leaving him with serious head injuries inflicted by a non-pupil. It is quite important to also note the view adopted by the Court with regard to the question of whether the victim could seek compensation from the school for these injuries. As Nicol J makes plain:

> I consider that it would be fair, just and reasonable to conclude that to some extent, at least, the school had a duty to take reasonable care to safeguard and protect Henry from attack by outsiders. ((2010, paragraph 119)

According to this line of reasoning, it would seem reasonable to infer that whilst it is important for schools to discharge their duties towards pupils, it is perhaps a step too far to suggest that the criminal law should invariably intervene when children are subjected to criticisms or unkind comments (*R v Ireland* (1998); *R v Morris* (1998)). There is also a real concern that extending the reach of the criminal law to prosecute all forms of conflicts between peers or the use of exclusion orders would be tantamount to adopting a "zero tolerance policy", which may unwittingly act as a disincentive for individuals to report bullying incidents to authorities (House of Commons, 2011; Sampson, 2002: 24).

Malicious Communications Act 1988

One frequent question raised by schools and parents is whether malicious or unpleasant comments posted on a victim's social networking account or distribution of false or unkind information about the victim can be the subject of criminal sanctions. For an actionable communication, Section 1 of the MCA 1988 must be satisfied. The section states that any person who sends to another person a letter, electronic communication or article of any description which conveys a message which is indecent or grossly offensive; a threat or information which is false and known or believed to be false by the sender or any article or electronic communication which is, in whole or part, of an indecent or grossly offensive nature is liable if his purpose, or one of his purposes, in sending it is that it should cause distress or anxiety to the recipient or to any other person to whom he intends that it or its contents or nature should be communicated (*Connolly v DPP* (2007)). The MCA gives a wide definition to the meaning of "electronic communication" and these include instant messages, texts, emails and any audio or video communication. The MCA is sufficiently flexible to address three types of malicious communications which children may be vulnerable to when using Web 2.0 technologies like email, IM and other communication tools:

1. Indecent or grossly offensive communication

When determining if the communication is indecent or grossly offensive a court will consider whether the communication offends the ordinary standards of decency and propriety (*R v Stanley* (1965)). A communication will be deemed to be "obscene" if on an objective assessment it is found to be shocking, lewd or indecent (*R v Anderson* (1972); *R v Straker* (1965)). Issues regarding the obscenity or indecency of the communication are left to the jury to determine (*R v Stamford* (1972)). It is not enough to show that the communication is merely offensive. Following *DPP v Collins* (2006), it was made clear that the message must be grossly offensive, and whether that is the case will depend on the standards of a democratic multi-racial society.

2. Threats via email or texts are also covered by the Act.

As noted previously, it is an offence to send any form of electronic communication (*R v Solanke* (1969); *R v Williams* (1986)). Section 1(2) of the Act does provide the person sending the communication with a defence. The provision states that a person shall not be found guilty if a threat was made to reinforce a legal demand and the sender had reasonable grounds for believing that he could send the email.

3. Sending information which is false and known or is believed to be false with the intention of causing anxiety or distress is also an offence under the MCA.

It is relevant to note here that information which could be viewed as "fair comment" or postings on websites which recount certain aspects of a private relationship or sexual encounters which is not lewd or grossly offensive but is calculated to cause embarrassment would fall outside this legislation.

In *Connolly v DPP* (2007) the accused was convicted of sending graphic photographs of aborted foetuses to pharmacies supplying contraceptive pills. The Court held that the conviction of the accused for sending an article which was indecent or grossly offensive did not abridge the rights under the Human Rights Act 1998, namely, Sections 9 and 10. Dyson LJ noted that the terms indecent and grossly offensive did not have a unique meaning for the purposes of the 1998 Act ((2007) paragraph 10).

Section 127 of the Communications Act 2003
The enactment of Section 127 of the Communications Act 2003 ensures that the types of activity covered by the MCA 1988 are similarly covered, where the communications take place through a public electronic communications network. This section criminalises two particular types of conduct. First, Section 127(1) criminalises messages or other matter sent through public electronic communications networks which are grossly offensive, or can be regarded as being of an indecent, obscene or menacing character. Any person who also causes such message or matter to be sent will be prosecuted under this section. Second, messages sent by public electronic communications network, which the sender knows to be false, or causes such a message to be sent; or persistent use of a public electronic communications network for the purpose of causing annoyance, inconvenience or needless anxiety to another will constitute an offence under this Act. In both instances, on summary conviction, the perpetrator can

be imprisoned for a term not exceeding six months or fined (not exceeding Level 5). A "public electronic communications network" is defined as an electronic communications network provided wholly or mainly for the purpose of making electronic communications service that is provided so as to be available for use by members of the public. It is important to make clear that the section only applies to the use of a communications network and service that have been provided and funded by the public. Section 127(1), it should be noted, aims to balance the rights to private life and the rights to freedom of expression enshrined in Articles 8 and 10 of the Human Rights Act 1998, respectively. The leading case is *DPP v Collins* (2006). The accused made a number of phone calls which were grossly offensive to the office of a Member of Parliament. Racially offensive telephone messages were also left by the accused. At first instance, the Leicestershire Justices dismissed the charges on the grounds that although the words used (i.e. "Wogs", "Pakis" and "Black Bastards") were offensive they were not of a gross nature. Lord Bingham observed that, unlike Section 1 of the MCA, Section 127 did not criminalise communications which individuals find annoying or offensive. The question whether a message is "grossly offensive" is one of fact and based on the "standards of an open and just multi-racial society, and that the words must be judged taking account of their context and all relevant circumstances" (paragraph 9). Furthermore, Section 127(1) will be triggered as soon the communication has been sent. This can be contrasted with Section 127(2) where there is explicit reference to the requirement of proof relating to the unlawful purpose and knowledge of the sender of the message. Lord Bingham was, however, keen to emphasise that some degree of culpability must be evidenced. As Lord Carswell made it clear, the essence of Section 127(1) is "whether reasonable persons in our society would find it grossly offensive" (2006: 21).

Protection of Harassment Act 1997

New communication technologies allow individuals to repeatedly target their victims through mobile phones, emails and social networking sites. For the conduct to amount to harassment, the following elements in Section 1, Protection of Harassment Act (PHA) 1977, must be established:

1. There must be a course of conduct. In other words, a single act or communication would not suffice. Section 7(3) states that a "course of conduct" must, in relation to a single person, involve conduct on at least two occasions in relation to that person. For example, in *Lau v DPP* (2000) it was held that where there was an interval between the first and the second act, both acts would not be regarded as a course of conduct. Where the interval between each act is not significant, the court may take the view that the incidents are sufficiently linked to constitute a course of conduct. In *Kelly v DPP* (2003), the offender left three messages in the

victim's voice mail. These three messages were left within a space of five minutes. The court held that the communications constituted a course of conduct. The "course of conduct" requirement will also be satisfied if the perpetrator sends an SMS text on one occasion and then follows up with an email or physical exchange. Finally, it needs to be shown that there is a link between each corresponding act before there can be said to be a "course of conduct". In *Pratt v DPP* (2001) Latham LJ stated that "prosecuting authorities...should ensure that what they are seeking the court to adjudicate upon can properly fall within the category of behaviour which is behaviour causing harassment of the other, not merely that there have been two or more incidents. The mischief which the Act is intended to meet is that persons should not be put in a state of alarm or distress by repetitious behaviour" (paragraph 12).

2. The course of conduct must constitute harassment. According to the Home Office, a course of conduct which alarms the victim or causes the victim distress will satisfy this requirement (Home Office, 2001). In *Majrowski v Guy's and St Thomas's NHS Trust* (2007), Lord Birkenhead noted that the Act was aimed at all forms of harassment wherever it occurs but noted that a distinction needed to be made between the upset and annoyances encountered in dealings with people and those which warrant the imposition of criminal liability (paragraph 30). In *Esther Thomas v News Group Newspapers Limited, Simon Hughes* (2001), Lord Phillips ventured to suggest that a much higher threshold was needed for prosecutions under this legislation:

> There are many actions that foreseeably alarm or cause a person distress that could not possibly be described as harassment. It seems to me that Section 7 is dealing with that element of the offence which is constituted by the effect of the conduct rather than with the types of conduct that produce that effect.

> The Act does not attempt to define the type of conduct that is capable of constituting harassment. "Harassment" is, however, a word which has a meaning which is generally understood. It describes conduct targeted at an individual which is calculated to produce the consequences described in Section 7 and which is oppressive and unreasonable. (paragraphs 29–30)

3. The accused must know or ought to know that the conduct amounts to harassment. Under Section 1(1)(b) if an accused knows that his actions constitute harassment, this requirement will be met. The section also provides an alternative, where an objective test can be applied. For example, a defendant's lack of awareness that his actions were harassing the victim will not be a defence if any reasonable person would regard the conduct as harassment. In *R v Colohan* (2001) it was stated that the reasonable person test would not include the particular characteristics of the

accused. The accused in this case sought to argue that his course of conduct was reasonable in view of the fact that he was diagnosed as a schizophrenic. This argument was rejected by the court on the grounds that permitting such an interpretation into the construction of the statute would prevent the PHA from achieving its primary purpose, namely, to give protection to victims of harassment. An accused convicted under the PHA faces six months' imprisonment or a fine. Where the accused has been convicted for the offence in Section 4, which is the course of conduct causing another to fear that violence would be used against the victim, the maximum term of imprisonment is five years or a fine (*cf.* Sections 1(2) and 4(4)).

It is well-known that many victims of crimes and witnesses find the criminal justice system intimidating, burdensome and slow. With the exception of blatant cases of abuse and victimisation, children tend to be reluctant to report incidents of online bullying and victimisation to parents or educators – uncertainty or lack of awareness as to their legal rights, embarrassment, and fear of parental or peer disapproval (Chamberlain *et al.*, 2010). One major drawback in using the criminal law to address the problems of peer victimisation is that in many instances, a prosecution is unlikely to be launched without the victim providing or obtaining relevant and admissible evidence in support of the claims. The absence of a "course of conduct" or evidence produced showing that the communication was fair comment or regarded as not being "grossly" offensive are just some of the difficulties victims face in satisfying the legal and evidentiary threshold. Peer victimisation through the use of Web 2.0 technologies may appear to upset the traditional balance struck in the provisions made by the criminal law. Some take the view that the criminal should intervene. Others regard the use of the criminal law as an inappropriate response when the harm perpetrated on the victim is not regarded as coming within existing rules on assault, harassment or malicious communications (Sampson, 2002). As the Anti-Bullying Alliance noted in its submission to the *Select Committee on Behaviour and Discipline in Schools*:[4]

> Bullying behaviour can be complex and difficult to manage. There are times where access to specialist intervention is vital–such as with cases of sexual bullying. There may also be a need for particular support for children who are vulnerable to bullying, or who have been damaged by bullying–and similarly there may be a need for ongoing intervention for children who display bullying behaviour... Evidence suggests that it is more beneficial to involve those agencies whose primary role is to address disruptive behaviours rather than generic agencies like the police.

Technology-mediated victimisation is just the latest series of deviant behaviour which can impair the emotional well-being of victims. Cases like *Tinker v Des Moines Independent Community* SD (1969), *Bethel School District No. 403 v Fraser* (1986), *Beussink v Woodland R-IV SD* (1998), *Morse v Frederick* (2007) and *JS v Blue Mountain* (2007) underscore the view that problems of ill-discipline and disregard of appropriate civil conduct and behaviour are not easily accommodated within the criminal justice system (*cf.* civil measures under Anti-Social Behaviour Act 2003: *R v Katinas (Paul)* (2010)). As Lord Birkenhead seems to imply in *Majrowski v Guy's and St Thomas's NHS Trust* (2007), individuals need to muster their own resources for self-help and resilience when dealing with the irritations, unpleasantness and annoyances that result from interacting with people, and that courts "are well able to recognise the boundary between conduct which is unattractive, even unreasonable, and conduct which is oppressive and unacceptable" (paragraph 30).

Of course, where victimisation involves a course of conduct amounting to harassment, there are sound reasons why Parliament has regarded that it is in the public interest to prosecute individuals who have embarked on the prohibited conduct on at least two occasions (under the MCA) or engaged in anti-social behaviour. None of this helps children particularly as

> the day-to-day adverse affects of bullying in damaging educational opportunities to students are as real as they are unnoticed...[and]...is a problem that affects the school performance, emotional well-being, mental health, and social development of school children. (*TK*, 2011: 6)

The Tellus4 Survey reported that two-fifths of the children surveyed had been bullied at least on a weekly basis, and that disability, age and ethnicity were often seen as contributory factors (Chamberlain *et al.*, 2010: 36–7). Mencap noted an increase in the victimisation of individuals with a learning disability. Eight of out of ten children with learning disabilities have been the subject of bullying incidents (Mencap, 2007). The Schools Health Education Unit surveyed young lesbian, gay, bisexual people about their experiences in school and found that over 65 per cent of the respondents had been the target of bullying (Hunt *et al.*, 2007). Pupils are entitled to protection under the Equality Act 2010, which requires schools and educators to take positive steps in preventing all forms of victimisation, harassment and discrimination. In practical terms, the Equality Act 2010 requires education service providers to adopt reasonable measures which safeguard pupils from all forms of victimisation, including those related to disability, gender, sexual orientation, race and religion. More disconcerting is the fact that pupils are now being excluded from schools for engaging in a range of misconduct. The recent data for "exclusions" show that there were 50 exclusions for bullying, 20 exclusions for racist abuse and 110 exclusions for sexual misconduct (DfE, 2010). Exclusions for persistent disruptive behaviour in primary schools were now averaging 200 in primary schools and 1,710 in State-funded secondary schools (DfE, 2010). In view of the fact that incidents of peer victimisation tend to be under-reported, there is much to be said for developing and enforcing acceptable standards of behaviour by schools in collaboration with law enforcement and local education authorities. Education providers in the United States and the United Kingdom, for example, have a statutory obligation to implement governance measures to promote the safety and well-being of pupils by eradicating peer victimisation. For example, § 32261(g) of the Californian Code makes explicit that peer victimisation of any form and perpetrated by Web 2.0 technologies will result in disciplinary sanctions. The Washington Revised Code (§ 28A.300.285) was enacted to deal with the limitations of existing criminal laws prohibiting peer victimisation and the varying successes of anti-harassment policies adopted by school districts. § 28A.300.285 aims to provide parents and students greater assurances regarding the safety protocols to be followed by all students; all education authorities are required to enforce the public interest in enabling students to learn and develop in a learning environment without fear of violence, intimidation and bullying. The State of Georgia has passed legislation requiring educational and school boards to adopt measures for enforcing safety rules and norms. For example, § 20–2-751.4 deals with bullying taking place within the school, at school-related events or activities and at designated school bus stops. Unlike the provisions contained in the criminal legislation the aim of these anti-bullying enactments (and like the one below) is to compel educators to adopt proportionate and timely responses to peer victimisation. Schools in England and Wales are required under the Education Act 2002 to demonstrate that they have implemented anti-bullying policies (e.g. whole school policies dealing with the reporting and investigation of bullying incidents, supporting victims, equipping staff with bullying management strategies, and communicating to staff and students the acceptable standards of behaviour required of them). The Department for Children, Schools and Families (DCSF) Guide *Safe to Learn* has been adopted by many schools (DCSF, 2007). The Guide advocates a "whole school" multi-stakeholder governance approach, which embeds the principles of equality, Personal, Social, Health and Economic Education (PHSE) and citizenship curriculum, respect and non-discrimination into its action plan (Tippett *et al.*, 2010: 85–90). A number of schools have adopted proactive anti-bullying strategies and measures (Howard *et al.*, 2010: 158–60). For example, Saint Cecilia's RC Infant and Nursery School in Liverpool organises home visits to families of children in the new intake, implements a playground buddy scheme and has set up a school council overseeing student welfare and well-being issues. The Woodside Community Primary in Dudley has anti-bullying strategies and support schemes involving all its staff and pupils. The Peatmoor Community Primary in Swindon has adopted similar schemes and provides an effective auditing and recording system for bullying incidents. It also makes available adult mediation services to its pupils. Finally, the Beavers Community Primary in Hounslow is a UN International Children's Emergency Fund (UNICEF)-accredited Rights Respecting School. It provides a buddy scheme, has a value-based curriculum and equips children with conflict management skills.

It is not possible to draw any firm conclusions regarding the effectiveness of all these positive measures aimed at reducing the level of peer victimisation experienced by children. That said, these policies could be regarded as proactive measures aimed at embedding extra-legal standards and mechanisms to complement the overarching regulatory framework provided by the criminal law. These proactive interventions are significant in that they now create obligations which local board of education authorities must comply with. For example, schools will now be required to make clear to all students the type of conduct which is now prohibited and the sanctions that accompany violation of school policies. Students and parents of students are expected to be notified of these rules and the information is to be included in student and parent handbooks. Teachers and school employees are also required to alert the school principal if they have credible information that a pupil may be the possible target of bullying. Most important of all, schools will be required to demonstrate that they now take peer victimisation seriously by developing procedures for counselling, reporting, investigating and disciplining. These anti-bullying enactments facilitate the creation of a MSIG framework, which enable schools to develop policies, measures and strategies that will create a toxic-free learning environment (New York Education Law, §§ 10–17 (2010)). The extension of the acceptable behaviour rules and norms both during school and after school hours is a clear recognition that as Web 2.0 technologies become an integral part of children's lives, there are significant opportunities for deviancy and victimisation to be perpetrated. Finally, the sanctions for violating school policies prohibiting bullying – counselling, parental/teacher intervention, suspension or exclusion – are preferable where clear violations of the criminal law have not taken place.

Some general comments can be offered by way of conclusion with regard to the interaction between criminal law rules and norms on the one hand and the role of schools in promoting greater awareness amongst children about their rights and responsibilities in managing their online and offline interactions on the other. First, the uncomfortable or uneasy truth, for those who view the First Amendment rights or the Judiciary as being obstructive, is that the criminal law does not provide sanctions for all forms of unpleasant speech (as noted above). This is probably a reflection of the balance the criminal law attempts to strike between the instances where State intervention is deemed to be necessary and those situations where there is an expectation that organisations, schools, parents and individuals develop effective strategies for managing risks encountered by children in their daily lives. This is one reading of the various pieces of legislation and measures noted above. These developments also seem to be in line with the balance struck between protected and unprotected speech. Indeed, the rules outlined in each of the areas of legislation correspond with the observations made by Supreme Court in *Tinker v Des Moines Independent Community School District* (1969). Mr Justice Fortas indicated that curbs on students expectations to express their ideas and thoughts need to be based on more than a "desire to avoid the discomfort and unpleasantness that always accompany an unpopular viewpoint" (393 US 503, 509). He emphasised that a student's freedom of expression was not absolute, and that in appropriate circumstances curbs imposed must be supported by demonstrable evidence indicating that other more important values in the education setting would be compromised (ibid). Where such evidence is forthcoming, limits on an individual's freedom of expression has been sanctioned by the courts. In *Morse v Frederick* (2007) a student alleged that his First Amendment rights had been violated by a ten-day suspension meted to him following his waving of a banner promoting drug use at an off-campus, school-approved activity. In holding that there was no violation of the student's First Amendment rights, the Supreme Court stressed that a failure to act would have undermined the school policy prohibiting illegal drug use and would have sent conflicting signals to students at this event. Second, the reference to demonstrable evidence showing a causal link between the conduct and the harm suffered suggests that alternative strategies need to be pursued which ensure that a child's learning environment continues to be free from harassment and discrimination. Third, it may very well be that schools, parents and law enforcement could work together to augment the existing legal standards by focusing on those activities which continue to cause considerable anxiety amongst children and which can impair their ability to take full advantage of the educational and development opportunities offered in school. It has already been remarked previously that schools have a legal basis for proscribing conduct which can materially and substantially undermine the proper conduct of educational activities.

Online intermediary: Filtering and liability issues

Before examining the principal regulatory framework that defines the scope of an online intermediary's responsibility for safeguarding children in relation to exposure to illegal or inappropriate content, under the Electronic Commerce Directive 2000/31/EC, it should first be noted that there is no disagreement that illegal content should be blocked by ISPs and online service providers. Just as in the offline environment, many will agree that children should not have access to illegal and adult content. It does not come as a surprise that children's access to illegal or age-inappropriate content has re-ignited the well-documented debates on mandatory filtering of illegal and harmful content (House of Commons, 2007–8). ISPs and online service providers are seen as increasing children's exposure to such content through the networks, communication platforms and services they make available. Kleinschmidt describes the relations between ISPs (broadly defined) and online users as founded on the performance of three functionalities: access, hosting and consumption (2010: 332). The reference by Kleinschmidt to a contractual nexus has a wider significance. First, it foreshadows the contractual, technical and regulatory measures that underpin the strategies for mediating contact, content and conduct risks. Second, increasingly children's exposure to risk-prone activities will require policymakers to also identify the context and levels in which each online intermediary can be expected to discharge its responsibilities as part of a MSIG strategy. Finally, when addressing content regulation and liability issues we need to also keep in mind that the online environment is now very much a conglomeration of services, markets and industries in the telecommunication, broadcasting and entertainment sector. Businesses like AOL, BT, Vodafone and O2, for example, provide voice, data and broadband Internet access packages to customers. A number of online intermediaries may provide nothing more than a communications infrastructure and system capabilities – for example, individuals can through subscription or membership upload content for storage or distribution. Other online intermediaries enable individuals to generate their own content or engage in a wide range of interactions with anyone with an Internet access (e.g. Facebook, MySpace and blogs). Increasingly, the growing market in entertainment and online gaming has resulted in a proliferation of online intermediaries making available software application and online multimedia communication platforms for individuals to play games, post videos and watch movies. Mobile phone providers, online gaming sites and social networking sites not surprisingly provide an array of services, including software applications, voice and network facilities. Despite the range of developments in new media and entertainment offline laws dealing with obscenity and child protection laws continue to be amenable for example to the issues raised by the use of the Internet to access, create, and store illegal and inappropriate content. In this context it should be noted that the BBFC has long adopted classification schemes that have informed the strategies adopted by online service providers and services in managing the flows of content across their networks or services. The current categories adopted by the BBFC are U, PG, 12A, 12, 15 and 18. Works which are rated "18" albeit legal are deemed to be unsuitable for children as they contain strong violence, frequent use of strong language and scenes of sexual activity and/or sexual violence. Individuals below the age of 18 years are not permitted to view or purchase films or videos of works rated at "18". The "15" category films cover a wide range of "grown up" issues and have in the past included sexual activity, paedophilia, rape, incest and genocide (e.g.

Little Children, The Woodsman, Doubt, Sex and the City and Schindler's List) (BBFC, 2011). The body classifies films on behalf of Local Authorities in this country, who in turn license cinemas under the Licensing Act 2003. One condition for licensing cinemas under the 2003 Act is that admission of children below the age of 18 years is to be restricted in accordance with the classification recommendations of the BBFC or the licensing authority. The Video Recordings Act 1984 provides the BBFC with the power to classify video works which are released as video recordings. Works within its terms of reference include films, video games and television programmes which are supplied on formats like tape, disc or other device capable of storing electronic data. Apart from videos, which are specifically exempted, all works must be classified by the BBFC. It is an offence to offer to supply unclassified material on video or DVD contrary to the provisions Video Recordings Act 1984. "Video on demand" content regulation in the United Kingdom is now overseen by the Association for Television on Demand (ATVOD). Increasingly, as videos are distributed in alternative formats (e.g. downloads or streaming) a voluntary classification scheme is provided under BBFC.online. The general principles of facilitating public access to a wide range of works and informed decision-making are, however, qualified in three main respects. First, the BBFC will not classify material if it either is in conflict with the law or has been produced through the commission of a criminal offence. Second, the BBFC may require selected parts of the work to be cut, if it is to be made available for screening in cinemas or distributed in a video or DVD format (e.g. moral harm, desensitising a viewer to the effects of violence, glorifying abuse, encouraging unhealthy fantasies amongst children) (cf. *R (on the application of British Board of Film Classification) v Video Appeals Committee* (2008)). Third, the BBFC may intervene to recommend a re-classification, if the material is likely to be viewed as unacceptable to general public opinion (e.g. filthy language may be deemed inappropriate for "12" rating). As a public authority, the BBFC aims to ensure that "regulated works" do not infringe child protection laws like the PCA 1978 and the OPA 1959 and 1964.

Content regulation issues can arise in a number of ways. For example, by virtue of Section 1(1)(b) of the PCA 1978, an online intermediary can be prosecuted for displaying indecent photographs (or pseudo-photographs), for being in possession of such contents or for facilitating access to others. Section 1(1)(d) of the PCA also makes it an offence to publish or cause to be published any advertisement likely to be understood as conveying that the advertiser distributes or shows such indecent photographs (or pseudo-photographs), or intends to do so. ISPs and newsgroups need to be on the alert for hosting discussion groups and forums which imply that they are a repository or venue for those with prurient interests in children or extreme pornography. Whilst it is understandable that online intermediaries can and should play an important part in reinforcing existing standards and laws, it would not have gone unnoticed that regulating content which may be age-inappropriate or potentially viewed as harmful is more problematic (*R (on the application of British Board of Film Classification) v Video Appeals Committee* (2008) – "classification with regard to Manhunt 2"). Many filtering strategies and liability rules attach particular importance to parents and educators determining the appropriateness of content for viewing by minors. One thing is clear: content regulation and legal standards and rules have been extended across a number of online service providers and bring within the child protection remit a diverse range of content, multimedia communication platforms and services. For example, in pursuance of obligations entered under the Cybercrime Convention and its protocols, guidelines have been provided to enable law enforcement and ISPs to coordinate their activities. ISPs make efforts to minimise the use of their services by third parties for criminal activities and report suspected criminal activity taking place on their communication platforms. ISPs rely on filtering software to regulate online content. For example, software is used to block or filter content by the use of blocklists. These blocklists may comprise blacklisted websites, IP addresses and Internet addresses (URLs). Some online service providers use deep packet inspection technology to identify and filter child pornography. The filtering technology can be used to monitor all forms of online traffic and information requests (e.g. search engines, websites, emails and downloading of content). Many ISPs and online service providers automatically filter information security threats and illegal content. Finally, as will be noted later, requests from law enforcement authorities to block and filter racist, hate and other illegal content are usually acted upon quickly by ISPs, mobile phone providers and social networking sites.

As can be seen from this brief account, filtering already operates at the network, product and search levels. The end-user interface is also provided with blocking and filtering functionalities. Online service providers increasingly provide users, including parents and educators, with software tools to assist them in determining the type of content that be accessed and viewed by children. The age and content classification categories, for example, provided by the BBFC and Pan European Games Industry (PEGI) equip parents with information so that decisions regarding children's access to online entertainment and computer games are consistent with safeguarding children's safety and well-being norms. In a recent survey it was suggested that many providers of games in eighteen European countries were incorporating child protection norms and principles into their practices (ISFE, 2010). Compliance with these codes is seen as minimising children's exposure to illegal or inappropriate user-generated content or adult website URLs. Parents, for example, are also provided with information relating to age-appropriate and content categories (e.g. violence, nudity, drug use, inappropriate language and discrimination). Additionally, like the BBFC, many online service providers provide parents with "extended classification information" so that they have a better understanding of the issues which informed the classification decisions. In passing, it should be noted that the Canadian Radio-Television and Telecommunications Commission (CRTC) does not regulate content on the Internet. Even though ISP filtering is not mandatory, the governance framework with regard to the regulation of content consists of a combination of national laws, industry codes of practice (i.e. Canadian Association of Internet Providers "Code of Conduct"), use of content filtering software and contractual terms (i.e. "Acceptance Use Policy"). The Project "Cleanfeed Canada" involves a MSIG approach comprising the Canadian Coalition against Internet Child Exploitation (CCAICE), a group which includes Cybertip.ca, ISPs, federal and provincial governments and law enforcement. Participating ISPs include major service providers like Bell, MTS allstream, TELUS, SaskTell, Rogers, Videotron, SHAW and Aliant. The content filtering process involves the creation and use of a regularly updated block-list of national and foreign-based URLs which contain child abuse images. These are made available to participating ISPs, who automatically filter the content without any end-user intervention. Project "Cleanfeed Canada" does not, however, maintain a log of traffic accessing the sites; ISPs, as is the case in countries like the United States, the United Kingdom and Australia, are not law enforcement agencies and filtering software is not regarded as a law enforcement tool. In Australia, the Broadcasting Services Act 1992 (Cth) (as amended) now subjects online intermediaries to regulatory oversight by ACMA. ACMA is responsible for monitoring the broadcasting, Internet and commercial content service industry (Section 5). It also undertakes investigations into reports from the public regarding illegal, prohibited or offensive on-line content, including those from the Internet and mobile phones. Prohibited content for the purposes of the Broadcasting Services Act 1992 (Cth) is defined by clause 20 of Schedule 7 if they come within the restricted content classification system adopted in this country. In 2007 ACMA drafted new rules, set out in the Restricted Access System Declaration 2007. The existence of fines for non-compliance with industry standards and codes of practice provides a sufficient incentive for removing illegal content online in particular (Coroneos, 2008). As online intermediaries make audiovisual media increasingly accessible through multimedia platforms a number of technological measures and codes of practice have been adopted.

The rules on filtering and liability of online service providers attempt to balance market innovation and child protection goals (McCarthy, 2010). To this end, policymakers have increasingly shown a preference for a MSIG strategy whereby online intermediaries assume a primary role in developing measures and policies that enhance the safety of children when using their services and communication platforms (ITU, 2009d,e; Dutton *et al.*, 2007). Akdeniz, in his review of the role of ISPs in this area of governance, advocates a more temperate approach since overregulation may have "a chilling effect on the development of the Internet" (2008: 231). There has been a preference amongst policymakers to require industry to develop online child safety measures that minimise children's exposure to contact, content and conduct risks. Some have expressed serious concerns about recent calls for ISPs to monitor and regulate online activity and communications. The frameworks favoured by EU policymakers comprises "hard" and "soft" law measures (e.g. laws and codes of practice). Many online intermediaries, national regulatory bodies and organisations now form part of the INHOPE network as part of the child protection MSIG policymaking strategy. Within the INHOPE network of hotlines, 26 European countries now work with law enforcement in removing illegal content found in the online environment. Additionally, the move towards self-regulation by the industry can be seen in part as a direct response to avoiding additional layers of regulatory intervention. Internet service providers and intermediaries like mobile phone and content providers, and social networking sites, are already subject to a range of industry-wide standards and regulations. The *European Framework for Safer Mobile Use by Young Teenagers and Children* has as one of its goals the implementation by mobile phone providers of technical and regulatory processes aimed at reducing the availability and supply of illegal content in the online environment. In 2009, major social networking site services providers subscribed to a set of principles which enable parents, educators and children to better manage online risks. These developments will be addressed in more detail in Chapters 6 and 7. Apart from a situation where an information services provider actively engages in the hosting, making or distribution of obscene or child abuse content, most online intermediaries within the EU adhere to the legal obligations set out in the Electronic Commerce Directive 2000/31/EC.

The principal framework regarding the liability issues of online information services providers is that set out in Articles 12–15 of the Electronic Commerce Directive 2000/31/EC. As the preamble to the EC Directive indicates:

The exemptions from liability established in this Directive cover only cases where the activity of the information society service provider is limited to the technical process of operating and giving access to a communication network over which information made available by third parties is transmitted or temporarily stored, for the sole purpose of making the transmission more efficient; this activity is of a mere technical, automatic and passive nature, which implies that the information society service provider has neither knowledge of nor control over the information which is transmitted or stored. (paragraph 42)

Online intermediaries can only lay claim to immunity if they bring their actions within a limited range of defences. The defences apply to information or intermediary service providers. An "information society service" is defined in terms of any "service normally provided for remuneration, at a distance, by means of electronic equipment for the processing (including digital compression) and storage of data, and at the individual request of a recipient of a service" (Art 2(a) of the Directive 2000). For example, where an information service provider is deemed to be a "mere conduit" in the provision of Internet access or provides transmission services, that provider will not be liable for illegal information transmitted but only if three conditions have been met. First, it must be shown that the provider had not initiated the transmission. Second that the provider did not have a part to play in the selection of the receiver of the transmission. Finally, that the provider did not assume any editorial role in the information transmitted. Under Article 13, no legal liability arises for the online information services provision in the absence of any interference in the communication, or if the provider

> acts expeditiously to remove or to disable access to the information it has stored upon obtaining actual knowledge of the fact that the information at the initial source of the transmission has been removed from the network, or access to it has been disabled, or that a court or an administrative authority has ordered such removal or disablement. (Article 13(e))

Whilst this automatic storage process will not trigger infringement mechanisms, a court order or notification from an administrative authority, in accordance with the legal rules of the Member State, can be relied upon to require a service provider to terminate or prevent an infringement. Article 14 addresses the situation where online intermediaries provide individuals and organisations with online facilities that enable them to store information. As a general rule, the online intermediary is not liable for information stored on the website of the recipient of the service if the following conditions are met:

(a) the provider does not have actual knowledge of illegal activity or information and, as regards claims for damages, is not aware of facts or circumstances from which the illegal activity or information is apparent; or
(b) the provider, upon obtaining such knowledge or awareness, acts expeditiously to remove or to disable access to the information.

In *Godfrey v Demon Internet Ltd* (1999) the failure by an ISP to act expeditiously after being notified of a possible defamatory posting being transmitted from its servers was deemed to give rise to civil liability. Of course, if the recipient of the service is acting under the authority of the online intermediary or if the service provider controls a website where content is uploaded different considerations may apply. In *Kaschke v Gray* (2010) Stadlen J declined to grant a summary judgment in favour of an information service provider with regard to a defamatory posting on a website controlled by it, since it was unclear whether the provider could demonstrate that it came within the hosting exemption. Additionally, the Article permits Member States' legal systems to enact procedures where a service provider could be required to terminate or prevent an infringement, either through removing or disabling access to information. To minimise potential exposure to legal liabilities, most members of the Internet Service Providers Association (ISPA) adopt a "notice and take down" policy. More controversially perhaps is Article 15, which states that online intermediaries are under no general obligation to monitor content. This exemption extends to online intermediaries and clearly has governance implications (e.g. there is no incentive to being proactive and monitoring illegal or harmful communications since this would result in the immunity being lost). However, paragraph 2 does provide a limited avenue for Member States to create mechanisms and procedures whereby information society service providers can be required to report to competent public authorities of alleged illegal activities undertaken by recipients of their services or identification of these recipients. These and related matters will be elaborated further in our discussion in Chapter 6. One criticism often made in relation to the 2000 Directive is that the "mere conduit" defence paradoxically prevents hosts of websites and online communication services who are best placed to deal with the type of illegal or inappropriate content before it is accessed by the individual from doing so. The effect of Articles 13 and 14 is that online intermediaries would be excluded from the immunity these provisions make available, should steps be taken to monitor online activity. In *Bunt v Tilley* (2006) Eady J held that the imposition of legal liability on an ISP would depend on there being demonstrable evidence of awareness of personal responsibility being assumed. Clearly, Article 13 presupposes the absence of knowledge as a condition precedent to the "mere conduit" defence, whilst Article 14 obligates hosting service providers to remove content or disable access to the services upon notification.

In the United States, 47 USCA § 230 deals with the position of online intermediaries liability for third party's actions. Section 230(c), for example, states that a provider or user of an interactive computer service shall not be treated as "the publisher or speaker of any information provided by another content provider". For the purposes of the Act, § 230 (f) (2) defines an "interactive computer service" as "any information service, system, or access software provider that provides or enables computer access by multiple users to a computer server". As a general rule the owner and operator of a social networking website is not regarded as an information content provider, and consequently can rely on the provisions under the Act as defence to civil and criminal actions (*Cubby v CompuServe* (1991); *Stratton Oakmont, Inc. v Prodigy Services Co* (1995); *Zeran v AOL* (2002) 159). In *Doe v MySpace Inc* (2007) an attempt by a parent to hold the social networking site liable for the harm suffered by her daughter was unsuccessful. The minor in this case met an online sexual predator on the social networking site. He lured her to an offline meeting and assaulted her. The Court held that the online intermediary was not an information content provider and consequently the civil suit against MySpace failed (2007: 850). The Court also observed, obiter, the plaintiff's claims were unwarranted, particularly as that the child "lied about her actual age to bypass the age requirement and then violated MySpace's express rules by giving out her personal information" (2007: 850).

§ 230(1) regards Internet service providers and social networking sites as "interactive computer service providers" and consequently they would not be treated as publishers or speakers of any information transmitted on their communication networks or services. § 223 provides online intermediaries with defences to criminal prosecutions arising from a third party's misuse of the communication networks and services to post, request or engage in any communication which is obscene, or child pornography, or used with intent to harass or victimise another individual. An online intermediary will not be found to have violated the provisions for hosting obscene child pornography or facilitate harassment by virtue of

> providing access or connection to or from a facility, system, or network not under that person's control, including transmission, downloading, intermediate storage, access software, or other related capabilities that are incidental to providing such access or connection that does not include the creation of the content of the communication. (§ 223(e)(1))

However, this defence is not available if the online intermediary is found to be complicit in the act of creating or shown to be engaged in knowing distribution of communications in violation of the statutory provisions. Under Federal Law, information service providers are under an obligation to report any information they obtain which indicates the violation of child pornography laws to CyberTipline at the NCMEC as soon as reasonably possible (42 USC 13032). In passing, it should be observed that many schools and libraries assume the role of "online gatekeepers" by utilising blocking and filtering technology to regulate content that is accessed by children at these venues. In the United States, the Children's Internet Protection Act (CIPA) provides a regulatory framework which addresses concerns about children's exposure to illegal or inappropriate content when accessing the Internet on school and library computers. In *United States v. American Library Association* (2003) it was held that the use of filtering software on computers in public libraries accessed by children did not abridge the free speech provisions. The use of such software was regarded as being consistent with the public interest in preventing children from accessing materials harmful to them from these terminals. Some legislatures in the

United States now require Internet service providers to provide filtering software to prevent transmission of harmful content to minors following a request from a consumer (Utah Code § 76–10-1231). Obligations also extend to the provision of a hyperlink to online sites, which provide free filtering software (Tex. Bus. & Comm. Code §§ 35.101 to 35.103), and to make available parental monitoring and filtering services and software (Nev. Rev. Stat. § 603.100 to 603.170). We can see similar trends taking place in other jurisdictions where legislation and codes of practice are used to create a flexible co-regulatory governance framework. One example is the Canadian Criminal Code, C-15A, which has been amended by Criminal Law Amendment Act 2001. Section 164.1(1) provides that if a judge is satisfied by information on oath that there are reasonable grounds for believing that an online intermediary has illegal content on its computer system, which can be accessed by third parties, a custodian of the computer system order can be issued to

(a) give an electronic copy of the material to the court;
(b) ensure that the material is no longer stored on and made available through the computer system; and
(c) provide the information necessary to identify and locate the person who posted the material.

In terms of future governance strategies or likely legal intervention regarding the role of online intermediaries, a debate needs to be had with regard to the availability of the "immunity" harbours for online services providers like social networking sites and mobile and content service providers like YouTube, Facebook and MySpace (APPCG, 2009: 5) One issue raised in the report published by the All Party Parliamentary Communications Group (APPCG) was whether sites, which enabled users to create, store and distribute user-generated content, should be expected to exercise greater care and vigilance. There have been concerns expressed by parents and educators that social networking sites and portals hosting user-generated content should be permitted to rely on the "mere conduit" defence when users of its services post malicious or harmful content. The ISPA UK takes a different view and suggests that there is a legitimate distinction to be made between the deployment of filters at a network level to capture child abuse content and the need for a proactive role being advocated in other cases (e.g. file sharing and inappropriate postings). According to Virgin Media:

> questions about when and how ISPs should act to deal with different types of traffic are as much to do with ensuring that we maintain customer confidence and opinion. The public's attitude towards management of their on-line behaviour is far from consistent. When it comes to

issues of child protection, or racist or terrorist websites, there is almost universal agreement that ISPs should take action. However in a number of other areas, there is far from unanimous agreement on the lengths to which ISPs should act. (APPCG, 2009: paragraph 42)

That the law should discourage "good Samaritans" may seem to be surprising, as the following response by the Children's Charities Coalition on Internet Safety to the House of Lords Select Committee indicates:

the Directive threatens to punish the responsible company that wants to engage proactively to do the right thing, and it rewards the provider who is happy just to sit back and wait to be told there is a problem. Again, that cannot be right. (House of Lords Science and Technology Committee, 2007–8: 25)

Evidentiary considerations

As voice, data and video signals become the medium through which online criminal activity take place, law enforcement authorities increasingly turn to communications data and intercept evidence as part of their investigation strategy. Under the Regulation of Investigatory Powers Act (RIPA) 2000, the interception of any communication of a person in the United Kingdom must be consistent with the rule of law (*Rotaru v Romania* (2000); *Liberty v UK* (2008); *Iordachi v Moldova* (2009)). In *Liberty v UK* (2008) the European Court of Human Rights made it clear that interception of communications must take into account an individual's human rights, in particular Article 8 of the ECHR. The enactment of RIPA 2000 is believed to have addressed some of the shortcomings of the previous law. Certain public authorities, including law enforcement authorities, are permitted to acquire communications data from Communication Service Providers (CSPs). The procedures for accessing the communication data are subject to the safeguards provided in RIPA and the Code of Practice. "Communications data" comprises the "who", "when" and "where" of a communication session (Interception of Communications Commissioner, 2010: 7). The request for communications data can be made to CSPs and ISPs. Public authorities made 525,130 requests to these organisations for the year ending December 2009. This number was an increase from the requests made in the previous year (504,073), and it is in large part attributed to police forces investigating Internet-related criminal activity, and consequently require access to communications data (ibid., 2010: 8). It is beyond the scope of this work to engage in an assessment of the RIPA. Instead, the focus will be on the nature of digital information and the use of entrapment by law enforcement in prosecuting individuals for child sex offences.

Digital evidence increasingly plays an important part in linking an offender to the crime. Casey describes digital evidence as "any data stored or transmitted using a computer that support or refute a theory of how an offense occurred or that address critical elements of the offense such as intent or alibi" (Casey, 2004: 12). The evidence comprises information stored on, received or transmitted by an electronic device, which can be used for investigation (Carrier *et al.*, 2003). For example, the history of MSN messages, the sending and receipt of web-based emails, IP addresses, access logins and the "sent folder", all of which can help investigators link the suspect to the crime scene. Without real evidence of crimes having taken place online, the allegations and complaints can descend to assessing the probative value of one person's word against another. Digital evidence can help minimise potential problems in prosecuting individuals for engaging in activities like online sexual solicitation, possession and distribution of illegal content and engaging children in non-contact sexual activity (Casey, 2004: 96–100). The absence of relevant and admissible data can prevent the court acceding to the prosecution's claim that a crime had been committed. For example, in *R v Grout (Phillip)* (2011) the accused was charged with the offences of engaging a child in sexual activity and inciting the child to engage in sexual activity. The facts can be summarised. Following a complaint made to the police in relation to text messages of a sexual nature being sent by the accused to a minor, the former was interviewed. The allegations made by the complainant were put to him and on the advice of his solicitor, the accused refused to answer any further questions. The accused was subsequently arrested and his computer and mobile phone was searched. Following the investigation, and in particular after the digital evidence was collected, law enforcement discovered that the available text and MSN conversations between the parties could not be used to support the allegation regarding the accused's violation of child sex laws. There were two reasons for the difficulties faced by prosecution. First, the accused's computer had been re-formatted before the arrest, and consequently the history of the entire MSN conversations linking him to the allegations made by the complainant was unavailable. Second, the difficulties were further compounded by the fact that the accused had deleted all the text messages he had sent to the complainant. It should have been apparent then, from the type and quality of evidence gathered, that if the accused was to be prosecuted successfully for the offences under Section 8(1) of the SOA 2003, something more than a complaint would have been required. Instead, prosecution decided to present the available evidence to the jury. The absence of incriminating digital evidence proved fatal. This case merely serves to illustrate the particular characteristics of digital evidence that can leave prosecution open to defence objections to both its relevance and its use in court.

With regard to digital evidence generally, questions regarding its authenticity, integrity and confidentiality may be grounds for rendering potentially incriminating evidence of online criminal activity seized from computers and websites inadmissible (*R. c. Boudreau-Fontaine* (2010); *US v Comprehensive Drug Testing II* (2010); *US v Runyan* (2001)). Consequently, as the Locard Exchange Principles (*Table 3.9*) show, it is important for prosecution to ensure that the integrity and authenticity of evidence linking the victim and suspect to the crime scene are not called into question or that its seizure does not violate the latter's constitutional or human rights.

The rules on admissibility and the processes for collecting, preserving and presenting digital evidence must be borne in mind during any investigation and prosecution phase (Walden, 2010: 604–6; Miller, 2003: 119). Carrier views digital evidence as comprising an important part of an investigation where the aim of the investigation is to identify, collect and analyse evidence that will enable questions about particular events or the criminality of the suspect's activities to be constructed (Carrier, *et al.*, 2006). Digital evidence now provides law enforcement with additional sources of information during the investigation process. For example, the offender's online sexual activities with regard to a minor in *R v KJ Butcher* (2009) only came to light when the parents stumbled on these communications on their child's computer. Following a search of the child's computer, law enforcement discovered a series of incriminating evidence linking the offender to the crimes for which he was subsequently convicted. The data provided by the ISP showed that the computer owned by the offender was used to communicate with the child at the relevant times when the conversations were deemed to have taken place, and that the offender was the

Table 3.9   Locard Exchange Principles

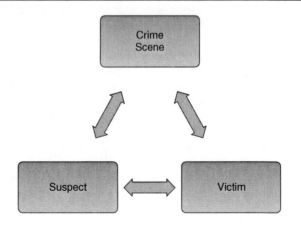

person engaging in the conversation which formed the substance of the charge. Other evidence extracted from the child's computer included logs of chat room conversations, messages which disclosed the making of several sexual overtures to the child (e.g. asking her to show her breasts via the web camera, which she acceded to, and discussions relating to the purchase and use of sex aids) and a series of communications attempting to persuade her to meet him for sexual activity. The communications also revealed that the accused was aware that the girl was a minor. The evidence gathered from both the computer and the child led to the accused being charged and convicted of causing or inciting M, a child under 13 years, to engage in sexual activity contrary to Section 8(1) of the SOA 2003, and causing or inciting a child to engage in sexual activity contrary to Section 10(1) of the SOA 2003. The computer can also provide valuable information of the "crime scene" or even indicate if the accused was the person who committed the crime using the computer. For example, in respect of a charge for possessing child pornography, images found on an accused's hard drive can be regarded in effect as constituting the crime scene (e.g. possession), and the evidence gathered in accordance with the principles on collection and preservation can be treated as relevant and admissible incriminating evidence (*US v Tucker* (2002)). In *US v Reniger* (2010), the ISP, Cox Communications was served with an administrative subpoena compelling a court-authorised disclosure of the account details of the user whose IP address was found to be making available child pornography content to other P2P users. It is, however, important that prosecution establish that the accused is guilty of the crime for which he is being charged. In *US v Beatty* (2009) the accused was charged for possession and distribution offences relating to child sexual images contrary to 18 USC §§ 2252(a)(2) and 2252(a)(4)(B), respectively. The accused was identified through his IP number when using a Gnutella file-sharing network. IP addresses are useful signifiers of location. After further investigation, the accused was traced to his home address and a warrant was obtained to search his premises and computer. The accused's computer was found to contain hundreds of illegal content involving children. However, failure to provide evidence linking the accused to the alleged offences can be fatal. In *R v Lamb* (2010) prosecution charged the accused for one count of making available child pornography content via the LimeWire software programme, contrary to Section 163.1(3) of the Criminal Code. Evidence was produced showing that a shared folder from the accused's IP address at certain specified times made available the illegal content and that the alleged activities could only have taken place on his computer. When the computer was seized from the accused's premises, it was found that the Port and GUID numbers matched the LimeWire programme from the particular installation. Crucially, the illegal content was not found in the shared folder of the accused's computer and prosecution was unable establish beyond reasonable doubt that it was the accused who made the child pornography content available on the day in question. It appears that the accused's computer was not password protected and that it could have been accessed and used by other persons living in the same residence. In other investigations, failure to obtain digital data in the form of history and chat logs prevented the successful prosecution of an accused. For example, in *Paul Savage v R* (2010) the Court of Appeal in the Supreme Court of Victoria held that three counts of committing an indecent act with or in the presence of a child under the age of 16 had to be quashed on the grounds that the evidence gathered from the mobile phones of a number of complainants and those of the suspect were insufficient to amount to evidence of offences having been committed. The Internet and communication technologies can also introduce a number of complications into the process of detecting, investigating and prosecuting offences against children. A report issued in 2009 by Statistics Canada pointed to the logistical and technological challenges facing law enforcement in Canada when investigating and prosecuting Internet child luring incidents (Laughlin *et al.*, 2009). The report covered investigations spanning the years 2006 and 2007. From the 464 cases of Internet child luring considered, it was found that 64 per cent of the incidents reported were not solved. Individuals can make use of anonymising software in chat rooms to make sure that conversations remain private. Additionally, access to content on the computer can be prevented by the use of encryption technology. The scale of the challenge facing law enforcement should not be underestimated. Collecting and preserving digital evidence can also pose obstacles during an investigation – portable storage devices containing valuable information can be removed from the crime scene or even concealed in file registries (Kerr, 2005: 537–40). Where encryption protections have been used by an offender, the process of gathering digital evidence may require the investigating team to ascertain whether the access restrictions relate to the user-resource level or those operating at software-network level (Walden, 2007: 282–3). Depending on the access protection controls adopted, the investigating officer may have to approach the offender, the organisation or the commercial online services provider to gain access to relevant digital evidence (*US v Wayerski* (2010)). In *R v J* (2009) the user-level access protection employed by the offender meant that law enforcement needed to only obtain a search warrant to gain access to the incriminating material on the computer. Difficulties may, however, be encountered where the information stored online or being transmitted is protected by encryption technology and/or located in servers outside the national jurisdiction. An example of the former situation can be seen in *R v Mara* (2009). The accused was part of an online group trading in child exploitation content. The technical challenge faced by law enforcement in this case emerged from the fact that the content traded on by the group was posted in newsgroups in binary files and hence could not be viewed by those who did not have an access "key". The "keys" were changed frequently and embedded an additional three levels of security (i.e. changing nicknames, changing newsgroup location, changing file extensions both manually and through an automated software programme specifically created for the purpose of avoiding detection by law enforcement). Law enforcement was, however, successful in gathering evidence of the accused having used his computer to access and transmit child abuse content from the Internet as well as recording indecent images of a child on designated dates, contrary to the provisions in Section 474.19(1) of the Criminal Code (Commonwealth), and Sections 210(1)(f) and (3) of the Criminal Code (Queensland), respectively. Had law enforcement not infiltrated the group, crucial evidence incriminating the accused would have been missed. Where the investigation involves the distribution of child pornography material on newsgroups and P2P sites, law enforcement has to collect and preserve a range of evidence (e.g. evidence of connection to the remote server, the IP addresses which are in plain view and deemed to be providing access to the illegal content, the jurisdiction in which the client is based, and activities associated with the distribution of the illegal content) (Liberatore *et al.*, 2010). Law enforcement authorities now set up specialised units to equip personnel with relevant investigatory techniques and skills. For example, crime scene technicians are trained to secure, collect and preserve evidence gathered at the crime scene. These are crucial processes owing to the fact that digital evidence can be easily manipulated, deleted from folders or concealed within folders in encrypted hard drives. To minimise the difficulties encountered by law enforcement, specialist forensic computing training is provided and guidelines are provided for collecting and gathering digital evidence. Section 49 of the RIPA also assists the investigation process; law enforcement can compel an offender to disclose usernames and passwords so that information stored on the computer can be accessed. However, the powers to compel disclosure are not unlimited. In *R v S and Another* (2008), it was held that the powers conferred by Section 49 of the RIPA permits disclosure of "any protected information", which includes "any electronic data which, without the key to the data (a) cannot, or cannot readily, be accessed, or (b) cannot, or cannot readily, be put into an intelligible form". When making an application under section 49(2) of the RIPA some evidence must be offered in support for the view that the person is in possession of a key to the protected information or that disclosure of the information is necessary for securing the effective exercise or proper performance by the public authority of its statutory power or duties. The two offenders in this case declined to comply with the disclosure notices on the grounds that the request violated their privilege against self-incrimination. The court held that disclosure of the "keys" of itself did not constitute "self-incrimination" as the privilege only applied to the contents protected by the encryption software (paragraph 24).

Police and Criminal Evidence Act 1984

The Police and Criminal Evidence Act (PACE) 1984 contains some key provisions that govern the investigation, collection and gathering of evidence. It is not uncommon for offenders to claim that incriminating digital evidence obtained from searches of premises and seizure of the contents exceeded the authority granted in the warrant or that the evidence relied upon by prosecution constituted hearsay (*R v Miah and Another* (2011)). Where the evidence is found on the computer or portable digital storage devices, guidance for the collection, gathering and processing of data is set out in the Association of Chief Police Officers' (ACPO) Guide (see later discussion). It is usual in cases involving complaints about sexual activity with children for the police to obtain a search warrant to search the premises of the accused and the surrounding area so that crucial evidence is not concealed, altered, destroyed or removed. A Justice of the Peace may, on an application for a search warrant, grant the request if the officer has reasonable grounds for believing that there is relevant material on the premises which is likely to be of substantial value to the investigation of the offence and will be admissible as evidence in the trial (Section 8 of PACE 1984; *Power-Hynes and another v Norwich Magistrates' Court and another* (2009)). In *R (on the application of Glenn & Co (Essex) Ltd) v Revenue and Customs Commissioners* (2010), it was held that the power to inspect documents included information stored on a computer or other storage device. Under Section 8(1) PACE, "material" which can be seized under a search warrant will include a computer and its hard disc (*R (on the application of Faisaltex Ltd) v Preston Crown Court* (2008)). Additionally, a warrant can be drafted to permit personnel with technical expertise to accompany the investigating officer conducting the search (Section 16 PACE 1984). The warrant can also specify that computers, webcams, videos and related communication and storage devices will be the subject of the search and seizure operation (Section 19 PACE 1984; *R (on the application of H)* (2009) paragraph 79; *cf. Redknapp and Another v Commissioner of the City of London Police and Another* (2008)). A police officer has a general power to seize materials found on premises if there are reasonable grounds for believing that it is evidence in relation to an offence which he is investigating or any other offence. In relation to computer and digital evidence, the material seized can be imaged or copied (*Cowan v Condon* (2000); PACE, Code B). The evidence gathered from the computer, cameras, mobile phones or media storage devices (e.g. images) are treated as "real" evidence (*DPP v McKeown* (1997)). However, evidence which purports to incorporate human statements can be regarded as hearsay (*R v Wood* (1982); Section 115 CJA 2003). More generally, most jurisdictions not only exclude digital evidence on the grounds of hearsay but also render similar fact evidence inadmissible. For example, if the evidence produced does nothing more than show that the accused, from his previous criminal conviction, is the type of person who has committed the offence for which he is now being tried, that evidence may be excluded (*R v Morelli* (2010); *HML v the Queen, SB v the Queen, OAE v the Queen* (2008) HCA 16, *R v H* (1995), Section 78(1) PACE 1984; *cf.* Sections 101(1)(d) and 107 CJA 2003). Prosecution's use of evidence gathered during the investigation phase can also be challenged on the grounds of hearsay or that the constitutional rights of the accused have been infringed. For example, in the United States the law governing electronic evidence in criminal investigations is principally found in the jurisprudence on Fourth Amendment and statutory privacy laws (Kerr, 2010). It is of particular interest to note the observation made in the US Court of Appeals for the Ninth Circuit in *US v Comprehensive Drug Testing II* (2010). The ruling suggested the need for a defined set of protocols, which ensured that searches undertaken by law enforcement authorities did not overreach the rights of the accused (at 1119). Under the plain view exception to the Fourth Amendment, law enforcement can seize relevant incriminating evidence if access gained to the venue was legal at the first instance and the evidence seized was readily apparent (Kerr, 2005). The courts in *US v Mann* (2010) and *US v Williams* (2010) appear not to have been inclined to restrict the ability of law enforcement to gather relevant incriminating evidence under the plain view exception to the Fourth Amendment (Ohm, 2011). In *Williams* (2010) a search warrant executed for a harassment charge was deemed not to preclude the licence authorising law enforcement to access files in the computer; following the search, a large volume of child abuse images was found in the computer. In *Mann*, the approach adopted suggests that ordinary approaches to the constitutional boundaries of search procedures may have to take into account the fact that computer files may be mislabelled or concealed within the directory to evade identification by law enforcement (2010: 782). The Court rejected the accused's argument that law enforcement exceeded the authority provided by the search warrant to gather evidence of voyeurism by accessing files which contained child pornography (2010: 781). It may be interesting to explore briefly the position in Canada. Evidence seized in contravention of an accused's constitutional rights under Sections 8 and 10(b) of the Canadian Charter of Rights and Freedoms (the Charter) can be rendered inadmissible. As a general rule, a search is reasonable if it is conducted in accordance with the rule of law (*R v Stillman* (1997); *R v Collins*, (1987)). In *R v Boudreau-Fontaine* (2010) the Court of Appeal held that derivative evidence gathered from a computer seized during an unlawful arrest was rightly held by the trial judge to be inadmissible on the grounds of a series of violations of the accused's rights – the absence of any reasonable grounds for arresting the accused and searching the computer, the act of compelling the accused to hand over the username and password information and the disregard of the accused's right to not self-incriminate himself. The accused was sitting in his car when he was approached by two police officers. He was asked to produce some identification and these were subsequently checked from the patrol car's onboard computer. The search results indicated that the accused had been previously charged with a number of offences including the distribution of child pornography and was on probation. As part of the probation order the accused was prohibited from accessing the Internet. There was some uncertainty whether the accused was in fact accessing the Internet when approached by the police officers. Notwithstanding their doubts, the accused was arrested and a search warrant was then issued to permit seizure of the contents in his car, which included the laptop. Based on evidence gathered from the computer and the unlawful search, the accused was subsequently charged with possession of child pornography and in breach of his probation order. The Court of Appeal made clear that for a seizure to be lawful, the items to be made the subject of the warrant had to be specifically described (2010: paragraph 50). As Doyon JA observed:

> In the present case, we are not faced with minor violations. They are serious... Rather, they are repeated violations of several Charter rights. The officers knew, or should have known, that their actions were contrary to the Charter. (2010: paragraph 59)

Principles of electronic-based evidence

A number of principles have been developed to ensure that relevant electronic-based evidence is not challenged on the grounds of its integrity and authenticity being compromised (see table below). The ACPO *Good Practice Guide for Computer-Based Electronic Evidence* now provides law enforcement with guidance to ensure that the best available evidence is presented in court (Tables 3.10 and 3.11).

Accordingly, the aim of gathering, recovering and presenting the evidence is to demonstrate to the court that the integrity of the evidence has not been impaired from the time these came into possession of the police (Ferraro *et al.*, 2005). In online grooming or peer victimisation incidents on social networking sites, given that many conversations are engaged in these environments using possibly different computers and devices, piecing together a case narrative from chat rooms, history or log of the conversation from computers, laptops and mobile phones is a complex and time-consuming process (Beebe *et al.*, 2005). If appropriate, the ISP of both parties would be contacted to identify dates and time when the offences were deemed to be committed. Finally, the forensic lab will also have to testify that standard procedures were complied with to ensure that the integrity of the data was not compromised (Carrier *et al.*, 2003). Ultimately, we need to keep in mind the goal of the digital investigation process – to enable a decision to be made as to whether legal prosecution should follow.

Table 3.10 Principles of electronic-based evidence

Principle 1

No action taken by law enforcement agencies or their agents should change data held on a computer or storage media which may subsequently be relied upon in court.

Principle 2

In circumstances where a person finds it necessary to access original data held on a computer or on storage media, that person must be competent to do so and be able to give evidence explaining the relevance and the implications of their actions.

Principle 3

An audit trail or other record of all processes applied to computer-based electronic evidence should be created and preserved. An independent third party should be able to examine those processes and achieve the same result.

Principle 4

The person in charge of the investigation (the case officer) has overall responsibility for ensuring that the law and these principles are adhered to.

Source: ACPO Good Practice Guide For Computer-Based Electronic Evidence (version 4) www.7safe.com.

Table 3.11 ACPO Principles

Application of ACPO Principles

Principle 1 in ACPO's guide is important as it ensures that the gathered evidence is preserved and not altered or modified. Relevant evidence would include the laptops, relevant removable media like external drives, modems, USB or memory sticks, digital cameras, documentation and printed media, and mobile phone. Additionally, by switching off the laptops and isolating them from any router, modem or network, this will ensure that the evidence on the hard drive is not altered, deleted or manipulated by remote access. Access to usernames and passwords is important to ensure that forensic examination can be conducted expeditiously.

Principle 2 is important in ensuring that the right personnel, procedures and venues are used to examine the digital evidence. Procedures for accrediting forensic experts, and standardizing mechanisms for collection, gathering and presenting digital evidence are covered in ACPO's guide. Additionally, the ISP of both parties should be contacted and relevant data of communications between the two parties examined.

Principle 3 is met where photographs are taken of the crime scenes, the laptops and any other visible evidence from the screen. A log of actions taken in respect of the laptops and the crime scene should be maintained.

Principle 4 advises the investigating officer to ensure that personnel appointed in seizing and examining the evidence are trained personnel.

Source: Adapted from ACPO's Good Practice Guide.

P2P and illegal content

One of the attractions of using P2P software is that they appear to offer users ready access to content. At any one time millions of files can be exchanged over the Internet and this raises practical law enforcement and policing issues. In essence, once P2P software is downloaded users can gain access to the files stored on the hard drives of other clients using the particular P2P software. A client wishing to gain access to an audio or video file needs to type in a keyword in the search function, the server then retrieves information of the request and if there are files matching the keyword, these are displayed on a list and the hard drives of the clients with those files are identified. Another benefit from using this software is that it enables individuals to leverage the Internet to gain access to files stored on the hard drivers of other users (known as clients). It should therefore not come as a surprise to discover that P2P software is used to exchange extreme pornography and child sex abuse material (*US v Phillips* (2010); *US v Jameson* (2010)). In 2003, US General Accounting Office (GAO) expressed concerns about the growth in P2P networks exchanging illegal content (GAO, 2003; Table 3.12). Using keyword searches of files associated with child sex abuse and pornographic content, it was found that over 42 per cent of the content exchanged on the networks consisted of child sexual abuse material.

This is a trend that is now being detected in a number of countries. In Brazil, following growing complaints that P2P networks were being used to exchange child sexual abuse content, the Brazilian Federal Police scanned the eMule file-sharing network for computers across the world engaged in illegal sharing of child abuse content (Faguendas, 2009; Table 3.13). The police used a software application to monitor paedophilia file-sharing activity

Table 3.12   P2P and file sharing of illegal content

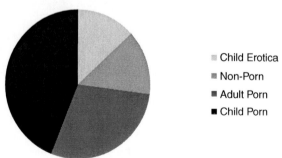

Child Erotica
Non-Porn
Adult Porn
Child Porn

Source: GAO, 2003.

Table 3.13   Scale of paedophilia activity on eMule P2P network

Country	Unique clients by user hash	Internet users (millions)	Clients (millions)
China	34,756	162,000,000	214.54
Italy	25,437	31,481,928	807.99
France	18,959	32,925,953	575.81
Spain	15,816	19,765,033	800.20
Germany	15,749	50,426,117	312.32
Brazil	13,725	39,140,000	350.66
United States	8,210	210,575, 287	38.99
South Korea	5,044	19,040,000	264.92
Poland	4,111	14,084,600	291.88

on this P2P network. The results correspond with similar criminal activity in other P2P networks. In a study of paedophile activities on the Internet, Latapy focused on paedophile activities on eDonkey, a well-known file-sharing software (Latapy, 2009). Using simple honeypot portals, it was reported that over a 32-day period, 24 distributed honeypots were advertising four files, and over 110,049 IP addresses were identified and 28,007 distinct files noted.

Sting operations and entrapment

Policing the Internet poses its own set of challenges, as criminal activity can take place in various communication venues – usenet, bulletin boards, Internet relay chats, discussion groups, mailing lists, social networking sites and virtual worlds. Until their eventual detection and prosecution, groups like Candyman, W0nderland Club and Marcy used multiple communication platforms for engaging in the commercial and sexual exploitation of children (Krone, 2005a,b). In 2007, a global paedophile ring was disbanded after law enforcement successfully infiltrated this group (Moore, 2007). Police sting operations enable law enforcement to deter and prosecute offenders for violating national laws (Casciani, 2011). For example, the Queensland police launched Task Force Argos to investigate grooming activities in on-line chat rooms (The Age, 2010). Police sting operations involve the use of deception by law enforcement to catch potential offenders (*US v Williams* (2010)). In relation to online solicitation activities by adults, a sting operation will involve a police officer acting as a potential victim. By pretending to be a child, the undercover officer aims to collect relevant evidence as part of the investigation (High, 2005). The decision to launch a police sting operation can result from a complaint made by a minor regarding an online sexual solicitation incident. Alternatively, law enforcement may target particular venues in the online environment where paedophiles and other criminals are likely to operate (e.g. chat rooms and social networking sites). One legal issue that invariably arises in relation to the use of police sting operations is the fine distinction between pre-emptive deterrent police activity and State-induced breach of the criminal law. Courts in the United States have considered the issue of entrapment in relation to police stings carried out in the online setting. Entrapment is a substantive defence in the US federal courts. In *Sherman v US* (1957) it was held that the presumption of "legislative intent" meant that Congress could not have intended its statutes to be enforced by luring innocent persons into committing crimes. In the United Kingdom, as in Australia, entrapment is not a substantive defence (*R v Sahin* (2000)). It is not open to an accused to use entrapment as a defence to a criminal charge by claiming that he was induced to commit the crime by the police. That said, a court might, however, stay the proceedings if the conduct of the police was seen to be an abuse of process. It is also a course advocated in Canada, following the Supreme Court ruling in *R v Mack* (1988). The Supreme Court stressed that if the accused was not engaged in criminal activity, the opportunity provided by the police officers to commit the crime will be a form of entrapment justifying a stay in the proceedings. The burden of proof is on the accused who alleges an abuse of process in the form of police entrapment. Justice Lamer stressed that an abuse of process can arise from one of two acts. First, where the authorities provide an accused with an opportunity to commit an offence without any prior evidence that the accused was already engaged in criminal activity. Second, even if there was reasonable suspicion or the authorities were acting in the course of a bona fide inquiry their conduct will be deemed to be an abuse of power if the accused is actively induced into committing the offence for which he has been charged. The distinction between "random virtue testing" (which may be an abuse of process) and a query pursuant to "a bona fide investigation" is important (*R v Holland* (2011); *R v Juneja* (2010)). For example, an unsolicited email to the accused offering to purchase child pornography could be seen as an example of "random virtue testing" if there is no reasonable suspicion that the email address or website was being used to distribute child pornography. An example of a bona fide investigation would be when a law enforcement officer who has infiltrated an online child sex ring to enquire about the availability of live streaming of child sexual abuse media or victims for sex tourism activity. Even though there may be no "specific" evidence that the individual approached was engaged in sex tourism or live streaming of child sexual abuse, the inquiry would appear to be a bona fide attempt in investigating the commission of criminal acts (*R v DGF* (2010)). With regard to the position in the United Kingdom, the leading case for entrapment is the House of Lords ruling in *R v Sang* (1980). In *R v Sang*, the Law Lords ruled that relevant admissible evidence could not be simply excluded on the grounds that the methods employed by the police were unfair or unlawful. Section 78 PACE 1984 now reverses the decision regarding the admissibility of unfairly obtained evidence. The statutory provision provides that a court has the residual discretion to exclude evidence on which the prosecution proposes to rely if, having regard to all the circumstances, the admission of the evidence would have such an adverse effect on the fairness of the proceedings that it ought not be admitted. This is not dissimilar to the approach adopted in Australia following rulings in *Ridgeway v the Queen* (1995) and *R v Thomas* (2006). The present procedural rules governing the admissibility of evidence can be found in the Evidence Act 2008, Sections 135–8. The High Court in *Ridgeway* (1995) suggested that in cases where entrapment is shown to be present, the trial judge has the discretion to exclude evidence from the investigation, if the methods employed were found to be unlawful or improper ((1995) paragraphs 14–18). Police conduct which induces a state-created crime (e.g. entrapment) is viewed by the Judiciary as being unacceptable and improper. As Lord Nicholls indicated in *R v Loosely* (2001):

> It is simply not acceptable that the state through its agents should lure its citizens into committing acts forbidden by the law and then seek to prosecute them for doing so. That would be entrapment. That would be a misuse of state power, and an abuse of the process of the courts. (paragraph 1)

In deciding whether conduct amounts to a state-created crime, consideration is given to all the circumstances of the case and whether the conduct of the police or other law enforcement agency was so seriously improper as to bring the administration of justice into disrepute. It is sometimes assumed that any evidence resulting from Internet sting operations will give rise to claims of entrapment and consequently may be excluded under Section 78 of PACE 1984. This is a misleading view of the law as it currently stands in the United Kingdom. In *R v Looseley* (2001), Lord Nichols cited with approval the observation of Lord Taylor of Gosforth CJ in *R v Smurthwaite* (1994) that Section 78 did not displace the common law rule that entrapment does not of itself provide a defence. Consequently, when faced with evidence gathered from an Internet police sting which is used to charge the accused with a crime, the judge may now make an assessment, in the light of the conduct and exchange between the undercover officer and the accused, whether the offender was enticed to commit a crime that he would not otherwise have committed, the methods employed, the nature of the offence and the officer's role in obtaining the evidence. The Court of Appeal in *Jones* (2007) provides another illustration of how English courts approach issues of admissibility when faced with defence claims that the admission of the evidence gathered through the use of sting or covert investigation strategies would have such an adverse effect on the fairness of the proceedings that it ought to be excluded. The police commenced investigations after being informed by a journalist that an anonymous individual had scribbled graffiti messages on toilet doors in trains. These messages aimed to entice children for sexual activity. One example of a message placed by the accused was as follows:

wanted for sex, girls from 8 to 13, text only [mobile telephone number]

A journalist contacted the number and received a text requesting the following information: her age, whether she was a virgin, her willingness to perform oral sex and a named picture of herself. The journalist informed the police, who then launched a sting operation. The undercover officer pretended to be a young girl by the name of "Amy", aged 12. Amy contacted the offender and was then requested to provide the information that was previously requested from the journalist. A meeting was arranged but it was one where the offender failed to turn up. The accused subsequently commenced communications with Amy during which time he indicated the sexual acts he would be engaging with her. The accused was arrested and charged with a range of offences under the SOA 2003. Of particular interest here is the court's response to the accused's claim that the proceedings had to be stayed on the grounds that the use of entrapment was an abuse of police powers. On appeal against conviction, Thomas LJ stressed that covert policing operations should not incite an accused to commit an offence (2007: paragraph 23). The key point here is the Court of Appeal's observation that police covert operations in this case did not go beyond responding to the information requested by the accused. We can infer from this observation that had the police instigated the communications (e.g. approaching the accused and indicating that Amy was available for sexual activity) there may have been an arguable case of entrapment. It is also clear, as confirmed by the approach of the Court of Appeal in *R v Jones*, that a balance has to be struck between the public interest in prosecuting individuals who entice minors for sexual activity and the competing public interest in protecting individuals from unlawful or unfair police activity (*A-G's Reference (No. 3 of 1999)* (2001) at 590 per Lord Hutton).

Sting operations have been employed in the United States to detect those who misuse the Internet to persuade or induce minors to engage in sexual activity (*The People v Karampal Singh* (2010); *Jacobson v US* (1992); *US v Brand* (2006). In *US v Orr* (2010) the accused was convicted under the provisions of 18 USCA § 2422 (a) and (b) – using an interstate commerce to attempt to persuade or induce a minor to travel to engage in sexual activity. The accused appealed on the grounds that he was entrapped. An affirmative defence of entrapment requires an accused to adduce the relevant standard of proof with regard to two elements: (1) the crime was induced by law enforcement; and (2) the accused lacked the disposition to engage in criminal conduct. The accused engaged in a series of online conversations with a person whom he assumed was a woman, a mother with two daughters. These conversations took place in a chat room, which hosted conversations on "Fetishes". The accused used the screen name "master_corpos1" and the women had the username "jenmomam". The accused intimated that he had been training his 12-year-old stepdaughter to perform sexual acts and inquired whether "jenmomam" was training her girls. He then suggested his willingness to help train her and her daughters. During the conversation, he persuaded her to move to Michigan with her children so that they could become his sexual slaves. The accused then proceeded to purchase train tickets for all three of them. Unknown to the accused, "jenmomam" was in fact a police officer conducting an online undercover investigation into child sexual exploitation. At the trial the accused did not rely on the defence of entrapment but sought to raise the judge's failure to deal with the defence as a ground for appeal. The Court concluded that any attempt to rely on the defence of entrapment would not have been successful since the accused had demonstrated, during the entire conversation, a commitment to train the two minors for sexual purposes and continued to maintain the view until his arrest. It was also held that the accused could not provide any evidence showing that law enforcement had in fact employed extraordinary pressure or made extraordinary promises indicative of an inducement to engage in criminal activity. We can contrast this covert policing operation with that in *US v Poehlman* (2000), where the undercover officer played an important role in turning the accused's original purpose of seeking sex with adults to that of engaging in sexual activity with minors. As the court noted:

> An improper inducement goes beyond providing an ordinary opportunity to commit a crime. An inducement consists of an opportunity plus something else – typically, excessive pressure by the government upon the defendant or the government's taking advantage of an alternative, non-criminal type of motive. ((2000), 692, 701)

In *US v Curtin* (2006) the accused was charged with travelling across state lines with intent to engage in a sexual act with a minor, in violation of 18 USC § 2423(b), and using an interstate facility to attempt to persuade a minor to engage in sexual acts, in violation of 18 USC § 2422(b). The court observed that the general tenor of the communications between law enforcement and the accused was one where the latter was clearly motivated by a desire to initiate a minor into the world of adult sex. The ruling in *US v Ross* (2010) provides another illustration of the effectiveness of sting operations, which comply with due process measures; the accused was charged with the offence of attempting to entice a minor for sexual activity (18 USCA § 2422(b)). The accused had Internet chats, email exchanges and phone calls with a person whom he believed to be a minor. He travelled to a location he thought was her home. His attempt to raise the defence of entrapment failed because there was no inducement provided by the undercover police officer. These cases illustrate a paradox in the use of sting operations and its continued relevance to issues of admissibility – on the one hand that individuals should be held accountable for their actions; and on the other that individuals should not be improperly induced into committing criminal acts by the mere fact that they may be thought to have a tendency or disposition to commit criminal acts (Feinberg, 2003: 62).

Conclusion

This chapter has described and explained how the criminal law responds to contact, content and conduct risks resulting from children's consumption of Web 2.0 technologies and social media. The analysis undertaken – namely, the role and response of the criminal law in promoting trust and confidence – illustrates many of the governance challenges posed by digital information and the end-to-end architecture for policymakers, law enforcement, parents, educators and children. Some examples and case illustrations were also provided to highlight the legal and evidentiary issues as well as the forensic significance of using digital evidence in prosecuting individuals for violating child sexual abuse and exploitation laws. The deployment of covert and sting operations and investment in Hi-Tec Crime units for investigating, collecting and presenting digital evidence will continue to play an important role in enhancing the safety of children in the online environment. One conclusion reached in this chapter is that the judicial interpretation of its national laws and the successful investigation and prosecution of individuals found to have used Web 2.0 technologies to engage in child sex offences suggest that criminal law standards and rules can be extended to this new context of child protection policymaking. It is fair to say that the substantive rules put in place by governments are satisfactory (President's Working Group on Unlawful Conduct on the Internet, 2000). It has been shown that the problem facing policymakers is not so much to do with the application of its laws (though the extension of its laws beyond its national boundaries will continue to pose a challenge). One real challenge will be to assess how best the responsibility for implementing and enforcing existing legal standards and rules can be extended to the various stakeholders. Recognition of the limited role of the State and constraints on its ability to police and enforce its laws may re-energise efforts towards better coordinating MSIG strategies at national and international levels. Issues like content regulation and those resulting from other risk-prone activities may also require educators and parents to be more aware of their obligations and the extra-legal strategies that can be employed when assisting children to use the Internet in a safe and responsible manner (Case, 95–9).

4
Transborder Challenges to Enforcing Online Child Safety Laws

Overview

Cyberspace creates the impression of a space where multiple sovereign nations can assume jurisdiction whilst at the same time States find themselves struggling to enforce their criminal laws beyond their national boundaries (Perrit, 1996). The ease with which the Internet now enables individuals to procure children to engage in sexual activity, the difficulties in detecting and investigating online sexual exploitation, the lack of harmonised laws and the varying degrees of skill and expertise of law enforcement units exacerbate the feeling that this borderless and decentralised environment is incapable of being governed. Edwards laments the difficulties in assessing the effectiveness of national laws in disrupting the creation and distribution of illegal content and asserts somewhat inaccurately that "being seen to be 'doing something' about child pornography on the Internet remains a political imperative for most governments" (Edwards, 2010: 630). It is important, however, not to overstate the impact of the Internet on the applicability of existing jurisdictional principles and rules. Although there is increased potential for using the Internet and communication technologies to engage in the commercial and sexual exploitation of children across geographical boundaries, this chapter argues that the online environment does not introduce any additional jurisdictional challenges that had not been encountered previously. Before we can identify the nature of the jurisdiction challenges facing policymakers and law enforcement and their significance for child protection, an account will be provided of the basic principles governing the ability of States and its courts to assume jurisdiction over criminal acts, which have extra-territorial dimensions. An explanation will be provided of the rules that govern the decision by a State to either assert or decline jurisdiction over criminal acts both within its national boundaries and beyond. In the second part, the chapter will look at some of the principal legal instruments enacted by governments to deal with the extraterritorial criminal jurisdiction issues. Finally, an assessment will be made as to whether the online environment raises any significant governance challenges that require additional or novel regulatory approaches to resolving transborder criminal activities relating to the commercial and sexual exploitation of children. One conclusion reached is that many countries now take the view that online child safety governance requires a global response. The efforts made in reducing the jurisdictional and investigatory barriers suggest that international treaty instruments and informal cooperation measures may serve as an appropriate regulatory response to the transborder dimensions of online child sexual exploitation activity.

Criminal jurisdiction: Background

The concept of criminal jurisdiction

It is a general principle in international law that States have jurisdiction over acts taking place within their territorial boundaries. "Jurisdiction", as is often stated, is concerned with the exercise of legislative, adjudicative and enforcement powers of a State over persons, property or events (Akehurst, 1972–3). The jurisdiction to prescribe refers to the power of a State to enact laws and rules that govern the activities of persons or the interests of persons in things within its territorial boundaries and beyond. Adjudicative jurisdiction on the other hand is a term used to describe the authority of the State in subjecting persons or entities to judicial or administrative processes. Accordingly, this term describes the power, for example, of courts to adjudicate over persons or things. Finally, the jurisdiction to enforce is concerned with the State's authority to enforce compliance with its laws and regulations. The power to enforce laws or punish individuals for non-compliance can be executed through its judicial mechanisms or other administrative or executive procedures (Estey, 1997). In the event, for example, of an individual committing a crime in the United Kingdom but then fleeing to Australia, an application will be made to the destination country to have the offender extradited to face trial for the offences charged in the requesting State (*Liangsiriprasert v USA* (1991); *Treacy v DPP* (1971)). One view of the exercise of sovereign rights with regard to jurisdiction is that States do not enforce their laws outside their territory unless the conduct or activities come within the rules permitting them to do so under a Convention or the exercise of sovereign power beyond its territorial boundaries is seen as being consistent with customary international law or sovereign rights to self-determination (Knox, 2010: 351). The presumption against extraterritoriality is derived from the idea that since national laws are territorial, considerations of comity warrant legislative, executive and even judicial restraint (Estey, 1997: 178–80). That said, States have in a number of instances extended the reach of their laws for pragmatic or political reasons in areas like intellectual property and national security (Lowe, 1985, 732). Extraterritorial legislation can be regarded as either a puzzling contradiction or a "paradox of a world of multiple, sovereign authorities" (Desautels-Stein, 2008: 514). Within the context of criminal jurisdiction, the exercise by a State of its powers to prescribe, adjudicate and enforce its laws and punish offenders is regarded as being consistent with international law norms. As Berman correctly observes, criminal jurisdiction involves the exercise of "powers over people, so powers over individuals themselves (including their liberty), over their property, and over their activities" (Berman, 2003: 3). Whilst tribunals like the International Criminal Court have jurisdiction over particular areas like humanitarian law, national courts in the main assert jurisdiction over criminal law violations, which they can legitimately investigate and prosecute. A State can assume jurisdiction over criminal acts that take place within its territory, or in cases where there is a transborder element that a sufficient connection exists between the conduct complained of and its laws (*R v Smith (Wallace Duncan) (No. 4)* (2004)). As Lord Reid indicated in *Treacy v DPP* (1971):

> There is a strong presumption that when Parliament, in an Act applying to England, creates an offence by making certain acts punishable it does not intend this to apply to any act done by anyone in any country other than England. Parliament, being sovereign, is fully entitled to make an enactment on a wider basis. (1971: 537)

The following principles determine the State's authority to subject offenders to the criminal jurisdiction of its laws relating to the sexual exploitation of children:

Territoriality Principle
Active Personality Principle
Passive Personality Principle
Protective Principle
Universality Principle

Territoriality Principle

This is a fundamental principle governing criminal jurisdiction as recognised in the *Island of Palmas Case*:

> Sovereignty in the relations between States signifies independence. Independence in regard to a portion of the globe is the right to exercise therein, to the exclusion of any other State, the functions of a State. (RIAA II 829, 838)

According to the principle of territoriality, criminal acts taking place within the territory of a sovereign State are subject to the laws of the land. For example, a foreign national can be charged for crimes under the SOA 2003 if he or she has engaged in criminal acts in this jurisdiction. In such an instance, the identity or nationality of the perpetrator or victim will not be relevant to the issue of whether a State's assertion of jurisdiction over the incident is legitimate. It is the nexus between the acts and the place where the event in question takes place that will determine the basis upon which the State is able to assume jurisdiction (*R v Smith (Wallace Duncan)(No. 4)* (2004)). With many countries now concluding bilateral treaties which permit cooperation between law enforcement authorities, or subscribing to Conventions which aim to harmonise substantive and procedural rules for prosecuting crimes with a transborder element, the jurisdictional barriers to investigating and prosecuting individuals for crimes committed overseas are not as onerous as they once were (Hirst, 2003).

Active Personality Principle

A State's authority to assume criminal jurisdiction over its nationals can in certain circumstances extend beyond its territory, where elements of the crime are held to have taken place both within its territorial boundaries and beyond (Hirst, 2003; *R v Libman* (1985); *Treacy v DPP* (1971)). To avoid any uncertainty with regard to a State's ability to act extraterritoriality, statutory enactments make explicit reference to the existence of such a power. There are, for example, statutory provisions relating to extraterritorial criminal jurisdiction governing piracy (Section 2 Piracy Act 1837), war crimes (Section 1 Geneva Conventions Act 1957), hostages (Section 1 Taking of Hostages Act 1982), hijacking (Sections 1, 2 or 6 Aviation Security Act 1982), terrorism (Terrorism Act 2000) and torture (Section 134 CJA 1988). Within the context of this study, the exercise of a State's jurisdiction over the acts of its nationals in overseas countries, like the SOA 2003, Crimes Legislation Amendment (Child Sex Tourism Offences and Related Measures) Bill 2007 and PROTECT Act 2003, would be examples of legislation attempting to address a problem of national and global concern (Lavers, 2006: 68).

Passive Personality Principle

The issue of whether the nationality of a child sexual abuse victim should determine the assertion of extraterritorial jurisdiction is hotly debated (Beaulieu, 2008: 4–6; G8, 2007; *cf.* Hirst, 2003: 29–36). The most frequent argument offered against the assertion of extraterritorial jurisdiction is that the State's legitimate interests lie in respect of regulating the activities of its citizens (Lavers, 2006). This conception of the territorial principle is based on a model of a nation State that is concerned with the acts of its citizens and conduct taking place within its geographical boundaries rather than activities taking place in another State (Keitner, 2011: 56–8); the premise here being that the conduct engaged in by the national in the overseas country does not have an adverse or harmful effect within the home State (*Treacy v DPP* (1971)). However, in the final upshot the jurisdictional issues may turn on the construction of the particular legislative enactment (*R v Manning* (1998) 461, 476).

Protective Principle

The rationale for the protective principle is that States have the inalienable authority to exercise jurisdiction over persons or events situated in another jurisdiction when an act taking place outside its territory has or is likely to have an adverse effect on its security or interests (*R v Abu Hamza* (2006)). Clearly, the extent to which this principle applies will depend on the nature of the criminal activity concerned (Hirst, 2003: 115). As seen above, in relation to the extraterritorial reach of the laws, conduct like piracy, hijacking and terrorism are activities which can be included within the scope of the protective principle. In cases where jurisdiction is asserted, there is a close relationship between the protective principle and the "effects" test employed by States to justify the assumption of jurisdiction over an act that has taken place outside its territory (*US v Tollman* (2008)).

Universality Principle

According to the Princeton Principles on Universal Jurisdiction, a State may assert jurisdiction over a person notwithstanding the absence of any connecting factor, solely on the grounds of the nature of the act concerned (Sadat, 2001: 241–64). Universal jurisdiction for present purposes is described as "criminal jurisdiction based solely on the nature of the crime, without regard to where the crime was committed, the nationality of the alleged or convicted perpetrator, the nationality of the victim, or any other connection to the state exercising such jurisdiction" (Princeton University Program in Law and Public Affairs, 2001). Consequently, a State can assert criminal jurisdiction beyond its territorial boundaries, if the nature of the crime is such that it justifies the exercise of its sovereign authority (Colangelo, 2009: 881–926). The prosecuting State can as a consequence subject the individual to the machinery of the criminal law without regard to the place where the acts were deemed to have taken place or the nationality of the perpetrator concerned (Fry, 2002: 174). This exercise of State authority is subject to a number of due process safeguards – the requirement that the exercise of that authority is by a "competent and ordinary judicial body", the recourse to formal extradition hearings to ascertain whether an extraditable crime has been committed by the extraditable person and that the appearance of this person before a court of law in the requesting State does not violate established "international norms and standards on the protection of human rights" (*Akyol v DPP Zwole Lelystad Netherlands*

(2010); *Wenting v High Court of Valenciennes* (2009)). For example, under the Geneva Conventions Act 1957, individuals can be prosecuted for war crimes committed outside the United Kingdom (*Commissioner of Police for the Metropolis and Others, Ex Parte Pinochet* (2001); *R (on the application of Krstic) v Secretary of State for Justice* (2010)). With regard to the assertion of State sovereign powers, previously the consent of the Attorney General or CPS was not required in an application to issue a summons or warrant; the applicant merely needed to furnish evidence that an offence has been committed by the accused. The Ministry of Justice has recently announced that this procedure would now be reviewed (Hansard, 2010). Even though crimes against children are not regarded as being within the scope of the Universality Principle, signatories to the UNCRC, Cybercrime and CPC instruments undertake to implement key principles and rules into their national legal systems. Consequently, the criminalisation of particular forms of exploitative activity permits States to assume jurisdiction over a number of conduct or result crimes (e.g. child pornography, sexual solicitation and sex tourism). Individual States can assume jurisdiction even in situations where nationals have engaged in crimes against children in foreign jurisdictions. For example, under the CPC Convention, signatories can implement measures in national legislation which remove the substantive and procedural obstacles to prosecuting individuals for engaging in serious sexual offences abroad against foreign nationals (e.g. double criminality). Subscribers to the CPC Convention agree to "take the necessary legislative or other measures to establish jurisdiction over the offences established in accordance with this Convention, in cases where an alleged offender is present on its territory and it does not extradite him or her to another Party, solely on the basis of his or her nationality" (Article 25). One recent example of a national court assuming jurisdiction over foreign nationals in relation to the commercial and sexual exploitation of children is the successful prosecution of two Swedish nationals for engaging in human trafficking and online live web streaming pornography operations on the southern island of Mindanao, Philippines (SMH, 2011). The Cybercrime Convention is another example of an instrument creating a multilateral framework for regulating crimes mediated through ICTs. Countries subscribing to this Convention use its provisions as a framework for enacting legislation dealing with child pornography and other forms of sexual abuse of children. Like the CPC Convention, potential jurisdictional conflicts can, for example, be avoided with regard to prosecuting perpetrators engaged in CSEC in a destination country since each signatory assumes an obligation to "adopt such legislative and other measures as may be necessary to establish as criminal offences under its domestic law, when committed intentionally and without right" (Article 9(1)) Access to digital evidence located in a foreign jurisdiction can be enhanced as each party to the Cybercrime

Convention undertakes to implement legislative or other measures, which empower competent authorities to search or access:

a. a computer system or part of it and computer data stored therein; and
b. a computer-data storage medium in which computer data may be stored in its territory. (Article 19(1))

Where the commission of a child sex offence permits multiple States jurisdiction over the matter, parties are encouraged to coordinate their activities "with a view to determining the most appropriate jurisdiction for prosecution" (Article 22(5)). The Cybercrime Convention aims to reduce the opportunities for perpetrators to engage in forum shopping as Article 22(3) stipulates that parties shall adopt "such measures as may be necessary to establish jurisdiction" and that parties "cooperate with each other...through the application of relevant international instruments on international co-operation in criminal matters" (Article 23). These Conventions can be broadly seen as reflecting growing consensus amongst the international community that certain forms of sexual and commercial exploitation of children should be treated as crimes regardless of where they are committed.

Implications for investigation and prosecution

Jurisdiction rules are of direct relevance to the ability of a legal system to implement its child protection laws when there is a transborder dimension. Differences in the substantive laws on child pornography, the age of consent and the legal definition of a "child" can undermine investigatory and prosecution efforts in holding a potential offender to account, if national laws do not cover sexual offences committed against children in another jurisdiction (Berman, 2002: 311–23). Indeed, it is not uncommon for nationals prosecuted for engaging in child sex offences with a transborder dimension to raise issues regarding the court's jurisdiction or the applicability of the criminal laws to conduct taking place in another jurisdiction. It is argued that varying legal definitions of the age of consent can complicate investigation and prosecution decisions (Taylor *et al.*, 2003: 83).

Even though the CPC Convention defines a "child" as "any person under the age of 18 years" (Article 3(a)), Article 18 permits States to "decide the age below which it is prohibited to engage in sexual activities with a child" (Article 18(2)). Even varying approaches to the way crimes are defined can hinder attempts to prosecute a child sex offender (Podgor, 2004; Graham, 2000). Article 20(3) of the CPC Convention permits parties to define the age threshold and the types of prohibited conduct. These differences may have a bearing when attempts to have an offender extradited flounder on the grounds that the act concerned is not regarded as a crime in the responding/

destination State. The double criminality rule may prevent the responding State from treating the offence as an "extraditable crime". One could envisage a situation where a requesting State, which criminalises all forms of pornography, seeks to have an offender extradited from the United States for distributing pseudo-photographs of a virtual child in the former jurisdiction. Under US Federal Law, the possession of pseudo-photographs of children *per se* is not a criminal offence, unless these are regarded as contravening the child pornography legislation or the obscenity test under *Miller v California* (1973). Broadly, supranational and international policy instruments do provide an opportunity for States to overcome the potential problems that may arise from the transborder dimensions of child sex offence by harmonisation (Beaulieu, 2008). The Proposed Directive is one example of the use of regulatory instruments to harmonise child protection laws within EU Member States.

As a child protection measure, the ability of a State to investigate and prosecute citizens engaged in child sex offences in overseas jurisdictions has some advantages (Hirst, 2003). For example, States can now launch prosecutions, should the destination country not have sufficient law enforcement resources or expertise in investigating and prosecuting child sex offenders from the home country. Second, the legislation can also be pre-emptive in the sense that law enforcement in the home country can now make a timely intervention before the offender travels abroad to meet the child (or conversely, where an arrangement is made for the child to travel to the home country of the offender. *US v Seljan* (2007) is not only an example of the application of the nationality principle but it also serves to highlight how potential victims can be safeguarded by pre-emptive measures undertaken in the home jurisdiction where extraterritorial laws have been enacted. The accused in this case was a US national who was charged and convicted for a range of offences involving sexual misconduct with children based in the Philippines. He was stopped when he attempted to board his flight and subsequently arrested and prosecuted for a number of child sex offences; evidence was gathered showing that he was attempting to travel with intent to engage in illicit sexual conduct with a minor contrary to 18 US §§ 2423(b) and (e), enabled law enforcement to make a timely intervention and apprehend the offender. Finally, the ability of a State to enforce its criminal laws extraterritorially corresponds with one justification of the criminal law, which is to deter its nationals from engaging in criminal acts albeit in destination countries (*R v Klassen* (2008); Mody, 2001).

Two principles continue to proscribe the extraterritorial reach of national laws: (i) double criminality; and (ii) and double jeopardy. As noted previously, the use of bilateral treaty arrangements and supranational child protection instruments minimise the impact of these rules (see later). With regard to the latter, the principle *non bis in idem* espouses the ideal of fairness in criminal proceedings (*Connelly v DPP* (1964)). As the Advocate General Ruiz-Jarabo Colomer indicated in his Opinion:

> The decisive factor is not whether the right to impose a penalty is exercised under one legal system or under several legal systems, but that in order to know whether an act may be punished more than once, the person exercising the power to impose the penalty, must ascertain whether, with the various penalties, the same legal principles are being protected or whether, on the contrary, the values which are being protected are different. (Cases C-187/01 and C-385/01: paragraph 56)

In essence, the principle provides that a person who has been prosecuted for a criminal offence in one jurisdiction should not be subjected thereafter to multiple prosecutions in other jurisdictions for the same offence (Abelson, 2009: 1–38). The rationale for this rule, albeit the claims that victims of crimes are equally deserving of consideration by the criminal justice system, is that those prosecuted for serious crimes do not forfeit their entitlement to respect for humanity and dignity when in custody (Fletcher, 2003a: 581). Before the principle can be applied in the accused's favour, it must be shown that the proceedings were conducted in good faith and that the judgment reached by the judicial or relevant body was consistent with international norms and principles of due process. One effect of this principle is that a national returning to his country cannot be prosecuted for the same crime on the grounds of acquittal or that the sentence meted by the overseas court was lower than the punishment handed down in the country of residence. In *Bohning v Government of the United States of America* (2006), the appellant sought to challenge an extradition request from the United States on the grounds that in view of the specific provisions in Section 80 of the Extradition Act 2003, his extradition would violate the rule against double jeopardy. The appellant travelled to the United Kingdom from the United States and attempted to engage in sexual activity with a 13-year-old girl who lived in Birmingham. Following his arrest, his laptop was seized and incriminating evidence was subsequently discovered. The evidence included over 10,000 images depicting sexual abuse of children and babies; emails and chat conversations between the appellant and girls (including the minor in Birmingham). The appellant was charged with 20 counts of child sex offences, including possession of indecent material, distribution of an indecent photograph of a minor and publication of an article, contrary to the provisions under the PCA 1978 and the SOA 2003. Crucially, when drafting the indictment, prosecution ensured that the offences with which the appellant was being charged did not traverse those charges which were pending against him in the United States. Following the appellant's conviction and his serving of a custodial sentence, the US government sought his extradition for offences coming within a number of categories which were not the subject of the charges in the United Kingdom: (i) incitement of B and two other young girls, one resident in the United Kingdom and the other in the United States, to commit acts of indecency; and (ii) distribution and possession charges in respect of the material that had been found on the laptop. The Court of Appeal agreed that an offender could not be prosecuted twice for the same crime (paragraph 21). It, however, held that the double jeopardy rule did not prevent prosecution for separate offences, which arose out of the same facts (e.g. incitement), or to offences, which could have been but were not charged (ibid.). Consequently, the Court ruled that the extradition of the appellant did not violate the double jeopardy rule. The application of this rule in respect of an individual's acquittal of crimes outside the United Kingdom must now be reconsidered in the light of the reforms introduced by Part 10 of the CJA 2003 (Fletcher, 2003b). Sections 75–9 of the 2003 Act enable persons acquitted for "qualifying offences" to be retried where new and compelling evidence has emerged (*R v A* (2008)). Section 75 makes clear that Part 10 applies to acquittals. There are a number of points to be borne in mind with regard to re-trials of individuals acquitted of child sex offences in jurisdictions outside the United Kingdom. The first thing to be noted is that amendments to the scope of the double jeopardy rule only apply to serious offences regarded as "qualifying". Murder, manslaughter and rape are obviously included within this category. Acquittals in relation to offences involving sexual activity with a minor, however, will be deemed to be "qualifying" but only in the limited situation where the victim is below 13 years. This age restriction has obvious investigatory implications since it leaves those victims above the age threshold not only vulnerable to further sexual exploitation but also without any legal redress. Second, even if the age threshold is satisfied, an application has still to be made to the Court of Appeal for a ruling on whether the acquittal in a foreign court is a bar to a re-trial. This application to the Court of Appeal can only be made with the written consent of the Director of Public Prosecutions. Consent from the Director of Public Prosecutions will only be forthcoming if the prosecutor can demonstrate that the public interest will be served for the application to proceed, that the re-trial would not be inconsistent with the United Kingdom's obligations as a Member of the EU under Article 31 or 34 of the Treaty on EU relating to the principle of *ne bis in idem* and that "there is new and compelling evidence against the acquitted person in relation to the qualifying offence". The public interest requirement, for example, is unlikely to be met under Section 79, if there has been substantial media coverage of the incident, which is likely to make a fair trial less than probable, and the relative length in period between the alleged commission of the offence and the prospective re-trial is deemed to be excessive. Other considerations which may be relevant when determining the public interest issue will include the likelihood of the investigating officer or prosecutor adducing the new evidence during the earlier proceedings had they acted with due diligence or expedition. The burdens on law enforcement in discharging its obligations are considerable. The requirement for "compelling new evidence" could include DNA evidence, fingerprint or other incriminating evidence and new witnesses to the offence. In *R v A* (2008) the court held that new and compelling evidence must not only be relevant and admissible but it must be regarded as highly probative of the offender's guilt of the qualifying offence. Evidence of a confession obtained by unfair or improper means and if shown not to be substantial or highly probative would be a bar to an application to have the case re-tried (*R v Whittle (Barry Gordon)* (2010)).

Another principle that has implications for the successful investigation and prosecution of individuals found to have engaged in sexual offences against children in foreign jurisdiction is the double criminality rule. The rationale for the double criminality rule stems from the adherence to the principle – *nulla poena sine lege* – that there should be no punishment without law. Its application in extradition proceedings seems to be based on considerations of policy or political expediency (Griffith *et al.*, 2005). According to the double criminality rule, a UK national can only be extradited to face prosecution in the home country if the conduct engaged in during a visit to an overseas country is deemed to be a crime in both the home and the overseas country. The entry into bilateral treaties and conventions can modify the application of the double criminality rule and consequently ensure that offenders will have fewer opportunities for challenging extradition requests (*Canada (Attorney General) v Leamont* (2010). In the United Kingdom, the previous law which adopted the principle of double criminality for child sex offences committed by British citizens abroad has now been replaced by amendments introduced under the Criminal Justice and Immigration Act 2008, Section 72(1). Following these amendments, British nationals or those who are resident in the United Kingdom can now be prosecuted for sex offences committed abroad against anyone, even though the age thresholds in destination countries may be much lower than those in the United Kingdom (*R v Penner* (2010)). The substantive rules for age-specific offences will still continue to apply if these offences are committed abroad. These developments are also consistent with the provisions for harmonising child protection laws under the Council of Europe's Cybercrime Convention (paragraph 33). Countries acceding to the Convention can now prosecute offenders perpetrating crimes against children in destination countries (Smith *et al.*, 2004; *XYZ v Commonwealth* (2005)). Reference should also be made to the obligations entered into by States under the UNCRC and the Optional Protocol. Under Article 3(4) of the Optional Protocol, "each State Party shall take measures, where appropriate, to establish the liability of legal persons for offences" and to adopt measures that enhance transborder detection, investigation and prosecution of individuals engaged in CSEC (Article 10(1)). There is some evidence of countries taking their responsibilities towards eradicating CSEC seriously. Recently, a Memorandum of Understanding was concluded between Thailand and Cambodia to reform their laws and adopt necessary measures to prevent trafficking of children and women in particular (Article 8 MOU). The *Bilateral Cooperation for Eliminating Trafficking in Children and Women and Assisting Victims of Trafficking* conforms with the Universal Declaration of Human Rights, the Convention on the Rights of the Child, the Conventions on the Elimination of All Forms of Discrimination against Women and other international human rights instruments. Another example of the standard setting role of the UNCRC can be seen in the amendments introduced by the Australian government to its Commonwealth Criminal Code Act 1995 (1995 Criminal Code). The broad effect of the amendments would be to reduce the substantive and procedural obstacles facing law enforcement in prosecuting Australian nationals who plan to travel overseas to engage in sexual activity with minors below the age of 16, as a result of engaging in grooming or conducting procurement activities whilst in Australia (Section 272.15). In *R v ONA* (2009), the Court of Appeal in Victoria (Australia) stated that attempts to challenge the constitutionality of Section 16A(2) of the Crimes Act 1914 (Cth) or suggest that there was a legitimate distinction between persons who travelled overseas with the aim of engaging in sexual activities with minors and those who formed such an intention after arrival in the destination country were unfounded, and failed to recognise the growing social and political consensus regarding child sex activities like sex tourism. Child sex tourism (CST) can be described as "the sexual exploitation of children by offenders who travel away from their home in order to have sexual contact with children" (Parliament of the Commonwealth of Australia, 2010). The UN defines CST as "tourism organized with the primary purpose of facilitating the effecting of a commercial sexual relationship with a child" (UN, A/50/456, paragraph 54). CST is a growing industry – and Web 2.0 technologies enable individuals to publicise its services (ECPAT, 2008). Cybercafés, mobile phones, blogs and websites are some of the technologies used to identify locations, collect information of potential victims and book flights and accommodation in a foreign country (ECPAT, 2010: 38). With increased broadband access and Internet connectivity being made available in most tourist destinations, individuals can now access materials and even contact victims through mobile phones, chat rooms and IM (ECPAT, 2010: 45–8). As Neave JA stated unequivocally, the enactment of legislation criminalising CST is designed to "provide a real and enforceable deterrent to the sexual abuse of children outside Australia by Australian citizens and residents" (2009: paragraph 54). Like many of the enactments we have considered earlier, the Crimes Amendment Act 1995 is another illustration of children's rights norms and values setting the standards for legislative activity. New Zealand has also reviewed its national child protection laws. Under Section 144A of the Crimes Act 1961, it is now an offence to engage in any sexual activity with a child, which if done in New Zealand would be a crime. Additionally, under Section 144C of the 1961 Act, it is also an offence to assist or encourage others to travel overseas for the purpose of having sex with minors or to promote sex tours. Prohibited acts would now extend to booking tickets and reserving accommodation, organising transport to overseas destinations and producing advertising and promotional literature relating to child sex tours. Recently, a New Zealand national was found to have engaged in these activities and was prosecuted for facilitating CST (OCEANZ, 2010). The activities of the accused were subject to an undercover operation by the Police Online Child Exploitation across New Zealand (OCEANZ) unit. Sex tourism is a subset of a more general global problem of human trafficking (Meredith, 2010). Human trafficking of minors has been a long-standing issue (ECPAT, 2008). It has been described as a "modern phenomenon with ancient roots" (King, 2008: 369). It is beyond the scope of this chapter to undertake an examination of this area of child protection save for one example, which can be provided to illustrate the transborder issues resulting from the interaction between human trafficking and sex tourism. § 230.25 of New York's anti-trafficking legislation, for example, holds businesses to account if they provide "travel-related services knowing that such services include or are intended to facilitate travel for the purpose of patronizing a prostitute, including to a foreign jurisdiction and regardless of the legality of prostitution in said foreign jurisdiction". In *People v Barabash* (2006), the accused operated a tourism services business in New York under the name of Big Apple Oriental Tours (BAOT). Trips to Philippines were provided and "tour guides" were procured to bring the tourists to venues where women were available to have sex for money. Evidence was offered showing that the tour guides provided the tourists with specific instructions on how to engage in sexual activity with women for money. More importantly, the price of the package tour included the costs for having sex. These sums of money were alleged to have been forwarded to tour guides in the Philippines so that the women who engaged in sexual activity with the tourists concerned were paid for the services rendered. The absence of evidence proving the complicity of the proprietors proved to be fatal to the prosecution for this specific offence. Finally, two additional examples of extraterritorial legislation which reflect governments' attempts to punish those engaged in abusing children through sexual exploitation can be provided. These are Section 7(4.1) of Criminal Code in Canada and the United States' PROTECT Act 2003. Parts of the PROTECT Act 2003 incorporate the obligations under the Optional Protocol (18 USC §§ 2422–3) which was acknowledged to be the case in *US v Frank* (2007). The PROTECT Act 2003 does not apply retrospectively, as was noted by the court in *US v Jackson* (2007). In *US v Bianchi* (2010), the offender was prosecuted under 18 USC § 2423(c) for engaging in illicit sexual conduct in Moldova. The offender in this case engaged in the practice of travelling to foreign destinations with the aim of meeting and engaging in sexual activity with young boys. Between the periods of December 2003 and March 2005, the offender travelled to poverty-ridden areas in Moldova and Romania to engage in sexual activity with minors. The value and significance of extraterritorial legislation cannot be overemphasised. Another example of how obligations assumed under international conventions are mirrored in the adjudicative jurisdiction process is *R v Klassen* (2008). A Canadian national was prosecuted and convicted for importing child sex abuse material into the country. The Supreme Court held that the exercise of its extraterritorial legislation was consistent with Canada's obligations assumed under the Optional Protocol, namely, to "take such measures as may be necessary to establish its jurisdiction ... [w]hen the alleged offender is a national of that State or a person who has his habitual residence in its territory" (Article 4(2)(a)) (paragraph 56). Any other construction of the Criminal Code, according to the Supreme Court, would have been a derogation of its responsibilities as a sovereign State and as a Party to the Conventions protecting children from commercial and sexual exploitation:

> The universal principle reflects Canada's commitment under the Convention and the Optional Protocol to contribute to the suppression of the "significant" "widespread" and "continuing" exploitation of "particularly vulnerable groups," but within the limitations of both prescriptive (and adjudicative) jurisdiction and the nationality principle. ((2008) paragraphs 97)

Jurisdictional issues can also arise when an individual engages in criminal activity on websites located in another jurisdiction. It should be noted, however, that existing jurisdictional principles could be adapted to meet objections raised by an offender in respect of the competence of a court in adjudicating over a matter with a transborder element. In *R v Sheppard & Whittle* (2010), the court was faced with a situation where the appellants had posted racially inflammatory material on a website which was hosted on a server located in California. Publication of such content breaches the criminal laws in the United Kingdom, and arguably protected by free speech jurisprudence under the Federal Laws in the United States. The court held that the location of the web servers did not prevent the accused from being held accountable under UK criminal laws since the online materials were accessible to nationals in this jurisdiction. Consequently, the nationality principle was applied to subject the offender to UK criminal laws.

Notwithstanding the enactment of extraterritorial legislation by countries like Canada, Australia, the United Kingdom and the United States, the transborder nature of child sexual exploitation or abuse activities can pose a number of practical investigatory and procedural challenges (Perrin, 2010). Prosecution rates are notoriously low and these can be attributed in part to the lack of visibility (as the offences take place abroad) (Cotter, 2009). NGOs ascribe the low prosecution rate to the lack of priority given by States to the commercial and sexual exploitation of children from less developed economies, in particular to the growing problem of CST (Beaulieu, 2008; Healy, 1995). Not surprisingly, public policy concerns about the CSEC continue to be expressed with growing regularity in national and regional child protection forums (West, 2000). In a published report, ECPAT regarded the lack of progress made in protecting vulnerable children from its citizens a "national shame" (2006: 8). At the international expert meeting on combating CST it was noted that "[v]ery few child sex tourists are arrested, tried and sentenced" (ECPAT, 2009: 1). The visibility and detection challenges may be compounded by individuals meeting up with minors in the most innocuous of venues like public areas, hotel lobbies or the homes of the child victims (ECPAT, 2008). Even if information relating to the nationality of the individual has been obtained, the lack of awareness by the general public of the mechanisms for reporting suspicions of criminal activity engaged in by foreign travellers and the lack of trained law enforcement authority in these countries hinder proper investigation and prosecution of child sexual exploitation offenders (High, 2005). For example, offenders have been known to work as volunteers in developing countries assisting in education, health and other care projects, as a way of evading detection by authorities. In *US v Perlitz* (2010) the offender worked as a volunteer to assist "street children" and concealed his activities from staff at the organisation for over a decade.

Some efforts have been made by destination countries to deal with the problem of sex tourism. Countries like Thailand, Vietnam, Laos and Sri Lanka have implemented regulatory measures criminalising CST and human trafficking activities. Even though Thailand does not have specific legislation dealing with CST offences, some enactments passed by the legislators do criminalise activities that come within the sphere of CSEC. For example, the Measures in Prevention and Suppression of Trafficking in Women and Children Act, BE 2540 (1997), now provide law enforcement greater investigation powers to curb offences relating to human trafficking of women and children (Section 5). Under Section 7 of the Prevention and Suppression of Prostitution Act, B.E. 2539 (1996), any person or entity found to have advertised or make known to the general public "in a manner apparently indicative of importunity or solicitation for the prostitution of himself, herself or another person" can be imprisoned for a maximum of two years. Section 10 also subjects parents or persons who have responsibility for a minor below the age of 18 years to criminal prosecution for conniving in the child sex offences under Section 9. Prostitution and human trafficking, particularly involving children below 18 years, are criminalised in Laos (Articles 131–4). In Vietnam, legislation has been passed amending provisions in its Penal Code (No-37/2009/QIII2). Article 115 criminalises sexual activity with children below the age of 16. The amended Article 119 now criminalises "trafficking in humans" and Article 120, clause 2, is replaced with "against more than one child". Finally, in Sri Lanka, the Penal Code (Amendment) Act, No. 16 of 2006, inserted some important provisions into its legislation, notably Sections 360E (soliciting a minor below the age of 18 years) and 360C (trafficking).

Given the complexity of gathering relevant information, governments have begun to work closely with NGOs and child welfare organisations in foreign destinations. ECPAT continues to play an invaluable role in policing destinations frequented by individuals engaged in CST, and undertakes education and awareness-raising programmes and lobbying initiatives (ECPAT, 2010: 60–5). It has also established invaluable networks with law enforcement authorities from various countries like Australia, the United Kingdom, Canada, France, and the United States. In addition to detecting and identifying child sexual abuse activity in countries like Bangkok, Cambodia, and regions in Eastern Europe and South America, the decision to charge and prosecute a national in the country of residence is not as straightforward as might initially appear. One should not, for example, underestimate the difficulties in obtaining relevant and credible evidence that satisfies the rules on admissibility in countries like the United States and the United Kingdom. Law enforcement, in countries where the victim resides, may not have the resources or possess the skills or expertise in dealing with incidents of child sexual abuse. The gathering of physical and medical evidence of victims after the abuse may also be a problem if there are inadequate facilities and insufficiently trained personnel. Cultural and economic factors may also affect decisions to prosecute. Family members may be reluctant to provide evidence incriminating the offender or may have been complicit in the commercial sexual exploitation of the child (Garrard, 2006). Victims who are subject to sexual abuse and exploitation by foreign nationals may not come forward to give evidence against the offenders for fear of reprisals (*US v Bianchi* (2007)). Rules on hearsay and the thresholds regarding the types of evidence that may be received by the court have implications for decisions to prosecute. Another potential barrier to prosecuting individuals for engaging in CSEC is the requirement that the victim provide testimony in person either by attendance at the trial or through a live video link. Finally, without cooperation from the relevant authorities in the destination country, gathering relevant evidence and witnesses can impose considerable logistical challenges in terms of time, expertise and resources. In relation to the United Kingdom, the advice given by the CPS to prosecutors and investigators in the United Kingdom is that on receipt of the report of alleged child sex offences committed by UK nationals in the destination country, law enforcement should arrange with their counterparts to ascertain the best course of action (CPS, 2009). Where multi-jurisdictional elements are found to be present there may be practical reasons for not having the national prosecuted in the home country: the appropriateness of having the crime prosecuted in the place where the victims reside, the likelihood of prosecution succeeding should the case be heard in the foreign courts, the availability of testimony from victims and witnesses, where there are language differences, the lengthy process in having the testimonies translated into the English language, the availability of extradition and the benefits of separate trials. Requests for search and seizures of computers or servers located in foreign jurisdictions may take considerable to be processed. We have seen, however, that these obstacles are not insurmountable. The use of extraterritorial legislation and ratification of the Optional Protocol and the Cybercrime Convention can minimise the impact of the dual criminality rule on investigation and prosecution procedures. As the House Report leading to the enactment of the precursor to the PROTECT legislation noted:

> There would be no need for a sex tourism statute if foreign countries successfully prosecuted US citizens or resident aliens for the child sex crimes committed within their borders. However, for reasons ranging from ineffective law enforcement, lack of resources, corruption, and generally immature legal systems, sex tourists often escape prosecution in the host countries. It is in those instances that the United States has an interest in pursuing criminal charges in the United States. (House of Representatives, 2002: 3)

Reference should also be made to one of the outcomes to the G8 Justice and Interior Ministers' meetings in 2007 and 2008 which provide the requisite political impetus in assisting law enforcement to investigate and prosecute nationals engaging in the sexual exploitation of children abroad. The Ministerial Meeting adopted a paper – "G8 Experience and Recommendations: Implementation of Extraterritorial Jurisdiction for Sex Crimes against Children" (G8, 2008). Two recommendations from this document are of particular relevance in this context. First, it was made clear then that the principle of dual criminality should not prevent the prosecution of nationals engaging in sexual activity with children abroad, if the underlying sexual activity would have been an offence had it taken place in the home jurisdiction. Furthermore, it was also stressed that if the destination country sets the age of sexual consent lower than that of the home country, or if the legislation does not adequately deal with child prostitution, prosecutors should not be hampered from prosecuting their nationals and permanent residents who sexually abuse children. This is quite an important point. For example, with the exception of Section 15 of the SOA 2003, if a UK national engages in sexual activity with a child in the destination country, the fact that the age of consent in that jurisdiction was 14 years would now not be a defence. Additionally, the application of the double jeopardy rule and the limited inroads made by Part 10 of the CJA 2003 should be noted. Whilst the ECPAT report (Beaulieu, 2008) has been overtaken by some positive legislative developments, the central concerns about enforcing child protection laws in foreign jurisdictions against nationals of the home country are still relevant; more specifically, governments could do more to curb, deter and prosecute their nationals for exploiting and sexually abusing minors. It is important for destination countries which have a thriving sex tourism industry to enact legislation that defines the scope of sexual offences against children and to support law enforcement efforts in investigating and prosecuting offenders. CSEC still continues to be a problem in many tourist destinations. For example, NGOs claimed that resorts in Sri Lanka continue to attract both locals and tourists (US Dept of State, 2010a). Lack of funding in raising awareness is seen as contributing to the exploitation of children for sex in the country. It was suggested that South Africa was proving a popular destination for individuals seeking sexual activity with minors (US Dept of State, 2010b). This claim has been denied by the South African government. Russia too has been identified as a destination for sex tourism (US Dept of State, 2010c). Finally, sex tourism has been a particular problem for emerging tourist destinations like Madagascar (US Dept of State, 2010d). The growth of the tourism industry and the impact of the financial and economic crises on nationals have been seen as contributing to the problem of sex tourism in this country (US Dept of Labor, 2009).

In view of some of the jurisdictional constraints facing law enforcement in prosecuting transborder crimes, there has been a noticeable trend in the development of regional and international policing and information sharing networks (see later discussion in this chapter). For example, law enforcement agencies increasingly rely on covert operations to identify and investigate nationals suspected of engaging in the practice of CST. The US Immigration and Customs Enforcement Agency (ICE), for example, continues to expend its efforts in prosecuting US citizens engaged in sexual activity with minors in countries in the Far East like Thailand and Cambodia. ICE coordinates its investigations from its office in Seattle, which has links to the agency's offices in Bangkok and the Cambodian National Police, Anti-Human Trafficking and Child Protection unit. Much of its powers are derived from the PROTECT Act 2003, which enables the agency to enforce Federal Laws safeguarding children in overseas countries from the sexual predatory activities of US citizens. The Trafficking Victims Protection Act in 2000 also provides an additional set of provisions, which can be used to deal with child sex trafficking. In the Operation named *Twisted Traveler*, information provided to ICE law enforcement authorities by NGOs and the Cambodian government led to three Americans being arrested for engaging in sexual activity with minors in Cambodia (FBI, 2009). Two hundred suspected paedophiles were arrested by the Australian Federal Police (AFP) following a three-year investigation, which involved collaboration with national law enforcement agencies like CEOP, ICE, the European Police Office (EUROPOL) and the

Royal Canadian Mounted Police (AFP, 2011). In *R v Cafferata*, 2008 YKTC 93, the accused was identified as one of a number of Canadians who subscribed to child pornography websites. The identification was part of an international child pornography investigation, known as *Project Emissary*, which began in the United States with Canadian involvement. For completeness a brief overview of some of the positive measures aimed at overcoming the investigation and prosecution obstacles in child sexual abuse cases with a transborder dimension will be provided. These are mutual legal assistance (MLA), information exchange between judicial and law enforcement authorities, and extradition.

Mutual legal assistance

The Crime (International Co-operation) Act 2003 replaces the United Kingdom's MLA legislation, contained in Part 1 of the Criminal Justice (International Co-operation) Act 1990. This Act implements the MLA provisions of the Schengen Convention and more particularly the Convention on Mutual Assistance in Criminal Matters. Article 1 of the Convention provides that Contracting Parties undertake to afford each other, in accordance with the provisions of this instrument, the widest measure of mutual assistance in proceedings with regard to offences the punishment of which, at the time of the request for assistance, falls within the jurisdiction of the judicial authorities of the requesting Party (Rackow *et al.*, 2010). MLA is a mechanism made available to law enforcement and prosecutors to obtain information and assistance from their counterparts in another jurisdiction (*Rantsev v Cyprus* (2010); Pati, 2010). Within the EU, the policy for promoting free movement of European citizens has led to a corresponding focus by policymakers in developing mechanisms for greater cooperation between law enforcement authorities and mutual recognition of decisions taken by judges in national legal systems of member states (Sepper, 2010). Requests for mutual assistance are understandably subject to a number of formal mechanisms. For example, requests have to be made by competent judicial authorities to their counterparts. The types of mutual assistance provided include requests to receive witness or expert testimony via a televised or video link, executing letters rogatory, controlled deliveries and conduct of surveillance operations on behalf of the requesting judicial authority. Responses to requests can, however, take time and delays can undermine the pace of investigation and in some instances have seriously undermined prosecutions. For example, a prosecution against a British national failed after Gloucestershire police's request to extend the time period for gathering and collecting evidence was turned down at the Bristol Crown Court on 15 June 2010 (Beddoe, 2010). On a separate matter, it should be noted that the operation of MLA and extradition procedures will have to be re-examined within the context of the EU in the light of the anticipated reforms under the Proposed Directive (European Commission, 2010e).

UK Central Authority for the Exchange of Criminal Records

The UK Central Authority for the Exchange of Criminal Records (UKCA-ECR) provides an important information sharing service to Member States. The unit was established under the 2005 EU Council Framework Agreement. Member States inform each other of convictions of their nationals to other EU Member States. The information that is received is translated and placed in a database known as the PNC. Member States can serve requests seeking information of criminal records of other nationals in the EU. The type of information that can be the subject of the notification process as well as the request includes information about accused, suspects, victims and witnesses.

Extradition

"Extradition" is the process whereby a person is surrendered to a requesting State for criminal prosecution (*Ayaz v Italy* (2010)). In *New Zealand v Johnston* (2011), the court reiterated the point that extradition hearings are not concerned with the merits of the case against the person against whom the request for release has been made. Individuals can be extradited from foreign countries on the basis of an agreement reached between the two countries following a request to transfer the accused so as to enable the individual to be prosecuted in the national court. In *US v Clark* (2006), the offender was found to have engaged in sexual activities with minors in Cambodia. His activities were investigated by an NGO – Action Pour Les Enfants – whose role is to rescue children who have been sexually exploited by non-Cambodians. The Cambodian National Police investigated the complaint made by the NGO and subsequently charged him. The US government had the offender extradited after the Cambodian government acceded to the request. In *Ayaz* (2010) the court rejected the accused's appeal against his extradition to the requesting State (Italy) for child sex offences deemed to have taken place in Italy. The court held that his extradition did not violate the double jeopardy rule, since the European Arrest Warrant (EAW) did not cover the type of conduct for which he was originally sentenced in the United Kingdom. Extradition procedures within the EU have been speeded up with the introduction of the EAW (Herlin-Karnell, 2010: 824–35). The EAW was introduced by the Framework Decision and incorporated into UK law when the Extradition Act 2003 came into force at the beginning of 2004 (Council of the European Union, 2004a,b). A request to have a suspect or accused extradited from a Member State will follow if the competent judicial authority concludes at the extradition hearing that the offence for which the EAW has been issued relates to an extraditable offence, that the bars to extradition are not present and that the extradition does not violate the individual's rights under the ECHR (*Iwinski v Poland* (2011); *R (on the application of HH) v Westminster City Magistrates' Court* (2011)). One additional matter is worth raising here. Framework Decision, 2002/584/JHA, replaces the application of the double criminality rule with regard to the offence of sexual exploitation of children

and child pornography (Council of the European Union, 2004a,b). It is sufficient with regard to offences like child pornography and sexual exploitation
of children, if these are crimes in the issuing Member State for which there
is a custodial sentence or a detention order for a maximum period of at least
three years. The enactment of the Policing and Crime Act 2009, in particular
Part 6, needs to be noted, since it amends the Extradition Act 2003. Sections
67 and 68, for example, aim to expedite requests for extradition made under
the Schengen Information System. Articles 3 and 4, however, preserve the
double jeopardy rule (*Ayaz* (2010)). The Framework Decision does incorporate
some safeguards for the individual who is the subject of the EAW, including
those relating to consent and legal representation. Clearly, where there are
reasons to show that the grant of extradition will result in the accused being
subject to torture or degrading treatment on the grounds of gender, race or
nationality, reassurances need to be obtained that the ends of justice will
be served, should the extradition request be granted (*Coleiro v Malta* (2010);
Janovic v Lithuania (2011)).

Extraterritorial legislation: The solution?

As conventions, treaties and protocols relating to the protection of children
from sexual abuse and exploitation gain wider acceptance, it is becoming
apparent that national legal systems are responding to the governance challenges posed by transborder criminal activity mediated through Web 2.0
technologies. Many States now subscribe to the standard setting framework
of instruments like the UNCRC and the Optional Protocol. Extraterritorial
legislation is only one mechanism through which individuals engaging in
sexual offences against children in overseas jurisdictions abroad can be prosecuted by law enforcement authorities in national legal systems. Increasingly,
as information communication technologies are used to mediate the commission of offences against children, information sharing, bilateral treaty
arrangements and codes of practice now provide a more robust approach to
governance. To address some of the policing and enforcement issues raised
by CST, the support of the tourism industry has also been enlisted.

The Code of Conduct for the Protection of Children from Sexual Exploitation in Travel and Tourism

The Code of Conduct for the Protection of Children from Sexual Exploitation
in Travel and Tourism (the Code) was developed as part of the collaborative
venture between the tourism industry and ECPAT. Signatories to the Code,
consisting of tour operators, travel organisations, travel agents, hotels,
undertake to observe the following measures:

1. To establish an ethical policy regarding CSEC.
2. To train the personnel in the country of origin and travel destinations.

3. To introduce a clause in contracts with suppliers, stating a common repudiation of CSEC.
4. To provide information to travellers by means of catalogues, brochures, in-flight films, ticket-slips, home pages, and so on.
5. To provide information to local "key persons" at the destinations.
6. To report annually.

These principles also adhere closely to the expanding concept of child safety governance, which now embed the obligations under Article 34 UNCRC and the World Tourism Organisation's Code (European Commission, 1996a: 3). The European Commission has recently energised its efforts in creating a more coherent policy towards eliminating CST in its Proposed Directive (European Commission, 2010e). Under the Proposed Directive, Member States will be expected to align their national laws with the standards and principles of the CPC Convention and amend their rules on jurisdiction "to ensure that child sexual abusers or exploiters from the European Union face prosecution even if they commit their crimes outside the European Union, in particular via so-called sex tourism" (ibid.: paragraph 9).

Conclusion

It is possible to identify the principles applicable to a State's exercise of its jurisdictional authority. First, States have jurisdiction over criminal acts taking place within their territory. This jurisdiction extends to criminal acts of foreign nationals within its territory. Second, States have jurisdiction over its nationals. Third, where a crime has a transborder element, more than one State may have jurisdiction over the event in question. Consequently, the presumptive rule in many national legal systems is that its criminal jurisdiction over the act will not have extraterritorial application unless there are specific provisions, which permit courts to assert jurisdiction over activities that take place beyond the geographical boundaries (Section 72 of the SOA 2003).

Criminal jurisdiction and online child sexual abuse and exploitation

Framing the problem: The exceptional nature of jurisdiction rules

From a criminal jurisdiction perspective, the Internet is not necessarily a phenomenon that poses fundamentally new legal issues or questions. Those who view cyberspace as a distinct environment posing complex jurisdictional challenges point to the case *La LigueContre Le Racisme Et L'AntisemitismevYahoo!* (2001). The case has generally been regarded as epitomising the jurisdictional conflicts that can be created by online activities. We should however recall that a sovereign State always has jurisdiction over criminal acts taking place within its territorial boundaries. Neither is the extension of these rules to online activity to be regarded as inconsistent with long-established jurisdiction principles (*R v Sheppard & Whittle* (2010)). Both rulings illustrate that existing jurisdiction principles continue to apply in the online environment. For example, jurisdictional issues can arise with regard to the publication of illegal content on websites. In the United Kingdom, the OPA 1959 makes it an offence to "publish" an obscene article or to have an obscene article for publication with the aim of commercial gain (Section 2 of the OPA 1959). Publication on the Internet would raise potential jurisdictional issues along the lines encountered in *R v Sheppard & Whittle* (2010). In both *Perrin* (2002) and *Fellows and Arnold* (1997), the judicial view appears to be that the act of making available and the potential accessibility of the content within the national jurisdiction would be sufficient to hold the offender liable. The use of file-sharing software to access, distribute and download child abuse content via file-sharing software, albeit its transnational dimensions, is still amenable to jurisdictional principles and rules. For example, the question may arise as to whether there can be a "public place" where the crimes in question are said to take place on websites. *R v Sheppard & Whittle* (2010) provides one possible response to this question. Another can be found in the Indecent Displays (Control) Act 1981; a website would be deemed to be a place where the public "have or are permitted to have access (whether on payment or otherwise)" (Section 1(3)). The fluid nature of information flows is not regarded as curtailing the ability of courts to assume jurisdiction. In *US v Lynn* (2011) the offender was charged with a number of offences for receiving, distributing and possessing child pornography contrary to 18 USCA § 2252(a)(2), 2252(a)(4) (B). The use of file-sharing software to download visual depictions of child pornography was corroborated by evidence showing that the content had been accessed in Washington and London, and consequently satisfied the interstate commerce element. We have previously noted that Section 72 of the SOA (2003) allows the courts to subject UK nationals to its laws even if sexual offences have transborder dimensions. In *R v Penner* (2010) the offender appealed his convictions for making indecent photographs of children,The offender was a Canadian national, and one of the issues before the Court of Appeal was whether the indecent images found on his computer were made in the United Kingdom. The Court of Appeal hypothesised that had there been an issue as to whether the child abuse content was downloaded outside United Kingdom, prosecution would have been able to rely on Section 72 of the SOA 2003. This statutory provision prevents an offender from using the transborder nature of the crime as a defence to prosecution in the United Kingdom, as long as it is shown that the act of downloading the photographs is an offence in both jurisdictions (paragraph 15).

Why do we hear that cybercrimes are undermining these principles? Brenner has suggested that

> [c]ybercrime challenges the principles law and has traditionally used to determine when a nation has jurisdiction to prohibit certain conduct and to sanction those who engage in the prohibited conduct. (Brenner, 2006: 189)

Those who regard the decentralised characteristics of the Internet as undermining criminal jurisdiction principles make two assumptions that can be questioned. First, that the transnational character of the Internet somehow transforms the character of online activities from their offline versions. Second, those existing jurisdictional principles which emerged in a defined time period are somehow outdated in the online environment. These assumptions would appear to hold true, as Brenner suggests, when one considers the transnational harms resulting from the Love Bug virus (ibid.). The virus was unleashed from the Philippines and impaired many computers across the globe. Brenner is right to claim that events like the criminal act of unleashing malicious code as having a number of consequences for the ability of a State to assert its criminal jurisdiction beyond its territory. Two additional points need to be noted, however. First, transborder criminal activity may be problematic if countries have different substantive and procedural criminal laws. Second, a particular conduct occurring in a foreign jurisdiction harming citizens of other nationalities can give rise to multiple countries asserting jurisdictions. It is true that theoretically the global reach of the Internet will lead to questions regarding the application of laws and its reach – but these are neither novel issues nor do the issues raised pose insurmountable difficulties for judges in determining the application of jurisdiction rules and its criminal laws (*R v Sheppard & Whittle* (2010); *cf. Justin Paul Savage v R* (2010)). A more relevant line of inquiry would be to begin with a consideration of the difficulties in securing compliance with national child protection laws when the Internet is used to engage in the sexual exploitation of children and related activities (Hersh, 2001: 1831). What this line of inquiry suggests is that in an environment of de-centralised networks and information flows, national legal systems will continue to face investigatory challenges due to different legal rules applying to the protection of children, difficulties faced in identifying criminal activity or problems encountered with collecting digital evidence stored on servers or websites hosted in various jurisdictions. The difficulties faced in respect of the latter, as Wall observes, stem from the fact that information networks reduce the risks of detection and accountability (Wall, 2007: 119–26). Indeed, the scale of the deviant activity cannot be disassociated from the fact that Web 2.0 technologies now make available to individuals opportunities to explore privately their sexual desires without fear of being detected by national law enforcement authorities (Quayle *et al.*, 2002). Additionally, there are numerous ways of concealing online identities and engaging in criminal activities (e.g. registering domain names with false information, encryption, anonymisation tools and services, providing false details when setting up accounts on social networking sites). Another governance concern is the increased use by criminal organisations of the Internet to share illegal content and support child sexual abuse activities. The media spotlight on the discovery of the global child pornography network following Operation Cathedral and the prosecution of its members illustrate that information security governance is an ongoing process. This investigation involved the efforts of High Tech Units in tracking the activities of individuals from 14 countries engaged in child pornography. The W0nderland Club's activities were highly organised and the group's leaders vetted membership into this group. The servers which were used by the group were frequently moved to avoid detection by law enforcement, and the leadership was clearly well versed with adopting state-of-the-art encryption and security protocols. Identifying the demand and supply channels in the Internet is a complex, resource-intensive process (Baartz, 2008; Grabosky, 2007a). The IWF in its recent report highlighted the growing demand for child sexual abuse content from a global audience (IWF, 2010b). In one instance a website which briefly hosted child sexual abuse content (before being taken down) received requests from 25,000 individual IP addresses worldwide. These requests were also received from mobile Internet accounts and gaming platforms.

Time to re-think the traditional law enforcement model?

In the light of what has been discussed it is apparent that the commercial sexual exploitation offences mediated through decentralised networks and electronic media require regulatory responses which effectively address the nuances of technology-mediated criminal activity (Dandurand *et al.*, 2007). It has been suggested that crimes mediated through technology have exposed the limitations of current crime control strategies. Unlike offline crimes, online criminal activity has a number of features that raise potential barriers to investigation and prosecution (Brenner, 2004). Brenner identifies three features which render regulating online criminal activity more problematic (2010: 39–47). First, the offender and victim are unlikely to be present in the same physical space and time. For example, many of the offline sexual crimes against children require the offender and the victim to be within proximity of each other. Second, cybercrimes may involve multiple offenders engaging in child sexual exploitation offences from multiple venues and using varied communication platforms. Child pornography rings have been known to provide live web streaming shows of children being sexually exploited to a global audience, whilst facilitating private on-line bulletin boards and chat rooms. Third, online criminal activity does not display the physical cues that define much of regular offline criminal activity.

Law enforcement and policing

The Internet enables criminals to avoid the reach of national law enforce-ment authorities by the expedient use of remote servers and vetting those accessing their services (Grabosky, 2007a). In addition to the ease with which detection can be avoided, the digitalisation of content also poses challenges for policing and investigation. As was noted in Chapter 3, decen-tralised communication networks, mobile computing and broadband tech-nology make available new avenues through which illegal content can be accessed (Grabosky, 2007b: 145–61). Advances in multimedia technologies and platforms enable child abuse and illegal content to be easily created, stored, reproduced and accessed (*R v Jewell and Gramlick* (1995)). The vol-umes of evidence that law enforcement have to process also make the in-vestigation and prosecution task burdensome (Smith *et al.*, 2004: 128–30). In *Saddler v R* (2009) the offender was charged and convicted of offences relating to possession of child pornography contrary to Section 91H(3) of the Crimes Act 1900. As part of the process for framing the charge and pro-viding supporting relevant and admissible evidence, law enforcement had to process 45,000 images, many of which were stored in portable media devices and external hard drives. The offender in *Hitchen v R* (2009) was found to be in possession of 729,000 child pornographic images and 2,700 video files depicting child pornography. These cases illustrate some of the challenges facing law enforcement as they attempt to investigate and frame the indictment appropriately. P2P networks, bulletin boards, chat rooms and websites now provide new channels and opportunities for evading detection by law enforcement. The anonymity and convenience commu-nication technologies provide has also contributed to the rise in demand for child sexual abuse content (Harrison, 2006). Sexual grooming can now be conducted privately, and the interactions between the perpetrator and victim be web-streamed easily across the Internet to like-minded individ-uals in the deviant community. Until his arrest, the offender in *R v Lee* (2010) was found to have downloaded onto his computer child pornography from file-sharing programmes. Most file-sharing programmes like "eMule" and "LimeWire" permit users to make contents available on a shared folder to other users of the programme from anywhere in the world and at any-time when the computer is switched on (*R v Johannson* (2008)). Email and IM now enable individuals to engage in other forms of child sexual ex-ploitation and abuse – human trafficking and sex tourism. The Canadian

Security Intelligence Service (CSIS) reported that the Internet continues to be used by criminal organisations to coordinate their activities (CSIS, 2007; FBI, 2008). Finally, communication networks enable users to connect with others, access and create content, exchange and share information and reinforce their deviant values (*R v Hopps* (2010), paragraphs 26–30). It is this scale of misuse of Web 2.0 technologies for hosting, accessing, communicating and exchanging information and the commercial gains derived as a consequence that has led to the Internet and communication technologies becoming a popular medium for organised criminal activity (Kim-Kwang, 2009). Online paedophile rings, for example, leverage the decentralised network structure of the Internet and fuel the market for CSEC. These organised groups operate subscription services for IRC web streaming of live child sexual abuse (ibid., 2009: 281). Additionally, Kim-Kwang is right to conclude that policing and enforcing online criminal activities are beyond the capabilities of individual national legal systems (2009: 282). Online child sex rings use specific Internet relay channels and P2P file-sharing networks to enable their members to create and distribute child sexual abuse content as well as produce literature which provides like-minded individuals with strategies and techniques for avoiding prosecution for child sex offences (Baartz, 2008). Access to these groups is tightly controlled through the adoption of secret vetting protocols. In a recent investigation, a global child pornography network was found to have had more than 12 million hits on its website from 170 countries (AFP, 2009). In *R v Hopps* (2010) the witness for the Crown, who was a member of the RCMP and ICE, noted that over 50,000 individuals were engaged in the global trade in child pornography and that legitimate company servers were hijacked to peddle the content (paragraphs 34–7). Law enforcement operations with particular expertise in high-tech crimes have noted an increase transborder criminal activity (AFP, 2008). In the United States, child abuse images are increasingly depicting very young children and increasing violence. Since 2010, the hotline Cybertips received 175,000 reports of online child pornography; between 1996 and 2007, there was an increase in child exploitation cases; prosecutions for child pornography cases between 1994 and 2006 rose to 82 per cent; and there was a correlation between child pornography and contact offences (HRC, 2011: 6).

These depressing findings should not lead us to assume that the challenges facing national legal systems and law enforcement require additional legislation. In recent years a number of law enforcement bodies have directed their strategies towards developing and improving their investigative skills and intelligence with the aim of disrupting online commercial and sexual exploitation channels. As indicated in Chapter 3, the online environment also provides "digital trails" which can assist law enforcement. In *T v the Queen* (2011), the incriminating evidence used to prosecute the offender for possession of child abuse content was found on his computer, memory stick and other digital portable storage devices. When commercial sexual exploitation activities are reported, the decision to prosecute and even the ability to prosecute will be influenced by three factors: relevant legislative authority, availability of evidence and intelligence sharing. In some respects the online environment creates "digital trails" which are particularly useful for law enforcement when investigating child sexual exploitation incidents. Some of the investigative techniques used to bring offenders before the courts are nothing more than good examples of law enforcement adopting appropriate investigation strategies, networking and coordination with other national policing agencies or organisations (see below). In *R v Collins* (2011) the offender was traced via the telephone which was used to access the website for the National Society for the Prevention of Cruelty to Children. In *R v Parnell* (2004) the accused was convicted of the crimes of attempted incitement to commit buggery, and attempted incitement to an act of gross indecency with a male under the age of 16. Unknown to the accused, the Sri Lankan authorities had intercepted his email. On his return to England, the accused was arrested and prosecuted under Section 2 of the Sexual Offences (Conspiracy and Incitement) Act 1996.

Policing networks

INTERPOL

This organisation has as its mission the prevention or combating of international crime by facilitating cross-border police cooperation, and supports and assists all organisations, authorities and services.[1] As part of its work, the International Criminal Police Organisation (INTERPOL) assists law enforcement in investigating and prosecuting individuals and organisations for crimes against children. One important contribution made by INTERPOL is the provision of trained investigators with access to the International Child Sexual Exploitation image database (ICSE DB) via a secure communication network. The database is funded by the European Commission and has received the backing of the G8. The INTERPOL Child Abuse Image Database (ICAID) was created in 2001 and now has over 520,000 images submitted by 36 Member States. Two examples can be provided to highlight the value of the database and information sharing policies as effective child protection measures. The first concerns two young girls, aged 9 and 11 years, who were sexually abused and filmed. A video of the abuse was found in Australia, where authorities requested the assistance of the INTERPOL General Secretariat to identify the language spoken and hence possibly the location of the victims. Following a lengthy investigation coordinated by INTERPOL, the child victims were located in Belgium and rescued. Their father and the abuser were subsequently arrested. The individual filming the abuse was traced to Italy and subsequently arrested. The second involves an investigation undertaken by a Canadian police officer who discovered a number of child abuse images. He approached INTERPOL to conduct some forensic image analysis. During the image analysis, an officer noted that some of the background items including the computer keyboard pointed strongly to the abuse images being made in Spain. The subsequent investigation led to the uncovering of a child rapist network operating in Spain and the identification and rescue of a further seven victims below the age of four years.

CIRCAMP

Apart from INTERPOL, COSPOL Internet Related Child Abuse Material Project (CIRCAMP) provides invaluable organisational support to law enforcement authorities investigating online child sexual exploitation.[2] The overall aim of the CIRCAMP network is to combine the resources of and improve coordination between law enforcement agencies in Europe. According to CIRCAMP, eleven Member States (Norway, Belgium, Denmark, Finland, France, Ireland, Malta, Spain, Sweden, Netherlands, UK) are now taking part in a law enforcement project aimed at preventing access to child sexual abuse material. CIRCAMP also cooperates and shares information with non-EU Member States and these now include Switzerland and New Zealand.

EUROPOL

EUROPOL is another organisation which supports law enforcement agencies in the EU Member States.[3] As criminals become more organised and skilled in evading detection by law enforcement through the use of sophisticated technologies and payment mechanisms, EUROPOL aims to support law enforcement agencies in Member States by providing intelligence analysis, by training of law enforcement and facilitating information sharing. A number of its services are directly relevant to enhancing the effectiveness of national law enforcement agencies in relation to CSEC. For example, to ensure that law enforcement and judges have the requisite skills and knowledge, EUROPOL organises an annual training course "Combating the Sexual Exploitation of Children on the Internet" focusing on the legal, investigatory and evidentiary issues in this regard. This training course is also made available to law enforcement agencies around the world. It is envisaged that by creating such a forum, greater awareness and understanding of the investigation and enforcement strategies to address technology-enabled crimes can be promoted, investigators can share their experiences and practices and networks for ongoing and future collaboration and coordination of law enforcement efforts can be improved. Since 2001, EUROPOL has used the Analytical Work File (AWF) to support investigations undertaken by Member States in dealing with criminal activity relating to the sexual exploitation of children. In 2007, the AWF was used to coordinate and support investigations undertaken under *Operation Koala*, which involved 29 countries within and outside the EU. Over 400 suspects were identified, and from the resulting investigation around 100 child sex offenders were

arrested. EUROPOL has a number of strategic arrangements with organisations outside the EU. The agreements include exchanging specialist knowledge, disseminating strategic intelligence, production of general situation
reports, sharing of information on investigative procedures and crime prevention methods, participation in training activities as well as providing
advice and support in individual investigations. An example of the latter
can be in seen in the agreement EUROPOL has with Australia. Its contact
point is the AFP. One of the areas for cooperation involves the "trade in
human beings", which covers the "subjection of a person to the real and
illegal sway of other persons by using violence or menaces or by abuse of
authority or intrigue, especially with a view to the exploitation of prostitution, forms of sexual exploitation and assault of minors or trade in aban-
doned children".

VGT

The Virtual Global Taskforce (VGT) comprises national law enforcement agencies coordinating their resources and intelligence to protect children from
online child abuse.[4] The VGT was set up in 2003 to deal with the global rise of
online child sexual exploitation activity. The current membership of the VGT
include EUROPOL, the AFP, CEOP, the Italian Postal and Communication
Police Service, the Royal Canadian Mounted Police, the US Department of
Homeland Security, INTERPOL, the Ministry of Interior for the United Arab
Emirates and New Zealand Police. The VGT enables investigations to be better
coordinated and facilitates information sharing at regional and international
levels. To date more than 200 commercial child sexual abuse websites have
been dismantled. The VGT engaged in an international investigation known
as *Operation Basket*. It commenced investigations as far back as 2006 following intelligence provided by the United States Immigration and Customs
Enforcement investigation. An important part of the investigation involved
the identification of the criminal organisation coordinating the commercial exploitation of online child sexual abuse content. During the course of
the investigation over 30,000 customers from 132 countries were identified.
Law enforcement authorities around the world including the Netherlands,
Germany, the Czech Republic, Belarus and Italy collaborated with the VGT. In
addition to engaging with law enforcement activity, the VGT now works with
over 96 countries to assist them in drafting UNCRC compliant laws.

CEOP

CEOP, the UK law enforcement agency, continues lead child safety issues in
the United Kingdom. It recently reported the dismantling of a paedophile
network on the social networking site Facebook (CEOP, 2010b). The UK national, Ian Green, was the subject of an international operation known as
Operation Ocean. The High Tech Operations Unit of the AFP provided CEOP
with intelligence regarding the activities of an individual in the United

Kingdom who was coordinating the making and distribution of thousands of child abuse images. Green used the anonymity the Internet provides to create false Facebook profiles, group accounts and email addresses to download and distribute child sexual abuse images and then proceeded to share these on his home page. CEOP managed to infiltrate this network despite the efforts of Ian Green to screen and monitor individuals who gained entry into the private groups on Facebook. Ian Green pleaded guilty to a range of offences under the PCA 1978 and for breaching his terms under the Sex Offenders Register. The AFP National Manager Commander Neil Gaughan observed that

> policing in this social networking environment is a challenge, but the co-operation during this operation demonstrates that international law enforcement is united in a global fight against online child exploitation material. (CEOP, 2010b)

Project Safe Childhood

In the United States, the Project Safe Childhood initiative was developed to combat child exploitation and abuse.[5] It was launched by the Department of Justice in 2006 and led by the United States Attorneys' Offices and the Criminal Division's Child Exploitation and Obscenity Section. In 2010, as part of an ongoing investigation, prosecutions were brought against an individual for transporting child pornography through an Internet bulletin board. At least 36 subscribers were found to have used this facility to trade in thousands of images and videos of child pornography. This case is particularly relevant to the discussion regarding the strategic significance of coordinating policing networks at a global level. This was an international investigation known as the *Lost Boy* online bulletin board. The investigation was launched in collaboration with international law enforcement agencies and it culminated in a number of individuals being prosecuted for a wide range of child exploitation offences. It was claimed that the Lost Boy network comprised members from the United States, Belgium, Brazil, Canada, France, Germany and New Zealand.

FCACP

Increasingly, law enforcement has expanded its investigation strategies by engaging with the banking sector and online intermediaries to disrupt the misuse of Web 2.0 technologies for commercial and sexual exploitation of children activities. In recent years, the Financial Coalition against Child Pornography (FCACP), comprising major banks, credit card companies, electronic payment networks, third-party payments companies, and online services companies, have provided invaluable support to law enforcement efforts in disrupting the growing commercial child sexual exploitation industry.[6] The European arm of the FCACP (European Financial Coalition (EFC)) was set up, partly in response to NGO and public concerns about the growth in commercial child sexual abuse websites.[7] FCACP has a global presence and networks with national law enforcement authorities across the world. This strategic development is largely the product of intelligence information obtained by law enforcement indicating that the child abuse industry was using the online environment to channel its funds and develop alternative payment mechanisms to avoid detection. The activities of the FCACP are coordinated by the NCMEC, which has a hotline for receiving anonymous reports about the websites engaging in commercial sexual exploitation – CyberTipline. A number of web hosting companies have also supported these efforts. For example, GoDaddy.com, which is one of the largest hosting companies in the world, collaborates with the FCACP. Recently, the Federal Deposit Insurance Corporation compiled a code of practice to establish due diligence standards members can use in the merchant application and verification protocols to detect child pornographers and prevent them from using the online payment channels to fund their practices. The "Internet Merchant Acquisition and Monitoring Best Practices for the Prevention and Detection of Commercial Child Pornography" can be seen as an illustration of how legal standards and principles governing the protection of children from commercial and sexual abuse can be extended to businesses. The guidance provides due diligence protocols, which can be used to process merchant applications and verify the accounts to ensure that these platforms do not provide an avenue for profiting from child pornography.

An international cybercrime treaty

In the light of the above discussion, it is not entirely clear whether reforms of the principles applicable to extraterritorial criminal jurisdiction will have a significant impact, when compared with, for example, efforts directed towards funding and supporting current governance measures like information sharing, promoting collaboration between NGOs, law enforcement and the financial sector and assisting communities and ethnic minorities who are particularly vulnerable to commercial and sexual exploitation. In view of the benefits in creating a safer online environment for children through greater cooperation and collaboration between law enforcement agencies and prosecuting authorities nationally, regionally and globally, there is an emerging view that national efforts to secure compliance with child protection laws would be better served by countries subscribing to a global treaty (Dandurand, *et al.*, 2007). These views are now being canvassed in different forums. At the Twelfth UN Congress on Crime Prevention and Criminal Justice a working paper prepared by the Secretariat explored the possibility of establishing a global convention on cybercrime.[8] Some doubt might be expressed as to whether an additional treaty may be what is required presently. The Cybercrime Convention, which came into force in 2004, involved six years of negotiation. It has been acceded to or ratified by 30 countries. Forty-seven countries have signed the Convention. The United Kingdom, Canada, Russia, Japan and Australia have yet to ratify the Convention.[9] Of those who have ratified it, 15 countries have indicated reservations to certain parts of the Convention. This Convention, as will be discussed in the next chapter, covers, amongst other crimes, the substantive and procedural rules on child sexual abuse images. Even though a global convention holds out the promise of a new standard setting framework, as anyone who has followed the progress of the Cybercrime Convention and the reservations placed by signatories will attest, obtaining global agreement on promoting judicial and law enforcement cooperation on topics like child pornography, prostitution and human trafficking is unlikely to be a straightforward matter.

Conclusion

Extraterritorial legislation has an important role in managing the transnational issues raised by nationals engaging in commercial and sexual exploitation of children in foreign jurisdictions. One conclusion reached is that the substantive "jurisdictional" challenges raised by the convergence in broadcasting, telecommunications and social media are not as problematic as might appear at first blush, when compared with, for example, the investigatory challenges facing law enforcement at this present time. In an environment of decentralised communication networks, where information can be easily created and distributed at a speed and scale that is unparalleled in history, it may be true to say that the "traditional mechanisms of international cooperation, including letters rogatory, mutual assistance and other formalities with roots in the 19th century and earlier, are ill-suited" (Smith *et al.*, 2004: 120). The Internet now makes it easier for individuals to engage in criminal activities from jurisdictions which either do not have effective policing resources or do not have laws protecting children from abuse and sexual exploitation. From a legal point of view the Internet does not impose any new substantive challenges to extraterritorial criminal jurisdiction principles. It has also been shown that the Internet can make the task of investigating and prosecuting offenders much easier, as law enforcement organisations share intelligence with each other. Information sharing, greater collaboration with the banking sector, NGOs, ISPs and the use of sting operations can significantly enhance the prosecution of child sexual abuse and exploitation offenders even when criminal deviants misuse de-centralised network structures and information flows.

5
Online Child Safety: International Cooperation and Policymaking

Overview

Safeguarding children from sexual harm and abuse is a global phenomenon. The MSIG framework consists of an expanding regulatory landscape of laws, treaties and conventions and involves a range of stakeholders and interests. The globalisation of risks, including those relating to the CSEC, has also resulted in harmonisation efforts and cooperation at national, regional and international levels (OECD, 2009). The UN and its institutions, the EU and the Council of Europe now provide important platforms for mobilising online child safety governance strategies and policymaking. The aim of this chapter is to reflect on some of the significant institutional governance responses to combating child sexual exploitation and abuse. It is not the intention to undertake a comprehensive analysis of these responses but, rather, the focus will be on the contributions these institutions make in defining the standards and principles which provide the benchmark for the MSIG policymaking activity (ITU, 2008b). The chapter has three parts. The first part describes the policymaking role of the UN within the framework provided by the UNCRC and highlights some of the principal regulatory and policy developments which continue to inform the way governments and stakeholders now approach online sexual exploitation and abuse of children. The second part considers the important role of the EU, with particular reference to the SIP. The final part describes the significance of the increasing contributions by the Council of Europe in this area of policymaking.

The United Nations and the Convention on the Rights of the Child

In May 2002, the UN hosted a Special Session of the UN General Assembly on Children (UN, 2002). The goal of the Special Session was to provide delegates with an opportunity to review the progress made since the World

Summit for Children in 1990. At the sixty-first session, a follow-up report to the Special Session of the General Assembly on children was presented (UN, 2006b). In this report, the General Assembly was informed that over 140 and 118 countries had signed the UNCRC and the Optional Protocol, respectively. One hundred and forty-six countries have now ratified the ILO Convention 138, whilst another 161 countries ratified the ILO Convention No. 182. The 2006 *Study on Violence against Children* is only one of many child protection initiatives undertaken by the UN and its organisations (UN, 2006a). It is an important study since it provides one of the most compelling accounts of the violence and abuse inflicted on children across the world. Its conclusions are both poignant and timely particularly as there is now growing momentum in encouraging governments to renew their commitments to promoting children's rights within their jurisdictions. These are important developments. Accession to international obligations is viewed as a prelude to signatory countries demonstrating their commitment towards enhancing the welfare and development of children in their national plans. Increasingly, safeguarding children from violence is regarded as an important limb in the Millennium Development Goals within the UN Development Assistance Framework. The UN's commitment to children's rights is well-known and the Special Session can be viewed as an appropriate illustration of how child protection governance strategies can evolve from the interplay between the UN, governments and civil society. The UNCRC, which lies at the core of the issues relating to children's safety and well-being, draws many of its central principles and norms from the Universal Declaration of Human Rights 1948. In the General Assembly Resolution, the UNCRC, its provisions and other human rights instruments were regarded as standard setting instruments. It is generally recognised that the realisation of the rights under the UNCRC would be dependent on States' willingness to cooperate and provide mutual assistance (Articles 4 and 28(3)). The preamble to the UNCRC regards children as beneficiaries of all fundamental human rights.[1] The key provisions of the UNCRC relevant to the subject of sexual exploitation of children are as follows. First, the Convention rights and obligations are owed only to a "child", who for the purposes of the UNCRC is any person below the age of 18 years (Article 1). Clearly, this is an important provision, as the substantive rights under the UNCRC do not extend to individuals beyond this age group. However, it should be noted that a number of countries have stipulated the legal age of the child at 16 years or even lower. This has obvious implications for the level of protection accorded to children in areas like online sexual solicitation, CST and child pornography. Second, States are vested with a number of obligations towards children, which is perhaps an acknowledgement that children live in a political, legal and social environment where institutions ultimately decide on issues that concern their development, safety and well-being. Third, children are envisaged as enjoying civil, political, economic, social and cultural rights. These are described as "protection rights", "participation rights" and "survival and development rights". Children who have particular needs or who are vulnerable are regarded as meriting additional protection. There are four principles which inform the standard setting role of the UNCRC: non-discrimination; the best interests of the child being a primary consideration in all decisions concerning children; the right to survival and development and respect for the views of the child. There have been considerable attempts made in integrating the human rights discourse into the subject of children's rights and an assessment of their normative foundations is beyond the scope of the book (Fortin, 2010).

Safeguarding children against violence is a fundamental principle in child protection. Article 19 of the UNCRC provides that States "take all appropriate legislative, administrative, social and educational measures" to protect children from all forms of violence. The UN continues to play an important role in addressing the scale of violence against children, in particular, by drawing attention to the commercial and sexual exploitation of children in society. States are urged, for example, to protect children from these forms of violence by taking "all appropriate national, bilateral and multilateral measures" (Article 34, UNCRC). Article 34 encapsulates much of the thinking that regards safeguarding children from violence as a human right and anticipates an important role for international, regional and national cooperation (Table 5.1).

The UNCRC also provides a framework where States voluntarily assume the obligation to realise the rights of children in society. The overriding principle is set out in Article 3, which elevates the best interests principle as a primary consideration for all actions concerning children. Signatories to the UNCRC commit themselves to furthering the best interests of the child

Table 5.1   Eight elements of a protective environment

Shaping attitudes, traditions, customs, behaviour and practices towards children
Governmental commitment to fulfilling protection rights
Creating a framework within countries so that child protection issues can be openly debated and discussed in various settings.
Relevant child protection legislation and allocating resources for enforcement
Creating appropriate human and institutional support infrastructures for those working or living with children
Promote information and safety literacy amongst children
Monitoring and Reporting Mechanisms
Services for recovery and reintegration, which uphold the respect and dignity of the child.

Source: UNICEF.

when formulating policies or taking decisions which have a direct or indirect bearing on children (Alston, 1994). The aim of Article 3 is to provide governments and adults in society with a benchmark against which their interactions with children and their decisions can be evaluated. Furthermore, the wording in Article 3 suggests that even if the child's best interests were determined, it is not decisive of the outcome to any action taken by public or private entities since other considerations may have to be taken into account. It is not surprising to discover that there is no comprehensive definition of what "best interests" might mean (Freeman, 2007). This is understandable, since the determination what is a child's best interests will need to be carefully considered alongside the obligations traditionally vested in the family in determining matters affecting the child's development, safety and well-being. This has not stopped attempts being made to articulate the scope of the principle. Some have suggested that it is misleading to think of "children's rights", since children are incapable of determining what is in their best interests (Purdy, 1994: 223–41). A common-sense view that certain limits be imposed specially on children would resonate very much with parents and educators (ibid., 1994: 224). Others have a more fundamental objection to the concept of children's rights (O'Neill, 1988: 445–63). O'Neill's objection can be traced back to the belief that children are not in the same category of groups of individuals where the recognition of rights is regarded as an instrument through which individuals can be freed from oppression (ibid., 1988: 461). Of course, we can take issue with the view that children should not be beneficiaries of rights on the basis that they are dependants rather than an oppressed group. O'Neill's thesis could, however, be viewed as emphasising the role of social norms in enhancing the relational aspect in the interactions that children have with their parents. Children, according to her, have a fundamentally different relationship with society and more specifically their parents (1988: 456–9). Her arguments about the central role of parents in providing children with an appropriate environment through which they can realise and develop their abilities and be nurtured raise a wider and well-discussed issue, the arguments about paternalism and autonomy (Fortin, 2010: 19–29). It is important to stress that notwithstanding the arguments about how we should view children and the way the enjoyment of their rights are realised in society, there is unlikely to be any disagreement that we should "take children's rights more seriously" (Freeman, 1992: 53). According to Freeman, the discourse on children's rights is compatible with societal understanding and expectation that whilst we should acknowledge that a child is an autonomous human being it does not foreclose interventions deemed necessary to safeguard its health and well-being (ibid., 1992: 67–8). Eekelaar has framed the autonomy/protection debate in terms of the interests that the law has or ought to uphold in the area of public policies which affect children (Eekelaar, 1986). One is inclined to agree with his characterisation of the debate. In tracing the emergence of the concept of children's rights in societies, he alerts us to instances where the law has, ironically, had to intervene not only in cases of violence and abuse towards children, but it has also, in extreme cases, had to curb the protective impulses that motivated many of the actions of loving and caring individuals (ibid., 1986: 162). The Safeguarding Vulnerable Groups Act 2006 illustrates the role of law in Implementing vetting protocols that protect children from coming into close contact with certain categories of individuals deemed to pose risks to their safety and well-being. When approaching the subject of children's rights, Eekelaar argues that we need to do two things. First, we need to articulate the interests, which can be made the subject of policymaking – basic, developmental and autonomy (ibid., 1986: 170). Second, given that children may not necessarily be in a position to make informed decisions, Eekelaar suggests that it is

> necessary therefore to make some kind of imaginative leap and guess what a child might retrospectively have wanted once it reaches a position of maturity. In doing this, values of the adult world of the individual adults will inevitably enter. This is not to be deplored, but openly accepted. It encourages debates about these values. (Ibid.)

A "basic interest" would be what we regard as core interests without which the developmental or autonomy interests cannot be fully realised. Basic interests are those which ensure that the child's physical, emotional and intellectual integrity is protected. Developmental interests will consist of those which a child can expect from society to enable it to maximise its innate abilities. Finally, autonomy interests could involve a child's expectation of its "freedom to choose his own lifestyle and to enter social relations according to his own inclinations uncontrolled by the authority of the adult world" (ibid., 1986: 171). According to Eekelaar the autonomy interest is subordinated to other interests, and he accepts that the interplay of each of the interests may in some contexts result in conflicts involving the State and parents. He uses the example of the case of *Gillick v West Norfolk and Wisbech Area Health Authority* to highlight an issue of contemporary relevance – the right of a child to make mistakes (1986: 182). The conflict in this case originated from a circular issued by the Department of Health and Social Security which stated that although it was desirable for a child to seek parental advice about contraception, a child under 16 could seek counselling and treatment with a doctor instead. On the specific issue of whether a child below the age of 16 had the capacity to give valid consent, the House of Lords by a bare majority ruled in favour of the child's autonomy interests (1986: 180).

To conclude this brief discussion of the best interests principle, it should be apparent that just as the end-to-end principle raises profound questions about how States should now address the governance challenges posed by technology-mediated offences against children, the best interests principle also raises policy issues regarding the basic, developmental and autonomy interests that ought to guide policymakers, parents and educators seeking to enhance the safety of children in the online environment. Some of these policy issues are already being encountered as policymakers attempt to deal with children's behaviour on network publics, "sexting" and access to "inappropriate" content. More specifically, in adapting legal, technological and social norms to the online environment, we in turn have to assess how best each of the interests can be balanced (e.g. access to content, development, social relations, expression and identity formation) when children and adults may have different expectations of how the former should manage their online activities. As children's rights become mainstream in policymaking activity and discourse, concerns about the encroachment into a child's autonomy will no doubt figure in tussles between parents and children, particularly as the former (as purchasers of mobile phones and computers) will define the ground rules for access and use of these technologies (Castells *et al.*, 2007: 147). With ever-increasing convergence between technology and mobile computing culture, parents and children have to wrestle "more often than not, the perceptions of threat are exaggerated in narrative accounts from both media coverage and interpersonal channels" (Castells *et al.*, 2007: 114). The parallels between the protection/autonomy concerns on the one hand and Beck's "risk society" and the individualisation of risk on the other are difficult to ignore.

One way by which States demonstrate their commitment to children's safety and well-being is through the development and implementation of policies, procedures and legislation, which provide the foundation "for the full and harmonious development of his or her personality, should grow up in a family environment, in an atmosphere of happiness, love and understanding" (UNCRC, 1989). The emphasis here being that whichever settings or contexts children find themselves in, there is an expectation that policymakers must, as a minimum, ensure that the basic and developmental interests are accommodated without undermining a child's ability to engage and participate in society. Additionally, it is also recognised that the opportunities for development, participation and enjoyment of human rights can be impaired if appropriate legal safeguards are not available to protect children's physical and emotional integrity. The key point to note here is the particular role of the State in creating a regulatory framework that enables all individuals in society to understand and comply with the established standards and principles.

Committee on the Rights of the Child

Clearly, some mechanism needs to be in place to ensure that the obligations assumed by the signatories under the UNCRC are complied with. The role of the Committee on the Rights of the Child (CRC) is particularly relevant here. Article 43 can be seen as one practical response towards creating a framework through which issues regarding the scope and implementation of the UNCRC by signatories can be addressed. The CRC consists of a body of experts who monitor and review the implementation by States of their obligations undertaken under the UNCRC. By acceding to the UNCRC, States agree to subject efforts made in complying with the obligations assumed under the UNCRC to scrutiny by the CRC. There are a number of benefits in having this regulatory oversight mechanism. Such a process, for instance, not only increases the likelihood of compliance but it also ensures that particular problems or issues regarding the implementation of the UNCRC that are specific to a particular culture or country can be identified and addressed. States are required to ensure that the reports submitted by them demonstrate clearly the relationship between the specific policies and measures implemented and the Convention obligations. A State submitting a report can, for example, identify the measures it has put in place to protect and promote the rights of the child. It may also be that the report will set out information regarding the steps already being taken to advance the safety and well-being of children. Finally, the report provides States with an opportunity to highlight particular problems encountered when fulfilling its obligations under the UNCRC. The CRC normally convenes three sessions per annum and publishes its findings in the form of comments on the issues raised by the report. An additional part of the CRC's remit is the monitoring of States' compliance with the obligations assumed under the two Optional Protocols to the UNCRC. The CRC also releases into the public domain its "General Comments" – which consists of its interpretation of human rights provisions and thematic issues. This communication serves to clarify particular aspects of the UNCRC or even identify matters that States and individuals need to have in mind when formulating governance responses affecting children. For example, in 2009, the CRC issued a General Comment No. 12, which addressed the paradoxical character of the legal and social status of children, and emphasised the fact that whilst children may not possess the autonomy of adults, States still had to regard them as legitimate subjects of rights (CRC, 2009). This General Comment supported the findings of the Secretary-General's 2006 *Study on Violence against Children*, and stated that children's views should be obtained or be given due weight in all aspects of managing their safety. Additionally, it was felt that a child's "right to be heard" had an important place in the formulation of governance strategies and measures (ibid., 2009: paragraph 120). One practical issue that is often raised in the reporting process is whether States have taken "all appropriate legislative, administrative and other measures" in accordance with their undertakings under the UNCRC. This is a particularly important issue when determining a State's compliance with its obligations under the UNCRC. According to the CRC, in its General Comment No. 5, governments need to undertake a two-stage process when determining compliance with their obligations under the UNCRC (CRC, 2003: paragraph 1). First, when implementing the measures *necessary* for the realisation of the rights, a State is required at the first instance to engage with all stake-holders, including children. During this period of engagement, not only has the State to seek the views of the stakeholders, but it is also required to demonstrate that its domestic legislation is compatible with both the letter and the spirit of the UNCRC and, more crucially, that these rules are being appropriately enforced. Second, when States submit their reports to the CRC, there is an expectation that the actions taken to comply with the UNCRC are clearly described and evidenced. The forms of evidence that can be offered include measures like campaigns and educational programmes which raise children's and the public's awareness of the UNCRC, disseminating the deliberations of the CRC and its Reports widely within the State, designating budgets and resources to establish children's representative groups and centres, creating opportunities for children's participation in policymaking and giving due weight to their views and concerns, enacting legislation which enables children's interests to be taken into account (i.e. health and education) and integrating child impact assessments into any legislative, policy or budgetary decisions. For example, the setting up of youth panels in online child safety policymaking is one illustration of the role of the SIP in embedding UNCRC standards and values amongst its Member States. Clearly, since many of the online child safety policies, for example, impact children, it is only right that they should have a say in the measures adopted to enhance their safety. By subjecting States to scrutiny from the CRC and, indirectly, to the electorate, it is also felt that greater awareness and understanding of UNCRC obligations will in itself provide States with the necessary incentive to be seen to be complying with its undertakings. The CRC also plays an important role in entering into a dialogue with the State during the reporting process by highlighting areas of good practice as well as recommending areas where specific attention is required.

It is encouraging to find that States have generally been responsive to the recommendations made by the CRC. Some illustrations can be provided by way of conclusion to the discussion on the work of the CRC. For example, following the dialogue during the consideration of the periodic reports, the United Kingdom informed the CRC that it would be withdrawing its reservations to Articles 22 and 37(c) of the Convention and indicated that it also planned to ratify the Optional Protocol before the end of 2008 (CRC, 2008a). The Optional Protocol was in effect ratified on 20 February 2009. The CRC has previously indicated in its Concluding Observations based on the reports submitted by the United Kingdom and Northern Ireland that the principle of the best interests of the child was not being adequately reflected in all legislative and policy matters affecting children, especially in the area of juvenile justice, immigration and freedom of movement and peaceful assembly (CRC, 2008b). The then government responded by making available on its website its views regarding the steps to be taken in response to the Committee's conclusions. During this meeting, broader issues regarding the government's commitment were also addressed together with the problem of the media's negative portrayal of children. The CRC also took the opportunity to make clear that "welfare" and "best interest" were not synonymous (CRC, 2008b: paragraph 23). In its 49th Report the CRC reiterated the need for the United Kingdom to ratify the CPC Convention, and increase its efforts towards integrating the best interests of the child principle in "all legislative and policy matters affecting children, especially in the area of juvenile justice, immigration and freedom of movement and peaceful assembly" (CRC, 2010: 64). Even though the recommendations have no legal force, States continue to implement the measures proposed by the CRC. Australia, for example, amended its Criminal Code by inserting new child pornography and child abuse offences. The new offences now ensure that individuals using the Internet to access, transmit, or produce illegal content with the intention of placing it on the Internet will now be prosecuted (CRC, 2005b: 97). After welcoming the efforts made by the State, the CRC also drew attention to its concerns about "the exposure of children to violence, racism and pornography, especially through the Internet" (CRC, 2005a: paragraph 33). Concrete recommendations made by the CRC assist States in guiding their implementation strategies. In response to the recommendations made by the CRC, ACMA initiated a series of studies and policy reviews aimed at promoting greater awareness of online safety issues and policies (e.g. filtering, media literacy and redress mechanisms) (ACMA, 2009b,c,d). Indeed, we see not dissimilar strategies being pursued by policymakers in the United States, Canada, the United Kingdom and other Member States in the EU in reviewing national legislation and MSIG strategies. Additionally, following the assurances given to the CRC regarding Australia's accession and ratification to the Optional Protocol, the government fulfilled its undertaking on 8 January 2007 (2005a: paragraph 78–9). We should also note the role of the Special Rapporteur on the sale of children, child prostitution and child pornography in making visible the issues meriting the attention of policymakers. The Special Rapporteur's mandate is to investigate the exploitation of children around the world and to submit reports to the General Assembly and the Commission on Human Rights. The Human Rights Council (HRC) passed a resolution providing the Special Rapporteur with an additional mandate to analyse the cultural and economic factors contributing to CSEC, to identify and promote best practices in combating this problem (HRC, 2007). In 2004, the then Special Rapporteur drew the attention of the General Assembly and the Commission on Human Rights to the scale of the prevalence of child pornography materials on the Internet and the lack of legislation dealing with this type of material, which prompted concerted international efforts to address the growing problem of CSEC (Commission on Human Rights, 2004). The Special Rapporteur also highlighted the important role of the CRC, when examining the reports submitted by governments on the implementation of the Optional Protocol; particular reference was made to its role in promoting a common understanding of the definition of pornography so that all signatories could adhere to common standards and principles (Commission on Human Rights, 2004: paragraph 119). Whilst there is a lack of consistency in the legal definition of "child pornography" or variance in the age for consenting to sexual activity, many of the concerns regarding the contact and content risks are gradually being addressed at national and regional platforms (2004: paragraphs 122–9). Anyone engaged in the creation, distribution and possession of child abuse material would be prosecuted (European Commission, 2010e, 2011b). A number of States have in place legislation that criminalises online sexual solicitation of minors. ISPs have developed monitoring and information sharing practices designed to reduce online access to illegal content. We also have specialised law enforcement units that deal with online safety and security. There are, however, areas identified by the Special Rapporteur which still require ongoing international consensus and collaboration (e.g. age of the "child", criminalising possession of "pseudo-child abuse images" and defining the scope of "child pornography"). Additionally, the effectiveness of efforts to disrupt the supply and demand for CSEC continue to be a concern (ECPAT, 2009). In 2006, the Special Rapporteur noted that there was a need for governments and policymakers to develop effective preventative strategies which targeted the demand for CSEC (Commission on Human Rights, 2006). This is a difficult area of governance, and the eradication of demand has been described as "a complex and multifaceted phenomenon" (ibid., 2006: paragraph 119). We have previously discussed some of the governance responses with regard to CSEC but the findings continue to be relevant to online child safety governance even to this day (ibid., 2006: paragraph 122). Whilst empowerment can lead to a reduction of CSEC, in many cases their eradication continues to be problem since the conditions which enable the demand to be met are deeply rooted in social structures of poverty, social inequality, armed conflict and even forced economic migration (ibid., 2006: 121). In 2009, the Special Rapporteur focused on the prevalence of child abuse images in the online environment (HRC, 2009a). The report reinforces many of the recommendations set out by the previous Special Rapporteur and those produced by World Congresses on CSEC. Significant differences in the definition of a "child" and "child pornography" were seen as hampering law enforcement efforts in prosecuting offenders. Some countries regarded the age of consent to sexual activity as defining the boundary between child pornography and those which were not (ibid., 2009a: paragraph 55). A number of countries did not have legislation that addressed virtual pornography or did not distinguish between erotica and child pornography (ibid., 2009a: 56–7). There are obvious limits to these fact-finding missions. In a report submitted to the HRC, the Special

Rapporteur informed the Government of India about some serious allegations surrounding child trafficking and police involvement in undermining the investigation and prosecution of offenders (HRC, 2009b: 40–9). Unfortunately, the Government of India did not provide a response to the allegations (ibid.). These reports, it should be said, are invaluable both in terms of raising public awareness to the various forms of CSEC and in appealing to the collective interests of States in dealing with the problem at the domestic and international level.

Optional Protocol on the sale of children, child prostitution and child pornography

The Optional Protocol is relevant to establishing standards and principles, particularly in relation to curbing the creation, production, distribution and consumption of illegal child abuse content. On 25 May 2000, at the 54th session of the General Assembly of the UN, the Optional Protocol was adopted and opened for signature by any State that was a party to the Convention or had signed it. The use of children for commercial sexual activity and abuse has long attracted condemnation from society (O'Connell *et al.*, 2001). It is true that Articles 32 and 33 of the UNCRC reflect the consensus that children should be provided protection from particular forms of commercial and sexual exploitative activities. There are some important qualifications, two which can be highlighted here. The inclusion of minimum age requirements for "economic exploitation and from performing any work that is likely to be hazardous or to interfere with the child's education, or to be harmful to the child's health or physical, mental, spiritual, moral or social development" can exclude a number of children and activities. Additionally, ascertaining a State's full compliance with both the wording and the spirit of the obligations assumed under the Convention is not a straightforward process as it may involve traversing into areas of social and economic policy (Article 32(2)).

Like the UNCRC, accession to the Optional Protocol illustrates yet again the growing recognition by many States of their ongoing role and responsibility towards protecting children and promoting their rights. The practical significance of subscribing to this instrument can be stated briefly. Ratification of the Optional Protocol helps States clarify the types of conduct that can be made the subject of criminal sanctions and identify applicable substantive and procedural standards for governance. For example, the Optional Protocol attempts to overcome the uncertainties surrounding the types and forms of child sexual exploitation that can legitimately be made the subject of a State's obligations in this area of child protection by identifying cases where public intervention is warranted. Any "act or transaction whereby a child is transferred by any person or group of persons to another for remuneration or any other consideration" will be prohibited (Article

2(a)). "Child prostitution" is defined as the use of a child in sexual activities for remuneration or any other form of consideration (Article 2(c)). Arguably, "sex tourism" would be covered, particularly where there is a commercial aspect to the supply of children to travellers from overseas for sexual activity. Signatories under the Optional Protocol undertake to pass criminal laws which prohibit acts relating to the representation of a child engaged in real or simulated sexual activities or any representation of the sexual parts of a child for primarily sexual purposes (Articles 3(1)(c) and 2). States which sign the Optional Protocol are also expected to undertake all necessary steps towards strengthening international cooperation and implementing measures to investigate, prosecute and punish offenders (Article 10). The engagement of the CRC, as noted previously, in respect of States' implementation of the Optional Protocol is designed to provide assurances that proper reporting mechanisms are in place, that compliance is given priority by States and that any emerging issues and difficulties are addressed in a timely manner. In its report on the 48th session, the CRC noted that it had received 43 initial reports under the Optional Protocol (CRC, 2009: paragraphs 14–22). In considering the initial report from the United States with regard to the Optional Protocol, the CRC acknowledged the contribution made by the Innocence Lost Initiative in combating child prostitution in the country (CRC, 2009: 47). Other measures regarded by the CRC as good practice included the enactment of the Trafficking Victims Protection Act 2000 (which enhanced the investigation and prosecution of individuals engaged in child sexual exploitation) and its re-authorisations in 2003 and 2005, the PROTECT Act of 2003, which expanded its extraterritorial criminal jurisdiction to prosecute State party's citizens committing sex crimes against children abroad and the Adam Walsh Child Protection and Safety Act, passed in 2006, which increased penalties for child sex offenders and eliminated the statutes of limitations for criminal offences against children. These measures adopted by the United States, more generally, can also be regarded as examples of timely and proportionate governance responses towards the practice of CSEC. Interestingly, the CRC also recommended in its report that the United States needed to better target its resources towards child trafficking and collection of data (King, 2008). The CRC was particularly "concerned that a focus on sale of children, child prostitution and child pornography is still lacking" (ibid: 50). This is an aspect that was also noted by the Special Rapporteur following a fact-finding mission to the United States in 2010 (HRC, 2011). Various stakeholders represented to the Special Rapporteur that "commercial sexual exploitation is a highly profitable industry, coupled with a low risk of conviction for abusers, and there is a pool of vulnerable children at risk of being used in such practices" (ibid., 2011: paragraph 12). Finally, another example of the standard setting outcomes in CRC engagement with States can be seen in its consideration of the report submitted by Korea. The CRC reported that the strategies for combating CST were hampered by the lack of a coherent plan and adequate funding (CRC, 2009). The State was encouraged to work closely in partnership with the tourism industry, NGOs and civil society organisations (ibid., 2009: 63). It was also observed by the CRC that there were inadequate steps taken by the State in raising the awareness of the general public and engaging with children in relation to their awareness and understanding of the risks posed by the Internet and other mobile communication technologies (ibid.).

To conclude, it suffices to acknowledge the extent of the obligations States voluntarily assume by subscribing to international obligations like those in the Optional Protocol and UNCRC and their willingness to engage with the CRC in adapting their legal and social infrastructures accordingly.

Other UN Agencies and organisations

By way of completeness, two other contributions from the UN should also be mentioned. The UN Educational, Scientific and Cultural Organization (UNESCO) is an agency which promotes collaboration among nations through education, culture, sciences and communication. It does not undertake projects which are overseen by the CRC but it has an indirect impact through educational programmes aimed at enhancing children's media and ICT literacy skills. This subject will be covered in more detail in a later chapter. UNESCO now collaborates with the International Telecommunications Union and the UNDP. On 21 December 2001, the UN General Assembly adopted the resolution (A/RES/56/183) which endorsed the organisation of the WSIS. UNESCO has hosted an Expert Meeting on *Sexual Abuse of Children, Child Pornography and Paedophilia on the Internet* in 1999 and shortly thereafter, on 20 September 2005, an awareness-raising round table on "Safety of children on the Internet" was organised jointly by the Russian Federation's National Committee for UNESCO's Information for All Program and Microsoft Corporation Russia and CIS branch. These meeting opportunities have two particular benefits. First, the events provide an important mechanism for raising public awareness of this area of child protection policymaking. Second, these communication platforms enable stakeholders from civil society and the private sector to exchange ideas and develop collaborative partnerships and strategies with each other.

Second, the UNICEF, ECPAT, the NGO Group for the Convention on the Rights of the Child together with the Government of Brazil recently launched the WC III in Rio de Janeiro on 25–28 November 2010. The aim of this conference was to provide delegates with an opportunity to review the progress made since the previous Congress in dealing with all forms of sexual exploitation and the emerging governance challenges facing stakeholders. More generally, the World Congress provides a platform where the private and public sector, together with representatives from governments and law enforcement, review their strategies for promoting international collaboration aimed at protecting children from sexual exploitation and abuse. Each World Congress has made some notable contributions towards the debates on online child safety governance. For example, the 1996 First World Congress against CSEC, which was held in Stockholm, brought to the attention of governments the scale and organised nature of CSEC (Newell, 2008). This Congress has been regarded as "seminal in breaking the taboo of CSEC and the silence permeating CSEC" (Muntarbhorn, 2001). At the Stockholm Congress, the delegates issued a declaration and an agenda for action, signalling both their commitment to the principles enshrined in the UNCRC and their resolve in strengthening international commitment in creating appropriate regulatory mechanisms to "put an end to the commercial sexual exploitation of children worldwide" (CSEC World Congress, 1996: paragraph 13). Following the meeting in Stockholm, the CRC participated in the open-ended working group looking at various aspects of the draft Optional Protocols (CRC, 1996). At least 34 governments had produced national strategies for dealing with CSEC with a further 26 in the process of developing national action plans (NGO Group, 2001). The Second World Congress in 2001 was held in Yokohama. At this Congress, delegates from more than 134 countries were presented with national strategies for combating child sexual abuse from 100 governments. The report from the General Rapporteur – Professor Vitit Muntarbhorn – noted the growth in the CSEC industry, in particular the national and transnational trafficking of children for sexual purposes (Muntarbhorn, 2001). The Stockholm and Yokohama Congresses affirmed the role and value of the UNCRC. Additionally, the Yokohama Congress reiterated many of the commitments and action plans highlighted in Stockholm. Finally, the WC III in Brazil identified five themes, which also highlights the multi-dimensional aspects of child sexual abuse: new dimensions of sexual exploitation; legal and enforcement; inter-sectoral policies; the private sector and corporate social responsibility and international cooperation. Following the extensive review of national and international responses to CSEC in the World Congress, the participants were unanimous in their call for governments to adopt and enforce national laws protecting children from commercial sexual exploitation (ECPAT, 2009). Some of the principal recommendations include the development of a model law and guidance for national governments, the need for States to make greater use of the General Comments by the CRC on all forms of child sexual exploitation and related abuse, the value derived from involving children in the governance process, the need to encourage countries to ratify the various international instruments in this field and efforts to be made in reducing the number of reservations made on ratification and developing mechanisms for securing compliance. In essence, the central message appears to be that States need to be responsive to the risks facing children in society, particularly from technology-mediated sexual exploitation and abuse. The involvement of the FCACP at the WC III Congress is significant particularly as the "commercial exploitation of children" industry is heavily reliant on financial institutions, credit card payment and merchant third-party payment companies for sustaining its economic and commercial viability (Hecht, 2008: 98).

Finally, to conclude this section regarding the efforts made by the UN in this area, a brief mention should be made of the UN Secretary-General's 2006 *Study on Violence against Children*. The study undertakes a systematic approach in examining the scale of violence suffered by children in society. The decision to undertake the study can be traced back to work commenced by the CRC during 2000 and 2001 (CRC, 2000, 2001a,b). During the general discussion days, which focused on the violence suffered by children in society generally, the Committee recommended that the Secretary-General be requested by the UN General Assembly to conduct an in-depth global study on violence against children. The Committee emphasised that the study

> should lead to the development of strategies aimed at effectively preventing and combating all forms of violence against children, outlining steps to be taken at the international level and by States to provide effective prevention, protection, intervention, treatment, recovery and reintegration. (UN Secretary General, 2001)

Some of the findings in the study resonate with the issues covered in this book. First, that the Internet and communication technologies increased children's exposure to risk of sexual exploitation and abuse from peers and adults (UN Secretary General, 2006: paragraph 80). Second, that new technologies make "sex tourism" both accessible and affordable to an unprecedented audience in a scale and level never encountered (UN Secretary General, 2006: paragraph 77). Third, that the mass media contributes to children's exposure to risks of sexual exploitation since they "sometimes portray as normal or glorify violence, including violence against children, in print and visual media including television programmes, films and video games" (UN Secretary General, 2006: paragraph 80). The Secretary-General recommended that countries continue in their efforts to combat the use of the Internet and communication technologies in the sexual exploitation and abuse of children and peer victimisation, engage parents, carers and children in media literacy and awareness-raising initiatives, encourage industry to promote design and standard setting efforts for child protection and increase the deterrence and punitive role of criminal laws (ibid., 2006: paragraph 114).

The above account of the role of the UN demonstrates the enormity of the online child safety governance challenge and the critical need for a MSIG strategy in responding to the many risks and threats encountered by children. It is not unreasonable to conclude that the UN regards its role as elevating the need for policy responses in promoting child welfare and development. Its institutional processes and agencies continue to encourage and support governments in their efforts to strengthen and promote children's rights. Within the context of online child safety policymaking, the EU and the Council of Europe have been instrumental in efforts to mainstream children's rights and child protection matters. A summary of these efforts will now be provided.

The European Union

The Treaty of Lisbon requires the EU to promote policies and measures which protect the rights of the child. It will be recalled that children's rights are already part of the EU discourse on human rights (e.g. Article 24 of the Charter of Fundamental Rights of the EU). It remains to be seen how the obligation to respect children's rights under the Charter will extend to children's interaction with the Internet in view of the fact that the 27 EU countries are also signatories to the UNCRC. There is no disguising the fact that in the post-Lisbon constitutional landscape, child welfare and development will continue to be at the forefront of the "Europe 2020" strategy (European Commission, 2010b). The European Commission (Commission) has provided leadership in the area of online child safety governance in terms of both formulating policies and ensuring their widespread acceptance and implementation by Member States. In this regard, particular priority continues to be given to the use of legal instruments to enforce child safety norms, requiring all Member States to create appropriate regulatory and incentive frameworks which promote a culture of safe and responsible use of Web 2.0 technologies and impressing on all stakeholders to ensure that their measures and policies continue to be relevant.

The EU governance landscape comprises a patchwork of policy communications, Directives, Conventions, national legislation, industry practices and awareness-raising initiatives (European Parliament, 2009). What follows is a brief account of the standard setting policies and measures. We can begin by noting that the trend towards establishing a coherent governance framework, for example, can be located in the emphasis placed by the Commission in engaging all stakeholders, at varying levels of involvement, with the task of promoting and embedding safe and responsible Internet use and principles. The SIP was developed to address the unique challenges posed by the Internet and communication technologies for Member States' ability to enforce laws regulating illegal and harmful content (European Commission, 1996b,c). A number of measures relevant to enhancing the safety of children have been implemented across Member States – blocking and filtering solutions, interception strategies and establishment of hotlines. Many of these measures also mirror those adopted by policymakers in other jurisdictions (ITU, 2009b, 2010b). The Green Paper issued by the

Commission also mapped some nascent ideas regarding the involvement of the private sector in the SIP (European Commission, 1996c). The standard setting agenda, at least with regard to enhancing children's safety, can also be seen in the development of programmes which broadened the strategies and measures used to enhance safety with the support of the ICT, broadcasting and telecommunications industry. The priority for the EU even to this day appears to be to encourage greater cooperation amongst all stakeholders, promote sharing of best practices and create incentives for self-regulation. The Commission's initiatives in respect of child safety over the past decade could be viewed as an attempt to achieve two goals – first, to encourage innovation in the audiovisual and information services sector; and, second, to reassure parents and children that media and services can be accessed and utilised without fear of exposure to illegal or harmful content. From the accounts provided above, the SIP can be regarded as providing an institutional setting for the MSIG framework at the EU level whereby the obligations and responsibilities are allocated to various stakeholders, with the Commission and Member States assuming the role as "risk managers" (Eurobarometer, 2006, 2007, 2008). The industry rather than the State is as a consequence regarded as having an important role in developing technological and content monitoring solutions relating to blocking and filtering child pornography and hate content (King, 2009). The overarching SIP framework enables policymakers to keep pace with emerging threats posed to children. It was felt that since the first Action Plan, the strategies for promoting Internet safety had to continuously respond to the governance issues raised by the growing convergence between social media and communication platforms. Between 1999 and 2004, the rapid growth in the digital economy and spread of communication technologies led to a reassessment of the strategies needed to achieve the objectives of the Safer Internet Plus Programme (European Commission, 2009a). In its proposal, the Commission noted that the emergence of broadband and growing processing power and storage capacity of computers and the ready availability of mobile computing would contribute to increased demand and supply of illegal content (European Commission, 2004). The Safer Internet Plus Programme was extended to include mobile and broadband content accessed through different online technologies, like chat rooms, instant messages, P2P technologies and online games (European Commission, 2006b, 2008). The objectives of the Safer Internet Plus Programme have not altered in any fundamental respect; the focus remains on combating illegal and inappropriate/harmful content, promoting a safer environment and raising public awareness (European Commission, 2010e; EU SIP, 2009). The European Parliament's contribution to the online child safety governance initiative should also be acknowledged (European Parliament, 2004). During the deliberations the European Parliament urged those implementing the Safer Internet Plus Programme to direct their regulatory measures towards developing design and information literacy solutions (European Parliament, 2009). The inclusion of software and product manufacturers in child safety governance has always been regarded as a necessary governance strategy; the industry was encouraged to provide users with all relevant information (i.e. rating systems and quality labels) so that children, parents and educators could make informed decisions on how best to manage online risks (Eurobarometer, 2007). Additionally, greater emphasis has been placed in engaging sector-specific industries as part of the online safety standard setting agenda (European Parliament and Council, 2006).

The emerging governance strategy is both reflexive and fluid and is very much evident in the general thrust of the recommendations and Directives passed in the EU and the activities pursued under the two SIPs. The impetus driving the child-centred policies, particularly the Safer Internet 2009–13 programme and the Proposed Directive, reflects an evolving understanding of the benefits of co-regulation, which involves the participation of all stakeholders approaching common goals in safeguarding children, underpinned by established standards and principles (European Commission, 2011e). This understanding can also be found in the 2006 Communication, which stressed that EU's strategies for children corresponded with the EU's and its Member States' commitments concluded at regional and international levels, including the ECHR, the UNCRC and its Optional Protocols and the UN Millennium Development Declaration (European Commission, 2006a). The Commission has now published its Action Plan that reiterates its continued commitment towards promoting and strengthening children's rights (European Commission, 2011b; *cf.* Eurochild, 2011). This is again another example of regional governance strategies mirroring the standards and principles set out in instruments like the UNCRC. Article 3(5) of the Lisbon Treaty, for example, whilst emphasising the values of respect and dignity makes clear that the protection of human rights, in particular the rights of the child, is to be promoted by the EU. The revised Treaty on the Functioning of the European Union now vests in the European Parliament and the European Council powers to adopt measures combating child sexual abuse and exploitation (European Commission, 2011b: 10–11).

The specific references in the Commission's *Agenda for the Rights of the Child* to protecting children from all forms of violence reflect the standard setting value of provisions in the UNCRC, in particular Article 19, which requires signatories to the Convention to promote the right of the child to be free from the risk of violence in a variety of settings – homes, schools and public places. The importance attached to harmonisation and the need to maintain existing regulatory frameworks under review reflect the growing convergence in the standard setting agenda in national, regional and supranational initiatives. An example of this can be seen in the Proposed Directive, which was issued by the European Commission in 2010 (European Commission, 2010e). The policymaking efforts appear to have been influenced by some of the issues identified in previous chapters, in particular concerns raised with regard to the reluctance of victims to report sexual abuse, the frustration expressed by law enforcement in investigating, prosecuting and punishing those engaged in child sexual exploitation and abuse, the barriers posed by jurisdictional principles like double criminality and double jeopardy, the inconsistencies in legal definitions of some of the more serious sexual offences and the prevalence of sex tourism. Accordingly, the implementation of the provisions in the Proposed Directive should address regulatory shortcomings in five main areas, which will only be summarised here. First, all serious forms of child sexual abuse and exploitation not covered by EU legislation would now be criminalised. These are "child sexual abuse", "sexual exploitation", "child pornography", and "solicitation of children for sexual purposes". A "child" is said to be any one below the age of 18 but Member States can reduce the age when children can be deemed to consent to sexual activity. "Child pornography" will now cover not only children below the age of 18 years but also any material that visually depicts "any person appearing to be a child, or realistic images of a non-existent child, engaged in real or simulated sexually explicit conduct". It is not without significance that the definition of child pornography also extends to *any* depiction for primarily sexual purposes of the sexual organs of a child, or of any person appearing to be a child or of realistic images of a non-existent child, which would also be deemed to be "child pornography". Article 4 will now regulate non-visual depiction of children. Member States are also required to criminalise the production, distribution, dissemination or transmission of child pornography. The act of offering, supplying or making available child pornography is to be treated as an offence. Those who knowingly obtain access to child pornography by any information system would also be prosecuted for child pornography offences. "Child prostitution" is also identified as a serious form of sexual exploitation under Article 3. The term is understood as meaning the use of a child for sexual activity where money or other form of consideration is given or promised in exchange for the child's sexual services. An offence will be committed where a person recruits or coerces a child into prostitution or engages in sexual activities with a child, where recourse is made to child prostitution. It is no defence to a charge for committing an offence of child prostitution for the accused to show that the consideration or promise was made to a third party rather than to the child. Those profiting from or exploiting a child for prostitution would also be committing an offence. Article 3 also regards recruiting or coercing a child to engage in pornographic performances as a form of sexual exploitation. A "pornographic performance" means an exhibition in front of a live audience, which can be either online or offline. The act of recruiting or coercing a child to engage in real or simulated sexually explicit conduct or live exhibitions of the sexual organs of a child for primarily sexual purposes are to be treated as crimes. The Article also regards those knowingly attending pornographic performances involving the participation of children as committing a criminal offence. These provisions are likely to be relevant in dealing with the increased use of live web streaming by the commercial and sexual exploitation of children industry. There are two limbs to Article 6. First, acts which are deemed to be abetting, aiding or inciting the offences under Articles 2–5 will be criminalised. Attempts to commit the offences in Articles 2–4 are also criminal offences. Article 6(3) now expressly deals with those engaged in the practice of facilitating the travel of nationals from Member States to engage in activities covered by Articles 2–5; the activities to be criminalised include

(a) the dissemination of materials advertising the opportunity to commit any of the offences referred to in Articles 2 to 5;
(b) the organisation of travel arrangements with the purpose of committing any of the offences referred to in Articles 2 to 5.

Second, transborder investigation and collection of evidence for prosecution will be simplified, particularly where the commission of the offence takes place in multiple jurisdictions. Under Article 12(1) decisions to commence an investigation into an alleged child sexual offence need not now be based on a report or an accusation made by the victim. The interests of the victim are further highlighted in Articles 14 and 15. NGOs have long urged governments and law enforcement to consider the interests of child victims of horrific sexual exploitation, and, more importantly, the necessity of requiring an investigation or prosecution to be dependent on a complaint being made by the victim (Quayle *et al.*, 2008: 90–1). Even if the victim has withdrawn her statements, it is conceivable that permitting investigation or prosecution would serve the public interest if sufficient evidence was available to convict the accused. At the last resort, use could be made of video testimony from the child, subject to the usual safeguards on hearsay and rules on admissibility. Article 12(3) also requires Member States to clarify the scope of the confidentiality rules imposed by the law on professions who have contact with children that may prevent them from reporting suspected child protection offences to the appropriate authority. One question that needs to be considered is whether there is any real or significant difference between Article 12(3) and (4) – since they both appear to appeal to an individual's civic and moral obligation to report suspected child offences. It should be noted that some legislatures outside the EU have already implemented mandatory reporting of child pornography obligations. For example, the House Bill 2463 in Oregon, US, now requires processors of photographic images and computer technicians to report child pornography. In 2009, Ontario enacted a new Child Pornography Reporting Act, which makes it a criminal offence not to report suspected child pornography. Third, EU nationals who travel abroad to commit sexual offences against children will now be subject to national extraterritorial criminal jurisdiction. In the previous chapter we examined some of the rules on extraterritorial criminal jurisdiction in Australia, Canada and the United States. Article 13 aims to resolve a number of procedural and jurisdictional obstacles addressed in Chapter 4. There is a clear recognition amongst EU policymakers that Member States can and should avail themselves of extraterritorial criminal jurisdiction in cases where there are multi-jurisdictional elements. Article 13(2) attempts to remove the possible issue of "where" the crime is deemed to have been committed when the Internet or other communication devices are used in CSEC. Where a national from a Member State commits a child sexual abuse offence in another country, the application of its extraterritorial criminal jurisdiction should not be made conditional on the acts being a criminal offence at the place where they were deemed to have taken place (Article 13(3)). The removal of the double criminality rule is also consistent with Article 4 of the Optional Protocol. In relation to crimes, where organised gangs are involved, Member States are encouraged to cooperate with the aim of prosecuting the accused in one Member State if possible. Where there is uncertainty or disagreement about the best course to take, Member States are advised to refer to the "Eurojust Guidelines" or any instrument or mechanism within the EU in order to facilitate cooperation between their judicial authorities and promote better coordination of actions. The Article sets out some factors which should inform the decision-making process: the nationality of the accused, the place where the crimes or offences were committed, the origin of the victims and the place where the accused was discovered or arrested. Fourth, victims' interests will now be accommodated to ensure that they do not suffer additional stress and trauma in having to give evidence in criminal proceedings. Article 15 requires Member States to put in place processes which centre on the victim's best interests. For example, following a report or complaint, experts will now be under an obligation to conduct the interviews expeditiously. As far as possible, the interview should be conducted in premises designed or adapted for this purpose. An adult or legal representative, preferably chosen by the child, should accompany the child victim. The "Eurojust Guidelines" recommends that in matters relating to child protection, reference should be made to the principles in the UNCRC and CPC Convention (e.g. General Comment 12 CRC/C/GC/12; General Comment 13 CRC/C/GC/13). Of particular relevance to policymakers in Member States in this context is the recommendation made by the HRC that child-sensitive community-based and legal mechanisms be adopted (HRC, 2011: 5). Fifth, Article 16 addresses the problem of recidivism by restricting offenders from accessing the Internet. Individuals convicted of serious child sexual offences identified in the Proposed Directive will now be subject to an assessment of the risks to re-offending or dangers they may pose to society. In a press release, leading NGOs indicated their approval of the Proposed Directive:

The Commission's proposal brings the existing legislation closer in line with the UN Convention on the Rights of the Child (UNCRC) and the Council of Europe's Convention on the Protection of children against sexual exploitation and sexual abuse. (NSPCC, 2009)

One provision that remains to be addressed is Article 21, which deals with content regulation mechanisms. This Article as presently drafted is hardly a model of clarity. The Explanatory Note states, however, that where Member States are unable to remove the webpages they need only take the necessary measures, which can include non-legislative steps. Countries like Belgium, Finland, Ireland and the United Kingdom, for example, adopt a voluntary filtering scheme. With regard to the United Kingdom, reports from the public regarding websites hosting child abuse content are passed to the IWF. If the IWF views the content as illegal, it makes a request to the ISP to have the page blocked to users in the United Kingdom. There are judicial safeguards built into the orders granted to block websites suspected of hosting or disseminating child pornography. Attempts in the United States to impose a mandatory filtering or blocking obligation have been challenged on constitutional grounds. In Australia, there is a co-regulatory model governing filtering and blocking. Schedule 5 of the Broadcasting Services Act 1992 and the Internet Industry Codes of Practice define the measures ISPs are expected to implement to protect the general public from illegal content. There is an "opt-in" filtering framework. ACMA can require a content service provider or ISP to remove or block access to prohibited content. It is worth recalling that the previous Council Framework Decision regarded Member States as having direct responsibility for implementing substantive and procedural rules regarding access to illegal content (Council of the European Union, 2004b). No reference was made to the obligations of Member States for direct intervention in blocking illegal content like child pornography. The Working Party on Substantive Criminal Law has previously called for a proportionate response on this issue (Council of the European Union, 2001: 3). At the first Working Group meeting, a number of Member States expressed reservations regarding their obligation to impose blocking measures. As a result of the meeting, the European Parliament proposed an amendment to the Council text which attempts to diffuse some of the political and ideological controversy (EDRI, 2011). Reference should also be made to the observation made by Advocate General Cruz Villalón in *Scarlet Extended v Société belge des auteurs compositeurs et éditeurs* (Sabam) (2011) that the deployment of mandatory filtering measures could arguably encroach into users' expectation of privacy to their communications and protection of personal data which are protected under the Charter of Fundamental Rights. This aside, the SIP aims to increase communities' and stakeholders' understanding and awareness of their responsibilities for enhancing children's online safety. Two examples can be provided. First, the Safer Internet Forum, for example, is an annual conference organised under the SIP. Some of the topics covered in the annual conference over the years included promoting online safety in schools, addressing the impact of convergence and online sexual abuse, sharing industry practices relating to the use of labelling and age-verification tools and developing safety strategies on social network sites. Second, the EU has continued to support the Safer Internet Day campaign since its inception in 2004. This campaign is seen as an awareness raising opportunity for children, parents, educators and society generally (INSAFE, 2009, EU SIP, 2009). Many of the aims to be achieved by promoting these initiatives complement other measures developed by the EU (e.g. promoting safer use of online technologies, increasing public awareness of risks and precautions and reducing the amount of illegal content being distributed online). The recent SIP efforts include targeting potentially harmful conduct like peer victimisation and "grooming". Finally, policymakers also recognise that children and their parents should be integrated into the MSIG framework. Media literacy and education campaigns are increasingly directed at assisting these groups of individuals (see later discussion on media literacy in Chapter 7).

Council of Europe

The Council of Europe has 47 member countries and is based in Strasbourg. Its primary mission is to develop and promote the rule of law throughout Europe. It has passed a number of standard setting instruments which have direct relevance for child protection. The ECHR, which led to the establishment of the European Court of Human Rights, allows individuals to apply to this Court where their fundamental rights have been violated. The European Social Charter (ESC) is another instrument aimed at securing an individual's social and economic rights. There is a monitoring body, known as the European Committee on Social Rights, which ensures that States comply with the ESC. The Committee of Ministers and the Parliamentary Assembly are vested with statutory powers and have over the years adopted a number of recommendations and resolutions regarding children's rights. These instruments do not have binding force but they are persuasive and are relied upon when developing policies in the States. Finally, accession to the Conventions is not limited to Member States. Requests for accession to the Council of Europe Conventions are also received by States outside the European Community. In the remainder of the section a brief account will be provided of two main Conventions, with particular emphasis on their standard setting significance for enhancing the safety of children in the online environment.

Council of Europe Convention on the Protection of Children against Sexual Exploitation and Sexual Abuse CETS No. 201

The Treaty opened for signature on 25 October 2007. It is open to all Member States, non-Member States, by the EU, and for accession by other non-Member States. The CPC Convention came into force on 1 July 2010. Thirty-two countries have signed the CPC Convention and 7 have ratified it. The European Commission has described the CPC Convention as constituting the "highest international standard for protecting children against sexual abuse and exploitation to date", with the Optional Protocol as the main international standard on a global scale (European Commission, 2010e). Subscribers to the CPC Convention are expected to adhere to three of its main objectives. First, to prevent and combat sexual exploitation and sexual abuse of children. Second, to protect the rights of child victims of sexual exploitation and sexual abuse. Third, to promote national and international cooperation against sexual exploitation and sexual abuse of children. These commitments again indicate the widespread acceptance by many signatories of the need to prioritise child protection and develop (and review) strategies for enhancing their safety. The CPC Convention covers various forms of child sexual abuse and this instrument is the culmination of its three-year programme *Building a Europe for and with Children*. The Council's Children's Strategy for 2009–11 is consistent with the fundamental values and principles of the CPC Convention, with one of its goals being to eradicate all forms of violence against children.[2] There are a number of features in the CPC Convention that mirror the issues previously discussed in the Proposed Directive, the UNCRC and the Optional Protocols. Chapter II, for example, deals with measures that aim to prevent all forms of sexual exploitation and sexual abuse of children. States are regarded as having a critical role in implementing the necessary legislative or other measures. These can include raising the safety and media literacy levels of the public, parents, educators, carers and children. The obligation to safeguard children also extends to the responsibility of the State for dealing with recidivism by repeat and potential offenders. The CPC Convention advocates a MSIG approach. Chapter III emphasises the value of involving professionals from across the public and private sector to promote information sharing and exchange at national and regional level (i.e. education sector, health sector, social services law enforcement and judicial authorities). According to the Explanatory Note issued by the Council, it is hoped that the offences set out in Articles 18–23 will promote greater harmonisation of laws amongst signatories and prevent criminals from engaging in sexual activity with children in jurisdictions, which may have lenient sentences or rules. Additionally, increased harmonisation is expected to reduce problems that may be posed by the principle of dual criminality and promote mutual assistance efforts between Member States. Article 20 deals with the offence of child pornography. The Explanatory Note shows that the drafters of the CPC Convention recognise the increasing ways technology can be used to exploit and victimise children. For example, the phrase "sexually explicit conduct" extends to real or simulated acts in relation to all forms of sexual activity. States can also reserve the right not to criminalise the conduct identified in paragraph 1.a and e to the production and possession of pornographic material, which consists *exclusively* of simulated representations or *realistic images* of a non-existent child. Interestingly, the exemption also extends to user-generated content created by children and possessed by them, but only where it is made with their consent and used solely for their own private use. The latter exception is a reference to the growing practice of sexting amongst children and young adolescents. The reservation in the case of the former is more controversial on the grounds that this exception may be falling below the standards previously set out in the Proposed Directive, which was overwhelmingly endorsed by leading NGOs. Article 25 and Chapter VI contains many of the approaches to jurisdiction, investigation, treatment of victims and prosecution advocated in the Proposed Directive. Chapter IX deals with provisions aiming to promote and enhance international cooperation. In cases where Member States do not have mutual assistance treaty arrangements or are in the process of negotiating agreements, Article 38, paragraph 3, allows for requests for assistance and extradition to be dealt with promptly. It should be noted that the Council of Europe has also made available regulatory instruments that serve the purpose of expediting the investigatory and information sharing objectives of law enforcement. The European Convention on Extradition (ETS 24), the European Convention on Mutual Assistance in Criminal Matters (ETS 30) and the two Additional Protocols to Extradition and Mutual Assistance serve as a reminder that timely intervention is critical to safeguarding potential victims and prosecuting offenders.

Convention on Cybercrime CETS No. 185

The Convention on Cybercrime came into force in 2004 and is regarded as an important instrument for promoting international cooperation, particularly in relation to combating sexual exploitation and abuse of children. The Cybercrime Convention can be seen as another governance response to the difficulties faced by national legal systems in policing the Internet and prosecuting criminal activity mediated through technology (Putnam/Elliott (2001)). A number of countries that signed the Cybercrime Convention have also drafted national legislation reflecting their commitments assumed under this instrument. In a working paper prepared for the UN Secretariat it was noted that the Cybercrime Convention provides a "set of principles for developing a legal framework for international cooperation in cybercrime investigations" (UN Secretariat, 2010). As noted previously, the Cybercrime Convention has provisions dealing with the offence of child pornography and sets out the procedural aspects of investigating and prosecuting individuals and organisations for child pornography (Gercke, 2006). Article 9 criminalises the exploitative activities discussed previously (e.g. producing, offering, distributing and possession). To ensure that the Cybercrime Convention obtains support from as broad a range of States with their own political and cultural needs, Article 9 permits each Party a right not to apply, in whole or in part, paragraphs 1, sub-paragraphs d. and e, and 2, sub-paragraphs b. and c. Like Article 9, Chapters II and III aim to facilitate greater harmonisation and cooperation between Parties. For example, Chapter II aims to promote standard setting processes involving the collection, preservation and presentation of digital evidence. Chapter III provides a framework for cooperation in the form of mutual assistance and extradition requests. To ensure consistency in the approach adopted in other Council of Europe treaties, Chapter IV of the Cybercrime Convention contains clauses which mirror many of the standard provisions found in those agreements. It will be observed that the Convention does not deal with other content-related offences like xenophobic or racist material (Gercke, 2009). The Council of Europe subsequently drafted the First Additional Protocol to the Convention on Cybercrime. In the Explanatory Report to this Protocol, it was pointed out that some countries would not have subscribed to the Convention, in view of the free speech implications resulting from the criminalisation of racist propaganda content.[3] There is no doubt that the Convention continues to play an important role in promoting a global strategic response towards eradicating the commercial and sexual exploitation of children. The provisions provide a framework that defines core principles which can inform national policymaking and legislative activity (Gercke, 2008; Callanan *et al.*, 2008).

A key governance question remains: can we do better? Despite the various global initiatives in promoting international cooperation and harmonisation, the scale of criminality does not appear to be receding (ECPAT, 2005). It may be thought if more countries subscribed to the Cybercrime Convention and other treaties seeking to protect children from sexual harm and abuse, that the scale and volume of the threats could be better managed. As discussed previously, many countries have yet to ratify the Cybercrime Convention. Others do not have the resources to implement and monitor the effectiveness of their laws (UN Secretariat, 2010: paragraph 33). Whether the challenges facing the continued role and effectiveness of the Cybercrime Convention could be overcome through the enactment of a Global Cybercrime Treaty is an issue that was noted in the previous chapter (UN Secretariat, 2010: ibid.). More importantly, the standard setting instruments that currently exist already introduce significant improvements into the way commercial and sexual offences are now being investigated and prosecuted. The Conventions and instruments identified in this and preceding chapters show the widespread recognition by States of the importance of enacting legislation, which sets out the conduct to be prohibited and the obligations of all stakeholders to minimise children's exposure to the risks of technology-enabled crimes.

Conclusion

The developments highlighted in this chapter illustrate the distinctive nature of online child safety governance, with its decentralised contexts and processes involving a number of online service providers, the ICT industry and the telecommunications sector coordinating their activities and collaborating with each other. It is not uncommon to find policymakers in various countries, regional and international forums developing policies and strategies aimed at coordinating governance efforts on a range of issues and policies (e.g. Internet and mobile phone use, network and access filtering and use of hotlines) (ACMA, 2009a,b). Online safety and security is also becoming an area of national policy. Reference has already been made to reports commissioned by governments in the United Kingdom, Australia and the United States on online child safety. Safety issues are now an important item on the Internet Governance Forum, convened at the UN Summit on the Information Society (WSIS) in Tunis (November 2005). The *Declaration of Principles Building the Information Society: A global challenge in the New Millennium* reiterates the global commitment to safeguarding children (WSIS, 2003: paragraphs 11 and 59). These expressions of policy intent illustrate some of the ways children's rights norms and the recommendations in the UN *Study on Violence against Children* help articulate the principles and values informing the role and functions of various stakeholders within the MSIG framework (Klein, 2004). The regulatory developments and initiatives promoted in the EU reflect a new commitment and confidence in its ability to forge partnerships and create incentives for all stakeholders to adopt the benchmark standards and principles provided by the UNCRC and the CPC Convention in particular. The governance strategies are very much in keeping with the thrust of the UN 2006 *Study on Violence against Children*, which is to safeguard children from all threats of violence. The need to ground policy responses on research, and increasing policymakers understanding of children and their parents/carers' actual use of technology is a welcome development. It is a development that has the endorsement of researchers and practitioners across the EU and the United States. One view of these developments is that online child safety governance is rightly regarded as a priority for national and international standard setting efforts (Gallagher, 2009). It may be somewhat harsh to suggest that a government's public pronouncements regarding its prioritisation of safeguarding children are nothing more than the rhetorical flourishes of self-serving bias (Maduro, 2007). That said, it would perhaps be more accurate to say that since 1999 considerable progress has been made in safeguarding children in the online environment. Even though many of the Conventions, treaties and policies are of a general nature, they do reflect a growing recognition that as Web 2.0 technologies become the primary medium for communication and interaction, the situation for children will worsen without timely and effective intervention (ITU, 2010b: 9). In the next chapter, we will consider some examples of how these instruments and legal standards provide an important framework for enhancing the safety of children in the online environment.

6
Online Child Safety, Civil Society and the Private Sector: Alternative Strategies

An overview

Whilst governments have an undoubted role to play in shaping child protection policy, increasingly, it is in the outcome of the interactions between governments, NGOs, voluntary organisations and industry where the tangible results of the policymaking debates and collaborations will emerge in homes, schools and communities (Dutton *et al.*, 2007). The question of how civil society, the private sector and the State respond to the transnational character of the threats facing children is a complex and challenging one (Giddens, 1990). It is not possible to do justice to the many issues raised by this question, nor is it possible to undertake a detailed examination of the role of NGOs and the industry in enhancing the safety of children at the domestic and regional level. That said, the neglect of these interactions in current online child safety policymaking justifies, at the very least, an attempt to explain their significance for MSIG (Falk, 1995; Grugel, 2003). Indeed, the increasing role of civil society in this area of child protection has contributed to the creation of a new climate for children's rights advocacy and development of collaborative transnational networks. To this end, the work of the UN and its related organisations, and the engagement of stakeholders in the three World Congresses and the SIP, demonstrates an important paradigm shift in the way transnational actors and civil society appear to assume responsibility for policing the online environment and enforcing child safety norms through the adoption of extra-legal strategies (ECPAT, 2009). Consequently, to understand online child safety governance, we cannot limit our focus to the efforts of law enforcement or legislation enacted by States. It is only by understanding the contributions made by non-State actors that we can gain some useful insights into the pivotal role of the MSIG strategy in enabling States to fulfil their national and international commitments towards children. Two questions will provide the focal point for this chapter. There is a particular need for everyone concerned in online child safety to have some understanding as to why NGOs, voluntary organisations and the private sector have increasingly become key actors in the online safety regulatory landscape. The second question relates to identifying the processes which enable children's rights principles and legal standards to become an integral part of the evolving MSIG framework. The chapter will begin with a brief account of the relationship between modernity, civil society and the State in relation to the protection of children from online sexual exploitation and abuse. It then integrates some of the insights offered by commentators like Ulrich Beck and Anthony Giddens, first introduced in Chapter 2, into the activities of some of the key international, regional and national organisations and explains their significance for the emerging MSIG model for safeguarding children in the online environment (Beck, 1992; Giddens, 1991). The final part of the discussion considers some of the self- and co-regulatory models of good governance being used to enhance the safety of children in the online environment. The chapter concludes with the observation that the MSIG model represents an apt example of reflexive modernisation (Ayres *et al.*, 1992). How we measure the effectiveness of this model will be an ongoing area of tension in online child safety policymaking (Eurochild, 2011).

Preliminary observations

There is at least at one level a noticeable desire amongst States and organisations to promote better rule making and governance in relation to children's exposure to potential risks and threats in the online environment. The policy reviews undertaken in the United Kingdom, Australia, the United States and Canada show an increasing willingness by States and international institutions to promote greater collaboration and cooperation amongst the various stakeholders (Hoffman, 2005). These developments may be explained in terms of neo-liberal approaches to governance; others who take a pragmatic outlook of transnational governance may be inclined to suggest that the rhetoric of good governance and efficient rule making is a reflection of the impact of globalisation on the ability of nation states to respond to domestic public policy issues in an effective and timely manner (Hann *et al.*, 1996: 1; Long *et al.*, 2009: 107–22). Even though States are seen as the primary political actors responsible for enacting regulations, it is generally acknowledged that their ability to secure compliance with rules and laws has diminished considerably over the past half century with the emergence of transnational non-State actors (Hall *et al.*, 2002). Some view the emergence of these transnational actors in global governance as an important aspect of democratisation (Bexell *et al.*, 2010; Benkler, 2006). Others are a little more circumspect and suggest that the diminution in the role of the State as perhaps tilting the balance in favour of the private sector and its economic interests. That said, the increasing role of civil society organisations in providing a countervailing force should not be underestimated (Schewick, 2010; Bexell *et al.*,

2010: 87; Beck, 2000; Baker *et al.*, 2004). Hoffman, whilst accepting that governance is a contested concept, regards the redistribution of the roles and responsibilities between the State, the private sector and civil society within the context of the Internet "as an open-ended, collective process of searching which aims to fill a global 'regulatory void' both conceptually and institutionally in a legitimate way" (Hoffman, 2005: 2). Notwithstanding these perspectives about governance, one thing is clear – the erosion of the boundaries between broadcasting, telecommunications and entertainment sectors poses us with some interesting insights into the way modernity brings into play non-State actors and institutional structures, processes and options for policymaking (Beck, 1997: 38; Golding, 2000; Porter, 2002).

Civil society, state and modernity

The capitalist framework for wealth creation and its international institutions provide an important backdrop to the way the Internet has now brought into the public spotlight the risks, threats and uncertainties surrounding children's exposure to social media and technology (Beck, 1992a,b). The opening up of online child safety policymaking to non-State actors is one example of how governance frameworks increasingly provide platforms for engagement with a wide range of stakeholders from the industry and civil society (Giddens, 1990). Like Giddens, we can regard these developments as indicative of a cultural attitude towards institutionalisation of the lifeworld. He uses the term "modernity" in a very specific sense, and refers to

> the institutions and modes of behaviour established first of all in post-feudal Europe, but which in the twentieth century increasingly have become world-historical in impact. (Giddens, 1991: 14–15)

This multi-faceted lifeworld consists of an array of actors, measures and policies at national, regional and supranational fora in addressing the risks faced by children's exposure to Web 2.0 technologies. The symbols of modernity are also very much in evidence: disintermediated interactions, the regulatory space becoming populated by the private sector and civil society, the dispersion of rule making amongst transnational institutions and actors at different fora (i.e. individualisation of risks) and the emergence of reflexive regulatory systems aiming to reduce risk and uncertainty.

The concept of civil society

There are a number of descriptions applied to the concept of civil society. For example, the concept can be used as a shorthand way of distinguishing the activities of community groups and NGOs from those traditionally ascribed to political institutions and systems (Keane, 1988, 2003). Another would be to emphasise its normative and instrumental characteristics which entails the "management of society that is 'bottom up' rather than 'top down' and that involves the struggle for emancipatory goals" (Kaldor, 2003: 142). In both accounts, the descriptions and attributes only provide a partial account of the essence of the concept. As many observers have noted, the civil society concept has long been a feature of democratic systems. Popular activism, public protests, human rights advocacy and even collaborative decision-making have been associated with orthodox conceptions of civil society (Keane, 1998). The ambivalence surrounding the concept of civil society may be due to its ahistorical character and the role played by political, cultural and legal traditions in shaping our understanding of the concept (Ehrenberg, 1999). For present purposes, the following description of civil society will be adopted, which is

> an intermediate associational realm between state and family populated by organisations which are separate from the state, enjoy autonomy in relation to the state and are formed voluntarily by members of society to protect or extend their interests or values. (White, 2004: 10)

This description attaches emergent properties within the concept of civil society, which can be usefully employed to depict the MSIG model for online child safety. It can be used to describe the mobilisation of various stakeholders into groups, from different parts of the world, each pursuing collective goals and values. The emergence of civil society as a response to governance issues with a public interest dimension is not a modern phenomenon (Becker, 1994). Its role in child protection is suggestive of an ideal type organisation comprising communities, volunteers and activists who are not constrained territorially and have increasingly taken a leading role in urging policymakers and industry to comply with established legal, treaty and convention obligations towards children (Beck, 1992a). Their increasing role in the discourse on online child safety policymaking at domestic, regional and supranational level provides an important counterpoint to the formal political and legal responses to issues like the CSEC. Civil society has an important role in terms of holding both governments and the private sector to account as well as raising public awareness of the key issues and concerns faced by children, parents and educators (ECPAT, 2008). One example of a thriving civil society community can be seen in the range of delegates from not-for-profit organisations participating in the WC III. It is probably accurate to say that these organisations pursue collective goals, with their raison d'être being defined by the normative foundations of human rights conventions like the UNCRC and its two Optional Protocols. The European NGO Alliance for Child Safety Online (eNASCO), which seamlessly weaves 17 children's rights NGOs from across the EU into a network node working for a safer online environment for children, is another example of civil society being mobilised to advance children's rights issues and policies. The use of the concept of civil society does not imply that organisations coming within this category have objectives that are fundamentally at odds with those of the private sector or the State (Held, 1995). Indeed, the very nature of a MSIG framework consisting of various State and non-State actors across the spectrum of society suggests the existence of shared aims between the participants (Dutton *et al.*, 2007: 71). To be sure, we have already seen in previous chapters the extent to which the State, civil society and the private sector have complementary goals in relation to safeguarding children. Consequently, the challenge for policymakers lies not only in coordinating the activities but also in finding solutions to any resulting tensions that may hinder the broad governance objectives in safeguarding children (Bexell *et al.*, 2010: 87). The integration of the FCACP into the MSIG framework can be seen as a necessary strategy since other stakeholders are least able to disrupt the financial channels which sustain the CSEC. From a multi-layered governance perspective, it becomes imperative that policymakers determine how best the roles and responsibilities of the stakeholders can be allocated efficiently and fairly. We will consider later how some of these interactions result in the convergence of governance strategies and responses (Beck, *et al.*, 1994). For the moment, we can turn to the significance of the institutions of capitalism and internationalisation of institutions for civil society participation and private sector engagement in online child safety policy-making (Jobert *et al.*, 2008).

The state, transnational actors and globalisation

The shift in political autonomy and rule making has been attributed to three parallel developments: the gradual decline in the role of the nation state in the face of global institutions like the IMF and the World Bank; the emergence of transnational corporations and the growing influence of NGOs (Berlie, 2009: 12). No one is likely to disagree with the fact that globalisation has led to the emergence of the phenomena where the State is now only one of a number of actors engaged in standard setting and governance activities. What interests us here is the relationship between the logic of the capitalist system of wealth creation on the one hand and the governance issues and difficulties raised by the globalisation of risks as a consequence on the other (Ohmae, 1990, 1995; Castells, 1997). Castells, for example, views the resulting phenomenon of complex interdependence as the product of the "globalisation of core economic activities, by globalisation of media and electronic communication, and by globalisation of crime" (Castells, 1997: 244). Whilst we may question whether the interconnected nature of economic, technological and cultural activities accelerated the erosion of the pivotal role of States, it is the child safety governance significance of these new dimensions of convergence that interest us at this moment (Hall *et al.*, 2002). Castells' point is pertinent to the extent that it highlights an important feature of modernity, namely, the intensification of the globalisation of systems of wealth creation, which also leads to institutions and organisations now having to manage the negative effects of network infrastructures and information flows (Beck, 1992a). Castells provides us with a powerful example of modernity, which chimes well with online child safety policymaking. He observes the ever-increasing commoditisation of children as sexual objects resulting from growing media coverage of child sexual abuse and exploitation, the increasing poverty and the breakdown in family infrastructures and the globalisation of "markets for everything, and from everywhere to everywhere, whether it be organized sex tours or audiovisual distribution of pornographic material worldwide" (Castells, 1998:160). Quayle, Loof and Palmer highlight in their report that young adolescents are complicit in the culture of commoditisation but through self-victimisation (Quayle *et al.*, 2008: 63). Techno-economic advances also create new channels for misuse and risk distribution as seen in the case of *R v Morelli* (2010). The offender was convicted for possession of child pornography contrary to Section 163.1(4) of the Criminal Code. What is particularly instructive, within the context of Beck's view of capitalist systems generating risks, is the offender's use of new technologies and the Internet to create illegal content and leverage the communication platforms for CSEC (e.g. Usenet, websites, social networking sites and file-sharing software programs) (FCACP, 2008). The vignettes above demonstrate the complex risk milieu of modernity that is now being replicated across deviant communities across the world. There is in this sense a market "for everything and everywhere" (Castells, 1998: 150). Consequently, the resulting public anxieties have been mirrored in a number of responses. NGOs continue to demand that the State and ICT industry fulfil their social and moral obligations towards children. New collaborations target the CSEC industry. The inclusion of the FCACP into the MSIG is just the latest in a series of reflexive responses aiming to disrupt the payment channels sustaining the CSEC industry. As reports point to the growth in the child abuse images industry policymakers have also increased their efforts in mobilising a global response to risk management – the harmonisation of rules protecting children from CSEC, use of policing networks and industry engagement (OECD, 2008b, 2009; IWF, 2010b). The traditional State-directed form of risk regulation has evolved to include new governance arrangements, which emphasise deliberation, participation and frequent use of risk assessment strategies (European Commission, 2001b). One final observation can be made about the role of market rules and norms in the production of risks. Risks are distributed unevenly and another aspect of modernity is the measures and strategies developed to reduce societal anxiety and fears. For example, the threats posed to children from the growth of sex tourism and the rise in demand for child abuse materials often involve victims from developing countries and those at the lower end of socio-economic class structures (ECPAT, 2009). Indeed, as the World Congress III reports from Rio illustrate, the growth of transnational criminal activity, the emergence of deviant cultures, the rise of sex tourism and child pornography serve as apt reminders of the "invisible hand" seeking to impose its own perverse logic on societies, economies and individuals least able to respond to the risks (ECPAT, 2008: 76–81). The continuing impact of Web 2.0 technologies on communities least able to address the risks are uncertain, but the locations for future commercial exploitation are not difficult to glean since

> [b]y the year 2015, half of the world's online population will reside in two countries: China and India. The take up of digital technology in Asia over the coming decade will be nothing short of dramatic. In all probability, the growth of online commerce will follow a parallel trend. This will provide unprecedented numbers of potential victims and prospective offenders. (Grabosky, 2007b: 157)

There are three points to be noted with regard to the significance of "technological innovations" for evolving online child safety governance clusters. First, the governance processes are embedded in the logic of capitalist systems of information flows and exchanges. Economic objectives will be pursued alongside social and cultural objectives (see Table 6.1).

Second, advances in communications can also lead to a "creative destruction" of governance strategies and measures. Third, since the "risk society" creates winners and losers, responding to the threats becomes a preoccupation of policymakers and organisations at national, regional and

Table 6.1   Government objectives for policies in the communication sector

Economic objectives

Promote and sustain competition and choice as a means of minimising price and maximising quality of communications services.

Encourage investment and innovation.

Maximise the contribution of the communication sector to economic growth and performance.

Efficient allocation of spectrum.

Social and cultural objectives

Affordable access to a universal service specified in terms of telephony, broadcasting and Internet access

Plurality of voices in the media.

Cultural diversity and national identity reflected in content.

Consumer protection and privacy.

Source: OECD, 2004: 6.

supranational levels. In the remainder of this chapter an attempt will be made to highlight the significance of some of the online child safety clusters within the MSIG framework.

The regulatory domain of online child safety

The emerging network of MSIG (non-State actors)

A cursory examination of the directories from the Child Online Protection Division of the ITU and the Family Online Safety Institute provides us with a snapshot of how non-state actors continue to organise themselves in the converging governance space in the age of modernity (Djelic *et al.*, 2006; Berlie, 2009; Table 6.2).

Table 6.2 Emerging governance networks

Location	Initiatives/organisations	Media literacy	Children's rights policy advocacy
International	Childnet International	✓	✓
	Save the Children International	✓	✓
	Internet Governance Forum	✓	✓
	Family Online Safety Institute	✓	✓
	End Child Prostitution and Trafficking	✓	
	Groupe Speciale Mobile (GSM)	✓	
	Microsoft	✓	
	Vodafone		
Europe	InSafe	✓	✓
	Keepcontrol	✓	✓
	Teachtoday	✓	
	Safer Internet Programme	✓	
	eNASCO	✓	
	European Network and Information Security Agency (ENISA)	✓	
	European Broadcasting Union (EBU)		
Austria	Confoki	✓	
	Handywissen	✓	
	Safer Internet Austria		
Ireland	Webwise	✓	
	Watch your space	✓	
Latvia	Netsafe	✓	
Poland	Nobody's Children Foundation	✓	✓

Continued

Table 6.2 Continued

Location	Initiatives/Organization	Media Literacy	Children's Rights Policy Advocacy
United Kingdom	Beatbullying	✓	✓
	BBC Webwise	✓	✓
	Childnet International	✓	
	Next Generation Learning	✓	
	Thinkuknow	✓	
	Action for Children's Rights		
Middle East and	Think Community	✓	
Africa	Cyber Peace Initiative	✓	
Lebanon	Little Horus	✓	
Egypt			
Asia	Be NetSmart	✓	
India	IndiaChild	✓	
Malaysia	Whoa	✓	
Singapore	ESecurity	✓	
Taiwan	Internet Safety Educator	✓	
	ECPAT Taiwan	✓	
North America	Canada Safety Council	✓	✓
Canada	Media Awareness Network	✓	✓
USA	Online Safety Week	✓	
	Common Sense Media	✓	
	Connect Safely	✓	
	PointSmartClickSafe	✓	
	McAfee Security Advice Center	✓	
	International Centre for Missing & Exploited Children	✓	
Australasia	Cybersmart Kids	✓	
Australia	KidSafe	✓	
New Zealand	NetAlert	✓	
	Netty's World	✓	
	Hector's™ World	✓	
	Net safe	✓	

The broad reach of the network of non-State actors is striking. Some reasons can be provided for the emergence of non-State actors in this sphere of governance. One explanation would be that the Internet has provided NGOs with a new communicative space for engaging with a wide audience. The policies and initiatives pursued by governments can be subject to increased scrutiny, child safety information can be uploaded on websites and blogs and information and ideas can be easily located through the use of search engines and RSS services (Longford *et al.*, 2007). The strategies adopted by civil society and NGOs in disseminating their online child protection proposals have also increased their visibility and presence (Nelson *et al.*, 2008: 2–3, 27). NGOs seek to frame their activities in terms of requiring the private sector and governments to fulfil their legal and UNCRC or treaty commitments towards children. Networking with major international human rights NGOs also enhances their influence (Scholte, 2002; Bexell *et al.*, 2010). The formation of international alliances provides NGOs with the widest possible access to expertise, resources and audiences. NGOs continue to play an active role in the online child safety consultation process. The Save the Children organisation makes regular representations at national, regional and international summits. Childnet International, a UK-based charity, uses its domestic and international networks to promote public awareness of online safety issues and has produced a number of education resources relating to peer victimisation. It was also one of the first members of the UK Council for Child Internet Safety (UKCCIS). Whilst Childnet has a domestic and regional presence, this organisation has an international limb in its child advocacy activities. Childnet has worked with ACMA and the Child Health Promotion Research Centre (CHPRC) at the Edith Cowan University (ECU) in Perth in contributing to online safety educational and awareness raising programmes for children. We have already seen the positive response of civil society organisations and the private sector in the SIP. These are trends which can be found replicated in other jurisdictions (OSTWG, 2010; ACMA, 2009a,b,c). The Canadian Centre for Child Protection (CCCP), which is a charity focused on promoting the safety of children, has actively promoted public awareness activities and education programmes on personal safety. It has two initiatives which involve collaboration with industry. For example, in partnership with TELUS, the Centre created a website promoting parents' and children's awareness of the potential risks accompanying the use of mobile phones and the steps that can be taken to manage these risks or prevent them from arising in the first place.[1] The website also has a mechanism through which mobile phone users can report online sexual abuse to the national hotline – Cybertip.ca. The Centre has also worked with the Canadian Wireless Telecommunications Association to create a website – textED.ca – aimed at educating children and young persons about responsible use of texting technology. In the United States, Congressional Hearings provide various stakeholders with an opportunity to bring particular issues to the attention of legislators (US Senate Committee, 2010). The Joint Select Committee on Cyber-Safety of the 43rd Parliament in Australia received 147 submissions from individuals and organisations on a range of online security and safety issues affecting children's use of the Internet and Web 2.0 technologies.[2] Non-State actors also use other avenues for mainstreaming child welfare and rights issues. Forums like the WSIS create opportunities for civil society to engage with industry and governments (including those from developing countries) in the governance process (WSIS, 2005: Item 65). The creation of the Internet Governance Forum as part of the Tunis Agenda envisages a forum for cooperation and engagement which "will be multilateral, multi-stakeholder, democratic and transparent" (WSIS, 2005: Item 73). Finally, the issues raised by contact, conduct and content risks also become the focal point of civil society activism (ASIL, 2007). Indeed, one has only to look at the sheer volume of online child safety awareness content created by NGOs to appreciate why policymakers and States have been keen to engage with civil society.

Regulatory opportunities and constraints

As Web 2.0 technologies and communication networks transform the market and social environment, good governance is now seen as an indispensable objective by policymakers and the private sector (OECD, 2004). Techniques like self-regulation and co-regulation are regarded as legitimate alternatives to State-directed regulation, particularly as these make possible flexible horizontal and vertical decision-making structures (OECD, 2010a,b). These processes have been regarded by some as a pragmatic response which involves roles and responsibilities being allocated to all stakeholders in the "information chain" (Cave *et al.*, 2008: 1–8; Fisher, 2010). The allocation of these responsibilities does not come free of tensions that already exist amongst the stakeholders regarding the implementation of child safety measures. As noted in Chapter 2, the end-to-end principle has shaped much of our thinking about governance and more specifically the options and strategies for content regulation and the Internet sector generally. The principle of non-intervention, which has contributed to the emergence of the Internet as a social and technological phenomenon, is the product of visionary policymaking and what Cerf described in his testimony as "policy judgment rested on an existing regulatory framework that allowed open and non-discriminatory access to the Internet" (US Senate Committee, 2006). In a report issued by the Working Group on Internet Governance it was noted that any governance arrangements must take into account the design principles that contributed to its creation and continued social and economic growth (WGIG, 2005: 24). Interestingly, Mueller's observation that Internet governance is a matter for its regulatory institutions and not state-mandated commands should not be taken to mean that policymakers are marginalised in regulatory decisions (Mueller, 2010: 11). NGOs continue to lobby policymakers, industry and the technical community to re-think the neo-liberal assumptions in the end-to-end principle (Klinke *et al.*, 2006). This uncompromising stance was very much in evidence in the submission made recently by eNASCO to the FTC in the United States:[3]

> Above all we need to stop thinking about the Internet as if it were, essentially, an adult medium for which special (meaning "irritating") provisions need to be made to take account of the fact that children will use it from time to time. Children and young people are a large, persistent and permanent group of Internet users.

However, creating "risk-free" zones through the deployment of cyber-equivalent safety measures and tools pose social costs on society and industry (Kuperman, 2008: 219–20; WGIG, 2005: 9). Kelly suggests that an over-emphasis on safety concerns may stall technological innovation since when "it comes to risk aversion, we are not rational. We select which risks we want to contend" (Kelly, 2010: 248). Notwithstanding the tensions that surround Internet governance, five key regulatory principles inform the MSIG standard setting process. The measures adopted are expected to be (i) transparent; (ii) accountable; (iii) proportionate; (iv) consistent; and (v) targeted (Department of Business, Information and Skills, 2009). These principles are used to frame risk-based decision-making which aims to promote trust and confidence and its corollary – reduce children's exposure to risks (Fisher, 2010). For example, transparency in the methods or measures adopted by social networking sites can promote trust and confidence if the information communicated relates to the steps that are being taken to identify and minimise children's needless exposure to conduct, contact and content risks. Consistency in the application of standards not only promotes certainty but also allows individuals to order their activities accordingly. The principle of accountability requires that online service providers in particular assume responsibility for the safety and well-being of individuals who use their products and services in accordance with reasonable standards of care. One benefit in using these principles, as opposed to legislation, within the ICT industry is that they enable online service providers to make operational decisions on how risks are to be managed, communicated and even allocated to its users (Hood *et al.*, 2001: 3). Industry standards for network security, Internet protocols and domain names practices also help define the way online safety incidents can be managed operationally. The role of the State in this context is to determine what constitutes an acceptable level of risk to be borne by both online intermediaries and users (e.g. EC Directive 2000/EC/31). Adherence to the principles of proportionality and efficiency also ensure that governance strategies are sustainable and scalable.

Managing the transition from "industrial" to a "networked" environment is challenging on two fronts (Hood *et al.*, 2001). First, policymakers have to confront the consequences of "the spontaneous appearance of qualitatively different systems and mechanisms" and consequently find it "necessary to 'rewire' the speed, efficiency and effectiveness of global governance" (Cave *et al.*, 2007: 30). Second, the idea that Internet norms and values should continue to prevail regardless of the harmful consequences is not an easy one to defend (Bohman, 1996; Knight *et al.*, 1997). As the extract from eNasco cited above makes plain, the question of what constitutes an effective risk management policy and strategy will be a constant source of arguments about regulatory capture and fairness in decision-making processes (Dahl, 1989: 305–6). That said, the evolving online child safety regulatory landscape, which emphasises governance rather than regulation by government, is, however, encouraging. A number of policy reviews have also recommended

Table 6.3   Business considerations

What are the risks faced by children in using the device, software or service?
To what extent are the risks encountered by children the product of lack of awareness?
What information do children need to help them avoid or manage these risks effectively?
What design solutions can be embedded in the services or devices?
What support or guidance do children and parents need?
How does industry deal effectively with public anxieties and concerns?
What strategies should each information service provider consider?
Will "moral panics" impact the trust and confidence of consumers (i.e. parents and children) have on the industry or individual product or services?

the benefits of adopting the MSIG strategy for enhancing the safety of children in the online environment (OSTWG, 2010; ISTTF, 2009; ACMA, 2009d; Table 6.3). It is not uncommon to find policymakers integrating deliberative and participatory risk management processes into sector-specific activities (e.g. mobile phones, social networking sites and online games), which seek to create a coherent risk management framework in measures like

a. Information Security Awareness;
b. Online Safety Design Solutions; and
c. Parental Controls.

Online intermediaries and mobile service providers now incorporate measures enhancing the safety of children in the online environment; these are significant obligations and need to be considered alongside intermediaries' response to "notice and take down" requests, filtering and blocking of illegal or problematic content.

There are four observations to be made. First, there is no "ideal" risk-based model or technique of regulation. Indeed, there are advantages and disadvantages in adopting direct, self- and co-regulatory strategies. Second, the use of a risk-based approach can be used to operationalise strategies and measures based on evidence of risks actually encountered by children or in its deliberative constitutive sense of prudential management principles (Fisher, 2010: 48–50). Third, policymakers need to make available incentive mechanisms which will encourage online intermediaries and service providers to promote socially valuable outcomes. Finally, managing a globalised networked economy requires governments to engage with various stakeholders and define the acceptable levels of risks users should be expected to bear in their daily online interactions and use of Web 2.0 technologies and services (Sunstein, 2005).

Managing risks and complexity: A reflection

The management of risk is a complex endeavour. The governance challenges encountered when broadcasting was "new technology" are not dissimilar to those faced by policymakers in safeguarding children in the online environment (Fleming, 1996; Marsden, 1999). Controlling the content of information broadcasted, whether on the Internet or analogue environment, requires a balance to be struck between "communication or freedom of expression" rights and the need to protect children and vulnerable groups from illegal content and age-inappropriate online video games (European Commission, 2008; Fisher, 2009). With the emergence of the Internet and the convergence of protocols, communications can now be transmitted through VOIP and Internet protocol television (IPTV) and standard setting activities now extend to these modes of communication and information flows. As the recent arguments regarding blocking obligations only make clear, the use of technology to secure compliance with legal rules and norms is a double-edged sword since it has the potential to erode the distinct boundaries of legislative, executive and judicial powers (Cave *et al.*, 2007: 21).

The proliferation of illegal and age-inappropriate content on the Internet has intensified the pressures on the ICT industry and online service providers and created tensions amongst the stakeholders. These tensions have not been alleviated. The IWF noted the increased volumes of illegal content now found on the Internet (IWF, 2010b). These findings mirror those also found by the Canadian Child Exploitation Center in 2009 (see Table 6.4).

The domain name system continues to be abused by individuals and organisations engaged in CSEC (CCCP, 2009; IWF, 2010b; Table 6.5).

Table 6.4   Child sexual abuse images from Canadian Child Exploitation Center (2009)

82.1 per cent of the images analysed by Cybertip.ca depicted very young, pre-pubescent children under 12 years
Of the 4,110 unique images assessed by analysts, over 35 per cent showed sexual assaults against children
77.6 per cent of webpages had at least one child abuse image of a child less than eight years of age, with many showing infants and toddlers being assaulted
Images of children less than eight years old most often depicted them being abused through sexual assaults
Children abused through extreme sexual assaults including bestiality, bondage, torture, and degrading acts such as defecation, mostly (68.5 per cent) occurred against children under eight years old
83 per cent of the images were of girl children

Source: Canadian Child Exploitation Center, 2009.

Table 6.5 Online websites hosting child abuse content

Top five countries hosting websites with child sexual abuse images	Top five countries hosting images of child sexual abuse	Top five countries selling materials on child sexual abuse websites
12,696 website incidents	4,110 unique images	800 commercial websites
United States 49.2%	United States 57.3%	United States 65.6%
Russia 20.4%	Canada 12.6%	Canada 8.7%
Canada 9.0%	Russia 7.5%	Russia 5.6%
Japan 4.3%	Netherlands 3.6%	Netherlands 2.9%
South Korea 3.6%	Spain 3.4%	Germany 1.8%

Source: Cybertip.ca.

The examples in Table 6.5 illustrate just some of the ways the logic of information flows introduce a degree of complexity and speed into the way issues and roles of governments, the private sector and civil society have to be reassessed and redefined, since in "a slower world, the blind forces of evolution could be relied on to adjust business and political models to meet such economic, political, cultural and environmental challenges" (Cave *et al.*, 2007: 30). The transformation in the public and private sector engagement in online child safety governance reflects in one respect the way "systems" operate. Cherry and Bauer use complexity theory to highlight the difficulty in developing sustainable policies in an environment of complex adaptive systems (Cherry *et al.*, 2004). They suggest that the nature of complex systems and the unpredictability of such systems create problems for policy prescriptions based on outcomes rather than processes. Consequently, managing risk in an environment of decentralised and complex network infrastructures eludes customised governance prescriptions in view of the range of stakeholders participating in the policymaking and deliberative process.

There are three particular responses to risk management in the age of modernity. First, policymakers seeking to develop and implement child protection policies now have to address the unintended and disruptive consequences resulting from those who seek to evade its rules through the use of encryption technologies, P2P networks and websites from locations that are outside the reach of national law enforcement authorities. Second, a more immediate policy challenge is to facilitate the process where international standards and principles for safeguarding children can be better coordinated within the MSIG framework. Third, as policymakers increasingly turn to legal, technical and educational solutions to promote safety norms, they cannot ignore moral hazards that may accompany precautionary and prudential risk management strategies (Van Asselt, 2005).

The MSIG model

What the preceding discussions highlight is not only the complex dynamics of MSIG but that the management of online risks in the various contexts and multimedia platforms will require

> the development and application by Governments, the private sector and civil society, in their respective roles, of shared principles, norms, rules, decision-making procedures, and programmes that shape the evolution and use of the Internet. (WGIG, 2005: 3)

The very intricacies of governance and the emotive nature of the issues raised by sex tourism, child pornography and online sexual grooming should alert us to the fact that we cannot neatly package governance polices or regard one regulatory technique as overcoming moral hazard issues and risks generated by poor decision-making skills. As Ayres and Braithwaite observe:

> Good policy analysis is not about choosing between the free market and government regulation. Nor is it simply deciding what the law should proscribe... It is this mix, this interplay, that works to assist or impede solution of the policy problem. (1992: 3)

Critically, the move from managing offline to online risks has led to two paradigmatic shifts in risk governance:

> First, science is increasingly needed to make these risks "visible". Theories, models and sophisticated measurements are needed where our senses fall short. Accordingly, the role of science has partly shifted from calculating hazards faced by people to assessing potential dangers that we do not experience. Second, current risk assessment is increasingly future-oriented. The main question has shifted from one of "what has happened in the past" (probability) as a basis for risk assessment to one of "what may happen in the future" (possibility). Accordingly, risk assessment is increasingly affected by all kinds of uncertainties pertaining to future developments that cannot be ignored. (Van Asselt *et al.*, 2009: 362)

The UK approach

The United Kingdom continues to regard self- and co-regulation as appropriate regulatory strategies for online child safety. One practical benefit in using codes of practice as a governance strategy in relation to hotlines, mobile phone and content providers and social networking sites is that they vest in sector-specific businesses and industries the responsibility for developing and implementing risk management and risk communication decisions, with relevant government oversight. Additionally, given that parental and children's concerns may be related to age-inappropriate and culturally sensitive online content, the law provides an overarching regulatory framework leaving online service providers some degree of flexibility in the way they deploy technical and design solutions and risk communication measures. For example, online service providers are encouraged to make available parental software control tools and relevant information to users like parents, educators and children to help them identify content and services that are exclusive to adults only. The UK government, like many others, has focused on creating appropriate mechanisms to encourage businesses and the ICT industry to undertake an ongoing assessment and review of the policies and measures adopted, with State-mandated measures at one end of the regulatory spectrum and standard setting reporting processes and codes of practice by non-State and corporate actors on the other end (OfCom, 2008a,b). The IWF can be seen as an apt example of how concerns about some online risks can be operationalised and devolved to parties best able to manage them (IWF, 2008, 2010a). Interestingly, managing children's exposure to illegal content and minimising availability of such content are regarded as important online child safety governance objectives.[4] The IWF is funded by the Internet industry and the EU and has a diverse membership of around 100 members, which include Internet service providers, mobile operators and content service providers, search engine operators, social networking sites, IT and software companies and online payment companies. The IWF also works closely with the UK government, law enforcement authorities both in the United Kingdom and abroad and international organisations like INHOPE. The IWF fulfils an important role in the creation, distribution and consumption of child abuse content and child sexual abuse material. Its remit involves the reporting of criminal online content to the police and operates the "notice and take down" process. The "content" comprises child sexual abuse images hosted online anywhere in the world; adult content regarded as criminally obscene and hosted in the United Kingdom; content inciting racial hatred which is hosted in the United Kingdom and non-photographic child sexual abuse images hosted in the United Kingdom. The last category was included into the remit of the IWF following a request made by the Ministry of Justice in 2009. Sections 62–9 of the Coroners and Justice Act 2009 now include non-photographic visual depictions of child sexual abuse in the form of computer-generated images within its category of prohibited content. The IWF is not purely a UK "notice and take down" issuing body for child sexual abuse content. The organisation makes available to the UK Internet industry and online service providers a twice daily updated list of websites which host illegal images of children, advertisements and links to the content. The UK Internet industry subscribes to the *Code of*

Practice for Notice and Takedown of UK Hosted Content. This document serves as a standard setting tool. It describes the responsibilities assumed by ISPs for ensuring the safety and security of its customers with regard to exposure to illegal online content. The expectation that members comply with the obligation to implement *appropriate measures* in response to notices suggests that policymakers recognise that there is no perfect security solution. The guidance provided by the Code is advisory in nature and describes the obligations in a manner which can be reasonably understood and complied with. For example, Appendix 2 defines policies that members need to adopt when hosting newsgroups. The IWF also advises ISPs not to carry newsgroups that are normally regarded as promoting or linking to content of a paedophilic nature. Finally, to assist companies, IT and HR and legal professionals, the IWF provides these professionals with relevant and appropriate information aimed at raising their awareness of the precise scope of the organisation's authority and remit, the law on child sexual abuse and the mechanisms for reporting and measures which ensure compliance with legal standards and rules. The focus on due diligence implies that not only is security governance an ongoing process but that demonstrating compliance with industry standards is an important governance measure. Updating of keywords and phrases used to locate sexual abuse content online to members allows ISPs to adopt responsive measures aimed at minimising the availability of and accessibility to such content. The work undertaken by the IWF has an impact at the regional and international level. Foreign-based ISPs and hosts of websites use the information provided by the IWF to reduce the number of portals where child sexual abuse content are located. The IWF also notifies national and international news providers and ISPs of cases involving online newsgroups which host and advertise child sexual abuse content. Finally, the IWF provides its staff and partners with best practice guidelines relating to the collection and processing of potentially illegal indecent images of child sexual abuse. To avoid potential prosecution under the PCA, a Memorandum of Understanding was concluded between the CPS and the ACPO.[5] The aim of the Memorandum is to facilitate good governance in terms of collaboration and information sharing between those engaged in collecting, investigating and prosecuting offences relating to the creation and distribution of child abuse images. The continued importance of the IWF needs to be seen in its ability to balance societal expectations that risks be managed on the one hand and industry's recognition that early identification of the problems and the steps to be taken are critical to securing compliance with their obligations and responsibilities on the other.

The Canadian approach

The CRTC is an independent organisation responsible for the regulation and supervision of the Canadian broadcasting and telecommunications systems. It reports to the Minister of Canadian Heritage who in turn is accountable to Parliament. Whilst the CRTC works to ensure that its citizens can gain access to the Internet through their telephone service, its remit does not extend to regulating online content.[6] The Canadian Association of Internet Providers (CAIP) is a non-profit organisation which represents Internet service providers in the country. The Code of Conduct requires all its members to observe the laws and cooperate with the law enforcement authority. Its value in standard setting and promoting compliance and timely responses to threats and risks are very much in line with the points raised with regard to the IWF. Industry regulation is achieved through a mixture of laws and best practices.[7] The Government of Canada set up a national hotline in 2004. Cybertip.ca received a five-year funding agreement with Public Safety Canada. Its remit is to receive reports from the general public on matters relating to the sexual exploitation of children. The website is owned and operated by the CCCP. Cybertip.ca works closely with law enforcement partners from across the Internet and telecommunications industry. It has a much wider role than the IWF in that it is the organisation that also receives reports on online sexual exploitation of children.[8] The matters that come within its remit are child sexual abuse images and material, online sexual grooming (luring), child exploitation through prostitution, travelling to sexually exploit children and child trafficking. Cybertip.ca is a member of INHOPE. Cybertip.ca's processing of reports is not dissimilar to those adopted by IWF or other hotlines. For example, following a report, Cybertip.ca assesses whether the report is within its remit and cross-references the complaint with Canada's Criminal Code. If a complaint involves a child victim, the report is designated as priority and work is undertaken in processing the report. The report also draws on web research and makes available relevant information which will assist law enforcement in investigating the incident. Cybertip.ca undertakes a significant amount of public awareness campaigns. For example, to encourage the public to report incidents of child sexual exploitation, the organisation conducted a campaign across the major states in Canada. The campaign "I Reported It" aimed to raise public awareness about the crucial role played by individuals in society in reducing online child sexual exploitation by reporting incidents to Cybertip.ca. It is perhaps reasonable to suggest that the self-regulation approach pursued in Canada appears to regard the division of responsibilities as a strategy for addressing the problems raised by the ready availability and distribution of illegal content. For example, the *Act respecting the mandatory reporting of Internet child pornography by persons who provide an Internet service 2010* provides a regulatory framework relating to the reporting duties of persons who provide an Internet service to the public if they are informed about an Internet address where child pornography may be accessed by the general public or if they have reasonable grounds to believe that their Internet service is being or has been used to commit a child pornography offence (Section 3).

The Australian approach

ACMA ensures that the communication industry complies with the obligations under the relevant legislation.[9] Apart from being a member of INHOPE, ACMA also addresses issues relating to the mobile and fixed line telecommunications sector. Since the inception of ACMA, the telecommunications industry has developed schemes that resemble co-regulation in the sense that the non-attainment of the objectives results in intervention by Government regulators (Lindsay *et al.*, 2008). The Communications Legislation Amendment (Content Services) Act 2007 creates a content regulatory system and has introduced a new Schedule 7 into the Broadcasting Services Act 1992. Schedule 7 of the BSA brings within its governance framework stakeholders like the Internet industry (e.g. the Internet Industry Association Content Services Code) and content service providers (e.g. the Restricted Access Systems Declaration 2007) (Lindsay *et al.*, 2008: 31.5). Broadly, ACMA's regulatory oversight covers service providers that are "carriers", "carriage service providers" and "content service providers". It is suggested that the consumer protection policy is balanced by the importance ACMA attaches to promoting innovation and competition in the industry. Even though the MSIG strategy aims to provide a coherent and principled framework to the regulation of online content, there are difficult policy issues that remain to be addressed (which are not unique to this jurisdiction):

> Questions remain about the extent to which it has correctly balanced the competing policy objectives in this area. While it is important to ensure that children are appropriately protected from unsuitable content, it is also important to ensure that adults are free to access content and to foster an innovative local content industry. (Lindsay *et al.*, 2008: 31.27)

The co-regulatory strategy is also evident in the regulation of Internet and mobile phone content (Schedules 5 and 7 of the BSA 1992). ACMA maintains a register of codes of practice and standards made under the relevant legislation. One scheme overseen by ACMA relates to the protection of children from illegal and inappropriate content. There are codes of practice for Internet and mobile content. Breaches of the codes by ISPs or mobile content providers will constitute a breach of the relevant legislation. For example, under the three revised Internet content codes of practice registered under Schedule 5 of the Broadcasting Services Act 1992 (Schedule 5), ISPs and Internet content hosts are required to implement appropriate strategies for managing the use of the Internet by minors, to make provision for end users' use of filtering and other content management tools and to provide online safety information. In the event of an ISP being deemed not to have taken the appropriate measures, ACMA may issue a compliance order, and if this is not acted upon to the satisfaction of the authority, an offence will be deemed to have been committed under the legislation.

What is interesting about each of these national approaches to managing online risks is the multi-level and distributive characteristics of online child safety governance. The central features of collaboration, identification of the subject matter for regulatory intervention and participation of State, civil society and industry provide a blueprint for MSIG models at regional and international levels (Klinke, 2009: 406). Two considerations continue to inform the MSIG framework adopted by policymakers from each of the jurisdictions considered above. First, since the pace of technological innovation can expose the shortcomings of any national legal system, and its rules, codes of practice will continue to be regarded as providing sufficient flexibility and adaptability. Second, self-regulation not only enables the industry to assume direct responsibility for managing consumer concerns and needs, but the inclusion of civil society in the deliberative process will ensure a measure of democratic participation and accountability.

The business case for collaboration and cooperation

Search engine operators, social networking sites and mobile phone producers are actively engaged in reassuring policymakers and consumers that their products and services can be used safely and securely. Google, for example, launched its flagship website supporting parents and children in their efforts towards adopting safe search practices. It also provides users with tools which can be used to raise concerns and report problems.[10] Facebook, the social networking site, continues to promote safe social networking norms.[11] It has recently launched a *network publics* type social reporting platform where users are effectively provided with an opportunity to develop and promote appropriate social norms within their communities. To address the trust deficit that sometimes promotes insecurity on social networking sites, design solutions have also been integrated into user's pages to enable them to make visible, communications that are hurtful or unpleasant, through the use of report or help buttons. This recent governance measure can be seen as an attempt to create and sustain a positive environment for promoting acceptable community norms and values, in the light of growing concerns about peer victimisation occurring on social networking sites (White House, 2011). The social networking site has also incorporated Microsoft's PhotoDNA "hash" technology, which helps moderators detect any illegal child abuse images uploaded on its platforms (Allen, 2011).

The involvement of the private sector in assuring parents and children that reasonable efforts have been taken to ensure the safety of their services and products is perhaps another example of how businesses are embracing their social and ethical obligations towards consumers, which include children (Carroll *et al.*, 2010). Proactive involvement in child safety can of course be viewed as a strategy to elevate brand status and avoid public criticism (Bhattacharya *et al.*, 2004; Carroll *et al.*, 2010). That said, the responsiveness of business organisations to consumer expectations regarding their safety can be viewed as being consistent with the stakeholder or enlightened shareholder value governance model (Whetten *et al.*, 2002). There are two aspects informing this broad view of corporate actors' attitudes towards Internet governance in this area of child protection. First, there is growing public expectation that reasonable online safety measures be adopted. Many online intermediaries and technology providers, for example, continue to emphasise the value and importance of responding to children and parental expectations that the services and products they provide either adhere to or even surpass the safety benchmarks put in place by legislation. Second, organisations now increasingly integrate child safety norms into their business models. One exposition that advocates these ideas is the "media dependency" theory (Heslin *et al.*, 2008). The authors suggest that, and one which is very much in keeping with the well-established narrative on corporate social responsibility, promoting consumer trust and confidence can enhance product awareness and reduce opportunities for adverse reactions that may result from ignoring the views of children, parents and policymakers on sensitive issues like access to illegal or inappropriate content, online sexual solicitation and peer victimisation (Einwiller *et al.*, 2010). It is suggested that in a highly competitive environment it would be perverse if social networking sites and mobile phone providers were shown to be lacking sensitivity to parental anxieties and fears about the safety of their children (Ball-Rokeach *et al.*, 1976; Morton *et al.*, 2001). The "media dependency" theory, it should also be noted, is premised on the idea that the media provides an important channel through which information about risks encountered on social networking sites and online safety incidents generally are communicated to consumers. The theory suggests that since the private sector is particularly sensitive to portrayals of risks associated with their products or services, they tend to be particularly proactive in responding to consumer concerns and fears (Einwiller *et al.*, 2010). We may be assuming too much about the interdependencies that emerge in the realm of online child safety policymaking between the media, civil society and the private sector. That said, the media dependence theory does at least help us recognise how and why organisations like Microsoft, Vodafone, Google and the various social networking and mobile phone service providers have been proactive in demonstrating their commitment towards implementing child safety and security measures (Porter, 2006; Carroll, 1991). Their engagement with child protection policymaking and development of industry best practices correspond with a discernible trend in online child safety policymaking activity which "structures, guides and controls human and social activities and interactions beyond, across and within national territories" (Djelic *et al.*, 2006: 6). The governance implications for ICT, mobile computing and online service providers are evident.

For example, mobile phone and content service providers now not only meet the market needs for affordable and innovative products and services, but they also address consumers' safety needs and concerns. It can be said that the relations between social networking services providers and their users are also evolving into one where values like trust and confidence are seen as an integral part of the business–consumer relationship.

The role of civil society in Internet governance

From a constitutional perspective, the private sector and civil society are not regarded as political actors, and consequently require appropriate institutional infrastructures which facilitate their participation and engagement in national and international policymaking (Latzer, 2009). Some examples can be provided. The deliberations during the Byron Review, the Culture, Media and Sport Committee's inquiry on *Harmful Content on the Internet in Video Games* and the House of Lords Science and Technology Committee on *Personal Internet Security* benefited from views expressed by industry, child welfare organisations and researchers from the United Kingdom and beyond (Byron, 2008; Culture, Media and Sport Committee, 2008; House of Lords Select Committee on Science and Technology, 2007). The US Government's National Telecommunication and Information Administration in pursuance of the PROTECT Act 2003 established an OSTWG to review and evaluate the efforts made by industry in enhancing the safety of children. The Act specified that the Working Group must comprise at least 30 members who are representatives from the relevant sectors in industry, public interest groups and other appropriate groups and Federal agencies (OSTWG, 2010: 1). The move to create participative processes and panels of "experts" is also embedded in international instruments. For example, Article 9 of the CPC Convention views cooperation between civil society, industry and governments as an integral part of online child safety governance. The Prague Declaration on "Safer Internet for Children", which was adopted during the Ministerial Conference "Safer Internet for Children – fighting together against illegal content and conduct on-line – can be seen as one illustration of the interplay between civil society and industry in online child safety standard setting activity (Council of the European Union, 2009b). Supranational organisations regard engagement with stakeholders as an opportunity for capacity building and mainstreaming children rights and protection issues. The OECD continues to promote the MSIG model. In June 2008, a Ministerial consensus was reached indicating that governments had to work with other stakeholders, including civil society, the private sector and the Internet technical community (OECD, 2008). On 15 April 2009, the OECD and Asia Pacific Economic Cooperation (APEC) convened a symposium which brought together a wide range of participants from civil society with the aim of sharing information and best practices on the protection of children.[12] The delegates unequivocally endorsed the MSIG model:

[a]lthough approaches may differ from country to country, it is significant to involve various stakeholders and to promote international cooperation between the government and the private sector ... It is also important to spark international debate by cooperating with other global institutions and fora. (OECD, 2009: paragraphs 21 and 32)

Finally, the EU has long advocated engagement with civil society and the private sector. The SIP, for example, provides a platform where stakeholders can exchange information about practices in the area of online child safety. The *EU Kids Online II* stakeholders' forum, for example, invited participation from a cross-section of society (e.g. academics, industry child welfare organisations, parent groups and governments) across 21 countries. The strategy was adopted with the aim of providing policymakers with recommendations appropriate to the needs of individual countries (Jorge *et al.*, 2010).

Enhancing trust and reputation in the age of modernity

The widespread engagement by industry in enhancing the safety of children eases the burden and responsibility on policymakers to continuously enact laws in response to technological advancements and emerging threats. In the area of online child safety, social networking sites, ISPs, mobile phone and content providers and the telecommunication and broadcasting industry have adopted a wide range of measures to promote public confidence in their products and services. Online service providers and ISPs have also shown a willingness to work with law enforcement and policymakers. Many social networking sites now have filtering and reporting mechanisms to enable risks and problems to be identified. Sites like Facebook and MySpace provide users with information on how to seek redress for peer victimisation and report suspicions of grooming activity or problematic behaviours like self-harm and anorexia (Table 6.6).

One consequence of the MSIG approach is the concerted effort made by businesses to communicate and justify their risk management processes and decisions. Risk management and ongoing dialogue with the various stakeholders is seen as an important governance strategy. As Jovanic remarks:

Information on the nature and extent of risks and its management is fundamental for shaping public opinion and helps to build trust in the proposed responses and in those who are entrusted with the mission to manage them. (Jovanic, 2010: 290)

Modernity has led to the opening up of a global governance space, which has made the adoption of an MSIG framework a necessity. Three reflexive regulatory responses will be noted here for completeness. First, from a business or corporate perspective, promoting trust and confidence in its products and services is now very much a part of its standard setting activity and business

Table 6.6   Mainstreaming online child safety in the private sector

	Risks	Blocking/filtering/ rating/reporting	Media literacy
News Corporation/ MySpace	Content Contact Conduct	MySpace ParentCare	Safety Tips for Children and Parents
Vodafone	Content Contact Conduct	Tools built into device Parental settings	Vodafone Parents/ Children Guide Click Clever Click Safe tool
PointSmartClickSafe. org Cable and Television Industry			Education Program for Parents
AOL	Content Contact Conduct	Age-appropriate settings Parental controls for online surfing IM and email programming Activity Reports Online Reporting System	Safety Programs
Comcast.net		Parental Software Controls	GetSmart Safety Programs for Parents and Children (age appropriate)
Google Inc/ YouTube	Content Conduct	SafeSearch Filter Digital Hashing	Family Safety Centre
Microsoft – X-Box and Windows	Content Contact Conduct	Parental/Safety Settings Report functionalities	Family Safety Information
Symantec		Norton Online Family	Family Online Safety

models. Second, the presumptive governance strategy appears to be that the formation of alliances with States and civil society is a sustainable business strategy providing reciprocal benefits to all stakeholders. Third, notwithstanding the challenges posed by the Internet's technical infrastructure, the widespread acceptance of security standards and principles by the ICT industry in particular becomes an important aspect of online child safety policymaking. Increased media and policy spotlight on online child safety issues has no doubt made a significant difference in the way the ICT industry and the various online service providers now approach child safety issues and more specifically demonstrate their commitment to promoting trust and confidence amongst their users. In addition to the public awareness campaigns, many online service providers also use filtering content technologies to deal with illegal and problematic content and more general information security threats posed by malware, viruses and phishing. Yahoo!, Google, AOL and other online service providers now make available technological software controls that filter content – Safe Search tools, privacy controls to manage information that can be accessed by third parties, abuse reporting mechanisms so that breaches of its terms of use are reported and anti-spyware and malware tools. For example, AOL has embedded child safety standards into its business model. Design solutions have been embedded into the access layer to ensure that users can connect to the Internet safely. In addition to the online safety educational material and parental control mechanisms, the company also incorporates filtering software and safety incident reporting mechanisms on its email service and on the services it provides to parents and children. British Telecommunications (BT) is another example a company integrating child safety rules and norms into its business model (EUROPA, 2007b). It offers subscribers, parental control software and educational materials. BT also works closely with the IWF and automatically blocks access to websites hosting child sexual abuse content. Google, the search engine operator, launched its Family Safety Center on 9 September 2010.[13] The information awareness portal is the culmination of the process of consultation with parents and leading child safety organisations.

Some brief observations can be made with regard to the three governance challenges addressed by the Internet industry: first, the integration of child safety design and technological principles into business models; second, the necessity of translating these principles into meaningful measures and processes that end users can understand and, third, compliance with legal and industry standards. In respect of the latter, it should be noted that in a number of cases, businesses have shown a willingness to exceed current legal standards by focusing on the issues raised by consumers, parents and NGOs. Initiatives like increasing user awareness of the risks accompanying the use of the Internet, mobile phones, search engines and social networking sites; promoting accessibility; the deployment of targeted technical solutions relating to content and contact management and empowering parents and educators are now regarded as industry best practices. These responses aim to reassure parents and children that the risks attributed to the logic of information flows and networks and the nature of digital information can be minimised by adopting appropriate and reasonable technological, design and informational solutions. We can now turn to the governance responses aimed at enhancing the safety of children in two areas – mobile phone and content providers and social networking sites. The aim here is to illustrate how the MSIG framework can be deployed in relation to two technologies: mobile phones and social networking sites.

MSIG model case study 1: Mobile phones

The *European Framework for Safer Mobile Use by Younger Teenagers and Children*, concluded on 6 February 2007, can be seen as an attempt to supplement existing legal obligations protecting children, in particular from risks of victimisation and exposure to illegal and harmful content.[14] Most leading mobile phone and content providers in the EU subscribed to the Framework, including, Deutsche Telekom Group, Go Mobile, Hutchison 3G Europe, Orange Group, Telecom Italia SpA, and Vodafone Limited (EUROPA, 2007a). Signatories to the Framework undertake a number of obligations to safeguard children. These include the implementation of media literacy programmes; provision of tools which ensure that access to adult content can be controlled; creation of classification schemes which enable parents, for example, to make informed decisions on content to be accessed by their children, and, finally, to support law enforcement in its efforts to restrict the use of mobile phones to distribute illegal content (Table 6.7). Finally, the Framework also links the obligations assumed by signatories to ongoing EU online safety objectives, and are encouraged to work closely with INSAFE and INHOPE.

The Framework identifies the principles that guide mobile phone and content providers when implementing and reviewing the child safety measures adopted by them. Unlike statutory rules, which prescribe the prohibited conduct, signatories undertake the responsibility for implementing the measures that will achieve the goals set out in the Framework. For

Table 6.7   MSIG model for mobile phone safety

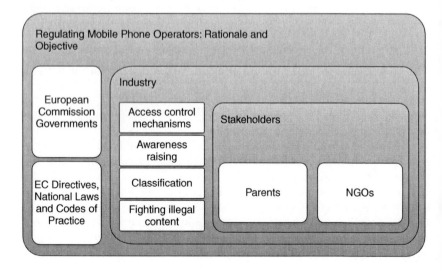

example, mobile phone providers agree to adopt "appropriate" mechanisms to control access to illegal or age-inappropriate content. Measures adopted by mobile phone providers include the provision of tools and information that enable parents to make informed choices on the services and content which can be made available to their children. Other measures include the provision of filtering solutions and billing control mechanisms. Whilst mobile and content providers are provided with flexibility in terms of the classification frameworks they adopt, they are, however, encouraged to ensure that the standards of review for classifying content are consistent with those prescribed by relevant national legislation and regulations. At a minimum, mobile phone providers are expected to ensure that parents can make informed choices regarding their children's use of mobile phones. The Framework also enlists the support of policy makers, trade associations and other organisations to provide regulatory oversight on the effectiveness and appropriateness of the measures adopted by the mobile phone providers. Safeguards are also built into the Framework to ensure that consumers' privacy and freedom to access content are not undermined.[15] The protection of children's privacy and the surveillance strategies adopted by online services providers including mobile phone operators are areas of governance attracting the attention of child welfare organisations and data protection agencies (Nairn *et al.*, 2009; Article 29 Data Protection Working Party, 2010; European Parliament, 2009b, 2010; FTC, 2010a,b). With regard to conduct, contact and content risks, mobile providers undertake to adopt or support the creation of "notice and take down procedures", if appropriate legal authorisation is obtained with regard to the removal of illegal content. Finally, in addition to the points above, accountability and oversight processes are also embedded into the Framework. Safeguarding children is viewed as an ongoing process involving in particular the collaboration between mobile phone operators, content service providers, law enforcement and parents. An annual review process of the measures adopted by individual mobile phone providers is undertaken to ensure compliance with obligations assumed under the Framework. During the public consultation exercise it was made clear that the responsibility for promoting safe use of mobile phones should also involve parents, carers and public authorities (European Commission, 2006a). The integration of these stakeholders into the governance process is a clear acknowledgement that good governance involves the participation of all stakeholders. Apart from the wider representation this governance strategy now makes possible, mobile phone providers are also provided with an opportunity to engage in productive dialogues with users and address any ongoing or emerging safety concerns in a timely manner. Oversight and accountability are achieved in a number of ways. First, the Framework requires the review process to be undertaken together with European and national stakeholders like the European Commission, INHOPE and INSAFE. Second, the implementation of the measures by individual Member States in the EU is kept under annual review. GSM Europe works with the European Commission in monitoring the implementation of the Framework (GSM World, 2007). Third, the implementation review reports are published on GSM's website.[16] The website also has links to national industry frameworks and plays an important role in raising awareness of the mobile community and the general public to current and emerging online safety issues and measures. The development of the Framework is an important governance response and there have been three reviews of the performances of each of the signatories. The latest implementation review covers the period January–June 2010. The widespread acceptance of the Framework by 83 signatory companies across the EU and their implementation in 25 EU Member States are welcome developments (GSM Europe, 2010a). In governance terms, there is in effect an industry network subscribing to safe and responsible use of mobile phones, which extends to approximately 96 per cent of all mobile subscribers in the EU (GSM Europe, 2010b). Since the signing of the Framework, there has been a noticeable trend in mobile and content providers' increased willingness to adhere to the obligations assumed under the Framework (GSM Europe, 2010b). In the 2009 implementation report, many mobile operators have adopted access control and classification systems (PriceWaterhouseCoopers, 2009). For example, 95 per cent of operators installed access control mechanisms or were in the process of implementing these measures (13 per cent) (ibid., 2009: 2). With regard to classification, over 80 per cent of the operators introduced classification systems or had policies regulating content accessible to adults only (57 per cent) (ibid.). The report also identifies areas where there appears to be a lack of concrete commitments within some national Codes of Practice in relation to discovery of illegal child images (as required by clause 14 of the Framework agreement), providing customers with mechanisms for reporting concerns (as required by clause 6) and reviewing safety standards once developed (as required by clause 18).

Some issues are worth exploring. A number of countries appeared to comply with clauses relating to access control mechanisms, which included age-verification checks at the point of sale or contract but these were not consistently implemented. At least 17 operators in the report could not confirm that checks were undertaken (GSM Europe, 2010b). The report also highlighted the fact that there was no EU-wide regulation that required all Member States to ensure that mobile operators and content providers made available software, which prevented minors from accessing adult content. Countries like the Czech Republic, Belgium, Finland, Germany, Italy and the United Kingdom had formal regulations that corresponded with the requirements of the Framework (PriceWaterhouseCoopers, 2009: 12). One aspect not covered by the Framework related to monitoring the effectiveness of the access control mechanisms. Forty-one per cent of the operators indicated that they actively monitored and reviewed the effectiveness of their access control mechanisms. Eighty per cent reported that they either monitored the systems or had in place notification systems that enabled problems to be reported to them. Many operators seemed to be compliant with media literacy and awareness raising initiatives (67 per cent) or planned to be fully compliant (16 per cent). Some even went beyond the requirements of the Framework. Orange UK and Vodafone Czech Republic had been particularly proactive in raising consumer awareness in respect of a range of online safety risks. With regard to mechanisms for reporting complaints or child safety incidents, though 28 per cent of the respondents indicated that they did not have a designated system for dealing with safety issues, a number of them offer customer services as a support mechanism. This is not a particularly satisfactory response, it should be said. It is in the area of illegal content that perhaps concerns are most often raised about industry's engagement with law enforcement. Even though 28 per cent stated that they were non-compliant with clause 13, which required collaboration with law enforcement authorities, a number of respondents responded appropriately by communicating with INHOPE. The variations in the responses with regard to reporting and blocking or takedown of illegal content can also be attributed to differences in national legislation. Finally, the overall impression of the implementation report was that signatories were adhering to the spirit of the Framework, efforts were made to engage and collaborate with other stakeholders and codes of practice were kept under review. It should also be noted that many of the awareness raising initiatives run by mobile operators also reflected contemporary concerns and issues like cyberbullying, "happy-slapping", theft, illegal file sharing and information security.

A summary can be provided with regard to the third implementation review of the Framework agreement and national implementation reports, which were published on June 2010:

(i) Access control mechanisms

The review not only reports that compliance by operators have been high but also draws attention to practices that either implement the Framework or exceed its standards. For example, Bulgarian operators now restrict mobile access to adult content. Access is permitted where age-verification checks have been passed (GSM Europe, 2010d: 5). Even where the age-verification changes show that the consumer is not a minor, access to adult content is only made available through the use of a password. Other access control mechanisms involve a screen display showing that content has been blocked with accompanying explanation, the requirement of a pin code to gain access to adult or age-inappropriate content and a warning page, with a legal disclaimer. The mobile operators in Greece, for example, provide subscribers with tools by which access control mechanisms can be activated for own-branded content (GSM Europe, 2010f: 5).

(ii) Classification of commercial content

Classification systems enable subscribers to make informed choices and decisions. The activation of access control mechanisms ensures that children are not inadvertently exposed to content deemed to be suitable for adults only (GSM Europe, 2010f: 6). The operators in Ireland have a more robust mobile content classification body (GSM Europe, 2010h: 3). All mobile phone operators are required to enter into a contractual obligation with an independent classification body. The remit of this body is to develop a framework for classifying commercial content, which is deemed to be unsuitable for minors. Additionally, mobile phone operators are required to ensure that the classification framework adopted by them is consistent with the standard of review used in other media; the parties undertake to treat content as age restricted where a similar classification has been adopted in other media like magazines, films, video and computer games (GSM Europe, 2010h: 10–11).

(iii) Raising awareness and education

In contrast to the second implementation review, there have been greater resources directed at raising awareness and providing parents with relevant information and support. In a number of countries, mobile phone operators engage directly with children and schools. Others, like the Latvian mobile phone operators, collaborate with NGOs in disseminating information about safe and responsible use of mobile phones (GSM Europe, 2010i: 2–4). The mobile operators in the United Kingdom work closely with organisations like CEOP and the NSPCC (GSM Europe, 2010j). All mobile operators (with the exception of 3UK) in the United Kingdom are involved in the development of the Teachtoday website. This portal serves to educate teachers, head teachers, governors and other staff about the Internet and its communication technologies.

(iv) Fighting illegal content on mobile Internet networks

Mobile phone operators with Internet connectivity rely on the list compiled by the IWF to block websites hosting illegal content. In the United Kingdom, all mobile operators use this blocklist to prevent inadvertent access to illegal child abuse content (GSM Europe, 2010j: 12). Mobile phone operators tend to comply with legally authorised "notice and take down" requests and block access to websites that are on the IWF list of sites hosting illegal content like child abuse, racist and obscene images. The mobile operators in Slovakia work closely with government authorities, the national safer Internet node and NGOs to eliminate illegal child sexual abuse media and undertake to facilitate the reporting of such content (GSM Europe, 2010k: 10). Many operators have also used the Framework to further enhance their efforts in promoting children's safe use of mobile phones. These include

monitoring and verifying that national Codes of Practice are being implemented, particularly where new products and services have been introduced
into the market (GSM Europe, 2010g: 9, 16), ensuring that marketing activities directed against minors adhere to consumer protection guidelines
(GSM Europe, 2010h: 24) and promote transparency in the provision of mobile services (GSM Europe, 2010i: 13).

In relation to clause 18, which deals with feedback from stakeholders, the
prospects look good in relation to the continued role of the Framework as a
review mechanism. The Hungarian Branch of the International Children's
Safety Service whilst commending the efforts made by the mobile operators in addressing the safety issues, highlighted the need for greater efforts
to be directed in promoting media awareness of the safety issues and information literacy (GSM Europe, 2010g: 15). John Carr, from the United
Kingdom, noted that mobile phone operators needed to address the privacy
issues raised by the provision of location-based services software for mobile
phones (GSM Europe, 2010j: 14). He also pointed out that in the United
Kingdom, bullying through mobile phones was still an area of concern but
felt that mobile phone operators had been particularly responsive to children and parent anxiety. The stakeholder for Bulgaria acknowledged that
its mobile operators were responsive to the safety concerns of children. It
was suggested however that mobile operators in this country still needed
to promote public awareness of online child safety through campaigns and
education, by participating in co-funding safer Internet initiatives and by
improving compliance efforts (GSM Europe, 2010j: 14).

In summary, the 2007 *European Framework for Safer Mobile Use by Younger
Teenagers and Children* prescribes a set of principles governing mobile phone
operators and content providers' relationship with children and their parents.
They are also expected to work with other stakeholders, including child protection organisations, with the aim of promoting the safety of children and
young persons. There are clear obligations imposed on mobile phone and
content providers to regulate children's access to content. These providers are
expected to support classification frameworks for commercial content based
on applicable national standards and rules. Classification of content, whether
accessible through telecommunications or not, are required to be consistent
with national standards regarding decency, appropriateness and legislation.
Mobile providers are expected to work closely with law enforcement in dealing with illegal content (e.g. child sexual abuse images) and are expected to
alert INHOPE or equivalent authorities when they encounter such content.
In supporting the efforts of law enforcement, mobile phone providers are
encouraged to support legally authorised "notice and take down" requests.
With regard to parental concerns about children's access to inappropriate
content, the Framework is sufficiently flexible in permitting signatories to
introduce measures that cater for individual and cultural needs.

MSIG model case study 2: Social networking sites

In 2008, the Home Office Task Force comprising key organisations from the United Kingdom, the United States and Australia produced a *Good Practice Guidance for Providers of Social Networking and Other User Interactive Services 2008* (Home Office, 2008). This document was the product of the collaborative efforts of government, industry, children's charities and voluntary groups and the law enforcement authority. A similar approach towards developing a unified response to the child safety issues raised by emerging interactive services can also be seen in the United States. Some of the measures identified in the ISTTF's Final Report with regard to enhancing the safety of children in the online environment provide a useful background to understanding the rationale and objectives of the EU Safer Social Networking Principles (SSNP) (ISTTF, 2008: Appendix A). The *Joint Statement on Key Principles of Social Networking Safety* identified four areas for coordinated action by social networking sites and its stake-holders: (i) the allocation of adequate resources to facilitate the contin-ued development of online safety tools that are accessible and effective, including online identity authentication technologies; (ii) the design of safety features on websites so that children's exposure to inappropriate contact and content are minimised; (iii) raising awareness about safe and responsible use of online services and technologies; and (iv) continued cooperation and collaboration with law enforcement authorities (ISTTF, 2008: Appendix A, 2–3).

In 2008, the European Commission convened some of Europe's major social networks as well as researchers and child welfare organisations to form a European Social Networking Task Force to discuss guidelines for the use of social networking sites by children. On 10 February 2009, follow-ing a public consultation exercise and the setting up of a European Social Networking Task Force, a document outlining the governance principles for social networking sites provided the basis for an agreement. Twenty of the main providers of social networking services signed the agreement, known as the *Safer Social Networking Principles* for the EU (European Commission, 2009d, 2010d; Table 6.8).

Like the Framework agreement on mobile phones, social network service providers undertake to implement reasonable and appropriate measures to enhance the safety of children. These obligations are couched in general principles, which do not differ in any fundamental respect from the recom-mendations we have seen in policy reviews undertaken by the Home Office and the ISTTF (Table 6.9).

On 9 February 2010, during the Safer Internet Day, the European Commission presented the findings of an independent assessment of the implementation of the SSNP for the EU. The report is in two parts: Part I and Part II. The evaluation is conducted in two phases. First, the report identifies the safety measures taken by signatories on these sites. Second,

Table 6.8   EU safer social networking principles

Principle 1: Raise awareness of safety education messages and acceptable use policies or users, parents, teachers, and carers in a prominent, clear and age-appropriate manner

Principle 2: Work towards ensuring that services are age-appropriate for the intended audience

Principle 3: Empower users through tools and technology

Principle 4: Provide easy–to-use mechanisms to report conduct or content that violates the Terms of Service

Principle 5: Respond to notifications of illegal content or conduct

Principle 6: Enable and encourage users to employ a safe approach to personal information and privacy

Principle 7: Assess the means for reviewing illegal or prohibited content/conduct

Table 6.9   MSIG model for safer social networking

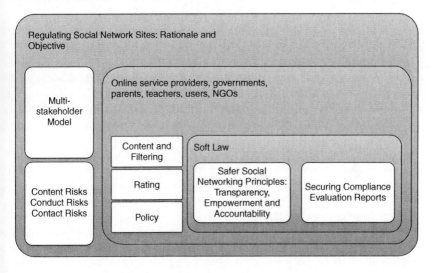

the independent assessors verify compliance with the SSNP. A brief account will be provided of the seven SSNPs.

Principle 1: Raise awareness of safety education messages and acceptable use policies to users, parents, teachers and carers in a prominent, clear and age-appropriate manner.

Signatories undertake to raise awareness of safety education messages and acceptable use policies to users, parents, teachers and carers in a prominent, clear and age-appropriate manner. It is important to recognise the rationale of this objective, namely, to enable individuals make informed choices about the product and services made available on the social networking site. The focus on promoting awareness and information literacy is based on the premise that risks encountered by children may be attributed to the lack of relevant and accessible information. The emphasis on social networking site providers' obligation to make relevant and accessible information available clearly places the onus on them to ensure that their users clearly understand the safety and risk management issues. The guidance provided in the SSNP mirrors some of the key recommendations made in the Home Office Task Force document, namely, those relating to signposting information about the services and online safety resources in a clear and accessible manner and that these are appropriate for various age groups between the 13- and 18-years-old category. The reference to providing information in a clear and accessible manner should lead to many sites now using videos and other media to communicate safety information in a clear and effective manner. Under the SSNP, site providers also undertake to clarify the boundaries of acceptable and unacceptable behaviour in a way that young users can understand.

Principle 2: Work towards ensuring that services are age-appropriate for the intended audience.
Compliance with the obligations under this principle aims to address 3 specific governance challenges: minimise risks of minors accessing age-inappropriate content and services, ensuring that underage users do not register as users and empowering users. The principle first of all aims to ensure that children do not encounter or access age-inappropriate information. Users with accounts on social networking sites can access content in a number of ways: search directory under the classification categories of interests, content and links posted by peers. Concerns about exposure to inappropriate contact are now addressed at the design stage and include the use of default settings to ensure that adults do not discover the profiles of users below the age of 18 years through a public search directory. Other measures to enhance the safety of children on social networking sites comprise those which exclude certain adult or age-inappropriate categories from search directories on the sites (i.e. status of relationships, body type, orientation and height). In relation to preventing children from accessing inappropriate content, filtering software (i.e. hashing technology) can be used to ensure that children do not upload or distribute inappropriate images. Other design solutions include the use of blocking technology to prevent minors from accessing age-inappropriate advertisements relating to tobacco, alcohol and general classified advertisements intended for an adult audience.

Principles 3, 4 and 6: Empower users through tools and technology; Provide easy-to-use mechanisms to report conduct or content that violates the Terms of

Service; and Enable and encourage users to employ a safe approach to personal information and privacy.

There is a degree of overlap between these three principles and those considered earlier. The safety objectives in promoting children's awareness of online risks resulting from engaging with electronic data can be further enhanced if tools are also made available to enable children to manage online safety incidents in an appropriate manner. Subscribers to the SSNP undertake to provide users with tools to ensure that strangers do not contact them, facilitate identity verification for "friend" requests, prevent tagging of personal photos, provide greater control over user-generated content and empower users to define their audiences (Table 6.10).

With regard to contact risks, site providers undertake to adopt measures that minimise the risks of children being contacted by adults. As noted

Table 6.10   Empowering children through design solutions

Risks	Design tools	Solutions
Peer victimisation	Profile settings	Content/identity management – consider perceptions on online users/peers
Contact and conduct risks	Privacy settings	Layered content/identity management Basic privacy settings for – "Friends Only" Customised privacy settings for posts, communications with family, mobile phone details
Contact and conduct risks (i.e. sexting)	Sharing Content	Content management (i.e. photos, comments on posts and walls, and status updates)
Risks associated with divulging Mobile Phone and Home Address (e.g. contact, content, conduct risks)	Contact Settings	Define peer group (i.e. Friends Only) with access to IM and email Block settings to be reviewed
Marketing, control of personal information, privacy	Application	Content management (i.e. limit use of personal information/content by friends, remove public search) Block inappropriate applications

Source: Adapted from Connect Safely, 2010.

above, the guidance advocates the use of educational material and technological tools to enable children to maximise the developmental opportunities as well as managing content, contact and conduct risks. Additionally,
reporting mechanisms and processes for quick responses to complaints and
concerns can enhance trust and confidence amongst users, parents and
educators. Many of the solutions implemented in response to the commitments under the SSNP have also been the subject of previous SIP initiatives
(European Commission, 2009a,b). Recently, Facebook launched its social
reporting facility enabling users to report incidents of inappropriate behaviour or misuse of content to their friends (Facebook, 2011). These initiatives
will increasingly be regarded by others in the industry as setting the benchmarks for good governance.

*Principles 5 and 7: Respond to notifications of Illegal content or conduct and
Assess the means for reviewing illegal or prohibited content/conduct*

Children and parents will have confidence in managing online safety
incidents and risks if they can also rely on timely responses to reports of
illegal content or online safety incidents. The obligation under principle 5
is informed by the rationale that expeditious investigation of notifications
of illegal content or abusive conduct can be an effective response in managing and responding to users' concerns about their safety and well-being.
The provisions dealing with furthering collaboration with law enforcement
ensures that potential threats to child victims, where online grooming is
concerned, can be eradicated and offenders prosecuted. The guidance document also offers some practical examples of implementing the moderation
and review processes. To this end, the work undertaken by the Home Office
Internet Task Force in 2005 – *Good practice guidance for the moderation of
interactive services for children* – is regarded as providing a standard setting
framework for social networking site providers (Home Office, 2005) (see
later discussion on "Media Literacy"). Many social networking site providers demonstrate compliance by using human and/or automated moderating
tools, filtering software and user-generated reports.

The seven principles under the SSNP provide a framework which allows individual social networking services providers to address the trust deficit and
online safety issues that may arise when children access and use their services. As discussed in earlier chapters, network publics and the affordances
provided by new technologies create numerous opportunities for misuse.
One advantage in having these principles is that they provide a benchmark
against which social networking services providers' compliance with these
obligations can be evaluated. Additionally, the SSNP also provides a flexible governance framework since it allows individual social networking sites
the opportunity to assess which safety measures are reasonable, appropriate
and even necessary. For example, sites like YouTube, Flickr and Dailymotion
are essentially communication platforms for users to upload or watch content like videos and photographs and consequently require reporting and

design solutions. By way of contrast, Club Penguin and Barbiegirls.com are designated sites for children, which may require extensive use of moderating, filtering and age-verification solutions and regular risk assessment reports.

Findings of an independent assessment of the implementation of the Safer Social Networking Principles for the EU

Subscription to the SSNP in itself will not enhance the safety of children or promote trust and confidence in social networking sites. It is important that site providers view online child safety governance as an ongoing process. Consequently, a mechanism is needed to ensure that subscribers to the SSNP are in effect clear as to their obligations – that they continue to take reasonable and appropriate measures to safeguard children on their social networking sites and have in place mechanisms for reviewing the effectiveness of their online child safety policies and measures. One way by which the EU ensures compliance with the obligations under the SSNP is through the conduct of a periodic review. The findings from the periodic review are published by the European Commission in a Report made available on the EU SIP website (Staksrud *et al.*, 2010). In preparing the most recent Report, a group of national researchers, hired by the Commission, visited the sites and assumed the role of fictional children aged 11 and 15 years. The information obtained by the researchers included those aspects relevant to safeguarding children from contact, content and conduct risks: the location of safety information; the accessibility of the information and whether it could be easily comprehended by a child; empowerment tools like blocking users or declining a friend request; pre-approval features for postings of pictures, posts and comments on a profile; privacy settings; and the ease with which profiles and information of minors on the sites were discoverable on the search directory. In addition to this, the researchers also sent a request to the site with the aim of assessing the quality and speediness of the response. Twenty-five websites were tested, and these included Arto, Bebo, Dailymotion, Facebook, YouTube, Xbox Live, Windows Live, MySpace, Piczo, Habbo Hotel, Yahoo! Answers and Yahoo!Flickr. Table 6.11 highlights whether the sites were "partially compliant", "compliant", "not compliant" or were not tested in relation to the seven principles under the SSNP.

The Report found that many of the services provided safety information for all users, minors, parents and educators (ibid., 2010: 19). The information provided varied from textual content to audio, photographs and video. Generally, the safety and privacy information were easily located, with some service providers being particularly proactive whilst in a small number of cases the "terms of service" were not easily discovered. However, in the case of 15 service providers, information for teachers was unavailable. Eleven sites provided information to teenagers that were accessible and comprehensible; it was felt that more effort was needed to provide young children with directed information on risk prevention measures and reporting

Table 6.11 Sample assessment of the self-declaration versus the measures implemented on the social networking sites

Signatories	P1	P2	P3	P4	P5	P6	P7	Comments/clarification
Bebo	C	C	C	Pc	Not tested	C	Not tested	
Facebook	C	C	C	Pc	Not tested	C	Not tested	Privacy and data protection issues remain an ongoing issue. Reporting mechanisms need to be made explicit and responsiveness to reports is slow Parental controls not available
Google	C	C	C	C	Not tested	C	Not tested	Safety options could be made explicit
Microsoft Europe (Windows Live and Xbox)	Pc	C	C	C	Not tested	C	Not tested	Accessibility of safety information via terms of service
MySpace	C	C	C	C	Not tested	C	Not tested	Extensive use of Parental Control Tools and Relevant accessible information
Yahoo!Europe	C	C	C	Pc	Not tested	C	Not tested	Moderation and Automated Responses notifying receipt of complaint Safety information needs to be targeted to specific groups

C, compliant; Pc, partially compliant.

Source: Report covers a sample of sites tested with key aspects summarised.

mechanisms (ibid., 2010: 20–1). The Report does not make clear what age groups came within the category of "children" and "teens". In relation to the information relating to online risks, most sites provided information about online bullying, hate speech, risks associated with divulging personal information and dangers of posting inappropriate or suggestive photographs on profile pages. From the sites tested, it was particularly noticeable that a number of service providers had very little or no information about the risks posed by sexual solicitation, self-harm and accessing illegal child images (ibid., 2010: 22). YouTube was seen as an example of good practice in relation to providing easy access to all relevant safety information. Sites like Habbo Hotel, Hyves, MySpace, YouTube and Zap provided safety information regarded as being accessible to children. Principle 2, which deals with age-appropriate services, was regarded as being implemented by most services, with information stipulating the age requirements for accessing services (ibid., 2010: 24). Many sites used technical and legal mechanisms to restrict minors' access to age-inappropriate information. The reviewers felt that more effort could have been made in providing parents with access to technological control tools on these sites (ibid., 2010: 25). Age verification and authentication of the identity of those registering on social networking sites continue to pose a challenge. In a recent survey by Consumer Reports, *2011 State of the Net Survey*, it was found that 7.5 million out of 20 million minors from the United States with Facebook accounts were below the age of 13 years (Consumer Reports, 2011). Facebook's registration policy states that users must be at least 13 years old. This social networking site provider is alleged to remove at least 20,000 underage users each day (Smith, 2011). At a hearing before the Joint Select Committee on Cyber-Safety, Facebook indicated that it was making considerable efforts in removing underage minors on its Australian sites (ABC News, 2011). This is an issue addressed in the report made by the examiners under the SSNP. It was reported that out of the 20 sites examined, seven applications were registered without email verification. In relation to three service providers, which were restricted to minors below 11 years of age, sign up was refused, with 17 service providers indicating that the refusal was due to age restrictions. The researchers used fictional birthday dates to re-register onto sites (i.e. indicating that the child was much older) where registration was previously refused on the grounds of age restriction. In seven instances, registration was approved by a simple change of the birthday date or age (ibid., 2010: 26). Sites like Bebo, Facebook, Microsoft XBOX Live and MySpace were held to have effective measures implementing age-restriction controls. The researchers found that principle 3 was not fully implemented by the sites tested. Even though many sites made available privacy and related information control settings, the fact that these were not set as default meant that some personal information was still visible to users and information of minors was still discoverable in user and general public directories (ibid., 2010: 27–8). Users in some instances could easily post comments on a profile whilst other sites had in place pre-approval/moderating tools (ibid., 2010: 29). That said, many services provided tools which allowed users to delete or remove postings and photographs on their own profile. A number of sites provided an alert service to users, notifying them when a picture containing them had been tagged on other people's profiles (ibid., 2010: 31). It seems that sites like Facebook and Myspace have made some progress in addressing the requirements under this principle. To assess whether the sites tested took users safety concerns seriously, the researchers sent the following message: "I am writing to you because someone is sending me scary messages. What should I do about this? Please help me" (ibid., 2010: 32). The message was sent from the registered profile of both a fictional 11-year-old and a 15-year-old child. The lack of an effective response from the sites could be explained by the fact that most sites have a pre-determined procedure for processing assistance and prescribe the type of concerns and likely risk management steps to be taken (e.g. bullying, grooming, harassment and illegal content). The researchers expressed disappointment that in a number of cases no acknowledgement to the request was received. Where links for reporting mechanisms were made available on sites it was found that response times varied from 24 hours to one week. Thirteen sites did not reply to the message requesting assistance while seven responded within 7 hours (ibid., 2010: 33). Google (YouTube), Myspace and Microsoft were regarded as examples of best practice in relation to responding to the underage user. ARTO, Bebo and Facebook were some of the sites deemed to have appropriate report mechanisms and found to acknowledge reports sent by users (Staksrud *et al.*, 2010: 34). Anecdotal accounts of response times suggest that more effort needs to be made by social networking site providers in this area. Generally, attempts to ascertain the response and reaction times to notices are important since a failure to address concerns promptly can often lead to minors being left without support during the interim. Returning to the implementation report, for ethical reasons principle 5 could not be evaluated, and the researchers could not submit reports of illegal content and conduct. Many sites appear to have encouraged users to adopt a safe use approach to personal information (principle 6) (ibid., 2010: 36). Users could use tools to alter their privacy settings and were provided with information which enabled them to make informed choices and decisions about the content they made available about themselves or posted online (ibid., 2010: 37). Bebo, MySpace, Habbo and IRC Galleria were identified as having exemplary practices. The Report noted that more could still be done by social networking site providers in publicising how users could terminate their accounts (ibid., 2010: 38–9). Finally the researchers relied on the self-declarations in establishing the sites implementing principle 7 (as was the case for principle 5), owing to ethical considerations.

Both case studies illustrate how the responses of online intermediaries and content service providers can help inform and define the way risks are identified, processed and managed. The implementation reports also highlight some unique aspects of online child safety governance. For example, the participation of researchers and experts in using social networking sites draws attention to the prudential measures that can be adopted at the network, design and educational levels. Within the context of risk assessment and management, the findings from the Framework and the SSNP implementation reviews also illustrate the benefits in providing regulatory oversight in the form of "testing" and engagement with the principal stakeholders (e.g. children, parents and educators). The fact that great strides have been made by mobile phone operators and providers of social networking services, for example, in developing technical solutions and communicating the online safety risks to parents and children is in part the result of regulatory pressure and efforts made by NGOs in highlighting concerns about risks associated with these products and services.

Conclusion

This chapter has provided one way of approaching and understanding the MSIG framework comprising the State, the private sector and civil society. The complexity introduced by the transnational nature of online risks and the nature of Internet communication infrastructures necessitates the adoption of flexible and reflexive regulatory strategies that operate at different levels and contexts. The use of Beck's ideas also illustrates how the management of risks and the processes for deliberation and participation become an important focal point of civil society activism and government concern. Increasingly, it seems likely that it is through these interactions that measures to assess, manage and communicate risks will be identified and inform governance policies and strategies. The two case studies illustrate the role of the EU in advancing the MSIG model for online child safety. These case studies also underscore Beck's conception of the risk society, particularly in view of the complexity in managing convergence and the processes for risk management, deliberation and participation involving civil society, industry and policymakers. Convergence in technology and social media implicates intermediaries who are deemed to be carriers and distributors of illegal content and these problems will have to be confronted at some stage in the immediate future. The "contamination" of the carrier model by those who engage in child sexual abuse and commercial exploitation has blurred the boundaries between telecommunication and child protection policies on the one hand and on the other hand has made domestic and international policymaking dependent on the integration of civil society and industry into the process of identifying and implementing sustainable solutions (Wu, 2004). It is unclear whether the EU and civil society organisations will continue to accept the age-verification problems or poor responsive times as either inevitable or a cost to be borne by minors. The reports furnished under the Framework and the SSNP should be cross-referenced with additional findings and reports undertaken in other jurisdictions. It is true that the proceduralisation of risk through the development of the Framework and SSNP enables policymakers to engage fully with online service providers and draw on the resources of NGOs who have shown considerable commitment towards undertaking a comprehensive scrutiny of risk management processes and decisions. There are, however, dangers, particularly in relation to NGO involvement in this area of governance – the boundaries between arguments relating to manageable risks and uncertainty can become blurred as a consequence. This minor criticism should not detract from the useful contributions made by NGOs in ensuring that the deliberative processes retain their democratic credentials. Even though the governance issues surrounding mobile phone and social networking site providers broadly reflect the concerns raised by parents and children in the EU, it is fair to say that the findings from the two case studies also resonate very much with the thrust of current policymakers' thinking about online child safety governance in the United States, Canada and Australia. Whilst the issues chosen for analysis have been selective, this should not distract us from the central message that runs across this book and more importantly which formed the focus of this chapter, namely, that without engaging all stakeholders, any enterprise aiming to enhance the safety of children in a system that recycles risk will prove to be futile and the gains illusory.

7
The Child, Media Literacy and Online Safety Policy Implications

Overview

As Web 2.0 technologies and social media become an integral part of children's lives, media literacy is emerging as an invaluable policy response, particularly for safeguarding children in the online environment (Livingstone, 2004a,b: 5; Prensky, 2001; *cf.* NCTE 1975). Targeting media literacy measures at children is not new. Before the Internet, educational and media awareness initiatives were relied upon to inculcate in children critical literacy skills (Gill, 2007:18–38; Megee, 1997). Media literacy initiatives were also seen as helping counteract the negative developmental and psychological effects of television programmes and commercial advertising on children (Buckingham, 2007: 84–6; Nathanson, 2004). An important premise in media literacy policies is that individuals who do not have access to relevant information will be least equipped in managing Web 2.0 technologies and online safety incidents in a safe and responsible manner (Rideout *et al.*, 2007). This intuition is broadly correct, as is reflected in the importance attached by the European Commission, mobile phone and social networking services providers in educating users, children and parents on the online safety and security issues (European Commission, 2011b; ECDG, 2009). This chapter is primarily concerned with understanding the role of media literacy with regard to online child safety governance; it emphasises some of its key features within the context of converging information and social media communication platforms and network publics which have practical governance and regulatory implications. Whilst accepting the value of informed decision-making as a child protection strategy, the central argument pursued in this chapter is that youth culture, network publics, the affordances of information flows and digital information introduce new complications that policymakers cannot ignore. Indeed, the idea that media literacy empowers children to better manage online risks should not disguise the fact that often it is not the lack of information about Internet threats but poor decision-making skills and the absence of ethical norms that lie at the root of some of the online child safety governance issues (James *et al.*, 2008; Thornburgh *et al.*, 2002: 12–13). Recognition of this feature has important implications for what we can and should expect from media literacy programmes (Byrne, 2009).

Preliminary observations

Byron stressed the importance of incorporating media literacy activities into policies for enhancing the safety of children in the online environment (Byron, 2008: 108). Many will agree with this recommendation (Buckingham *et al.*, 2007; Burroughs *et al.*, 2009; Eurobarometer, 2007; European Commission, 2010c). Children's exposure to risk-prone activities like interactions on social networking sites, emails, virtual worlds and mobile phones introduces a qualitative aspect to the issues online safety education and awareness campaigns are meant to address (Byron, 2010). Online safety education is now provided to all children across the world where Internet connectivity is available (Aqili *et al.*, 2010).

Balancing children's newfound autonomy with concerns about their safety and well-being is a source of considerable tension at home and schools where Internet access is available (Castells *et al.*, 2007; Palfrey *et al.*, 2008; Butterfield, 2010). New technologies, for example, now make children's online activities and interactions less amenable to supervision by parents (Livingstone *et al.*, 2011). Parents and educators are rightly concerned about children's inadvertent exposure to age-inappropriate and harmful content (ITU, 2009b; Lenhart *et al.*, 2007b; Hargrave, 2009; Council of the European Union, 2009a). Some regard these tensions as emblematic of constructions of childhood, where "the child at risk stems from adults' sense of exclusion from children's digital culture… [since in] this context, adults may experience a sense of losing control, and for understandable reasons" (Buckingham, 2007: 85). It is also an observation that illustrates the implications of living in the risk society for parents, educators and children:

> Individualization within modernity entails the almost constant monitoring of risk, which pervades our sense of how to manage ourselves and the world. Risks may be produced by social conditions, but we are expected to assess and manage them as individuals… Risks to children are represented as inherently more grave than risks to adults: it is almost beyond debate that we should "protect" children, that any potential risk to children should be taken very seriously. As adults we can decide to take risks, or to balance risk against pleasure. (Jackson *et al.*, 1999: 88–90)

These views of childhood, autonomy and safety warrant a close examination of media literacy initiatives, as it has obvious implications for our expectations of its role and limits within the MSIG framework.

Media literacy and the discourse on empowerment

What is media literacy?

Media literacy has been described as "the ability to access, understand and create communications in a variety of contexts" (OfCom, 2006: 6). There are other conceptions of media literacy. The Learning and Teaching Scotland Department regards media literacy as incorporating information literacy and lifelong skills.[1] The Audiovisual Media Services Directive adopts a broader view of the concept, which includes "skills, knowledge and understanding that allow consumers to use media effectively and safely" (European Commission, 2007a: recital 47). More recently, the Commission described the ability to access the media in a variety of contexts as important skills for engaging with Web 2.0 technologies and digital media (European Commission, 2007b). O'Neill and Hagen place particular emphasis on informed decision-making as an important goal of digital media literacy. They suggest that the focus on the "digital" dimension is more appropriate, given children's disposition towards technological affordances in the networked environment. Accordingly, as active participants, children "should be equipped with the necessary critical and conceptual tools that allow them to deal with, rather than be protected from the media culture that surrounds them" (O'Neill *et al.*, 2009: 230). Media literacy has also become a catchphrase for celebrating children's new autonomy and freedom in the age of information networks. Others herald a new phase of citizenship and institutional affirmation of children's rights in the evolving EU constitutional landscape. Media literacy complements the Commission's *Agenda for the Rights of the Child* in terms of its developmental and participatory potential (European Commission, 2011b: 11). It is a view that has been endorsed by Viviane Reding, who regards media literacy as critical "for achieving full and active citizenship".[2] It has recently been suggested that media literacy embodies a set of functional, critical and social competences (Sonck *et al.*, 2011: 2). These attempts in defining media literacy are consistent with approaches by theorists who attempt to construct the concept in terms of its participatory, cultural, developmental or protective value. Livingstone suggests that media literacy, if it is to have any substance or normative content, must involve more than providing individuals with access to content – she attaches particular importance to individuals being provided with the necessary evaluative and analytical tools that will enable them to engage critically with information in its various forms and contexts (Livingstone, 2003a). It is not the aim here to map the varying senses in which media literacy is understood or attempt to suggest why one definition may be preferable to another. Livingstone's observations, however, merit elaboration in terms of the four functions media literacy is meant to serve within the context of children's behaviours and activities regarded as risk-prone (Livingstone, 2005b: 6). First, literacy is regarded as enabling individuals to gain access to the technologies, information and online services. Second, adopting a critical stance towards the content will appreciably enhance the individual's engagement with Web 2.0 technologies and content. Third, individuals will become active participants in their interaction with digital content and technologies. Fourth, though not made explicit, individuals will be able to respond to the cultural and ethical challenges resulting from participation in network publics.

If the Internet, as some seem to assume, does nothing more than blend "old" media into "new" ways of communicating and interacting, then the apparent or perceived qualitative differences are perhaps distinctions without a difference (Penman *et al.*, 2007). This is not the case in reality, since informed decision-making and managing risk-prone activities place additional demands on participants in network publics as well as the private sector who are the primary providers of the technology and services that children now consume (Livingstone *et al.*, 2011: 45–8; Fox, 2008; Ofsted, 2010). As many observers of network publics have long commented, technological affordances also require individuals to take into account the reaction of visible and invisible audiences to their actions and conduct (Ito *et al.*, 2008; Hinduja *et al.*, 2008).

Web 2.0, media literacy and public policy objectives

The role of government is particularly important in ensuring that online child safety remains an important priority in the governance agenda. As countries continue to develop their human and technical infrastructure in the digital economy, promoting trust and confidence is seen as playing a critical role in national strategies for competitive growth and nation building (OECD, 2010a: 42; DCMS, 2009: 169–73). There is growing consensus that informational illiteracy can undermine the ability of individuals to engage fully with the Internet and reduce the range of cultural, social and economic opportunities the networked society makes possible (ACMA, 2009a: 29; DCMS, 2009: 189–90). This trend towards embedding media literacy in national programmes, as noted previously, is evident in many OECD economies. Countries have embarked on education and awareness raising campaigns (ACMA, 2009a,b; Fujino, 2009, 2007). ACMA, in its review of international developments in broadband and communication policy, commented on the significance of the interaction between media literacy, information security and a country's competitiveness (ACMA, 2009a: 29–30, 40). ACMA has undertaken a number of media literacy programmes aimed at shaping national policy interventions and regulations for the digital economy. Some of its initiatives include the promotion of young persons' use of Web 2.0 technologies and social media, promoting safe and responsible use of digital media and raising general awareness of ICT competences and skills (ACMA, 2007, 2009a,b, 2010a). Between 6 and 11 June 2010, ACMA hosted a national online security awareness week for all Australians, including children.[3] On 10 May 10 2010, Canada launched a public consultation aimed at formulating a digital economy strategy for Canada.[4] A task force involving multiple stakeholders will be vested with the responsibility for creating a National Digital Literacy Strategy. The National Broadband Plan for Connecting America views the development of digital literacy skills as a condition precedent for integrating Americans fully into the digital economy. These ideas and themes resonate much with the current direction in online child safety governance. The OSTWG published its final report and emphasised the value of a MSIG strategy towards online safety and literacy (OSTWG, 2010: 5). In the United Kingdom, OfCom, which operates under the authority granted by the Communications Act 2003 to regulate the broadcasting and communications sector, is of a similar mind. It works with a number of stakeholders from the private and public sector, as well as government departments and not-for-profit organisations, in promoting media literacy initiatives in the United Kingdom. The European Commission has also been instrumental in driving media literacy policies. In 2010, the Commission published its Communication, *A Digital Agenda for Europe*, where the promotion of trust and confidence amongst its citizens was seen as part of a broader strategy towards empowering individuals and enabling them to take advantage of the various opportunities provided by the digital economy (European Commission, 2010a: 24–5, 2010c,f). The Commission has also spearheaded a series of media literacy initiatives, one of which includes empowering children and minors in their use of the Internet and communication tools appropriately and safely (European Commission, 2009c). In the report published by the Commission, media literacy was seen as having an instrumental role, not least in developing the "critical capacities" of children and young persons in relation to their use of the Internet and communication technologies in all areas of their lives (2009c: 86). In the remainder of this chapter, an attempt will be made to describe some of the strategies for implementing media literacy policies.

The logic of information flows, media literacy and online child safety

Online child safety education and awareness raising initiatives are now firmly grounded in national, regional and supranational fora. On 13 November 2008, the UN Secretary-General Ban Ki-moon announced the setting up of the International Telecommunication Union's Child Online Protection (COP) initiative (ITU, 2008b). The COP initiative brings together stakeholders from the private and public sector, including UNICEF, the UN Interregional Crime and Justice Research Institute and the UN Institute for Disarmament Research. Raising awareness and capacity building are seen as critical to promoting and sustaining a culture of safe and responsible use of the Internet. The *Tunis Commitment* affirmed the indivisibility of human rights and regarded access to ICT, information and capacity building as key to creating an inclusive information society (WSIS, 2005). This Commitment has the broad support of governments, the private sector, civil society and international organisations in working towards implementing the undertakings set out in the *Geneva Declaration of Principles and Plan of Action*.

There are two models which are used to promote online safety education. The first is the "protection/precaution" model, which focuses on the contact, content and conduct risks and the measures to be taken in minimising exposure to these (Penman *et al.*, 2007). It is quite common in such a model for a prescriptive approach to be taken in managing children's access to and use of Web 2.0 technologies (e.g. "acceptable use policies" relating to ICT use, technological and design solutions and online safety awareness instruction). The emphasis here is on reinforcing the rules for safe and responsible use of Web 2.0 technologies and digital media. The COP initiative, for example, advocates greater parental and educator oversight in managing the online activities of very young children. Strategies include communicating the rules for accessing the Internet and utilisation of technological safety tools. For older age groups, it is more common to see online safety education programmes which adopt the "precaution/evaluative" model. Online safety education programmes targeting this age group aim to strike a balance between reinforcing protective risk management measures and encouraging reflective skills and values; children, educators and schools are seen as part of the "whole school" approach towards promoting safe and responsible use of communication technologies (Ofsted, 2010; OSTWG, 2010; ACMA 2009a,b). This model also attaches particular importance to building citizenship and resilience values (see "information security" discussion). A variant of the "precaution/evaluative" model is the "child-centric" governance model that defines the issues to be addressed by parents and educators for the age groups 5–7, 8–12 and 13 and above (ITU, 2009b). The guidelines deal with strategies and measures that can be adapted to deal with the cultural and developmental needs of children and young people. Broadly, online safety education measures adopted in jurisdictions where children are exposed to Web 2.0 technologies strive to uphold the UNCRC and the Tunis Commitment regarding the "the role of ICTs in the protection of children and in enhancing the development of children" as well as taking steps to "strengthen action to protect children from abuse and defend their rights in the context of ICTs" (WSIS, 2005: paragraph 24).

Framing the governance challenge for media literacy

It goes without saying that governance strategies and measures aim to ensure that children, parents and educators possess functional, information security and risk management competences. The qualitative dimension of the risks and the nature of digital information have practical implications for the delivery of media literacy programmes (ITU, 2009b,c). For example, as a result of Web 2.0 technologies becoming readily accessible and ubiquitous, we cannot view safety and security simply in terms of securing and monitoring physical spaces inhabited by children, since information flows now make possible for risks to be encountered in various contexts (e.g. home, school, virtual worlds, and social networking sites) and at different levels in the network infrastructure (e.g. game consoles, mobile phones and Internet) (Livingstone *et al.*, 2011: 51–2). Consequently, one objective of media literacy must be to help children make informed decisions about how online safety incidents are to be identified and managed. Another objective would be to educate children to realise that seeking appropriate assistance from responsible adults when needed is a legitimate option. Too often, anecdotal evidence suggests that children are fearful of reporting concerns and online safety incidents to parents and educators. In short, media literacy measures need to accommodate the nuances of engaging with youth culture, digital media and Web 2.0 technologies, particularly as mobile computing and information networks already create considerable challenges for online service providers, ISPs and parents in acting as "digital gatekeepers" (Hersh, 2001). Online monitoring tools and software are far from being infallible (European Commission, 2011a). In a recent study released by the European Commission under the SIP, it was found that a number of filtering software and parental control tools were less than effective on social networking sites and blogs (European Commission, 2011a). The study also reported that only 25 per cent of parents employed content regulation software. Other findings included the shortcomings in regulating age-inappropriate content on Smartphones and game consoles. To complicate the governance challenges further, studies on the dynamics of network publics and the affordances of Web 2.0 technologies also provide us with an understanding of why online safety messages may either go unheeded or appear to be ignored by children (Byrne, 2009; Livingstone *et al.*, 2008a,b). boyd suggests that some children's exposure to risks were contributed by the fact that they did not regard the safety messages as relevant to them or their daily lives (boyd, 2008b: 269–73). Some children, it appears, regard parental oversight of their online activities as an intrusion into their privacy and freedoms. Children's perception of online safety education and media constructions of risks cannot be underestimated. According to the psychological reactance theory, individuals faced with curbs on their freedom will experience reactance and consequently reassert their choices, which have the effect of diluting the effect of the restrictions (Brehm, 1966; Byrne *et al.*, 2011). Online safety messages and parental controls when perceived as intrusions may result in children developing "work around" strategies like creating false social networking site profiles, setting up of multiple email accounts and circumventing filtering controls and settings (Dillard *et al.*, 2005; Mitchell *et al.*, 2007c). In other instances, children's misplaced sense of their own safety and security can contribute to their inadvertent exposure to online safety incidents (Cox Communications, 2010). The recent phenomenon of sexting illustrates how a combination of all these factors can contribute to young adolescents assuming that online safety messages do not apply to them. Conversely, even if children do recognise the relevance of online safety messages, these may still be resisted (Byrne *et al.*, 2009). As Byrne and Hart argue:

> Boomerang effects also emerge in media literacy interventions... that are intended to reduce stereotypical attitudes generated from viewing media messages may sometimes increase prejudicial responses when compared to a control group. (Byrne *et al.*, 2009: 8)

The "boomerang effect" may also provide some explanation for the miscalculations by children which expose them to online incidents like peer victimisation and inadvertent exposure to age-inappropriate content in emails and websites (Lenhart *et al.*, 2007c). That said, we should resist the impulse in viewing all children's responses to online safety messages and guidance in negative terms. Children may in fact develop their own risk management strategies and solutions. According to the recent findings in a EU study 60 per cent of children who encountered sexual messages online discussed the matter with persons other than their parents (Livingstone *et al.*, 2011: 83) Notwithstanding the risk-prone nature of many of the online activities, children were found to utilise a wide range of risk management tools and strategies – defining their audiences through the use of privacy settings, blocking unsolicited or unwanted "friend" requests from persons outside the peer group, ensuring that only limited number of individuals gain access to user-generated content and reporting online safety incidents to responsible individuals and organisations.

What this brief account of children's approach to information and online interactions indicates is that framing the regulatory problem that media literacy is expected to resolve is not as simple as it might first appear. The governance challenges facing media literacy programme development is further compounded by the fact that the benefits of increased accessibility, mobility, replicability and instantaneity offer for learning and development can always be abused (Lenhart *et al.*, 2007c). Accordingly, information security competences (and ethical or citizenship values) need to be seen as a subset of media or digital literacy skills (O'Neill *et al.*, 2010: 18). We need, however, to be cautious about engaging in any form of technological determinism. As studies regarding children's use of Web 2.0 technologies continue to emphasise – risks arise in different contexts and settings and affects children differently (Livingstone *et al.*, 2010a, 2011). Given that children also respond and react to risks differently (i.e. gender, ethnic minority, special education needs) media literacy strategies need to avoid the image of all children as invariably coming within the category of vulnerable and incompetent individuals (Byrne *et al.*, 2009). It may very well be that better targeting of children who are likely to benefit from specific online safety resilience measures should be regarded as a policy priority and resources allocated appropriately in supporting any initiatives. It is beyond the purpose of this book or the chapter to address the online child safety governance issues that impact those children who come within this category of "at risk" individuals (Chamberlain *et al.*, 2010; Mencap, 2007; Office of the Children's Commissioner, 2006).

The interaction between information security literacy and media literacy

For media literacy to fulfil the standards envisaged in the UNCRC and the values highlighted in the *Tunis Commitment*, three areas needed to be addressed when deploying a hybrid of "regulators" (e.g. State, industry, civil society, parents and educators) and strategies (e.g. mandatory, self- and co-regulation) (Ofsted, 2010). First, the measures must aim to enhance ICT competences and knowledge of Web 2.0 technologies (functional literacy). Knowledge and understanding of the tools for using web browsers, instantaneous modes of communication and the affordances of Web 2.0 technologies are a pre-requisite to equipping children with the strategies for risk management (ITU, 2009b). Children will not be able to make informed decisions about how best risks can be managed in a safe and responsible manner if they do not have an understanding of Web 2.0 affordances and terminology. Drawing on studies and surveys under *the UK Children Go Online* programme, it was suggested that children do not possess the same analytical or evaluative skills with regard to engagement with digital content, when compared with adults (Livingstone, 2003a,b; Livingstone *et al.*, 2005a,c). This, it should be noted, is not always related to online safety and covers generic media literacy issues. The second matter to be addressed is that relating to raising children's awareness of the nature of digital information and problems associated with authentication and reliability (information security literacy). Whilst the promotion of functional literacy skills is important, safety and awareness raising strategies need to be seen as something more than requiring a technical solution to managing safety and online risks. The term "information security literacy" is not used in the sense of overcoming a child's perceived lack of cognitive and developmental ability to critically evaluate online information. We can understand "information security literacy" as a phrase used to denote an awareness and appreciation of the particular attributes of Web 2.0 affordances and the properties of digital information, which if misused, can potentially expose a child and its peers to online safety incidents (Butterfield, 2010). A lack of awareness of the functionalities of information networks can, for example, lead a child to readily assume that network publics constitute a defined audience, until he or she realises that information can be readily accessed, replicated and even distributed by and to visible and invisible audiences.

Disintermediation and anonymity also have important implications for a child's ability to authenticate and verify both the *identity of the users* the child *is connected with* and *those connected with him or her*. In a survey commissioned by Symantec, *Norton Online Family Report 2010*, which involved 9,000 online adults and children in the United States, Canada, the United Kingdom, France, Germany, Italy, Sweden, China, Japan, India, Australia and Brazil, it was found that media illiteracy and lack of information security skills were major factors impairing a child's ability to manage the risks encountered in settings like chat rooms, emails, blogs, search engines, gaming sites, virtual worlds and social networking sites (Norton, 2010). The release of the findings from the EU report on January 2011 provides some important insights into the media literacy skills of children within the 11- to 16-year-old age group (Livingstone *et al.*, 2011). The survey involved 23,420 children between the ages of 9 and 16, plus one of their parents and covered 23 Member States. For the purposes of the issues considered in this chapter, we can focus on one aspect of the findings relating to the responses of children to the eight digital safety skills deemed to be critical to minimising online safety incidents and risks (Table 7.1).

Table 7.1   Eight online skills and children's responses

	Boys 11–12 year old	Girls 11–12 year old	Boys 13–16 year old	Girls 13–16 year old	All
Bookmarking a Website	52	45	72	70	64
Blocking messages	45	46	72	72	64
Finding information on how to use the Internet safely	51	43	71	69	63
Changing privacy settings on a social networking profile	34	35	65	66	56
Assessing credibility of information found on websites	43	37	64	62	56
Deleting record of websites visited when surfing the Internet	37	29	63	59	52
Blocking unsolicited advertisements and mail	36	32	61	56	51
Changing filter preferences	15	12	41	29	28
Average number of skills	3.0	2.7	4.9	4.6	4.2

Source: Livingstone *et al.*, 2011: 27.

These eight skills are undoubtedly important and the findings can assist policymakers and educators better target the attainment of media literacy skills. The differences in the level of digital competences between the 11- to 12-years-old and the 13- to 15-years-old band should make clear that media literacy instruction needs to better engage children and effective strategies for measuring outcomes need to be developed. Findings that 28 per cent of the children surveyed were not confident in using access control tools to differentiate the quality of online content or that 34 per cent of children aged 11–12 years did not know how to alter the settings for managing disclosure and control of personal information on social networking sites need to be addressed through the use of practical exercises drawn from situations children are likely to encounter in their daily lives and experiences. The report concludes that some of the critical and safety skills still need to be more robustly embedded in current online safety education programmes (Livingstone *et al.*, 2011: 27). The focus on competences like the ability to adopt a critical stance on the quality of the information on websites, changing filtering and privacy settings, blocking unwanted communications and identifying safety information online are some of the skills children will have to master if they are to better engage with Web 2.0 technologies and social media confidently and safely. Clearly, education authorities and schools need to reassess the delivery, implementation and evaluation of media literacy programmes in the light of these findings (Livingstone *et al.*, 2011: 145–6). The Office for Standards in Education, Children's Services and Skills (Ofsted) will undoubtedly have an important role in auditing progress in this sphere of online safety education. It may very well be that more efforts will have to be directed at ensuring that parents and educators are equipped with the knowledge, skills and confidence in assisting children towards this end. Another explanation for these findings could very well be due to the fact that online safety education has until now been introduced to children far too late; educational interventions aimed at facilitating appropriate behavioural changes and attitudes need to be introduced when children first engage with Web 2.0 technologies (Livingstone *et al.*, 2011: 145).

Whilst the focus on ICT competences is important, online safety education must also address information security literacy issues like the manipulability, replicability and permanence of information. Other issues relate to the nature of information networks and the difficulties individuals encounter when differentiating between various forms of content. Ethical and moral dimensions of online behaviour can also be integrated into media literacy programmes (e.g. hacking, illegal file sharing, sexting and cyberbullying). The aim in seeking responses to the information security and ethical issues raised by children's participation in network publics is to educate children, parents and educators about the properties of information networks and to encourage them to evaluate technology from the perspective of their daily experiences and activities. The discussions generated between the child and the parent/educator can also be used to promote an understanding of the malleable nature of personal information, and identify the power imbalance and information asymmetries implicit in online interactions. As Turkle correctly observes, the view that childhood is a moratorium space may need to be re-thought since the permanence of data does not readily sit alongside with an online existence "that generates its own electronic shadow" (Turkle, 2011: 260).

Two additional observations can be made in the light of the findings from the EU study. First, the findings regarding a child's understanding and management of its privacy need to be approached with some circumspection. boyd and Hargittai rightly suggest that young adults' use of privacy settings depends on a number of factors: frequency of use, familiarity, confidence with technology and fear (boyd *et al.*, 2010). In their study of young adolescents on Facebook they noted some correspondence between children's confidence and familiarity with the communication platform and their ability in managing information accessed by their target audience. The authors also conclude that online service providers do not take into account sufficiently the fact that children who are most vulnerable may be least able to make effective use of their privacy settings on their social network accounts (boyd *et al.*, 2010). This is true but there is a much deeper issue. Turkle suggests that even though children's and adults' perceptions of privacy may not necessarily be identical, it does not obviate the need for parents and educators to engage children more fully in a wider discussion about how technology, privacy, and identity are being "re-wired" by online service providers (Turkle, 2011: 260–4). With regard to possessing critical skills which can assist children in differentiating the quality of information flows, the findings from the EU study do not make clear the process by which children actually engage with online content. This oversight needs to be rectified. One reason why children may inadvertently encounter age-inappropriate content from search results is that well-known information retrieval systems tend to be regarded as badges of credibility and trust (Hargittai *et al.*, 2010). This "leap of faith" is not unsurprising as Sundar observes that online content is now a composite of messages, categories and sources "embedded in the numerous layers of online dissemination of content" (Sundar, 2007: 74). Media literacy strategies must as a consequence start from the premise that children (like adults) adopt varying formal and informal content filtering strategies. An understanding of these processes is an important first step in supporting children in their attempts to differentiate the quality of online content derived from websites and search engine results (Metzger, 2007). If media literacy awareness initiatives are to attain their objectives, these complexities must be confronted, not only by the ICT industry but by online service providers. Accordingly, parents and educators need to be provided with the training and skills that enable them to understand the significance of website design, features and presentation, since these are attributes that young adults unconsciously take into account when evaluating web content (Hargittai *et al.*, 2010). A child's assessment of the credibility of material found online or its ability to differentiate the quality of online content can be derived from a wide range of sources and consequently any effective media literacy programme must reflect an awareness of cues children use when determining the credibility of online content in both formal and informal settings (Hargittai *et al.*, 2010: 487).

There are a number of benefits in integrating some of the observations noted above into existing online safety education and media literacy initiatives generally. For example, media literacy strategies can be used to identify concrete situations and affordances that are prominent in children's daily activities. Second, an understanding of children's use and perceptions of Web 2.0 opportunities and risks will ensure that children can be equipped with the knowledge and support that will enable them to reflect on their online activities (Donath *et al.*, 2004). Finally, information security education becomes an ongoing and relational activity where children can be engaged in a dialogue on not only what the risks are but also how risks arise and the rationale of many of the formal and informal rules and norms that can promote and sustain a culture of safe and responsible use. Engagement and continued dialogue will also ensure that parents and educators will be able to fulfil their roles as mediators should concerns arise (Livingstone *et al.*, 2011: 150–1). There is evidence from the wealth of information security material now made available on websites and those which are distributed in schools that the nuances of network publics and technological affordances are gradually being understood. Within the United Kingdom, organisations like Childnet, Beatbullying and CEOP now make available considerable information aimed at promoting children's, parents' and educators' awareness of existing and emerging information security risks (CEOP, 2010a). CEOP has recently produced educational material introducing children as young as five years of age to information security rules and concepts. The "Exposed" is one example of an initiative that helps children understand the persistence of data and its enduring implications for those engaged in the practice of sexting (CEOP, 2011). Complex data protection and privacy issues have also been addressed through the animation film – Lee and Kim's Adventure – which reinforce the security implications of the persistence and malleability of digital information. These are just two examples of resources that are now made available to children and parents – and crucially, for educators. The COP initiative has also provided online safety guidelines for parents, educators and children, which can be adapted accordingly (ITU, 2009b). These strategies and measures are increasingly reflected in the developments taking place across many jurisdictions including Australia, the United States and Canada and Member States in the EU.

One final point with regard to capacity building should be noted here. Should children be confused about the information they access online or encounter problems with regard to the use of social networking sites, mobile phones or other communications devices, it is imperative that they seek assistance from responsible adults (Livingstone *et al.*, 2011: 103–122). Many schools and child safety organisations provide information on how children can seek assistance or obtain redress. Even though there is evidence of children having recourse to peer mediation (i.e. CyberMentors), it is also important that measures are put in place which enable parents and educators to provide support and assistance (mediatory functions). Parents and educators have an important role in supporting and sustaining the standard setting activities covered in this book (National Foundation for Educational Research, 2009). Four reasons can be offered by way of support for integrating parents and educators into the MSIG framework, whilst noting some of the shortcomings expressed earlier. The first is that parents and educators spend by far the largest proportion of their time with children when they are at a developmental and formative phase. Admittedly, one is reliant on the child developmental model here in suggesting that adults can play an influential role in terms of both mediating ongoing and emerging issues encountered by children and promoting a culture of safety and civic responsibility (O'Neill *et al.*, 2010: 28–30). The role of parental oversight is based on the premise that parents' decisions and actions can have a positive impact on children's online interactions and consumption of Web 2.0 technologies (Livingstone *et al.*, 2011: 117–18; Byrne *et al.*, 2011). Researchers have long studied the strategies employed by parents and educators in mediating children's use of media (Livingstone, 2007, 2009c; Nathanson, 2004). In their survey of techniques adopted by parents in managing the online activities of children aged between 12 and 17 years, Livingstone and Helsper noted that the use of filtering and monitoring software solutions and social strategies like co-use, time and location restrictions varied according to parental styles, familiarity with ICT, age and gender of children (Livingstone *et al.*, 2008c, 2009a). Nathanson in a separate survey observed, however, that parents with negative conceptions of content screened on television were more active in mediating children's access to such content (Nathanson, 2002). This is also likely to be true in the case of parents whose view of children's interaction with Web 2.0 technologies are largely informed by media stories which sensationalise and magnify online risks and threats facing children (Livingstone *et al.*, 2011: 118; Byrne *et al.*, 2011). It is particularly helpful that online service providers now coordinate their activities with those of parents and educators by making available filtering and monitoring software, and instructional material focusing on specific age groups (Livingstone *et al.*, 2011: 148; Eastin, 2008). However, it should be noted that finding an effective strategy for engaging parents and carers must continue to be an important governance priority. Surveys suggest that some parents seem to be unaware of the online safety issues, underestimate the risks faced by their children or are less than confident in using online filtering tools and safety measures (Livingstone *et al.*, 2010b: 102–22; Livingstone *et al.*, 2011: 111–14). Children also reported that informing parents about past online safety incidents did have some influence on mediation strategies (Livingstone *et al.*, 2011: 116–19). Interestingly, the recent findings in the EU study relating to the differences between children and their parents' accounts of the online safety incidents experienced provide an insight into the complex interplay between reactance, parent–child mediation strategies and children's reporting of risky behaviour and online safety incidents (Livingstone *et al.*, 2011: 66–71, 77–78; Lee *et al.*, 2007; Liau *et al.*, 2005, 2008). The study also found that only a quarter of the children surveyed found the mediation efforts of parents to be helpful (Livingstone *et al.*, 2011: 115). Children in Turkey, Ireland and Bulgaria, for example, viewed parental mediation efforts as being overly restrictive when compared with experiences reported by children from Hungary and the Netherlands (ibid., 2011: 117). A number of possible explanations have been offered for these findings – parents lacking relevant ICT competences and knowledge; the appropriateness of parental mediation strategies and the availability of alternative mediatory and coping strategies (ibid.). Second, by including parents and educators in media literacy strategies, this can only serve to ensure that these stakeholders have a better understanding of the contexts and situations where timely interventions may be needed. Third, parents and educators can also provide the ICT industry, child welfare organisations and policymakers with insights into the issues and challenges that concern them with regard to their experiences and those of their children. The inclusion of parents and educators into online child safety governance can also provide policymakers with an opportunity to better coordinate their strategies, so that a principled and coherent approach towards online safety education can be delivered. Engaging parents and educators in the process has another relevance. Children's access to the Internet continues to be determined by parents and educators, and, consequently, if the broader goal is to ensure that children are able to realise the considerable benefits that the Internet and its technologies make possible, parents and educators need to have a better understanding of Web 2.0 technologies and the cultural dimensions of network publics (Livingstone *et al.*, 2009b: 3–11, Castells *et al.*, 2007).

The ecology of media literacy networks

The evolving governance model

Media literacy as a governance strategy towards enhancing the safety of children is based on three assumptions. First, the effectiveness of current online child safety strategies can be enhanced, if information about the risks and threats accompanying the use of the Internet and communication tools enables problems to be addressed at source. The unique characteristics of Web 2.0 technologies and its ready availability require an understanding of the different contexts and levels in which risks may be encountered. Second, that access to relevant safety and information security materials can promote trust and confidence. Third, children, parents and educators, at a philosophical or principled level, become part of the MSIG strategy. The emerging governance framework for media literacy consists of stakeholders drawn from various groups in society and a hybrid of instructional strategies and activities aimed at raising the awareness of children, parents and educators. One central theme running through debates and discussions on enhancing the safety of children is that children, parents and education need to be provided with information, tools and strategies in helping them make informed choices relating to the management of risks and online safety incidents. We have already seen the particular role of the EU and the United Kingdom in adopting measures aimed at promoting trust and confidence in the use of Web 2.0 technologies. The diverse range of strategies, measures and policies relating to media literacy prevents us from undertaking a critique of the governance approaches across the various jurisdictions. That said, it is clear that different stakeholders are actively engaged in addressing the trust and confidence issues which can enhance children's online experiences. Since many of the safety and risk concerns emerge from the environment where children congregate and the type of technologies that they use – mobile phones, virtual worlds, social networking sites and blogs – their status as consumers of technologies also has important policy implications for information services providers, organisations, industry and regulators (Lim *et al.*, 2010). The self-regulatory models for raising information awareness considered in Chapter 6 leave room for children to assume much greater responsibility for managing their online interactions in a safe and responsible manner. It will be recalled that the Byron Review recommended the delivery of an e-safety curriculum and the setting up of the UKCCIS (Byron, 2008: 70). UKCCIS was set up and published its online child safety strategy for the United Kingdom. UKCCIS has recently provided a series of industry best practice guidelines relating to moderation of interactive chat services for children, safe search practices, good social networking principles and best practices for chat services, IM and Internet connectivity content and hosting.[5] The governance strategies noted above are also reflected in online child safety policymaking in other jurisdictions (ACMA, 2009b,c). In the United States, the OSTWG was established to review the current initiatives promoting online safety and make recommendations (2010: 19–29). The Report of the Working Group was published on June 2010 and one of its recommendations was that children should be taught media literacy (OSTWG, 2010: 32). Media literacy consequently becomes part of the MSIG strategy. Many of the initiatives considered in that chapter will not be rehearsed here. It is now accepted that the ICT industry and businesses have an important role in promoting greater user awareness of their products and services, identifying the risks associated with these products and services, describing the measures for addressing emerging problems and informing users of their legal rights. As noted above, the European Commission has embedded media literacy strategies into its policymaking framework (European Commission, 2006a,b). For example, in developing media literacy initiatives, organisations in the Member States must take into account Recommendation 2006/952/EC, which includes promoting media literacy to teachers, trainers and children (European Parliament and Council, 2006). The Council of Europe has been proactive, as reflected in the publication of an online version of the Internet Literacy Handbook and a guide for teachers – *Through the Wild Web Woods* (Council of Europe, 2009, 2010).

Media Literacy, empowerment and human rights: A comment

Media literacy can be seen as part of the MSIG strategy on many fronts – enabling children to maximise the opportunities that communication tools provide for their personal development and lifestyles choices; promoting participation with peers and the wider community; facilitating the acquisition of skills that enable them to become responsible individuals and citizens and laying the foundations for their future engagement in the digital economy (Burroughs *et al.*, 2009). Benkler argues that our traditional views of media literacy and historically the exclusion of illiterate individuals from developmental opportunities can in part be attributed to the dominance of centralised, proprietorial industrial models favoured by policymakers and educators. He suggests that the transition into the networked information economy illustrates how policymaking and interventions by the State, in relation to media literacy, mark an important shift in thinking about the interaction between digital competence, literacy and human development (Benkler, 2006: 14). It must be right that equipping individuals with information that enhance their ability to access, understand and critically evaluate information will facilitate their ability to participate effectively in the information society (Burroughs *et al.*, 2009: 156–7; Livingstone, 2004b). Whether it is "old" or "new" media, literacy has strong normative foundations (Reguero *et al.*, 2010). As Jenkins correctly states, "[e]mpowerment comes from making meaningful decisions within a real civic context" (Jenkins *et al.*, 2009: 12–13).

This is the participatory and democratic ideal, which is also enshrined in the *Alexandria Proclamation*, which emphasises the value of literacy as a means through which individuals can realise their potential and engage effectively in their communities and societies.[6] Notwithstanding the force of the empowerment rhetoric that accompanies online child safety governance, there are compelling reasons for circumspection (Harris, 2005). The rhetoric of empowerment is never far from debates on whether the aim of media literacy should be to protect children from all potential harm (Hobbs, 1998). One view is that media literacy should not be framed purely as binary discourses of "risks" and "protection". Such a strategy, Hobbs suggests, is based on contestable assumptions, namely, that the function of media literacy education is to "inoculate" children from the negative influences of media (ibid., 1998: 19). In his review of the history of media education in the United Kingdom, Buckingham notes how the gradual democratisation of the curriculum resulted in a corresponding move towards protectionism (Buckingham, 1998). Concerns about the influence of popular culture on children resulted in a culture of inoculating students, as noted above, from the harmful or injurious effects of media (1998: 36). Even though media educators have since moved on from the defensive approach to understanding media, the Internet has re-ignited some of these old fears and concerns. It may be ill-advised to draw parallels between previous experiences in media education and emerging online child safety governance strategies. That said, we cannot ignore the fact that online safety education is continuously confronted with a number of these competing public policy goals (e.g. empowerment, autonomy, surveillance, blocking technology and restrictions on access) (Marx *et al.*, 2008). Buckingham has advocated going beyond the characterisation of the media literacy audience in binary terms of the sophisticated/vulnerable child and urges policymakers to focus on children's daily experiences and knowledge (1998: 37–8). Equally, media literacy cannot be separated from the constitutional dimension, which underpins childhood. The question of what is in the child's best interests has been dealt with previously (Fortin, 2006; Choudhry *et al.*, 2005). In that discussion, it was shown that the boundaries between what parents and educators regarded as being in the best interests was in some circumstances capable of being subjected to judicial or extra-legal oversight. The core principle providing the basis for media literacy is that communication is a basic human right (O'Neill, 2010). The *United Nation's Declaration of Human Rights*, for example, gives particular prominence to the needs of individuals as human beings to develop their abilities, and requires policymakers to ensure that their policies promote these goals. Children are, of course, not excluded from these expectations. If media literacy is to realise its normative ideals, it must at its core adhere to some fundamental precepts relating to children's rights – a particularly difficult task given that defining what constitutes age inappropriate content or inappropriate behaviour may be culturally dependent and made more difficult as ascertaining when childhood begins and ends is becoming practically impossible. These practical and legal difficulties also implicate our interpretation of the scope of Article 13 of the UNCRC, which recognises the child's right to freedom of expression, and that includes the freedom to seek, receive and impart information and ideas of all kinds, irrespective of whether they are oral, in written or in print, in the form of art or through any media of the child's choice. Access to the technologies and media is a pre-requisite to facilitating the realisation of this freedom.

As noted previously, the UNCRC and the *Tunis Commitment* envisage the State and society's commitment to enabling children develop their abilities and potential. More importantly, the *Tunis Commitment* calls on governments, the public and private sector and civil society to empower "young people as key contributors to building an inclusive Information Society" (WSIS, 2005: paragraph 25). Media literacy policymaking, and the strategy of empowerment, cannot be viewed outside the social milieu where children and their identities are socially constructed. Livingstone suggests that whilst the efforts of national media regulators and regional institutions like the EU aim to democratise children's engagement with new communication technologies and services, she counsels us to look carefully at the economic and political imperatives that are currently driving the media literacy policy agenda (Livingstone, 2008c: 58). It may very well be the case that "smart" regulation and the discourse on "stakeholder" participation may be the metaphorical "fig leaf" used to clothe the logic of capitalist imperatives. The politics of media literacy may be even more complex. Gill suggests that interest group politics characteristically tend to dominate policymaking and regulatory intervention since "[s]afety regulators, child protection and accident prevention agencies will want to see reductions in accidents, injuries, cases of abuse and neglect and other types of adverse outcome" (Gill, 2007: 82). Interestingly, notwithstanding the intentions of governments, civil society and the private sector the strategy reinforcing risk aversion is characteristic of "risk protestors" who regard the uncertain nature of the harm inherent in children's risk-prone activities as justifying regulatory oversight (Van Asselt *et al.*, 2009: 360).

Media literacy and the online context: An emerging paradigm

Media literacy strategies seem to be hindered by three particular deficiencies:

> The first is that it does not address the fundamental inequalities in young people's access to new media technologies and the opportunities for participation they represent (what we call the participation gap). The second is that it assumes that children are actively reflecting on their media experiences and thus can articulate what they learn from their participation (the transparency problem). The third is that it assumes children, on their own, can develop the ethical norms needed to cope with a complex and diverse social environment online (the ethics challenge). (Jenkins *et al.*, 2006: 16)

We have considered the participatory and transparency aspects in the discussion above but the reference to the "ethics challenge" accompanying children's engagement with Web 2.0 technologies is of contemporary relevance and can be elaborated by reference to a report issued by the Ofsted early in 2010 (Ofsted, 2010). The report was based on a small survey on how well schools were engaging students with online safety practices. Ofsted was asked to evaluate online safety training in schools. Its principal findings can be summarised. First, it was found that most schools had addressed the "participation gap" by ensuring that all children had access to ICT facilities and acquired basic competences. Without access to communication technologies and relevant knowledge of how the Web 2.0 system functions, building a sound base for promoting confidence is likely to be an uphill struggle. Confidence emerges from having both the knowledge and opportunity to engage with Web 2.0 technologies in a supportive environment. Second, many media literacy programmes were found to have adequately integrated children's experiences into the functional skills sessions, ensuring as a consequence that children were provided with a reflective space for engaging with the issues resulting from their participation in network publics ("transparency gap"). Finally, the inclusion of well-informed parents and educators was seen as creating opportunities where children could be engaged in a discussion on the role and place of ethical norms in their interactions with peers and social media ("ethics challenge"). It is not entirely clear from the report what addressing the "ethics challenge" entails other than creating a framework for deliberative engagement. Before delving into this issue some brief comments can be made. Too often, an overemphasis on the problems of information asymmetry and the individual's reluctance to intervene in cases of peer victimisation lead to an underestimation of the value of engaging children with the responsibilities and ethical challenges that result from their being part of an online community and culture (Livingstone *et al.*, 2005a). Without a basic understanding of the communication system, the tools for interaction and the ethical challenges faced by children, parents and educators cannot begin to understand what it means to be safe or how safety can be compromised in various venues and settings inhabited by children. For example, Shariff alludes to the importance of fostering a collaborative approach to addressing the problems posed by peer victimisation and the value of education (2009: 127–56). However, before media literacy can be used to promote appropriate and reflective responses from children, we need to not only address the deficiencies outlined in the extract quoted above but we also have to articulate clearly what being safe and responsible means within the cultural environment of network publics. Turkle, for example, highlights the way breaches of civic or non-political norms are viewed by children as part of

> [c]elebrity culture, [which] is all about transgression and rehabilitation. (These young people's comfort with "bullying" their peers is part of this pattern – something for which they believe they will be forgiven.) (Turkle, 2011: 262)

Media literacy strategies also have to address the new socialising structures that constitute children's environment of collapsing audiences and contexts (Castells *et al.*, 2007: 141; Livingstone, 2008a). Consequently, media literacy strategies need to embrace an MSIG approach where

> gatekeeping institutions, including local government, schools, libraries, and even families broker initial access to technologies, while educators and other adults are poised to provide the technical skills that permit a basic level of participation and the social and ethical skills that can nurture "good participation". (James *et al.*, 2008: 42)

This is, however, easier said than done since the role of the Internet as a democratising tool has also to be considered within the context of a patriarchal society (Lankes, 2008: 108). It is not an exaggeration to say that managing this transition in the way children now redefine their values and norms is a process that will take considerable investment in time and thought (Spielhofer *et al.*, 2009; Ipsos, 2009; Ofcom, 2008c, 2009). There is a discernible trend, however, towards addressing some or all three challenges at varying degrees of success. Educators and child welfare advocates and policymakers from the United States, the United Kingdom, Canada and Australia focus on the principal risks facing children and the steps to be taken. The information awareness strategies display some common features: (a) identifying key online safety incidents; (b) categorising audience and age groups (i.e. children, educators, parents and carers; age and gender) and outlining formal and informal redress mechanisms. The Next Generation Learning Portal is an example of an information portal providing parents, educators and children with information about the way Web 2.0 technologies can be used both at home and at school, with particular focus on education.[7] The site provides a wide range of information for children, parents and educators. It is not limited to online safety education, but also highlights some of the benefits in using technology both in the home and in classrooms. This site contains useful information on how technology can be used in the classroom and provides guidance for those who use the Internet when studying at home. Indeed, this is a dominant theme in the "Oh, Nothing Much Report" which is designed to encourage parents to engage with children with regard to their day in school.[8] There are links from the site to online safety resources at Thinkuknow.[9] Age-specific materials are grouped into resources for those aged between 4 and 7, 8 and 10 and 11–16 years. There is also a set of materials for those with special educational needs. Sites like the BBC and Childnet continue to devote resources aimed at providing parents and children with information about online safety. For example, the topics covered on the CBBC website include safety tips on gaming, use of chat rooms, social networking sites and IM.[10] Childnet International has an education portal focusing on digital citizenship and provides useful information for parents with older children.[11] Apart from parents, educators are also provided with resources aimed at raising their awareness of online safety issues. The online portal Teachtoday provides teachers, head teachers, governors and other members of the school workforce with information on new technologies and its possible use in schools.[12] One by-product in providing members of the teaching profession with this resource is to enable them to facilitate, support and manage children's use of the Internet and related technologies effectively. The Teachtoday site also provides bulletin boards and help functions to assist teachers with queries to questions or safety issues likely to be encountered in the educational context. The online portal was developed as part of a collaborative venture involving industry (e.g. social networking sites and mobile phone companies) and the teaching profession. The B4USurf site adopts a similar approach.[13] This portal is aimed at young people in the Asian region, in particular Singapore. The programme known as the "Cyberwellness Framework" provides a modular series of topics dealing with the threats and opportunities encountered by young persons online. The topics also integrate the cultural values and sensitivities of parents and children from this region. The contents of the site are produced in collaboration with the Business Software Alliance, and the programme targets children in the age groups 11–12, 13–16 and 17–19 years. There are suggested lesson plans which educators can use. For example, the lesson on "Blogging and use of social networking sites" focuses on individuals' responsibility for their online behaviour. Media literacy instruction includes student participation in developing acceptable use policy for blogs and social networking sites. The portal also provides parents with information about the "Cyberwellness Framework". In Australia, there have been a series of enterprising initiatives promoting media literacy in relation to online safety issues (CWG, 2010).[14] Responsibility for implementing government's policies in this area are devolved to a number of organisations including the Department of Broadband, Communications and the Digital Economy (DBCDE) and ACMA. The involvement of these agencies offers the benefit of a coherent "joined up" approach towards cybersafety education. The Stay Smart Online website, for example, provides a centralised information portal for online safety education and a free alert service for subscribers. ACMA, whom we have already mentioned previously, launched a website, Cybersmart, which provides online users with online safety information and advice and also has a presence on YouTube.[15] Like many of the social networking and child welfare organisations in the United Kingdom, the website provides a mechanism for reporting illegal and suspicious activities. Australia has its own version of Thinkuknow, which works closely with Microsoft, the AFP and ninemsn.[16] The CWG also takes soundings from the Youth Advisory Group in developing its cybersafety education and awareness raising policies. On 16 May 2011, ACMA announced a professional development programme for its educators (ACMA, 2011). This is a free accredited programme aimed at providing educators with a comprehensive understanding of children's engagement with Web 2.0 technologies and educators' obligations in enabling children to manage their online activities in a safe and responsible manner. In Alberta, Canada, the Alberta Children and Youth Services provides online safety education information for children and families. For example, the badguypatrol site (http://www.badguypatrol.ca/) is an interactive site which uses play and story narratives to teach children aged between 5 and 10 years critical Internet safety skills. Some of the issues covered include privacy and the dangers of anonymity. The website http://www.weron2u.ca/ provides teenagers with a granular perspective of online risks and threats drawing on actual techniques used by online sexual predators and provides an interactive game involving blocking of unwanted contacts and true life stories of children who have met online contacts offline. Finally, the Prevention of Child and Youth Sexual Exploitation Committee of the Government of Alberta set up a website, http://www.getwebwise.ca/, aimed primarily at families and provides resources on online child safety. The Media Awareness Network has developed a website, Be Web Aware (www.bewebaware.ca), which provides families with relevant online safety information. This website was created in collaboration with Bell and Microsoft Canada. In Australia, the search engine provider Google and the computer software company Microsoft worked closely with government and NGOs in providing all stakeholders, including children, parents and educators, with online safety education. The social networking site, MySpace Australia, delivered an interactive cyberbullying education campaign and competition for Australian high school students in 2009. This campaign was hosted jointly with SonyBMG, the Daily Telegraph, Kids Help Line and the New South Wales Education Department.

A closer look I: Hector's World™

One project that encapsulates the role and value in providing parents, educators and children with relevant and accessible information is the education and public awareness programme known as Hector's World™.[17] Hector's World™ is an online portal which contains a wide range of learning resources for children aged 2–9 years. A distinctive feature of this portal is its online safety education strategy aimed at providing children, parents and educators with relevant online child safety information. More specifically, the strategy of bridging education and entertainment works well with the use of animations, interactive multimedia formats, storylines and identifiable characters. The site also provides material aimed at encouraging parents and educators to reinforce important safety and citizenship rules and values (Butterfield, 2010: 109–19). Most of the resources provided on the site seem to reflect an understanding of the way children learn and engage with the Internet and technology. Hector's World™ has clearly identified learning objectives founded on "core" values, which underpin the program for lifelong "digital citizenship", namely, "respecting yourself, respecting others, caring for yourself and caring for your community". "Digital Citizenship" is regarded as bringing together the issues of safety, information literacy, media literacy and digital literacy. The media and information literacy components aim to promote many of the goals we ascribe to "media literacy" – namely, the development of skills required when dealing with information and media. "Digital literacy" is concerned with providing children with accessible information about the Internet and some of its communication and search functions. "Cyber safety" covers contact, conduct and content risks and focuses on information asymmetries which contribute to a child's exposure to online safety incidents. This module also provides children with an opportunity to draw on their personal experiences when reflecting on the problems encountered in differentiating information flows (Kolb *et al.*, 2000). For example, there is a short animation storyline involving the disclosure of personal information. Animated characters are used to provide a story narrative regarding the dangers of disclosing too much information and the steps that can be taken to mediate risks (i.e. through the use of pseudonym). The subject of cyberbullying (e.g. "You are not alone") is presented in two formats – an interactive video and a music video. The narrative storytelling strategy, which situates the subject within a context that a child can relate with, is central to reinforcing the safety issues and messages. One of the characters (Ming) is bullied when her photo is defaced and distributed to others. Hector and his friends note Ming's state of distress and respond in a positive way. An opportunity is provided by a temporary pause during the animation, for parents or educators to engage with children and seek their thoughts on how Ming might be feeling and ascertain what Hector and his friends could do by way of support. The session also introduces children to the way digital images can be manipulated, distributed and uploaded onto websites. The other matter that is addressed quite well is the provision of clear information on how children can seek assistance should they encounter problems. Often children who experience online incidents may be embarrassed or anxious about informing their parents or educators. This website provides useful information on steps children can take to either resolve problems by themselves or seek assistance from responsible adults. In building "resilience", children need to be given the means and opportunities to take steps in managing and addressing risks they encounter. In the episode on cyberbullying, Hector and his friends inform a responsible adult. The conduct of Hector and his friends is aimed at instilling in children a sense of community and the type of conduct expected from children as members of a community. Reference is also made to the actions of the "bullies", and children are encouraged to articulate reasons why such forms of behaviour (even though intended as a prank or a joke) may be inappropriate. It is quite important, in the context of Hector's World™, that the bullies apologise to Ming for defacing the photo and distributing it to others. Hector's World™ also adopts appropriate narratives for older children, with the focus again being directed at raising awareness, encouraging the adoption of acceptable social norms and reflection and providing information about the mechanisms for redress and grievances. These values also correspond very much with the idea of a digital citizen and reinforce the important roles that parents and educators can play in inculcating norms of safety and responsibility and help them target the right behaviours at a very early age in a child's online experiences.

We can close this discussion by offering a brief snapshot of one model that addresses the "participatory", "transparency" and "ethical" components highlighted by Jenkins.

A closer look II: The good play mode, cybermentors and Claire's story

Good Play is part of the GoodWork® Project which aims to showcase institutions and individuals who produce work that are academically rigorous and which are seen as making meaningful social contributions to practitioners. The Good Play project is intended to provoke in the inquisitors an informed discussion of the "ethical fault lines" that have emerged as a result of children's online experiences and interaction with social media (James *et al.*, 2008; Jenkins *et al.*, 2009). Whilst media literacy policies ordinarily focus on access, understanding, evaluation and creation, the Good Play project views the interaction between youth and the Internet in terms of eliciting ethical issues from "online conduct that is both meaningful and engaging to the participant and responsible to others in the community in which it is carried out" (Jenkins *et al.*, 2009: 15; James *et al.*, 2008: 44). One consequence of approaching the ethical issues raised within this framework is that it enables participants to adopt a child-centric perspective of interactions in network publics and their response to the participatory, transparency and ethical challenges inherent in their leisure time activities on social networking sites, gaming sites and mobile phones. The challenges can be approached from various dimensions – identity, privacy, ownership and authorship, credibility and participation (James *et al.*, 2008: 5). The Good Play approach is particularly relevant to media literacy in that it does not adopt a fundamentalist conception of safety or responsible use – rather, it aims to foster a dialectic engagement between children, parents and educators, which places the child's development, needs, experiences and expectations within the broader environment of social and cultural norms and values. Consequently, an expansive view of ethics is adopted which includes "respect/disrespect", "morality/immorality" and "individual behavior to role-fulfilment" (James *et al.*, 2008: 7). Values like respect, tolerance, accountability and civic responsibility figure prominently as these are seen as being invaluable to the discourse on children's understandings on a range of issues – racism, disability, religion, gender and sex. Even though it is not possible to do justice to the complex dynamics of this project in the summary, we can speculate on the operation of the Good Play methodology in one possible situation – peer victimisation on social networking sites. The following is a case study adapted from the Beatbullying project:[18]

Claire had an account on the popular social networking site MySpace. Over a period of time Claire built up a network of friends, which included classmates from years gone by and which brought her into contact with "friends of friends". Claire was unsure how it all started, but she discovered some posts on her profile page which were critical of her. Things gradually worsened – the comments posted on her profiles and photos became more vindictive and personal. Some of these postings were subsequently distributed to other children in Claire's school. Two months after the negative postings started, Claire logged onto her MySpace account and found the following message: "I just want you to know what a fat, evil, sadistic cow you are. I want to see you to suffer as slow and painful a death as possible." The insults covered both her off-school and her on-school activities (Beatbullying, 2009).

We can deconstruct this entire episode into the formal language of criminal law rules, or even conduct a media literacy session around this "worst case scenario". The Good Play approach provides a complementary strategy, which can be used to situate information security and media literacy concepts within a broader social context, which is alert to the cognitive, moral and character development of children:[19]

Can or should young people be allowed to present their identities for public display?

How do we engage with children about the value of feedback, particularly on social networking sites?

Are there disadvantages to a child's emotional well-being and personal development, where feedback becomes a primary factor in identity formation?

How do we engage with children who now use the anonymity provided by the Internet to participate in activities in which they would not ordinarily engage in?

Does computer-mediated conduct like peer victimisation become norms as a result of face-to-face mediatory opportunities being absent? Are offline bystanders proactive in enforcing acceptable social norms?

What are the implications of Claire's experiences when drafting a school-wide policy and who should participate in this process?

Is Claire herself culpable?

These are difficult questions and admittedly do not present us with easy answers. This is or has never been claimed to be the goal of the Good Play approach since it requires children to

> consider their roles in various online contexts, understand the responsibilities that are implied by them, and imagine the larger implications of various judgments. (James *et al.*, 2009: 89)

It is not possible to deal with these and the earlier questions posed in any meaningful detail, save for the observation that the absence of clearly delineated ethical norms and poor decision-making skills lies at the root of concerns about children's exposure to some of the "contact", "conduct" and "content" risks. To be sure, a more robust approach to online safety education would require educators to adapt some of the principles from the "12 Guiding Principles of Exceptional Character"[20] formulated by the International Center for Leadership in Education or those developed by the Heartwood Institute ("The Seven Universal Ethical Attributes").[21] The "Seven Universal Ethical Attributes" (i.e. courage, loyalty, justice, respect, hope, honesty and love) can, for example, be adapted to reflect the dilemmas faced by children as bystanders to cyberbullying.[22] Issues like sexting, illegal file sharing of copyright works, peer victimisation and unauthorised hacking can be based on principles like "honesty", "compassion" and "contemplation". For example, the disintermediated nature of the online environment may lead to individuals engaging in acts that they would not ordinarily be involved with in the offline environment (and vice versa). Conversely, cyberbullying may be prevalent because of the anonymised nature of online interactions or the result of the perpetrator or bystander's lack of empathy (Ohler, 2011; Office of the Children's Commissioner, 2006; Chamberlain *et al.*, 2010; Mencap, 2007).

Indeed, it can be said that the Good Play approach embodies to varying degrees some if not most of these principles and values when calling on parents and educators to reflect on key governance issues raised by questions like:

> How can we "ensure that all students benefit from learning in ways that allow them to participate fully in public, community, [creative,] and economic life?" How do we guarantee that the rich opportunities afforded by the expanding media landscape are available to all? What can we do in schools, after-school programs, and the home to give our youngest children a head start and allow our more mature youths the chance to develop and grow as effective participants and ethical communicators? (Jenkins *et al.*, 2009: 117)

Conclusion

Media literacy and public awareness campaigns will continue to be an important public policy response to concerns about children's vulnerability to online risks and harms. We should, however, be under no illusion about the role and value of media literacy. The premise that raising the awareness of parents and children will enhance the safety of children is valid to the extent that we accept that many of the actual risks (e.g. encountering unsolicited content which is illegal or inappropriate) or harm encountered by children are attributable to the lack of relevant accessible information relating to the management of online risks and incidents. More online safety education will not necessarily lead to transforming behaviours of children and young adolescents. Children will still continue, despite their participation in media literacy programmes, to make decisions that adults may regard as irresponsible or immature (Byrne *et al.*, 2011). Perhaps, more significantly, the discussion has highlighted the value of integrating the "ethical fault lines" paradigm into online safety education strategies. We cannot, however, ignore that some "mistakes" made by a child can have drastic safety and well-being consequences on a scale and intensity never previously encountered. That said, we need an honest, responsible and mature approach towards media literacy. Framing the debate in terms which conflate uncertainty with risks can only lead to more calls for surveillance and legal and regulatory intervention, which do not necessarily enhance the safety and well-being of children (Sampson, 2002). One enduring message from the Good Play approach is that media literacy must involve teaching and educating children that Web 2.0 technologies bring with them opportunities, risks and responsibilities (Ohler, 2011).

8
Concluding Thoughts: The Tethered Child

Safeguarding children in the online environment opens up a new dimension for governance – network publics and the affordances of Web 2.0 technologies expose children to potential vulnerabilities. The need for a coherent and principled response from all stakeholders in enhancing children's safety in the online environment received its most high-profile advocate – President Barack Obama. The Summit at the White House reiterates an important aspect of online child safety governance – we need to continue to develop MSIG strategies which enhance the safety of children since the limitations on national legal systems are manifest (White House, 2011; Chamberlain *et al.*, 2010). If we accept the premise that the law is unable to provide a perfect resolution to the threats facing children in an increasingly networked society, one rational strategy would be to focus our governance efforts in coordinating the activities of all stakeholders in society and ensure their compliance with established rules and principles. In this closing chapter I wish to bring together some key issues and themes highlighted in the book.

Childhood, convergence and the risk society

We now have a wealth of research to draw from with regard to what children do online, the technological affordances that increase the range and avenues for communication and the resulting safety issues. Numerous studies and policy reviews point to children being immersed in Web 2.0 technologies, and more crucially from a very early age (Berson, *et al.*, 2010; ACMA, 2009e). Even though network publics provide children with new spheres for development, experimentation, learning and identity formation, it is also becoming apparent that the idea of Web 2.0 technologies providing a moratorium space for children to grow up needs to be reassessed (Turkle, 2011). Convergence in multimedia technologies and their ready accessibility provide children with new spaces for interaction and identity formation, which may even accelerate the "disappearance of childhood". It is too early to draw any conclusions as to how best we can harness the

developmental opportunities these technologies make possible whilst minimising children's exposure to the worst excesses of the networked society.
One thing is already becoming clear – mobile phones, social networking
sites, virtual worlds and online games are now becoming evocative objects
for children (Turkle, 2007; Jackson *et al.*, 2009). Turkle has long remarked
that children now view their online relations and experiences through
computer screens, artificial personas (avatars) and mobile phones (Turkle,
1999). These identities and experiences are an aspect of what many have
come to regard as the second "self" – children now regard the virtual environment as defining their identities and lives (Livingstone *et al.*, 2011).
As the "virtual" become inseparable from the daily activities of children,
Beck's observations regarding the paradox of the logic of capitalism seems
all the more poignant – the individualisation of risks leads to society being
preoccupied with the risks associated with children's interaction with Web
2.0 technologies (Beck, 1999). We are also reminded that "[f]or teenagers it is their orientation to online communication that may pose risks as
much as they open up opportunities" (Livingstone *et al.*, 2011: 106). This
may be correct – in fairness, it is an observation that is equally true for
adults as well as children (Turkle, 2011: 260–1; Livingstone *et al.*, 2005b).
As individuals increasingly regard the Internet as an environment for socialisation and development of their personal relations, their orientation
towards information flows and affordances will invariably expose them to
all manner of risks. This is the Faustian bargain we make when we become
tethered to information networks (Turkle, 2011, 182–6). The tendency to
regard children as a homogeneous body of individuals that justifies paternalism may be a view that will increasingly be hard to sustain as children
seek new experiences and opportunities presented by ubiquitous mobile
computing technologies, with or without parental oversight. Conversely,
the scale and the irreparable nature of some of the content, conduct and
contact risks may require a more nuanced approach to safeguarding children. In Chapter 2, some reasons were offered to help us understand why
paternalistic attitudes are pervasive and its significance for the risk-based
approach to governance explained. As media spotlight continues to sensationalise children's vulnerabilities – stories of children committing sui-
cides, online sexual grooming and peer victimisation – we need to remind
ourselves that in our postmodern society, risk management has become
an important preoccupation of policymakers, and society generally (Fry,
2009). Online child safety governance, however, poses policymakers with
formidable challenges since there is a societal expectation that interventions are needed as children are

> an especially vulnerable audience – easily influenced and exploited, at
> risk from all sorts of grubby commercial interests, and particularly from
> those who peddle violence and pornography. (Buckingham, 2007: 85)

These expectations are already creating tensions within the MSIG framework on a range of subjects: filtering, age verification, monitoring of online content and the boundaries of "content deemed to be inappropriate". Beck's "risk" thesis provides us with one rhetorical framework for understanding the factors motivating our increasing reliance on digital gatekeepers and the criminal law in reducing the risks faced by children (Beck, 1998). Risk consciousness is pervasive, and perhaps most clearly illustrated by society's image of the pathological child (Furedi, 1997; Beck, 1992a). One is struck very much by the parallels between online child safety discourse and accounts of community safety initiatives involving the characterisation of youth deviant behaviour (e.g. anti-social behaviour), which have attracted the interest of the media and the political establishment. It therefore comes as not too much of a surprise that children's online interactions are problematised (e.g. risk-prone behaviours) and every risk-prone activity is now placed under constant scrutiny (ITU, 2010a,b). Online safety is not purely a legal issue but is now seen as requiring political, technological and cultural engagement (OECD, 2008c). The State is now one of a number of actors engaged in managing the risks faced by children in the online environment. This departure from an era where risk regulation was the province of the State and its institutions is a feature of the risk society. As Beck correctly observes:

> The sociology of risk reconstructs a techno-social event of its (im)materiality. Where risks are believed to be real, the foundations of business, politics, science and everyday life are in flux... The concept of risk reverses the relationship of past, present and future. The past loses its power to determine the present. Its place as the cause of present-day experience and action is taken by the future, that is to say, something non-existent, constructed and fictitious. We are discussing and arguing about something which is not the case, but could happen if we continue to steer the same course as we have been. (1997: 137)

This is particularly true. Each chapter in this book can be viewed through the lens of Beck's risk society. Risk is obviously not a new heuristic (Hood *et al.*, 2001). However, it is argued that the intersection of technology, youth culture and risk has led to traditional discourses on children's safety and well-being being replaced by another discourse – "multi-stakeholder", "governance", "resilience" and "safety". Governance now requires all stakeholders to engage in managing both risks and uncertainty associated with technological affordances like chat rooms, mobile phones and social networking sites (Ito, 2008). The objectives outlined in the Byron Report (and one which is also found in policy reviews across the EU, the United States, Canada and Australia) highlight the salience of the politicisation of online child safety governance: "risk-prone" activities, "safe" spaces and "risky" behaviours (Howitt, 1995; Jenkins, 1997; Buckingham, 2007). Such is the extent of parental anxiety that children are encouraged not to give out their personal information and they are constantly reminded through the media and online safety awareness initiatives of the dangers of online sexual predators, notwithstanding that many children take precautions like blocking strangers and use their privacy settings on social networking sites to control third party access to their online communications and user-generated content. Indeed, managing uncertainty has become as important as managing the threats posed by the Internet and its affordances. This way of thinking has become so entrenched in contemporary discourse that it is hard to imagine that the media, educators and parents were once filled with a not dissimilar anxiety about unsupervised children in public places and playgrounds (Graham, 2010). It is little wonder that adults and children tend to disagree on how best autonomy and security issues are to be negotiated (Castells *et al.*, 2007; Byrne *et al.*, 2011). These flows of information now constitute the new risk paradigm not in the sense of new hazards but in the intensity in policymaking efforts in managing complexity and uncertainty.

New communication technologies and the platforms for engagement reconfigure the way individuals and more particularly children engage in these spaces (boyd, 2010: 39–46). One thing is apparent. As children increasingly become tethered to their devices and online environments, parents are understandably anxious about their children becoming victims of bullying, being inadvertently exposed to age-inappropriate content or groomed by online sexual predators. Policymakers and educators continue to be concerned about the corruptive influences of the world beyond the school environment and growing reports of covert bullying and deviancy (House of Commons, 2011). Convergence, in summary, presents society with a complex set of challenges and decisions for child protection policymaking (Livingstone *et al.*, 2005a; OECD, 2008a). Before we turn to the broader question that online child safety governance raises, it is worth noting in passing the findings from the interim report funded by the EU SIP (Livingstone *et al.*, 2011). The study also found that even though older children tend to encounter more online risks, children can and do take responsibility for managing risks and have developed coping strategies (2010: 106). These are not isolated findings – policy reviews undertaken in the United States, Canada and Australia report the developing culture of safe and responsible use amongst children. With regard to the mediation efforts of parents and educators, ACMA, in its ongoing research on children's use of the Internet and social media, concluded that parents were now better equipped to manage and support their children's Internet use (ACMA, 2009b,c). Even though the strategies for raising public awareness and engaging industry, educators, parents and children are having some effect, it is also clear that a number of parents are either ignorant or suffer from apathy with regard to online safety matters. The EU Kids Online II Report also produced the worrying finding that many parents continue to underestimate the on-line risks actually encountered by their children (Livingstone *et al.*, 2011). For example, a number of parents seem to be unaware that their children have seen adult content online (inadvertently or otherwise), been subjected to peer victimisation or fail to recognise signs of distress resulting from the child's online experiences. Understanding the factors contributing to parents' underestimation of risk is a complex undertaking – media literacy strategies can and should be revisited to overcome these shortcomings.

Policymaking that views children as victims run the risk of viewing the best interest principle through the construct of a deficit model of child-hood – children as passive, vulnerable and incompetent individuals (Gill, 2007: 15–16). Gill, in his examination of the impact of parental risk aver-sion on children's development, concluded that such attitudes can inhibit the attainment of life-long problem-solving and risk management skills (ibid.). He uses the example of media panics created by playground in-juries to illustrate some of the ways insulating children from such risks can create moral hazards. The lack of a balanced perspective to children's interaction with the Internet imposes an onerous burden on the State and its legal system – direct State regulation and intervention are not sustain-able solutions given the ubiquity and mobility of information flows in the networked society (Sunstein, 2005, 2007). For many young adolescents an environment increasingly regulated by adults is sometimes viewed with frustration – particularly as it implies that children cannot be trusted to manage their online activities in a safe and responsible manner (Ofsted, 2010). It is important that these misgivings about societal reactions to children's engagement with Web 2.0 technologies are not misconstrued. None of the foregoing is intended to cast doubts on the need to protect those who are most vulnerable or deemed to be at risk – commercial and sexual exploitation of children is an act which deprives children of their fundamental right to be brought up in an environment free from violence (Mencap, 2006; Hunt *et al.*, 2007; Beatbullying, 2009). Harassment, bullying and physical and emotional violence need to be curbed (McLaughlin *et al.*, 2011). Individuals, including children, should not be subjected to violence on the grounds of their disability, race, gender, and religion (Mencap, 2007; Office of the Children's Commissioner, 2006). That said, we should also be wary of transposing fears and anxieties nurtured by media sen-sationalist reporting and avoid reflecting these concerns in the way we react to children's online activities and interactions. There is no risk-free zone either in the offline or in the online environments. In making these observations, the long-standing arguments about the social construction of childhood must also be borne in mind. In fact, it is difficult to disen-tangle these arguments from debates regarding the unique or exceptional nature of the risks that Web 2.0 technologies are regarded as creating for children (James, *et al.*, 1997).

Legal regulation

The criminal law continues to be regarded as an appropriate policy response in allaying public anxiety and disquiet about children's exposure to illegal content and online sexual solicitation. The State is seen as playing an important role in protecting its citizens, particularly those who are most vulnerable (Ashworth, 2000: 225). Laws governing the distribution of images of child sexual abuse images, sexual exploitation of children by nationals travelling to overseas countries and sexual activity with minors serve to reassure society that individuals who violate these rules will be held to account. Admittedly, in some jurisdictions, the criminal laws protecting children are not enforced effectively, and support for victims is far from ideal. These are well-documented problems and occur for a range of reasons – poor social infrastructures, corruption and lack of skilled law enforcement personnel. Much has been made about the Internet and cyberspace confronting regulators, law enforcement, parents and educators with an insurmountable challenge for the ability of the criminal law to protect children (ECPAT, 2008). These fears and concerns should, however, be kept in perspective – it is worth remembering that many online criminal activities originate in offline contexts (Palfrey *et al.*, 2008: 83–106). Two provisional observations can, however, be made in this regard. First, many child safety concerns expressed in relation to children's participation in network publics mirror those encountered in traditional child protection policymaking (Madge *et al.*, 2007: 13; Postman, 1983: 80–1). Second, and it is particularly true here, parental fears about managing invisible risks and uncertainty have elevated the role of the State both as a manager of risks and as an assessor of the levels of risk that children can reasonably be expected to assume (Ashworth, 2009: 89; Beck, 1992a: 73; Van Asselt *et al.*, 2009). It is of course right that policymakers should continue to assess the applicability of their criminal laws in dealing with the criminal acts of its citizens both at home and abroad. Mobile computing and communication technologies make possible new avenues through which children can become victims as well as perpetrators of harm and violence. As Chapters 2 and 3 highlighted, the fact that online child safety has been viewed as a problem of enforcement has perhaps created the impression that criminal law standards and rules operate only within a specific regulatory domain – law enforcement, legislators and courts. As the discussion has shown, the evolving MSIG framework illustrates the extent to which adoption of appropriate regulatory strategies can lead to a more fluid and timely (if not effective) response to many of the governance challenges faced by children in the online environment (Dutton *et al.*, 2007). This much is implicit, if one considers the public meetings convened by the House of Lords Select Committee in 2007 – following the enquiry into the state of information security it was suggested that software manufacturers and Internet service providers can and should assume a greater role in enhancing the security of individuals online (House of Lords Science and Technology Committee, 2007). The MSIG model can be regarded as a timely response, particularly as the rapid pace of technological innovations precedes the ability of individuals (particularly children) to develop norms of behaviour that help them identify and manage online risks (ibid., 2007: paragraph 6.36). The allocation of risk management and assessment obligations across the private sector, educators and civil society organisations is an acknowledgement that the State cannot be expected to regulate risks facing children entirely on its own. For example, the requirement that schools and educators now demonstrate their compliance with societal expectations that children take advantage of learning and developmental opportunities without fear of victimisation is an important part of the standard setting agenda in this area of governance. The use of educators and schools to create a culture of safety and security should not be seen as a failure of the criminal law or public mistrust in legal rules and norms. To be sure, parents, educators and schools can in essence shape children's use of Web 2.0 technologies and inculcate appropriate social norms and attitudes. The governing body within schools is required under Section 88 of the Education and Inspections Act 2006 to establish policies which promote good behaviour and discipline amongst pupils. Developing appropriate social norms within schools may also be a preferable solution rather than "exclusion" from schools or litigation since "[t]echnology is employed in efforts to humiliate, deprecate, or isolate…the point is to show who has social power. It's all about creating and reinforcing hierarchies".[1] One example of how schools and other stakeholders can respond in a timely and effective way in arresting the pernicious threat posed by peer victimisation to children can be gleaned from the recommendations accompanying a study concluded in Australia (Cross *et al.*, 2009). The strategies proposed in the study include media literacy and awareness-raising programmes, the promotion of civic responsibilities and resilience and engaging parents, educators and children. Other risk management strategies include the regulation of mobile phone use, counselling and targeting behavioural issues that lie at the root of bullying. In England, the Bottisham Village College adopts a "whole school positive culture" policy, which defines the standard of behaviour expected of staff and pupils.[2] The Marlborough School uses personal development curriculum to foster citizenship and equality values amongst staff and pupils in promoting a positive learning environment.[3]

One conclusion reached from the analysis undertaken with regard to the role of the criminal law in Chapter 3 is that an approach which characterises children as a homogenous body of vulnerable individuals in need of protection runs the real risk of underestimating the complex ways children now navigate and manage the affordances made available by Web 2.0 technologies. In constitutional terms, an indiscriminate approach towards implementing child safety policies can undermine or even encroach into a child's legitimate expectations of privacy and self-determination. Indeed, like Corsaro, we can observe that children's participation in network publics is a collective process and not simply a form of socialisation that internalises "adult skills and knowledge" (1992: 161). In other words, respecting children's fundamental rights without compromising the public interest in protecting a child from harm and abuse involves a recognition that

> children discover a world which is endowed with meaning and that they help to shape and share in their own developmental experiences by their interactive responses. (1992: ibid.)

Finally, in practical terms, the real danger accompanying the generalisation of children's vulnerability to online threats is that it perpetuates an expectation that legal intervention is necessary and perhaps distracts us from directing our efforts in identifying and supporting those who are most at risk and in need of assistance (Rosen, 2007: 136–8). A related concern is that increased regulatory intervention may produce unintended consequences like encouraging children to take needless risks or discourage them from reporting or seeking assistance when online risks are encountered (Byrne *et al.*, 2011).

As we have seen, network infrastructures and digital information pose problems for policing and enforcement – equally, these challenges can be addressed by adopting strategies and measures which complement the role of the law in this area of governance (e.g. codes of practice for social networking sites and mobile phone operators). And in some instances, questions may be legitimately raised as to whether criminalising particular forms of behaviour is the most effective governance response. Any attempt to extend the reach of the criminal law to cover all forms of peer deviance, unhelpfully described as "cyberbullying" or "sexting", merely serves to obscure both the rationale of the criminal law and the extent to which the State can be reasonably expected to intervene in protecting its citizens from harms or risks resulting from their daily risk-prone activities. The decision by 45 State legislatures in the United States to enact anti-bullying laws requiring schools to work with students, parents, law enforcement and local communities would appear to be an appropriate governance response.[4] This situation aside, it is not an exaggeration to say that the decentralised architecture of the Internet and the emergence of online services providers add to the complexities of policing, investigating and enforcing criminal law rules and norms with regard to the commercial and sexual exploitation of children (Kim-Kwang, 2008). According to Jenkins, "[t]he biggest single problem facing police is simply recognizing and understanding the nature of the child porn world on the Net" (2003: 215). We need not adopt a dystopian view of protecting children in the online environment. The earlier chapters highlighted instances where law enforcement have used networked technologies to exchange information with other national authorities, harnessed the anonymity offered by the online environment to entrap individuals and gathered incriminating evidence from ISPs (Krone, 2005b,c). Even in the area of peer victimisation, online incidents which otherwise may have gone unreported or unnoticed can now be detected by parents reviewing the information stored on message folders on the computer, mobile phones or social networking sites. The examination of investigatory and evidence gathering techniques in Chapter 3 suggests that the very features that promote deviant and criminal activity can be used by law enforcement in holding offenders to account. Other strategies adopted to minimise exposure to illegal content include modifying the design architectures of the affordances provided in networked technologies (e.g. hotlines, alert buttons and privacy controls) (IWF, 2010b). Technology-aided identification of victims in child abuse images and tracing of credit card transactions are some of the investigatory tools used by law enforcement (ECPAT, 2009: 95).

Policing and enforcing national laws in a networked environment is an ongoing problem for information security generally (*R v Hopps*). The earlier chapters identified the strategies adopted by a number of online intermediaries (e.g. IWF, social networking sites and mobile phone providers) in assisting law enforcement. The APPCG conducted an inquiry into the regulation of online traffic with particular reference to the role of ISPs. One of the issues examined was whether the current self-regulatory model should be maintained, modified or replaced. A difficulty often faced when urging ISPs to adopt a more proactive stance in modifying the transmission of communications is the issue raised with regard to the resulting loss of immunity provided by Articles 12–14 EC Directive 2000/31. Notwithstanding the immunity provisions, and the lengths to which online intermediaries can or should be expected to enhance the safety of its consumers, the assumption of additional responsibilities on online intermediaries is already under way (ITU, 2008b, 2009d). The chapter on the role of the private sector in promoting consumer trust and confidence through the assumption of voluntary obligations in protecting children is one such example (OECD, 2010a). Ultimately, a balance has to be struck between empowerment and protection concerns – and more importantly, some further clarification will be needed as to what can be legitimately expected from online intermediaries in enhancing the safety of children in the online environment (OSTWG, 2010; ACMA, 2009a,b).

The MSIG model

It has never been so easy for individuals and criminal organisations to gain access to children for their sexual gratification or victimise them (OECD, 2009). The Internet also makes it easier for individuals to engage in criminal activities from foreign jurisdictions, which either do not have effective policing resources or do not have laws protecting children from all forms of abuse and sexual exploitation (Grabosky, 2007a,b). One outcome of the increasing trend in approximating national laws and the establishment of procedures for investigation and collection of evidence (digital or otherwise) is that these go some way towards minimising the difficulties faced by law enforcement in prosecuting individuals, in cases where the criminal activity has transborder dimensions (European Commission, 2010e). A number of countries have enacted extraterritorial legislation to prosecute those nationals found to have engaged in CSEC in foreign jurisdictions (High, 2005). Despite concerns expressed by NGOs about the impediments posed by extraterritorial criminal jurisdiction principles, the "jurisdictional problem" should not be overstated. In fact, the logistical challenges faced by High Tech law units when investigating and processing offences continue to be a primary cause of complaint amongst national law enforcement authorities as they attempt to keep pace with online criminal activities. This is not to say that reforms to existing criminal jurisdiction principles will not be welcome. It is hoped that the Proposed Directive will make a significant impact on the day-to-day activities of law enforcement in prosecuting individuals for engaging in criminal activity with a transborder element (European Commission, 2010e). In the discussion on transborder and investigatory challenges, it has been shown that the Internet can actually make the task of investigating and prosecuting offenders much easier, as law enforcement organisations share intelligence with each other. Information sharing, greater collaboration with the banking sector, NGOs, ISPs and the use of sting operations are some of the notable reflexive governance responses.

National laws now have to accommodate the significance of the end-to-end architecture for the MSIG and risk-based regulatory strategies (Klinke, 2009; Fisher, 2010; OECD, 2003). The emerging MSIG deliberative and decision-making processes now draw on experts, researchers and NGOs to identify optimal risk management strategies at four levels:

1. The convergence between digital, broadcasting and telecommunication markets and its impact on business models.
2. The development of regulatory frameworks based on national, sector- and Internet-specific boundaries.
3. The emergence of contact, content and conduct risks and their significance for regulatory options and choices.
4. National, regional and international policy developments.

Online child safety, it should be said, is now regarded as part of a broader discourse about the obligations of governments and society generally in ensuring that children grow up in an environment where they are not abused or exploited (OECD, 2008c). States have also been active in demonstrating their support in addressing the threats of sexual violence and abuse to children. To this, we should also add the considerable work undertaken at the HRC and the UN General Assembly in advocating a rights-based approach to children's rights (ECPAT, 2009). The efforts of civil society and the considerable work undertaken by NGOs, the World Congress, the European Commission and the Council of Europe, the UN and the OECD together with the support of national governments suggest that great strides continue to be made in enhancing children's safety in the online environment. Reference has been made to the role of the EU on this front and the standard setting value of instruments like the CPC Convention, the Cybercrime Convention and the UNCRC. Harmonisation of child protection policies, greater law enforcement collaboration and the extensive work undertaken by NGOs now take place at many levels and contexts (European Commission, 1996a; European Financial Coalition, 2010b; FCACP, 2008; FBI, 2008; Gercke, 2008). The emergence of transnational actors and international institutional infrastructures for decision-making has three significant consequences for online child safety governance. First, State-mandated approach to centralised governance is now expanded to include reflexive assessments of risks and the formulation of regulatory responses which are transparent and capable of being measured for their negative impacts. It is particularly relevant to note that the Eurobarometer Surveys on children's experiences of their use of social networking sites and mobile phones are increasingly being grounded on evidence of perceived and actual risks (Eurobarometer, 2005, 2007, 2008). This phenomenon, as Keohane and Nye argue, has opened up the regulatory space, where States frequently engage with transnational actors and civil society in debates about governance, accountability, transparency and standards (1998: 81–94). Whether and to what extent non-State actors exercise the type of influence in defining the policy and standard setting agenda in child protection is of course a moot point (Strange, 1996). Second, self- and co-regulation are deemed to be the default governance strategies, since these are meant to cohere with rational, efficient and legitimate approaches to balancing innovation and child protection issues. Online child safety governance policymaking and strategies consequently need to take into account three aspects in current communications regulatory arrangements: (1) the shift from an industry to a information/network-based framework; (2) the existence of a common regulatory framework for the carriage of communications services; and (3) the regulation of a diverse array of content delivered from multiple venues and communication platforms (OECD, 2004: 17). Third, the collaboration between civil society and the private sector is seen very much as an enterprise that will promote trust and confidence (ACMA, 2009d; OfCom, 2008a).

Childhood in the digital world

In the analysis of some of the principal areas of online child safety policy-making, it was suggested that three goals have to be pursued in tandem – equipping children and their carers with appropriate media literacy skills, embedding child safety norms in the architecture of the Internet and the need to strike a balance between safety and empowerment issues. The Byron Report in 2008, the studies in the United States by the ISTTF and the OSTWG in 2008 and 2010, respectively, and the three reports on online risk and safety in the digital economy published by ACMA in Australia between 2008 and 2010 have called for an MSIG approach to online child safety policymaking. Each report advocates media literacy as an important instrument for enhancing children's safety. In Chapter 7, it was argued that media literacy initiatives need to take into account children's perspectives of the affordances of networked publics, their views on online safety issues and their risk management strategies (Livingstone *et al.*, 2011). The Thornburgh Commission may have had this aspect very much in mind when it observed that

> teaching a child to swim and to exercise good judgment about bodies of water to avoid has applicability and relevance far beyond swimming pools – as any parent who takes a child to the beach can testify. (Thornburgh *et al.*, 2002: 224)

There is still quite a lot of work to be done in this respect (Livingstone *et al.*, 2007). In a recent study it was noted that schools in the United Kingdom varied in their approaches towards online child safety (SWGFL, 2010: 1) This must be an area of concern – the lack of information security literacy and understanding of network affordances can only perpetuate the widening gulf between children's out-of-school experiences and their school activities and experiences. Whilst promoting greater awareness of the Internet and the significance of its affordances for privacy, identity and security, it should not be overlooked that education and promoting children's awareness of information security issues are by themselves insufficient. That said, there are two points that need to be highlighted. First, online safety in this context is not simply concerned with reducing the information deficit in parents and children. Second, developmental issues needed to be taken into account (Goswami, 2008; Livingstone *et al.*, 2004, 2011). If we start from the premise that children are not passive subjects, the focus of media literacy strategy must surely be directed at educating children in the broadest sense of the word (Byrne *et al.*, 2009; Livingstone, 2008b). In Chapter 7 we considered how media literacy might be conceptualised through the use of an "information security" approach and, more importantly, the benefits of integrating the framework provided by the Good Play project. By focusing on children's experiences, parents and educators, as online gatekeepers, can use the

Good Play model to promote citizenship values and decision-making skills (Smetana, 1995; Ohler, 2010). Younger children, particularly those below the age of 13, may need a slightly different policy response (ITU, 2009b,c,d; ACMA, 2010b). The approach adopted in Hector's World™, Cybersmart and CEOP's educational adventure series illustrates how education and ethical values can be imparted by simple strategies focusing on children's experiences of Web 2.0 technologies in their daily lives – there is now a good case for introducing online safety and citizenship education to children at a much earlier age (Butterfield, 2010; Livingstone *et al.*, 2011; ACMA, 2009f). This is not to say that there is a "one size fits all" approach, given the fact that children vary across cultures and develop at different levels (Goswami, 2008: 2–4). The Good Play model, discussed in the previous chapter, provides us with one approach that parents and educators can consider when responding to the needs and expectations of children in the networked society (Moore, 2010). Even though older children by nature tend to resent what they perceive as unnecessary adult interference, parents and educators need to think more creatively on how best they can mediate and impart appropriate skills and social norms to children (Ohler, 2010; Byrne *et al.*, 2011). Admittedly, this is not easy, particularly as network publics are increasingly regarded as a defining environment for children's identities and integration into participatory cultures (Livingstone *et al.*, 2011).

Media literacy strategies also remind us of the power imbalance that has long defined relations between adults and children in society (Castells *et al.*, 2007). Adults are the ultimate arbiters of how and when the Internet can be accessed – but constant monitoring and surveillance is not an entirely sustainable strategy, since children can access Web 2.0 technologies and social media from a variety of locations. Stories of children using workarounds, creating fake accounts in social networking sites with parents as their "friends" and accessing inappropriate online content at friends' homes or mobile devices suggest that promoting good decision-making skills requires persistence, empathy and commitment. There is something more that parents and educators need to do, which is to engage more fully with Web 2.0 technologies and grapple with the "ethical fault lines" identified in the Good Play project. One hesitates in advocating a particular parenting style that promotes safe and responsible use, but it is clear that more effort needs to be made in engaging parents, since (together with educators and children's peers) they are best placed to make timely interventions and inculcate appropriate values and practices in their charges (Bronfenbrenner *et al.*, 2000).

Conclusion

Society has long struggled with the "childhood" question (Aries, 1973). Protective and precautionary impulses that characterise the patriarchal framework are difficult to overcome. One of the biggest fears of parents is that the harms they hear perpetrated on children in the online environment may be inflicted on their own children. The anxiety faced by all parents is unlikely to come to an end. The end-to-end architecture, the flows of information and the collapsing of contexts have reversed the presumptive norms defining child protection policies in the pre-Web 2.0 environment. Many of the online child safety governance challenges that we see mediated through communication technologies arise at two levels. First, those which result from the generation of risks from the misuse of Web 2.0 technologies. Second, those which can broadly be regarded as resulting from individuals ethical choices in response to the disintermediated and anonymous dimensions of online interaction, identity formation and participation. It is safe to say that policymakers, educators and parents are still very much in the early stages of working out the protective parameters of children's online and offline activities. Enhancing the safety of children in the online environment is a particularly formidable challenge and the quest for an effective governance framework is likely to generate further intense public policy debates and arguments (Hersh, 2001). Whatever choices we make about children's engagement with the Internet and the networked environment, we need to accept that there is no metaphorical *Walden Pond* for children.[5] Thoreau would have been first to admit that had the Internet existed during his time, keeping the online and offline lives of individuals separate would have required more than signposting – "No (Harmful or Inappropriate Content and) Technology beyond This Point". Information networks now blend broadcasting, entertainment and social spaces and lead to collapsing audiences and contexts – we now have the opportunity to equip children with the skills and values demanded from Web 2.0 technologies. Perhaps, like Kelly, we should be mindful of the First Law of Technological Expectation: "The greater the promise of a new technology, the greater its potential for harm as well" (Kelly, 2010: 246). A failure to acknowledge this says much about living in the risk society and will have implications for the way we continue to define childhood and children's interaction with Web 2.0 technologies and social media.

Notes

Foreword

1. For the time being the US Government maintains a residual role in the management of the global internet through its continued engagement with the Internet Assigned Number Authority (IANA). ICANN "currently performs the IANA functions, on behalf of the United States Government, through a contract with United States Department of Commerce's National Telecommunications and Information Administration (NTIA)"http://www.ntia.doc.gov/files/ntia/publications/fr_iana_furthernoi_06142011.pdf.

2 Regulating Risks and Web 2.0 Technologies: Convergence, Technology and Social Policy

1. Available at http://tinyurl.com/44aezo4 (accessed on 20 March 2010).

3 Online Sexual Grooming of Children, Obscene Content and Peer Victimisation: Legal and Evidentiary Issues

1. The CPS and ACPO signed a Memorandum of Understanding (MoU) in 2004. The MoU sets out the process by which indecent images of children are to be handled, so that the defence under Section 1B of Protection of Children Act 1978 can be relied upon. The MoU provides guidance to the Police Service, CPS and others involved in the Internet industry, in order to create the right balance between protecting children and effective investigation and prosecution of offences. Section 46 of the Sexual Offences Act 2003 creates a defence to the offence of "making" under the 1978 Act, where a person "making" such a photograph or pseudo-photograph can prove that it was necessary to do so for the purposes of the prevention, detection or investigation of crime, or for the purposes of criminal proceedings.
2. See http://tinyurl.com/62nnfnz (accessed on 20 March 2011).
3. Ibid.
4. http://www.publications.parliament.uk/pa/cm201011/cmselect/cmeduc/516/516vw51.htm

4 Transborder Challenges to Enforcing Online Child Safety Laws

1. The following account is taken from http://tinyurl.com/yho7kc6 (accessed on 20 March 2011).
2. The following account is taken from Cospol Project [Online]. Available at www.circamp.edu (accessed on 20 March 2011).
3. The following account is taken from http://www.europol.europa.eu/ (accessed on 20 March 2011).
4. http://www.virtualglobaltaskforce.com/what_we_do.asp.

5. The following account is taken from http://tinyurl.com/2bgnnh (accessed on 20 March 2011).
6. The following account is taken from http://tinyurl.com/3pok3el (accessed on 20 March 2011).
7. The following account is taken from http://tinyurl.com/6gsqv2y (accessed on 20 March 2011).
8. See 15 A/CONF.213/1 at http://tinyurl.com/5t5w49q (accessed on 20 April 2011).
9. See http://tinyurl.com/6jzfvrq (accessed on 20 March 2011).

5 Online Child Safety: International Cooperation and Policymaking

1. See http://www2.ohchr.org/english/law/crc.htm.
2. See http://tinyurl.com/5tdb7qj (accessed on 23 March 2011).
3. Ibid. Explanatory Report to the First Additional Protocol to the Council of Europe Convention on Cybercrime No. 4

6 Online Child Safety, Civil Society and the Private Sector: Alternative Strategies

1. www.mobility.protectchildren.ca/app/en/.
2. http://www.aph.gov.au/house/committee/jscc/tor.htm.
3. See http://www.enacso.eu/ (accessed on 14 September 2010).
4. The following account on the Internet Watch Foundation is based on the materials found on its website. Available at www.iwf.org.uk (accessed on 23 March 2011).
5. MoU between Crown Prosecution Service (CPS) and the Association of Chief Police Officers (ACPO) concerning Section 46 of Sexual Offences Act 2003.
6. Broadcasting Regulatory Policy 2009–329, Public Notice 1999–84 and Telecom Public Notice 99–14 and Exemptions are described in Exemption order for new media broadcasting undertakings (Public Notice CRTC 1999–197) and Exemption order for mobile television broadcasting undertakings (Broadcasting Public Notice CRTC 2007–13).
7. CAIP Supports the Government of Canada's Strategy on Illegal and Offensive Content on the Internet: Promoting Safe, Wise and Responsible Internet Use. For background see Paul A Pierlott, Self-Regulation of Internet Content: A Canadian Perspective http://www.isoc.org/inet2000/cdproceedings/8k/8k_2.htm.
8. The following account draws on the information provided on www.cybertip.ca.
9. The following account draws on information and report sourced from http://tinyurl.com/6fqavmw (accessed on 20 March 2011).
10. www.google.com/familysafety.
11. https://www.facebook.com/safety.
12. www.oecd.org/sti/ict/children.
13. www.google.com/familysafety.
14. Available at http://tinyurl.com/3r5sec (accessed on 12 January 2010).
15. It is not possible to address the interplay between privacy and security concerns, raised, for example, by location-based services and other marketing applications integrated into mobile phone packages. See Privacy and Electronic Communication (EC Directive) Regulations 2003 and the Commission's A comprehensive approach on personal data protection in the European Union (COM(2010) 609) framework.

16. Resources available at http://www.gsmeurope.org/safer_mobile/news.shtml.

7 The Child, Media Literacy and Online Safety Policy Implications

1. http://www.ltscotland.org.uk/curriculumforexcellence/responsibilityofall/literacy/principlesandpractice/definition.asp.
2. Quoted in press release: Media literacy: Do people really understand how to make the most of blogs, search engines or interactive TV? Available at http://europa.eu/rapid/pressReleasesAction.do?reference=IP/07/1970 (accessed on 31 March 2011).
3. See http://www.acma.gov.au/WEB/STANDARD/pc=PC_312155.
4. See http://de-en.gc.ca/home/.
5. Materials can be found on the re-designed home page: http://www.education.gov.uk/ukccis.
6. Available at http://unesdoc.unesco.org/images/0014/001429/142919e.pdf (accessed on 23 October 2010).
7. See http://www.nextgenerationlearning.org.uk.
8. See http://www.nextgenerationlearning.org.uk/en/ohnothingmuch/.
9. See http://www.thinkuknow.co.uk/.
10. See http://www.bbc.co.uk/cbbc/.
11. See http://www.childnet-int.org/.
12. See http://www.teachtoday.eu/.
13. See http://www.b4usurf.org/.
14. The following account on Australian developments is a selective account from Consultative Working Group on Cybersafety: Submission to Joint Select Committee on Cybersafety, 9 July 2010 (V2.1 15 July 2010). Available at http://www.aph.gov.au/house/committee/jscc/subs.htm (accessed on 31 March 2011).
15. See http://www.cybersmart.gov.au/.
16. See http://www.thinkuknow.org.au/.
17. See http://www.hectorsworld.com/island/index.html.
18. Acknowledgement to Beatbullying for permission to use this story. The case study has been adapted for the purposes of the discussion.
19. The following are drawn from the case studies used in Jenkins *et al.* (2009) and adapted to suit this scenario.
20. See http://www.leadered.com/guiding_princ.html.
21. See http://heartwoodethics.org/1-approach/framework.asp (accessed on 31 March 2011).
22. See http://heartwoodethics.org/1-approach/framework.asp (accessed on 31 March 2011).

8 Concluding Thoughts: The Tethered Child

1. See *"Bullying" Has Little Resonance with Teenagers* [Online]. Available at http://tinyurl.com/3v25tpf (accessed on 20 February 2011).
2. See http://tinyurl.com/6k8v8j2.
3. See http://tinyurl.com/6x8xzwu.
4. See http://www.bullypolice.org/.
5. http://www.walden.org/

Select Bibliography

ABC News. (2011) Facebook privacy chief defends cybersafety measures [Online]. Available at http://tinyurl.com/5wkb8x2 (accessed on 25 April 2011).

Abelson, A. (2009) Prosecute/Extradite Dilemma: Concurrent Criminal Jurisdiction and Global Governance. *UC Davis Journal of International Law and Policy*, 16(1), 1–38.

ABS. (2009) Children's participation in cultural and leisure activities, Australia [Online]. Available at http://tinyurl.com/3hczoco (accessed on 11 November 2010).

ACMA. (2007) *Media and Communications in Australian Families 2007: Report of the Media and Society Research Project*. Sydney, Commonwealth of Australia: ACMA.

ACMA. (2009a) *Australia in the Digital Economy: Trust and Confidence*. Sydney, Commonwealth of Australia: ACMA.

ACMA. (2009b) Click and connect: Young Australians' use of online social media, quantitative research report [Online]. Available at www.acma.gov.au (accessed on 20 March 2010).

ACMA. (2009c) Click and connect: Young Australians' use of online social media – 02 Quantitative research report [Online]. Available at www.acma.gov.au (accessed on 20 March 2010).

ACMA. (2009d) *Online Risk and Safety in the Digital Economy*. Sydney, Commonwealth of Australia: ACMA.

ACMA. (2009e) *Use of Electronic Media and Communications: Early Childhood to Teenage Years*. Sydney, Commonwealth of Australia: ACMA.

ACMA. (2010a) Trends in media use by children and young people [Online]. Available at www.acma.gov.au (accessed on 10 March 2010).

ACMA. (2010b) Cybersmart parents: Connecting parents to cybersafety resources [Online]. Available at www.acma.gov.au (accessed on 2 November 2010).

ACMA. (2011) New online national program trains teachers in cybersafety [Online]. Available at www.acma.gov.au (accessed on 20 May 2011).

ACPO. ACPO Good practice guide for computer-based evidence (version 4) [Online]. Available at http://tinyurl.com/3fz7xdm (accessed on 12 February 2011).

AFP. (2008) National child porn operation nets 90 people [Online]. Available at http://www.afp.gov.au/ (accessed 5 June 2009).

AFP. (2009) Annual Report, 1 July 2008–30 June 2009 [Online]. Available at http://www.afp.gov.au/ (accessed on 20 March 2010).

AFP. (2011) 184 Suspects arrested in international child abuse investigation [Online]. Available at http://www.afp.gov.au/ (accessed on 12 April 2011).

Akdeniz, Y. (2008) *Internet Child Pornography and the Law: National and International Responses*. Farnham, UK: Ashgate Publishing Company.

Akehurst, M. (1972–3) Jurisdiction in International Law. *British Yearbook of International Law*, 46, 145–258.

AMF. (2009) Young people and technology: A review of the current literature (2nd edition) [Online]. Available at http://tinyurl.com/44yje5v (accessed on 20 November 2010).

APPCG. (2009) Can we keep our hands off the net? [Online]. Available at http://tinyurl.com/3ecvf6t (accessed 13 January 2010).

Allen, E. (2011) Facebook to use Microsoft's photoDNA technology to combat child exploitation [Online]. Available at http://tinyurl.com/3cpmfna (accessed on 15 May 2011).

Alston, P. (1994) The Best Interests Principle: Towards a Reconciliation of Culture and Human Rights. *International Journal of Law and the Family*, 1, 15–16.

Aqili, S., & Nasiri, B. (2010) Technology and the Need for Media Literacy Education in the Twenty-First Century. *European Journal of Social Science*, 15(3), 449–456.

Archard, D. (2004) *Children, Rights and Childhood*. Abingdon, UK; Routledge.

Aries, P. (1973) *Centuries of Childhood*. Harmondsworth, UK: Penguin.

Article 29 Data Protection Working Party. (2010) Opinion 2/2010 on online behavioural advertising 00909/10/EN WP 171.

Ashworth, A. (2000) Is the Criminal Law a Lost Cause? *Law Quarterly Review*, 116, 225–256.

Ashworth, A. (2004) Social Control and "Anti-Social Behaviour": The Subversion of Human Rights? *Law Quarterly Review*, 263–291.

Ashworth, A. (2009) Criminal Law, Human Rights and Preventative Justice. In B. McSherry, A. Norrie & S. Bronitt (Eds). *Regulating Deviance: The Redirections of Criminalisation and the Futures of Criminal Law*. Oxford, UK: Hart.

ASIL. (2007) Roundtable – A Multiplicity of Actors and Transnational Governance. *American Society of International Law Proceedings*, 101, 469–480.

Ayres, I., & Braithwaite, J. (1992) *Responsive Regulation: Transcending the Deregulation Debate*. Cary, NC, USA: Oxford University Press.

Baartz, D. (2008) *Australians, the Internet and Technology-Enabled Child Sex Abuse. A Statistical Profile*. Australia: Australian Federal Police.

Baker, G., & Chandler, D. (2004) *Global Civil Society – Contested Futures*. London: Routledge.

Ball-Rokeach, S. J., & DeFleur, M. L. (1976) A Dependency Model Of Mass-Media Effects. *Communication Research*, 3, 3–21.

Battersby, L. (2008) Sexting: Fears as teens targeted [Online]. Available at http://tinyurl.com/43stc3v (accessed on 12 March 2011).

BBC. (2009a) Teens targeted in Net safety push [Online]. Available at http://tinyurl.com/4xrfaac (accessed on 5 November 2010).

BBC. (2009b) Profile: Josef Fritzl [Online]. Available at http://tinyurl.com/4yt5zba (accessed on 12 March 2010).

BBC. (2009c) Teens targeted in Net safety push [Online]. Available at http://tinyurl.com/3wxx8dm (accessed 20 March 2010).

BBC. (2010a) Paedophiles increasingly access images from webcams [Online]. Available at http://tinyurl.com/3bbavtf (accessed on 10 August 2010).

BBC. (2010b) Apology for daughters raped by Sheffield man [Online]. Available at http://tinyurl.com/3pvs7y (accessed on 3 March 2011).

BBFC. (2011) Classification [Online]. Available at http://tinyurl.com/3q5gyl6 (accessed on 16 April 2011).

Beatbullying. (2009) *Virtual Violence: Protecting Children from Cyberbullying*. London: Beatbullying.

Beaulieu, C. (2008) *Extraterrestrial Laws: Why They Are Not Really Working and How They Can Be Strengthened*. Bangkok: ECPAT International.

Beck, U. (1992a) *Risk Society: Towards a New Modernity*. London: Sage Publishing.

Beck, U. (1992b) From Industrial Society to the Risk Society: Questions of Survival, Social Structure and Ecological Enlightenment. *Theory, Culture and Society*, 9, 101.

Beck, U., Giddens, A., & Lash, S. (1994) *Reflexive Modernization: Politics, Tradition and the Aesthetic in the Modern Social Order*. Cambridge: Polity Press.

Beck, U. (1997) *The Reinvention of Politics: Rethinking Modernity in the Global Social Order*. Cambridge: Polity Press.

Beck, U. (1998) *Politics of Risk Society*. Cambridge: Polity Press.

Beck, U. (1999) *World Risk Society*. Oxford: Polity Press.

Beck, U. (2000) *What Is globalization?* Cambridge: Polity Press.

Beck, U. (2002) The Terrorist Threat: World Risk Society Revisited. *Theory, Culture and Society*, 9(4), 35–55.

Becker, M. (1994) *The Emergence of Civil Society in the Eighteenth Century: A Privileged Moment in the History of England, Scotland, and France*. Bloomington: Indiana University Press.

Beddoe, C. (2010) ECPAT UK criticizes verdict on child sex tourism case [Online]. Available at http://tinyurl.com/3t6jo5o (accessed on10 March 2011).

Beebe, N., & Clark, J. (2005) A Hierarchical, Objectives-Based Framework for the Digital Investigation Process. *Digital Investigation*, 2(2) 146–166.

Benkler, Y. (2006) *The Wealth of Networks: How Social Production Transforms Markets and Freedom*. New Haven, CT: Yale University Press.

Berlie, L. (2009) *Alliances for Sustainable Development: Business and NGO Partnerships*. London: Palgrave Macmillan.

Berman, F. (2003) Jurisdiction: The State. In P. Capps, M. Evans, & S. Konstadinidis (Eds). *Asserting Jurisdiction: International and European Legal Perspectives*. Oxford: Portland.

Berman, P. S. (2002) Globalization of Jurisdiction. *University of Penn Law Review*, 151, 311–546.

Berners-Lee, T., & Fischetti, M. (2000) *Weaving the Web: The Past, Present and Future of the World Wide Web by Its Inventor*. New York: Texere.

Berson, I., & Berson, M. (2010) *High-Tech Tots: Childhood in a Digital World*. Charlotte, NC: Information Age Publishing.

Bexell, M., Tallberg, J., & Uhlin, A. (2010) Democracy in Global Governance: The Promises and Pitfalls of Transnational Acts. *Global Governance*, 16(1), 81–101.

Bhattacharya, C. B., & Sen, S. (2004) Doing Better at Doing Good: When, Why and How Consumers Respond to Corporate Social Initiatives. *California Management Review*, 47, 9–24.

Blumenfeld, W., & Cooper, R. (2010) LGBT and Allied Youth Responses to Cyberbullying: Policy Implications. *International Journal of Critical Pedagogy*, 3(1), 114–133.

Blumenthal, M., & Clark, D. (2001) Rethinking the design of the Internet: The End-to-End Arguments vs. the Brave New World. *ACM Transactions on Internet Technology*, 1(1): 70–109.

Bohman, J. (1996) *Public Deliberation. Pluralism, Complexity, and Democracy*. Cambridge and London: MIT Press.

Boston Globe. (2010) Teen's suicide prompts a look at bullying [Online]. Available at http://tinyurl.com/3lhfsag (accessed on 12 January 2011).

Bovill, M., & Livingstone, S. (2001) Bedroom Culture and the Privatization of Media Use'. In S. Livingstone & M. Bovill (Eds). *Children and Their Changing Media Environment: A European Comparative Study*. Mahwah, NJ: Lawrence Erlbaum Associates.

boyd, d. (2007) Why Youth Social Network Sites: The Role of Networked Publics in Teenage Social Life. In D. Buckingham (Ed). *Youth, Identity, and Digital Media*. Cambridge, MA: MIT Press.

boyd, d. (2008a) Why Youth Social Network Sites: The Role of Networked Publics in Teenage Social Life. In D. Buckingham (Ed). *Youth, Identity, and Digital Media*. Cambridge, MA: MIT Press.

boyd, d. (2008b) *Taken Out of Context American Teen Sociality in Networked Publics*. Berkeley: University of California.

boyd, d. (2010) Social Network Sites as Networked Publics: Affordances, Dynamics and Implications. In Z. Papachariss (Ed). *Networked Self: Identity, Community, and Culture on Social Networking Sites*. UK: Routledge.

boyd, d., & Hargittai, E. (2010) Facebook privacy settings: Who cares? *First Monday*, 15(8) [Online]. Available at http://tinyurl.com/3vky8uh (accessed on 20 April 2011).

Brackenridge, C., & Fasting, K. (2002) Sexual harassment and abuse in sport: The research context. *Journal of Sexual Aggression*, 8(2), 3–15.

Brehm. J. (1966) *A Theory of Psychological Reactance*. New York: Academic Press.

Brenner, S. (2004) Toward a Criminal Law for Cyberspace: Distributed Security. *Boston University Journal of Science & Technology Law*, 10(1), 1–109.

Brenner, S. (2006) Cybercrime Jurisdiction. *Crime, Law and Social Change*, 46, 4–5, 189–206.

Brenner, S. (2010) *Cybercrime: Criminal Threats from Cyberspace*. Santa Barbara, California: Praeger.

Bronfenbrenner, U., & Evans, G. (2000) Developmental Science in the 21st Century: Emerging Questions, Theoretical Models, Research Design and Empirical Findings. *Social Development*, 9(1), 115–125.

Buckingham, D. (1998) Media Education in the UK: Moving beyond Protectionism. *Journal of Communication*, 48, 33–43.

Buckingham, D. (2000) *After the Death of Childhood: Growing Up in the Age of Electronic Media*. Cambridge: Polity Press.

Buckingham, D. (2007) *Beyond Technology: Learning in the Age of Digital Culture*. Cambridge, Polity Press.

Buckingham, D., Whiteman, N., Willett, R., & Burn, A. (2007) The Impact of the Media on Children and Young People with a Particular Focus on Computer Games and the Internet. UK: DCSF.

Burroughs, S., Brocato, K., Hopper, P., & Sanders, A. (2009) Media Literacy: A Central Component of Democratic Citizenship. *The Educational Forum*, 73(2), 154–167.

Butterfield, L. (2010) Hector's World™: Educating Young Children about Life Online. In I. Berson & M Berson (Eds). *High-Tech Tots: Childhood in a Digital World*. Charlotte, NC: Information Age Publishing.

Bryant, C. (2009) *Adolescence, Pornography and Harm*. Australia: Australian Institute of Criminology.

Bryce, J. (2010) Online Sexual Exploitation of Children and Young People. In Y. Jewkes & M. Yar (Eds). *Handbook of Internet Crime*. UK: Willan Publishing.

Byrne, S. (2009) Media Literacy Interventions: What makes them Boom or Boomerang? *Communication Education*, 58(1), 1–14.

Byrne, S., & Hart, P. (2009) The "Boomerang" Effect: A Synthesis of Findings and a Preliminary Theoretical Framework. In C. Beck (Ed). *Communication Yearbook*. 33, Mahwah, NJ: Lawrence Erlbaum Associates.

Byrne, S., & Lee, T. (2011) Toward Predicting Youth Resistance to Internet Risk Prevention Strategies. *Journal of Broadcasting and Electronic Media*, 55(1), 90–113.

Byron, T. (2008) Safer children in a digital world: The report of the Byron Review [Online]. Available http://www.dcsf.gov.uk/byronreview (accessed on 10 June 2010)

Byron, T. (2010) *Foreword, Do We Have Safer Children in a Digital World? A review of Progress since the 2008 Byron Review.* Nottingham: DCSF.

Calder, M. (Ed) (2004a) *Child Sexual Abuse and the Internet: Tackling the New Frontier.* Dorset, UK: Russell House Publishing Ltd.

Calder, M. (2004b) The Internet: Potential, Problems and Pathways to Hands-On Sexual Offending. In M. Calder (Ed). *Child Sexual Abuse and the Internet: Tackling the New Frontier.* Dorset, UK: Russell House Publishing Ltd.

Callanan, C., & Gercke, M. (2008) Study on the cooperation between service providers and law enforcement against cybercrime – Toward common best-of-breed guidelines? [Online]. Available at http://tinyurl.com/3qvkyr2 (accessed on 4 March 2011).

Carrier, B., & Spafford, E. (2003) Getting physical with the digital investigation process. *International Journal of Digital Evidence*, 2(2) [Online]. Available at http://tinyurl.com/3u99w2p (accessed on 22 November 2010).

Carrier, B., & Spafford, E. (2006) Categories of Digital Investigation Analysis Techniques based on the Computer History Model. *Digital Investigations*, 121–130.

Carroll, B. (1991) The Pyramid of Corporate Social Responsibility: Toward the Moral Management of Organizational Stakeholders. *Business Horizons*, 34, 39–48.

Carroll, A. B., & Shabana, K. M. (2010) The Business Case for Corporate Social Responsibility: A Review of Concepts, Research and Practice. *International Journal of Management Reviews*, 12(1), 85–105.

Casciani, D (2011) World's largest paedophile ring uncovered [Online]. Available at http://tinyurl.com/3ukcwa3 (accessed on 12 April 2011).

Casey, E. (2004) *Digital Evidence and Computer Crime: Forensic Science, Computers and the Internet.* London: Academic Press.

Castells, M. (1997) *The Power of Identity.* Oxford: Blackwell.

Castells, M., Fernandez-Ardevol, M., Qiu, L. C. J., & Sey, A. (2007) (Eds). *Mobile Communication and Society.* Cambridge, MA: MIT Press.

Cave, J., Marsden, C., Klautzer, L., Oranje-Nassau, R., Rabinovich, C., & Robinson, N. (2007) Responsibility in the global information society: Towards multi-stakeholder governance [Online]. Available at http://tinyurl.com/3vtn9gv (accessed on 4 January 2010).

Cave, J., Marsden, C., & Simmons, S. (2008) Options for and effectiveness of Internet self- and co-regulation [Online]. Available at http://tinyurl.com/3qtj8oy (accessed on 4 January 2010).

CCCP. (2009) Child Sexual Abuse Images: An analysis of websites by Cybertip.ca [Online]. Available at http://www.cybertip.ca/app/en/ (accessed on 20 June 2010).

Centre for Digital Futures. (2010) Digital futures report [Online]. Available at http://tinyurl.com/3mgfd36 (accessed on 12 January 2011).

CEOP. (2009) Strategic overview 2008–9: *Making Every Child Matter ... Everywhere.* London: CEOP.

CEOP. (2010a) *The Way Forward, Cm 7785.* London: Home Office.

CEOP. (2010b) International paedophile network smashed as private Facebook group infiltrated [Online]. Available at http://tinyurl.com/3naddrl (accessed on 26 August 2010).

CEOP. (2011) Exposed [Online]. Available at http://tinyurl.com/3pkc4rj (accessed on 12 March 2011).

Chamberlain, T., George, N., Golden, S., Walker, F., & Benton, T. (2010) *Tellus4 National Report.* London: Department for Children, Schools and Families.

Cherry, B. A. & Bauer, J. M. (2004) Adaptive Regulation: Contours of a Policy Model for the Internet Economy. Paper presented at the 15th Biennial Conference of the International Telecommunications Society Berlin, Germany.

Chisholm, J. (2006) Cyberspace Violence against Girls and Adolescent Females. *Annals of New York Academy of Science*, 1087, 74–89.

Chong, E. (2010) Jailed for sexual grooming [Online]. Available at http://tinyurl. com/3zowfuk (accessed on 1 February 2011).

Choudhry, S., & Fenwick, H. (2005) Taking the Rights of Parents and Children Seriously: Confronting the Welfare Principle under the Human Rights Act. *Oxford Journal of Legal Studies*, 25(3), 453–492.

Cohen, S. (1972) *Folk Devils and Moral Panics: The Creation of the Mods and Rockers.* London, UK: MacGibbon and Kee.

Colangelo, A. (2009) Universal Jurisdiction as an International False Conflict of Laws. *Michigan Journal of International Law*, 30(3), 881–926.

Commission on Human Rights. (2004) Report on the sale of children, child prostitution and child pornography, E/CN.4/2005/78.

Commission on Human Rights. (2006) Report on the sale of children, child prostitution and child pornography, E/CN.4/2006/67.

CRC. (1996) Report on the 11th Session, January 1996, CRC/C/50.

CRC. (2000) General discussion day on the state of violence against children. Report on the 25th session, CRC/C/100.

CRC. (2001a) Recommendations adopted following the general discussion day on violence within the family and in schools. Report on the 28th session, September/ October 2001, CRC/C/111.

CRC. (2001b) General discussion day on violence within the family and in schools. Report on the 28th session, CRC/C/111.

CRC. (2003) General comment No. 5. General measures of implementation of the Convention on the Rights of the Child, CRC/GC/2003/5.

CRC. (2005a) Consideration of reports submitted by states parties under Article 44 of the Convention. Concluding observations: Australia, CRC/C/15/Add.268.

CRC. (2005b) Written replies by the government of Australia concerning the list of issues (CRC/C/Q/AUS/3, CRC/C/129/Add.4.

CRC. (2008a) Summary record of the 1355th meeting. Third and fourth periodic reports of the United Kingdom of Great Britain and Northern Ireland, CRC/C/SR.1355.

CRC. (2008b) Consideration of reports submitted by states parties under Article 44 of the Convention. Concluding observations: United Kingdom of Great Britain and Northern Ireland, CRC/C/GBR/CO/4.

CRC. (2009) Report on the Forty-Eight Session, CRC/C/48/3.

CRC. (2010) Report on the Forty-Ninth Session, CRC/C/49/3.

CRTC. (2009) Public Notice CRTC 1999–197[Online]. Available at http://tinyurl. com/3c8sg56 (accessed on 20 April 2011).

Consumer Reports. (2011) Five million Facebook users are 10 or younger [Online]. Available at http://tinyurl.com/3vmacez (accessed on 19 May 2011).

Coroneos, P. (2008) Internet Content Policy and Regulation in Australia. In B. Fitzgerald, F. Gao, D. O'Brien & S. X. Shi (Eds). *Copyright Law, Digital Content and the Internet in the Asia-Pacific*. Sydney: Sydney University Press.

Corsaro, W. (1992) Interpretive Reproduction in Peer's Cultures. *Social Psychology Quarterly*, 55(2), 160–177.

Cotter, K. (2009) Combating Child Sex Tourism in Southeast Asia. *Denver Journal of International Law and Policy*, 37 (3), 493–512.

Council of Europe. (2009) Internet literacy handbook [Online]. Available at http:// tinyurl.com/3n3xbw6 (accessed on 2 June 2011).

Council of Europe. (2010) Through the Wild Web Woods – Teachers' guide [Online]. Available at http://tinyurl.com/3qlflae (accessed on 12 January 2011).

Council of the European Union. (2001) Working party on substantive criminal law [Online]. Available at http://tinyurl.com/3lqlmqn (accessed on 12 April 2011).

Council of the European Union. (2004a) Framework decision. 2002/584/JHA.

Council of the European Union. (2004b) Framework decision. 2004/68/JHA of 22 December 2003.

Council of the European Union. (2009a) Protecting children from harmful content [Online]. Available at http://tinyurl.com/3qx3ho5 (accessed on 22 April 2011).

Council of the European Union. (2009b) Ministerial conference safer Internet for children [Online]. Available at http://tinyurl.com/3lxv55d (accessed on 2 June 2010).

Cox Communications. (2010) Teen online safety & digital reputation survey [Online]. Available at http://tinyurl.com/3fwcnn2 (accessed on 12 January 2010).

CPS. (2009) Child abuse: Guidance on prosecuting cases of child abuse [Online]. Available at http://tinyurl.com/3udzf9m (accessed on 25 November 2010).

Craven, S., Brown, S., & Gilchrist, E. (2006) Sexual Grooming of Children: Review of Literature and Theoretical Considerations. *Journal of Sexual Aggression*, 12(3), 287–299.

Critcher, C. (2008) Moral Panic Analysis: Past, Present and Future. *Sociology Compass*, 2, 1127–1144.

Cross, D., Shaw, T., Hearn, L., Epstein, M., Monks, H., Lester, L. & Thomas, L. (2009) Australian covert bullying prevalence study [Online]. Available at http://tinyurl.com/3d8dacj (accessed on 2 March 2011).

CSEC World Congress. (1966) Declaration and agenda for action [Online]. Available at http://tinyurl.com/3dddx9r (accessed on 12 June 2010).

Culture, Media and Sport Committee. (2008) Harmful Content on the Internet and in Video Games. Tenth Report of Session 2007–08 HC 353. London: The Stationary Office Limited.

CSIS. (2007) Transnational criminal activity: A global context [Online]. Available at http://tinyurl.com/3ksp4xu (accessed on 20 March 2010).

CWG (2010) Submission to Joint Select Committee on Cybersafety [Online]. Available at http://tinyurl.com/5tvqcmy (accessed on 12 March 2011).

Dahl, R. A. (1989) *Democracy and Its Critics*. New Haven and London: Yale University Press.

Dandurand, Y., Colombo, G. & Passas, N. (2007) Measures and Mechanisms to Strengthen International Cooperation among Prosecution Services. *Crime, Law and Social Change*, 47, 4–5, 261–289.

Davidson, J., Grove-Hills, J., Bifulco, A., Gottschalk, P., Caretti, V., Pham, T & Webster, S. (2011) Online abuse: Literature review and policy context [Online]. Available at http://tinyurl.com/3nbskru (accessed on 11 April 2011).

Defeis, E. (1992) Freedom of speech and international norms: A response to hate speech. *Stanford Journal of International Law*, 29, 57–130.

DCSF. (2007) *Safe to Learn: Embedding Anti-bullying Work in Schools*. Nottingham, England: DCSF.

DCSF. (2008) Youth cohort study and longitudinal study of young people in England: The activities and experiences of 17 year olds [Online]. Available at http://tinyurl.com/3brjqk4 (accessed on 21 May 2011).

DfE. (2010) Permanent and fixed period exclusions from schools in England 2008/09 [Online]. Available at http://tinyurl.com/4x72oy8 (accessed on 22 May 2011).

DCMS. (2009) Digital Britain Final Report Cm 7650. UK: HMSO.

Desautels-Stein, J. (2008) Extraterritoriality, Antitrust, and the Pragmatism Style. *Emory International Law Review*, 22 (2), 499–570.

DeRoche, E., & Williams, M. (2001) *Educating Hearts and Minds: A Comprehensive Character Education Framework* (2nd ed). Thousand Oaks, CA: Sage.

Dertouzos, M. (2001) *The Unfinished Revolution: Human-Centered Computers and What They Can Do for Us*. New York: Harper Collins.

De Saint, A. (2004) International Cooperation in Law Enforcement. In C. Arnaldo (Ed). *Child Abuse on the Internet: Ending the Silence*. Paris: UNESCO Publishing.

Deutsche Welle. (2008) German detective calls for Internet reset button after webcam attacks [Online]. Available at http://tinyurl.com/3hl467k (accessed on 12 January 2010).

Dillard, J. P., & Shen, L. (2005) On the Nature of Reactance and Its Role in Persuasive Health Communication. *Communication Monographs*, 72, 144–168.

Djelic, M., & Sahlin-Andersson, K. (2006) *Transnational Governance: Institutional Dynamics of Regulation*. Cambridge: Cambridge University Press.

Donath, J. & boyd, d. (2004) Public Displays of Connection. *BT Technology Journal*, 22(4): 71–82.

Dutton, W. & Peltu, M. (2007) The Emerging Internet Governance Mosaic: Connecting the Pieces. *Information Polity*, 12 (1–2), 63–81.

Eastin, M. (2008) Toward a Cognitive Development Approach to Youth Perceptions of Credibility. In M. Metzger & A. Flanagin (Eds). *Digital Media, Youth, and Credibility*. Cambridge, MA: MIT Press.

ECPAT. (2005) *Violence against Children in Cyberspace*. Bangkok: ECPAT International.

ECPAT. (2008) *Young Persons' Guide to Combating Child Sex Tourism*. Bangkok: ECPAT International.

ECPAT. (2009) Report of the World Congress III against sexual exploitation of children and adolescents [Online]. Available at http://tinyurl.com/37pku4r (accessed on 20 January 2010).

ECPAT. (2010) *The Use of Information and Communication Technologies in Connection with Cases of Child Sex Tourism in East and Southeast Asia*. Bangkok: ECPAT International.

EDRI. (2011) Net child abuse: Member States fiercely defend their right to do nothing [Online]. Available at http://tinyurl.com/454c3sm (accessed on 20 March 2011).

Edwards, L. (2010) Pornography, Censorship and the Internet. In L. Edwards & C. Waelde (Eds). *Law and the Internet*. Oxford: Hart Publishing.

Eekelaar, J. (1986) The Emergence of Children's Rights. *Oxford Journal of Legal Studies*, 6, 161–182.

Ehrenberg, J. (1999) *Civil Society: The Critical History of an Idea*. New York: New York University Press.

Einwiller, S. A., Carroll, C. E. & Korn, K. (2010) Under What Conditions Do the News Media Influence Corporate Reputation? The Roles of Media Dependency and Need for Orientation. *Corporate Reputation Review*, 299–315.

Lee, Ellie J. (2008) Living with risk in the age of `intensive motherhood': Maternal identity and infant feeding. *Health, Risk & Society*, 10 (5): 467–477

eNASCO. (2010) Submission by eNACSO to the FTC Review of the COPPA Rule [Online]. Available at http://www.enacso.eu/ (accessed on 12 January 2011).

Estey, W. (1997) The Five Bases of Extraterritorial Jurisdiction and the Failure of the Presumption Against Extraterritoriality. *Hastings International and Comparative Law Review*, 21, 177–208.

Eurobarometer. (2005) Special EUROBAROMETER [Online]. Available at http://tinyurl.com/3o36g2o (accessed on 20 March 2010).

Eurobarometer. (2006) Safer Internet [Online]. Available at http://tinyurl.com/3dhnl3u (accessed 20 March 2010).

Eurobarometer. (2007) Safer Internet for children: Qualitative study in 29 European countries [Online]. Available at http://tinyurl.com/3dhnl3u (accessed on 20 March 2010).

Eurobarometer. (2008) Towards a safer use of the Internet for children in the EU – A parents' perspective [Online]. Available at http://tinyurl.com/3dhnl3u (accessed 20 March 2010).

Eurochild. (2011) European Commission's Agenda on Child Rights lack ambition [Online]. Available at http://tinyurl.com/3wwdn25 (accessed on 12 February 2011).

EUROPA (2007a) Mobile operators agree on how to safeguard kids using mobile phones [Online]. Available at http://tinyurl.com/22txta (accessed on 10 February 2010).

EUROPA. (2007b) BT's response to the consultation on Safer Internet and On-line Technologies for Children [Online]. Available at http://tinyurl.com/44bqsbq (accessed on 10 February 2010).

European Commission. (1996a) Communication from the Commission on Combating Child Sex Tourism COM/96/0547 FINAL.

European Commission. (1996b) Communication on illegal and harmful content on the Internet, COM(96) 487.

European Commission. (1996c) Green Paper on the Protection of Minors and Human Dignity in Audiovisual and Information Services, COM(96) 483.

European Commission. (2000) Communication on the Precautionary Principle, COM(2000).

European Commission. (2001) European Governance. A White Paper. COM (2001) 428 final.

European Commission. (2004) Proposal for a Decision of the European Parliament and of the Council on establishing a multiannual Community programme on promoting safer use of the Internet and new online technologies, SEC(2004) 148] /* COM/2004/0091 final.

European Commission. (2006a) Towards an EU Strategy on the Rights of the Child, COM (2006) 367 final.

European Commission. (2006b) Commission opens public consultation on the protection of minors using mobile phones, IP/06/1059.

European Commission. (2007a) Audiovisual Media Services Directive [Online]. Available at http://tinyurl.com/4xywtwc (accessed on 20 March 2010).

European Commission (2007b) A European approach to media literacy in the digital environment [Online]. Available at http://tinyurl.com/3oswkjg (accessed on 12 January 2010).

European Commission. (2008) Directive and Communication on the Protection of Consumers, in Particular Minors, in Respect of the Use of Video Games, COM(2008) 207 final.

European Commission (2009a) Communication on the Final Evaluation of Safer Internet Plus 2005–2008, COM (2009) 64 final.

European Commission. (2009b) Commission staff working paper – Accompanying document to the proposal for a Council Framework Decision on combating the sexual abuse, sexual exploitation of children and child pornography, COM(2009) 135, SEC(2009) 355.

European Commission. (2009c) Study on assessment criteria for media literacy levels [Online]. Available at http://tinyurl.com/4x858yk (accessed on 4 March 2010).

European Commission. (2010a) A Digital Agenda For Europe, COM(2010) 245.

European Commission. (2010b) EUROPE 2020: A strategy for smart, sustainable and inclusive growth, COM (2010) 2020.

European Commission. (2010c) Digital Literacy European Commission Working Paper and Recommendations from Digital Literacy High-Level Expert Group [Online]. Available at http://tinyurl.com/3legpwv (accessed on 12 February 2011).

European Commission. (2010d) Making the most of social networking [Online] Available at http://tinyurl.com/3kg5pva (accessed on 12 February 2011).

European Commission. (2010e) Proposal for a directive on combating sexual abuse, sexual exploitation of children and child pornography, repealing Framework Decision 2004/68/JHA, COM 2010 94.

European Commission. (2010f) Digital agenda for Europe: What would it do for me? MEMO/10/199.

European Commission. (2011a) Benchmarking of parental control tools for the on-line protection of children SIP – Bench II [Online]. Available at http://www.yprt.eu/sip/ (accessed on 20 March 2011).

European Commission. (2011b) An EU Agenda for the Rights of the Child, COM (2011) 60 final.

ECDG. (2009) Study on assessment criteria for media literacy levels [Online]. Available at http://tinyurl.com/3zyf4lg (accessed on 12 February 2011).

EU SIP (2009) The Internet is fun. Keep it fun, keep control! Block bullying online! [Online] Available at http://tinyurl.com/4yllpnf (accessed on 12 November 2010).

European Parliament. (2004) Proposal for a Decision of the European Parliament and of the Council on establishing a multiannual community programme on promoting safer use of the Internet and new online technologies, SEC(2004) 148 /* COM/2004/0091 final - COD 2004/0023.

European Parliament. (2005) EC Decision No 854/2005/EC of the European Parliament and of the Council of 11 May 2005 establishing a multiannual community programme on promoting safer use of the Internet and new online technologies.

European Parliament and Council. (2006) Recommendation 2006/952/EC on the protection of minors and human dignity and on the right of reply in relation to the competitiveness of the European audiovisual and on-line information services industry.

European Parliament. (2009) Final evaluation of the implementation of the multi-annual community programme on promoting safer use of the Internet and new online technologies, COM (2009) 64 final.

Facebook. (2011) Details on social reporting [Online]. Available at http://tinyurl.com/68nrk73 (accessed on 12 March 2011).

Faguendas, F. (2009) Fighting Internet Child Pornography – The Brazilian Experience. *The Police Chief,* 76(9), 48–55.

Fairman, R., & Yapp, C. (2005) Enforced Self Regulation, Prescription and Conceptions of Compliance within Small Businesses: The Impact of Enforcement. *Law and Policy,* 27(4), 491–519.

Falk, R. (1995) *On Humane Governance: Toward a New Global Politics.* Cambridge: Polity Press.

FBI. (2008) Department of Justice launches new law enforcement strategy to combat increasing threat of international organized crime [Online]. Available at http://tinyurl.com/3e5wmu4 (accessed on 15 March 2010).

FBI. (2009) Three American men accused of traveling to Cambodia to have sex with children now en route to United States to face prosecution on federal "sex tourism" charges [Online]. Available at http://tinyurl.com/4xtg3o2 (accessed on 12 January 2011).

FCACP. (2008) Financial coalition against child pornography [Online]. Available at http://tinyurl.com/3pok3el (accessed on 23 November 2010).

FCC. (2011) National Broadband Plan: Connecting America [Online]. Available at http://www.broadband.gov/ (accessed 20 February 2011).

FTC. (2010a) OnGuardOnline.gov off to a fast start with online child safety campaign [Online]. Available at www.ftc.gov/opa/2010/03/netcetera.shtm (accessed on 21 April, 2011).

FTC. (2010b) Protecting kids' privacy online: Reviewing the COPPA rule [Online]. Available at http://tinyurl.com/42qajc5 (accessed on 10 January 2011).

Feinberg, J. (1987) *The Moral Limits of the Criminal Law Volume 1: Harm to Others*. Oxford: Oxford University Press.

Feinberg, J. (2003) *Problems at the Roots of Law – Essays in Legal and Political Theory*. New York: Oxford University Press.

Ferraro, M., & Casey, E. (2005) *Investigating child exploitation and pornography*. London: Elsevier Academic Press.

Finkelhor, D. (1984) *Child Sexual Abuse: New Theory and Research*. New York: Free Press.

Finkelhor, D., Mitchell, K., & Wolak, J. (2000) Online victimization: A report on the nation's youth [Online] Available at http://tinyurl.com/3bdb6dl (accessed on 12 March 2010).

Fisher, E. (2009) Opening Pandora's box: Contextualising the precautionary principle in the European Union. In M. Everson & E. Vos (Eds). *Uncertain Risks Regulated*. England: Routledge Cavendish.

Fisher, E. (2010) Risk Regulatory Concepts and the Law. In OECD (Ed). *Risk and Regulatory Policy – Improving the Governance of Risk*. Paris, France: OECD.

Flanagin, A., & Metzger, M. (2010) *Kids and Credibility: An Empirical Examination of Youth, Digital Media Use, and Information Credibility*. Cambridge: MIT Press.

Fleming, H. (1996) Media Ownership: In the Public Interest – The Broadcasting Act 1996. *Modern Law Review*, 60(3) 378–387.

Fletcher, G. P. (2003a) Against Universal Jurisdiction. *Journal of International Criminal Justice*, 1(3), 580–584.

Fletcher, M. (2003b) Some Developments to the ne bis in idem Principle in the European Union: Criminal Proceedings against Huseyn Gozutok and Klaus Brugge. *Modern Law Review*, 66(5), 769–780.

Fortin, J. (2006) Accommodating Children's Rights in a Post Human Rights Act Era. *Modern Law Review*, (69)3, 299–326.

Fortin, J. (2009) after Fortin, J (2006) (2009) *Children's Rights and the Developing Law*, 3rd edition. Cambridge: Cambridge University Press.

Fox, N., Ward, K., & O'Rourke, A. (2005) Pro-anorexia, weight-loss drugs and the Internet: An "anti-recovery" explanatory model of anorexia. *Sociology of Health & Illness*, 944–971.

Fox, S. (2008) Adolescence, Mobile Technology & Culture, Pew Internet & American Life Project [Online]. Available at http://tinyurl.com/3vxc5ut (accessed on 12 March 2010).

Freeman, M. (1992) Taking Children's Rights More Seriously. *International Journal of Law Policy and Family*, 6, 52–71.

Freeman, M. (2007) The Best Interests of the Child. In A. Alen, J. Lanotte, E. Verhellen, F. Ang, E. Berghmans & M. Verheyde (Eds). A Commentary on the United Nations Convention on the Rights of the Child. Leiden: Martinus Nijhoff.

Fry, C. (2009) Facebook bully Keeley Houghton talks of her regrets [Online]. Available at http://tinyurl.com/3mlmw37 (accessed on 11 February 2011).

Fujino, M. (2008) Information and Communications in Japan, White Paper [Online]. Available at http://tinyurl.com/3rny3rq (accessed on 12 March 2010).

Fujino, M. (2009) National broadband policies: 1999–2009 [Online]. Available at http://tinyurl.com/3jlta9j (accessed on 12 March 2010).

Fry, J. (2002) Terrorism as a Crime against Humanity and Genocide: The Backdoor to Universal Jurisdiction. *UCLA Journal of International Law & Foreign Affairs*, 7, 169–200.

Furedi, F. (1997) *Culture of Fear: Risk-Taking and the Morality of Low Expectations.* London: Cassell.

Furedi, F. (2001) *Paranoid Parenting: Abandon your Anxieties and Be a Good Parent.* London: Allen Lane.

G8. (2007) G8 experience in the implementation of extraterritorial jurisdiction for sex crimes against children [Online]. Available at http://tinyurl.com/3h27mah (accessed 10 October 2010).

Gallagher, P. (2009) Future developments in judicial cooperation in criminal matters. *ERA Forum* 9, 495–517.

GAO. (2003) File sharing programs: Peer-to-peer networks provide ready access to child pornography [Online]. Available at http://tinyurl.com/65afeyr (accessed on 10 June 2010).

Garland, D. (2003) The Rise of Risk. In R. Ericson & A. Doyle (Eds). *Risk and Morality.* Toronto: University of Toronto Press.

Garland, D. (2008) On the Concept of Moral Panic. *Crime Media Culture*, 4(1), 9–30.

Gardner, J. (1996) Justifications and Reasons. In A. Simester and A. Smith (Eds.) *Harm and Culpability.* Oxford: Oxford University Press, 1996.

Garrard, V. (2006) Sad Stories: Trafficking in Children – Unique Situations Requiring New Solutions. *Georgia Journal of International and Comparative Law*, 35(1), 145–174.

Gasser, U., Maclay, C. & Palfrey, J. (2010) Working towards a deeper understanding of digital safety for children and young people in developing nations: An exploratory study [Online]. Available at http://papers.ssrn.com/sol3/papers.cfm?abstract_id=1628276 (accessed on 12 January 2011).

Gerbner, G., & Gross, L. (1976) Living with television: The violence profile. *Journal of Communication*, 26, 172–199.

Gercke, M. (2006) The Slow Wake of a Global Approach against Cybercrime. *Computer Law Review International*, 140–145.

Gercke, M. (2008) National, regional and international approaches in the fight against cybercrime. *Computer Law Review International*, 7–13.

Gercke, M. (2009) Europe's legal approaches to cybercrime. *ERA Forum*, 10, 409–420.

Giddens, A. (1991) *Modernity and Self Identity: Self and Society in the Late Modern Age.* Cambridge: Polity Press.

Giddens, A. (1990) *The Consequences of Modernity.* Cambridge: Polity Press.

Gill, T. (2007) *No Fear: Growing Up in a Risk Averse Society.* London: Calouste Gulbenkian.

Gillespie, A. (2002) Child Protection on the Internet – Challenges for Criminal Law. *Child and Family Law Quarterly*, 411–426.

Gillespie, A. (2010) Legal definitions of child pornography. *Journal of Sexual Aggression*, 16(1), 19–31.

Golding, P. (2000) Forthcoming Features: Information and Communications Technologies and the Sociology of the Future. *Sociology*, 34, 165–184.

Goldman, S., Booker, A., & McDermott, M. (2008) Mixing the Digital, Social, and Cultural: Learning, Identity, and Agency in Youth Participation. In D. Buckingham (Ed). *Youth, Identity, and Digital Media*. Cambridge, MA: The MIT Press.

Goode, E. and N. Ben Yehuda (1994) *Moral Panics: The Social Construction of Deviance*. Oxford: Blackwell.

Google. (2010) Family safety [Online]. Available at www.googlc.com/familysafety (accessed on 21 April 2011).

Goold, B., Lazarus, L., & Swiney, G. (2007) Public protection, proportionality and the search for balance, ministry of justice research series, 10th June 2007 [Online]. Available at http://tinyurl.com/43nonwy (accessed on 12 March 2011).

Goswami, U. (2008) Byron Review on the impact of new technologies on children: A research literature review: Child development [Online]. Available at http://tinyurl.com/3goosmp (accessed on 12 February 2011).

Government of Canada. (2004) Smart regulation: A regulatory strategy for Canada [Online]. Available at http://tinyurl.com/4yvzees (accessed on 23 February 2011).

Government of Canada. (2011) *The Next Phase of Canada's Economic Action Plan: A Low-Tax Plan for Jobs and Growth*. Ottawa: Ontario.

Grabosky, P. (2007a) Requirements of prosecution services to deal with cyber crime. *Crime, Law and Social Change*, 47, 201–223.

Grabosky, P. (2007b) The Internet, Technology, and Organized Crime. *Asian Journal of Criminology: An Interdisciplinary Journal on Crime, Law and Deviance in Asia*, 2(2), 145–161.

Graham, J. (2010) Why Governments Need Guidelines for Risk Assessment and Management. In OECD (Ed). *Risk and Regulatory Policy – Improving the Governance of Risk*. Paris, France: OECD.

Graham, W. (2000) Uncovering and Eliminating Child Pornography Rings on the Internet: Issues regarding and Avenues Facilitating Law Enforcement's Access to Wonderland. *Law Review of Michigan State University Detroit College of Law*, 2000(2), 457–484.

Grant, I. (2009) Child safety takes precedence in Internet regulation debate [Online]. Available at http://tinyurl.com/3zgwwct (accessed 11 February 2010).

Griffith, G. & Harris, C. (2005) Recent Developments in the Law of Extradition. *Melbourne Journal of International Law*, 2, 6(1), 33–54.

Griffith, G., & Roth, L. (2007) Protecting children from online sexual predators, Briefing Paper no. 10/07. Parliamentary Library Research Service: NSW.

Griffith, G., & Simon, K. (2008) Child Pornography Law, Briefing Paper no. 9/08. Parliamentary Library Research Service: NSW.

Grugel, J. (2003) Democratisation Studies Globalisation: The Coming of Age of a Paradigm. *British Journal of Politics and International Relations*, 5(2), 258–283.

GSM Europe. (2010a) Safer mobile use [Online]. Available at http://tinyurl.com/5roz53c (accessed on 12 February 2011).

GSM Europe. (2010b) European framework for safer mobile use by younger teenagers and children [Online]. Available at http://tinyurl.com/5ualz9y (accessed on 12 February 2011).

GSM Europe. (2010c) National implementation report, national code for mobile operators on safe use of mobile services [Online]. Available at http://tinyurl.com/5udfzev (accessed on 12 February 2011).

GSM Europe. (2010d) National Implementation Report, the Bulgarian Code of Conduct on safer mobile use by children and younger teenagers [Online]. Available at http://tinyurl.com/6emwpj8 (accessed on 12 February 2011).

GSM Europe. (2010e) The Danish Mobile Operators' Code of Practice for the responsible and secure use of mobile services [Online]. Available at http://tinyurl.com/6as3nbd (accessed on 12 February 2011).

GSM Europe. (2010f) The Greek Mobile Operators' Code of Practice for the responsible and secure use of mobile services [Online]. Available at http://tinyurl.com/6k7uxal (accessed on 12 February 2011).

GSM Europe. (2010g) The Hungarian Mobile Operators' Code of Practice for the responsible and secure use of mobile services [Online]. Available at http://tinyurl.com/5uag2o7 (accessed on 12 February 2011).

GSM Europe. (2010h) The Irish Mobile Operators' Code of Practice for the responsible and secure use of mobile services [Online]. Available at http://tinyurl.com/6f3c34j (accessed on 12 February 2011).

GSM Europe. (2010i) The Latvian Mobile Operators' Code of Practice for the responsible and secure use of mobile services [Online]. Available at http://tinyurl.com/6ad6aop (accessed on 12 February 2011).

GSM Europe. (2010j) The United Kingdom Code of Practice for the self-regulation of new forms of content on mobiles [Online]. Available at http://tinyurl.com/69kjhcb (accessed on 12 February 2011).

GSM Europe. (2010k) National Code for mobile operators on safe use of mobile services [Online]. Available at http://tinyurl.com/5wplz2n (accessed on 12 February 2011).

GSM World. (2007) European framework for safer mobile use by younger teenagers and children [Online]. Available at http://tinyurl.com/6bgn9m7 (accessed on 12 February 2011).

Hall, R. B., & Biersteker, T. J. (2002) *The Emergence of Private Authority in Global Governance.* Cambridge: Cambridge University Press.

Haddon, L. (2002) Youth and Mobiles: The British case and further questions. *Revista de Estudios de Juventud,* 52, 115–124.

Handmer, J. & James, P. (2007) Trust Us and Be Scared: The Changing Nature of Contemporary Risk. *Global Society,* 21(1), 119–130.

Hansard. (2003) Sexual Offences Bill [HL]. HL Deb 01 April 2003 vol 646 cc1170–247 [Online]. Available at http://tinyurl.com/3l95sjp (accessed on 12 January 2011).

Hansard. (2010) March 4th, Column 118WS [Online]. Available at http://tinyurl.com/3d2rl48 (accessed on 13 March 2011).

Hargittai, E., Fullerton, L., Menchen-Trevino, E., & Thomas, K. (2010) Trust Online: Young Adults' Evaluation of Web Content. *International Journal of Communication,* 4, 468–494.

Hargrave, A. (2009) Protecting children from harmful content. Report prepared for the Council of Europe's Group of Specialists on Human Rights in the Information Society. Strasbourg, France: Council of Europe.

Hargrave, A., & Livingstone, S. (2006) *Harm and Offence in Media Content: A Review of the Evidence.* Bristol: Intellect.

Harris, N. (2005) Empowerment and State Education: Rights of Choice and Participation. *Modern Law Review,* 68, 925–957.

Harrison, C. (2006) Cyberspace and Child Abuse Images: A Feminist Perspective. *Affilia,* 21(4), 365–379.

Hasebrink, U., Livingstone, S., Haddon, L., & Ólafsson, K. (2009) *Comparing children's Online Opportunities and Risk across Europe: Cross-national Comparisons for EU Kids Online* (2nd ed). London: LSE.

Hawkins, R. & Pingree, S. (1983) Televisions influence on social reality. In E. Wartella, D. Whitney & Windahl, S. (Eds). *Mass Communication Review Yearbook,* Volume 5. Beverley Hills, CA: Sage.

Hawton, K., & James, A. (2005) Suicide and deliberate self harm in young people. *British Medical Journal*, 330, 891–894.

Healy, M. (1995) Prosecuting Child Sex Tourists at Home: Do Laws in Sweden, Australia, and the United States Safeguard the Rights of Children as Mandated by International Law? *Fordham International Law Journal*, 18, 1852–1923.

Hecht, M. (2008), Private Sector Accountability in Combating the Commercial Sexual Exploitation of Children. ECPAT International: Bangkok.

Held, D. (1995) *Democracy and the Global Order*. Stanford: Stanford University Press.

Henry, O., Mandeville-Norden, R., Hayes, E., & Egan, V. (2010) Do Internet-based sexual offenders reduce to normal, inadequate and deviant groups? *Journal of Sexual Aggression*, 16:1, 33–46.

Herlin-Karnell, E. (2010), European Arrest Warrant Cases and the Principles of Non-discrimination and EU Citizenship. *Modern Law Review*, 73, 824–835.

Herring, S. (2008) Questioning the Generational Divide: Technological Exoticism and Adult Constructions of Online Youth Identity. In D. Buckingham (Ed). *Youth, Identity, and Digital Media*. Cambridge, MA: MIT Press.

Hersh, M. (2001) Is Coppa a Cop Out – The Child Online Privacy Protection Act as Proof that Parents, Not Government, Should Be Protecting Children's Interests on the Internet. *Fordham Urban Law Journal*, 28, 1831–1878.

Heslin, P. A., & Ochoa, J. (2008) Understanding and developing strategic social responsibility. *Organizational Dynamics*, 37(2), 125–144.

Hier, S. P. (2003) Risk and Panic in late Modernity: Implications of the Converging Sites of Social Anxiety. *The British Journal of Sociology*, 54, 3–20.

High, J. (2005) The Basis for Jurisdiction over U.S. Sex Tourists: An Examination of the Case against Michael Lewis Clark. *UC Davis Journal of International Law & Policy*, 11(2), 343–372.

Hinduja, S., & Patchin, J. (2008). Personal Information of Adolescents on the Internet: A Qualitative Content Analysis of MySpace. *Journal of Adolescence*, 31(1), 125–146.

Hinduja, S., & Patchin, J. (2009) *Bullying beyond the Schoolyard: Preventing and Responding to Cyberbullying*. Thousand Oaks, CA: Sage.

Hirst, M. (2003) *Jurisdiction and the Ambit of Criminal Law*. Oxford: Oxford University Press.

Hobbes, R. (1998) The seven great debates in the media literacy movement. *Journal of Communication*, 48, 16–32.

Hoffman, J. (2005) Internet governance: A regulative idea in flux. Paper presented to European Consortium of Political Research, Budapest, September 2005.

Holloway, W., & Jefferson, T. (1997) The Risk Society in an Age of Anxiety: Situating Fear of Crime. *British Journal of Sociology*, 48(2), 255–265.

Holmes, J. (2007) Myths and Missed Opportunities. *Information, Communication & Society*, 12(8), 1174–1196.

Home Office. (2001) Home Office Circular 28/2001. The Protection from Harassment Act 1997.

Home Office. (2002) Protecting the Public: Strengthening protection against sex offenders and reforming the law on sexual offences. Cm 5668. Home Office, UK: HMSO.

Home Office. (2005) Internet Task Force. Good practice guidance for the moderation of interactive services for children [Online]. Available at http://tinyurl.com/3ks3h8v [materials are now archived] (accessed on 12 January 2010).

Home Office (2008) Good practice guidance for the providers of social networking and other user interactive services [Online]. Available at http://tinyurl.com/3p24q3f (accessed on 12 January 2010).

Hood, C., Rothstein, H., & Baldwin, R. (2001) *The Government of Risk: Understanding Risk Regulation Regimes*. Oxford: Oxford University Press.

House of Commons. (2007-8) Harmful content on the Internet and in video games. Tenth Report of Session 2007–08, HC -353 -I [Online]. Available at http://tinyurl.com/3sb5wvw (accessed on 21 January 2010).

House of Commons. (2011) 1st Report – Behaviour and Discipline in Schools [Online]. Available at http://tinyurl.com/3zqksgv (accessed on 21 April 2011).

House of Lords Science and Technology Committee. (2007) Personal Internet Security – Volume I HL Paper 165–I. London: The Stationary Office Limited.

House of Representatives. (1998) Protection of children from Sexual Predators Act of 1998 House Report No. 105–557 [Online]. Available at http://tinyurl.com/3hlgzap (accessed on 12 February 2011).

House of Representatives. (2002) Sex Tourism Prohibition Improvement Act of 2002 House Report No. 107–525 [Online]. Available at http://judiciary.house.gov/legacy/107-525.pdf (accessed on 12 March 2011).

Howard, S., Grigg, D., Pozzoli, T., Tippett, N., & Sadeghi, S (2010) The use and effectiveness of anti-bullying strategies in schools [Online]. Available at http://tinyurl.com/3mhd2ba (accessed on 13 March 2011).

Howells, K. (1995) Child sexual abuse: Finkelhor's precondition model revisited. *Psychology, Crime & Law*, 1(3), 201–214.

Howitt, D., & Sheldon, K. (2007) The role of cognitive distortions in paedophilic offending: Internet and contact offenders compared. *Psychology, Crime and Law*, 13, 469–486.

Howitt, D. (1995) *Paedophiles and Sexual Offences against Children*. London: Wiley and Sons.

HRC. (2007) Rights of the Child Resolution, HRC/7/29.

HRC. (2009a) Promotion and Protection of all Human Rights, Civil, Political, Economic, Social and Cultural Rights, including the Right to Development. Report submitted by Ms. Najat M'jid Maalla, Special Rapporteur on the sale of children, child prostitution and child pornography, A/HRC/12/23.

HRC. (2009b) Promotion and Protection of all Human Rights, Civil, Political, Economic, Social and Cultural Rights, including the Right to Development. Report submitted by Ms. Najat M'jid Maalla, Special Rapporteur on the sale of children, child prostitution and child pornography. Addendum Communications to and from Governments, A/HRC/12/23/Add.3.

HRC. (2011) Report of the Special Rapporteur on the sale of children, child prostitution and child pornography, Najat Maalla M'jid Addendum Mission to the United States of America, A/HRC/16/57/Add.5.

Hunt, R., & Jensen, J. (2007) The School Report: The Experiences of Young Gay People in Britain's schools. London: Stonewall.

INSAFE. (2009) Safer Internet Day 2009 [Online]. Available at http://tinyurl.com/6yf4ccs (accessed on 12 October 2010).

Interception of Communications Commissioner. (2010) Report of the Interception of Communications Commissioner for 2009. House of Commons, UK: Stationary Office.

Ipsos MORI. (2009) Children's and Young People's Access to Online Content on Mobile Devices, Games Consoles and Portable Media Players: Report Prepared for OfCom. London: Ipsos MORI.

ISFE. (2010) Video Gamers in Europe [online] Available at http://www.isfe-eu.org/tzr/scripts/downloader2.php?filename=T003/F0013/d6/1a/3401b53qaghqd4j25b2 ullin3&mime=application/pdf&originalname=ISFE_Consumer_Survey_2010.pdf (accessed on 12 September 2011).

ISTTF. (2008) Enhancing child safety & online technologies: Final report of the Internet Safety Technical Task Force to the Multi-State Working Group on Social Networking of State Attorneys Generals of the United States [Online]. Available at http://cyber.law.harvard.edu/pubrelease/isttf (accessed on 12 January 2010).

Ito, M. (2008) Introduction. In K. Varnelis (Ed). *Networked Publics*. Cambridge, MA: MIT Press.

Ito, M., Horst, H. A., Bittanti, M., boyd, d., Herr-Stephenson, B., Lange, P., Pascoe, C. J., & Robinson, L. (with S. Baumer, R. Cody, D. Mahendran, K. Martínez, D. Perkel, C. Sims & L. Tripp) (2008) Living and Learning with New Media: Summary of Findings from the Digital Youth Project. MacArthur Foundation, London: MIT Press.

ITU. (2008a) Use of information and communication technology by the world's children and youth: A statistical compilation [Online]. Available at http://www.itu.int/ ITU-D/ict/material/Youth_2008.pdf (accessed on 10 October 2010).

ITU. (2008b) ITU launches initiative to protect children online. Children are the most vulnerable users of the Internet [Online]. Available at http://tinyurl.com/3cysb4j (accessed 12 January 2010).

ITU. (2009a) Measuring the information society – The ICT Development Index [Online]. Available at http://tinyurl.com/3gqu3lb (accessed on 12 January 2010).

ITU. (2009b) Guidelines for children [Online]. Available at http://tinyurl.com/ yh4aon9 (accessed on 12 January 2010).

ITU. (2009c) Guidelines for parents, guardians and educators on child online protection [Online]. Available at http://tinyurl.com/yh4aon9 (accessed on 12 January 2010).

ITU. (2009d) Guidelines for industry on child online protection [Online]. Available at http://tinyurl.com/yh4aon9 (accessed on 12 January 2010).

ITU. (2009e) Guidelines for policy makers on child online protection [Online]. Available at http://tinyurl.com/yh4aon9. (accessed on 12 January 2010).

ITU. (2010a) The World in 2010 [Online]. Available at http://tinyurl.com/43f9rc8 (accessed on 12 December 2010).

ITU. (2010b) Children online protection: Statistical framework and indicators [Online]. Available at http://tinyurl.com/3bg4444 (accessed on 12 December 2010).

IWF. (2008) Annual report [Online]. Available at http://tinyurl.com/3nx65va (accessed on 12 January 2011).

IWF. (2010a) Operational trends [Online]. Available at http://www.iwf.org.uk/ resources/trends (accessed on 10 October 2010).

IWF. (2010b) Annual report [Online]. Available at http://tinyurl.com/3ez4o4b (accessed on 12 January 2011).

Jackson, L., Gauntlett, D. & Steemers, J. (2009) Children in virtual worlds – Adventure rock users and producers study [Online]. Available at http://tinyurl.com/3o6aacd (accessed on 20 October 2010).

Jackson, S., & Scott, S. (1999) Risk Anxiety and the Social Construction of Childhood. In D. Lupton (Ed). *Risk and Sociocultural Theory: New Directions and Perspectives*. Cambridge: Cambridge University Press.

James, A. & Prout, A. (1997) *Constructing and Reconstructing Childhood: Contemporary Issues in the Sociological Study of Childhood*. UK: Routledge.

James, A., Jenks, C., & Prout, A. (1998) *Theorizing Childhood*. UK: Polity Press.

James, C., Davis, K., Flores, A., Francis, J., Pettingill, L., Rundle, M. & Gardner, H. (2008) *Young People, Ethics, and the New Digital Media: A Synthesis from the Good Play Project*. MacArthur Foundation, London: MIT Press.

James, C., (with K. Davis, A. Flores, J. M. Francis, L, Pettingill, M. Rundle & H Gardner). (2009) *Young People, Ethics, and the New Digital Media: A Synthesis from the GoodPlay Project*. Cambridge, MA: MIT Press.

Jarvis, D. (2007) Risk, Globalisation and the State: A Critical Appraisal of Ulrich Beck and the World Risk Society Thesis. *Global Society*, 21, 1, 23–46.

Jasanoff, S. (1993) Bridging the Two Cultures of Risk Analysis. *Risk Analysis*, 13(2), 123–129.

Jenkins, H. (2006) *Convergence Culture: Where Old and New Media Collide*. New York: New York University Press.

Jenkins, H., Clinton, K., Purushotma, R., Robison, A. J., & Weigel, M. (2006) *Confronting the Challenges of Participatory Culture: Media Education for the Twenty-first Century*. Cambridge, MA: MIT Press.

Jenkins, H. (P. I.) with R. Purushotma, M. Weigel, K. Clinton & A. J. Robison. (2009) *Confronting the Challenges of Participatory Culture: Media Education for the 21st Century*. Cambridge, MA: MIT Press.

Jenkins, P. (1997) *Moral Panic: Changing Concepts of the Child Molester in Modern America*. New Haven: Yale University Press.

Jenkins, P. (2003) *Beyond Tolerance: Child Pornography on the Internet*. New York: New York University Press.

Jewkes, Y. (2010) Much Ado about Nothing? Representations and Realities Of Online Soliciting of Children. *Journal of Sexual Aggression*, 16(2) 1, 5–18.

Jobert, B. and Kohler-Koch, B. (2008) *Changing Images of Civil Society from Protest to Governance*. London: Routledge.

Jones, G. (2009) Teens driven to suicide by cyber bullying. [Online]. Available at http://tinyurl.com/3uguhqk (accessed on 12 April 2011).

Jorge, A., Cardoso, D., Ponte, C., & Haddon, L. (2010) Stakeholders Forum general report. LSE, London: EU Kids Online.

Jovanic, T. (2010) Some Paradigms of Regulation of Risks to Society. *Annals of the Faculty of Law in Belgrade – Belgrade Law Review*, 2010, 285–307.

Kaldor, M. (2003) *Global Civil Society: An Answer to War*. Cambridge: Polity Press.

Keane, J. (1988) *Civil Society and the State: New European Perspectives*. London: Versa.

Keane, J. (2003) *Global Civil Society?* Cambridge: Cambridge University Press.

Keitner, C. (2011). Rights beyond Borders. *Yale Journal of International Law*, 36(1), 55–114.

Kelly, K. (2010) *What Technology Wants*. London: Viking.

Keohane R. & Nye, J. S. (1998) Power and Interdependence in the Information Age. *Foreign Affairs*, 77(5), 81–94.

Kerr, O. (2005) Digital Evidence and the New Criminal Procedure. *Columbia Law Review*, 105(1), 279–318.

Kerr, O. (2009) *Computer Crime Law*. St. Paul, MN: Thomson West.

Kerr, O. (2010). Ex Ante Regulation of Computer Search and Seizure. *Virginia Law Review.*, 96(6), 1241–1293.

Kim-Kwang, R. (2008) Organised crime groups in cyberspace: A typology. *Trends in Organized Crime*, 11(3), 270–295.

Kim-Kwang, R. C. (2009) *Online Child Grooming: A Literature Review*. Canberra, Australia: Australia Institute of Criminology.

Kincaid, J. R. (1998) *Erotic Innocence: The Culture of Child Molesting*. Durham, NC: Duke University Press.

King, S. (2008) Human Trafficking: Addressing the International Criminal Industry in the Backyard. *University of Miami International & Comparative Law Review*, 15(3) 369–388.

King, R. (2009) Hate Crimes: Perspectives on Offending and the Law.

Kolb, D. A., Boyatzis, R. E., & Mainemelis, C. (2000) In R. J. Sternberg & L. F. Zhang (Eds). *Perspectives on Cognitive, Learning, and Thinking Styles*. NJ: Lawrence Erlbaum.

Klein, H. (2004) Understanding WSIS: An Institutional Analysis of the UN World Summit on the Information Society. *Information Technologies & International Development*, 1, 3/4, 3–13.

Kleinschmidt, B. (2010) An International Comparison of ISP's Liabilities for Unlawful Third Party Content. *International Journal of Law and Information Technology*, 18(4), 332–355.

Klinke, A., Dreyer, M., Renn, O., Stirling, A., &Van Zwanenberg, P. (2006) Precautionary Risk Regulation in European Governance. *Journal of Risk Research*, 9(4): 373–392.

Klinke, A. (2009) Inclusive Risk Governance through Discourse, Deliberation and Participation. In M. Everson & E. Vos (Eds). *Uncertain Risks Regulated*. England: Routledge Cavendish.

Knaak, S. (2009) Contextualising Risk, Constructing Choice: Breastfeeding and Good Mothering in Risk Society. *Health, Risk & Society*, 12, 345–355.

Knight, F. (1921) *Risk, Uncertainty and Profit*. Boston: Houghton Mifflin.

Knight, J., & Johnson, J. (1997) What Sort of Equality Does Deliberative Democracy Require? In J. Bohman & W. Rehg (Eds). *Deliberative Democracy. Essays on Reason and Politics*. Cambridge and London: MIT Press.

Knox, J. (2010) Presumption against Extrajurisdictionality. *American Journal of International Law*, 104, 351-396

Kontostathis, A., Edwards, L., & Leatherman, A. (2010) Text Mining and Cybercrime. In M. W. Berry & J. Kogan (Eds). *Text Mining: Applications and Theory*. Chichester, UK: John Wiley & Sons.

Kowalski, R. M., & Limber, S. P. (2007) Electronic Bullying among Middle School Students. *Journal of Adolescent Health*, 41, S22–S30.

Kravets, D. (2009) U.S. manga obscenity conviction roils comics world [Online]. Available at http://www.wired.com/threatlevel/2009/05/manga-porn/ (accessed 28 May 2010).

Krone, T. (2005a) Concepts and terms. High tech crime brief no. 1 [Online]. Available at http://tinyurl.com/3udfq2l (accessed on 23 April 2011).

Krone, T. (2005b) International police operations against online child pornography [Online]. Available at http://tinyurl.com/3nzxhhx (accessed on 20 April 2011).

Krone, T. (2005c) Queensland police stings in online chat rooms [Online]. Available at http://tinyurl.com/3l86gj5 (accessed on 20 April 2011).

Kuperman, A. (2008) Mitigating the Moral Hazard of Humanitarian Intervention: Lessons from Economics. *Global Governance*, 14(2), 219–240.

Lacey, N. (2007) Legal Constructions of Crime. In M. Maguire, R. Morgan, & R. Reiner (Eds). *The Oxford Handbook of Criminology*. Oxford: Oxford University Press.

Lamborn, S., & Steinberg, L. (1993) Emotional Autonomy Redux: Revisiting Ryan and Lynch. *Child Development*, 64, 483–499.

Lane, N. (2008) Mobile social networking: Communities and content on the move. [Online]. Available at www.informatm.com (accessed 20 October 2010).

Lankes, D. (2008) Trusting the Internet: New Approaches to Credibility Tools. In M. Metzger & A. Flanagin (Eds). *Digital Media, Youth, and Credibility*. Cambridge, MA: MIT Press.

Lanning, K. (1992) *Child Molesters: A Behavioural Analysis*. Washington, DC: National Center for Missing and Exploited Children.

Latapy, M. (2009) Measurement and analysis of P2P activity against paedophile content [Online]. Available at http://antipaedo.lip6.fr/ (accessed on 2 February 2011).

Lastowka, G. (2010) *Virtual Justice: The New Laws of Online Worlds*. New Haven: Yale University Press.

Latzer, M. (2009) Convergence Revisited: Toward a Modified Pattern of Communications Governance Convergence. *The International Journal of Research into New Media Technologies*, 15, 411–426.

Laughlin, J., & Taylor-Butts, A. (2009) Child luring through the Internet [Online]. Available at http://tinyurl.com/3gg99h8 (accessed on 12 March 2010).

Lavers, Troy. (2006) Jurisdictional Issues in Extraterritorial Criminal Law. In C. P. M. Waters (Ed). *British and Canadian Perspectives on International Law*. Martinus Nijhoff Publishers.

Lee, N. (2001) *Childhood and Society: Growing up in an Age of Uncertainty*. Maidenhead, UK: Open University Press.

Lee, S. J., & Young-Gil, C. (2007) Children's Internet Use in a Family Context: Influence on Family Relationships and Parental Mediation. *CyberPsychology & Behavior*, 10(5), 640–644.

Lenhart, A. (2005) Protecting teens online [Online]. Available at http://www.pewinternet.org/PPF/r/152/report_display.asp (accessed on 10 May 2010).

Lenhart, A. (2007) Cyberbullying and online teens [Online]. Available at (http://www.pewinternet.org/PPF/r/216/report_display.asp (accessed on 27 June 2010).

Lenhart, A. (2009) Teens and sexting [Online]. Available at http://www.pewinternet.org/Reports/2009/Teens-and-Sexting.aspx (accessed on 10 April 2010).

Lenhart, A., & Madden, M. (2007a) Social networking websites and teens [Online]. Available at http://www.pewinternet.org/pdfs/PIP_SNS_Data_Memo_Jan_2007.pdf (accessed on 23 February 2010).

Lenhart, A., Madden, M., Macgill, A. R. & Smith, A. (2007b) Teens and social media [Online]. Available at http://www.pewinternet.org/Reports/2007/Teens-and-Social-Media.aspx (accessed on 23 February 2010).

Lenhart, A., & Madden, M. (2007c) Teens, privacy & online social networks: How teens manage their online identities and personal information in the age of MySpace [Online]. Available at http://www.pewinternet.org/PPF/r/211/report_display.asp (accessed on 23 June 2010).

Lenhart, A., Kahne, J., Middaugh, E., Macgill, A., Evans, C., & Vitak, J. (2008) Teens, video games and civics [Online]. Available at http://www.pewinternet.org/Reports/2008/Teens-Video-Games-and-Civics.aspx (accessed on 23 June 2010).

Lessig, L. (2004) *Code: Version 2.0*. New York: Basic Books.

Liau, A., Khoo, A., & Ang, P. (2005) Factors Influencing Adolescents Engagement in Risky Internet Behavior. *CyberPsychology & Behavior*. 8(6): 513–520.

Liau, A., Khoo, A., & Ang, P. (2008) Parental Awareness and Monitoring of Adolescent Internet Use. *Current Psychology*, 27(4), 217–233.

Liberatore, M., Erdely, R., Kerle, T., & Levine, B. (2010) Clay Shields Forensic investigation of peer-to-peer file sharing networks. *Digital Investigation*, 95–103.

Lim, S., & Clark, L. (2010), Virtual worlds as a site of convergence for children's play. *Journal of Virtual Worlds Research* [Online]. Available at https://journals.tdl.org/jvwr/article/view/1897/1165 (accessed on 10 January 2011).

Lindsay, D., Rodrick, S., & de Zwart, M. (2008) Regulating Internet and convergent mobile content. *Telecommunications Journal of Australia*, 58(2–3), 31.1–31.29.

Ling, R. (2008) *New Tech, New Ties: How Mobile Communication Is Reshaping Social Cohesion*. Cambridge, MA: MIT Press.

Livingstone, S. (2003a) The changing nature and uses of media literacy, Media@LSE Electronic Working Papers, No. 4 [Online]. Available at http://tinyurl.com/6jqqeq9 (accessed on 21 November 2010).

Livingstone, S. (2003b) Children's Use of the Internet: Reflections on the Emerging Research Agenda. *New Media & Society*, 5, 147–166.

Livingstone, S. (2004a) What Is Media Literacy? *Intermedia*, 32(3), 18–20.

Livingstone, S. (2004b) Media Literacy and the Challenge of New Information and Communication Technologies. *The Communication Review*, 7, 3–14.

Livingstone, S. (2005a) *Audiences and Publics: When Cultural Engagement Matters for the Public Sphere*. Portland, OR: Intellect.

Livingstone, S. (2005b) Media literacy – Challenges ahead [Online]. Available at http://eprints.lse.ac.uk/archive/00000551 (accessed on 12 April 2011).

Livingstone, S. (2007) Strategies of Parental Regulation in the Media-Rich Home. *Computers in Human Behavior*, 23(2), 920–941.

Livingstone, S. (2008a) Taking Risky Opportunities in Youthful Content Creation: Teenagers' Use of Social Networking Sites for Intimacy, Privacy and Self-Expression. *Media & Society*, 10, 393–411.

Livingstone, S. (2008b) Internet Literacy: Young People's Negotiation of New Online Opportunities. In T. McPherson (Ed). *Digital Youth, Innovation, and the Unexpected*. Cambridge, MA: MIT Press.

Livingstone, S. (2008c) Engaging with Media – A Matter of Literacy? *Communication and Critique*, 1(1), 51–62.

Livingstone, S., & Bober, M. (2004) UK children go online: Surveying the experiences of young people and their parents [Online]. Available at http://personal.lse.ac.uk/bober/UKCGOfinalReport.pdf (accessed on 21 November 2010).

Livingstone, S., & Bober, M. (2005a) UK Children Go Online: Final Report of Key Project Findings. London: LSE.

Livingstone, S., van Couvering, E., & Thumin, N. (2005b) *Adult Media Literacy: A Review of the Research Literature*. London: OfCom.

Livingstone, S., Bober, M., & Helsper, E. (2005c) Active Participation or Just More Information? *Information, Communication and Society*, 8(3): 287–314.

Livingstone, S., Bober, M., Buckingham, D., & Willett, R. (2006) *Regulating the Internet at Home: Contrasting the Perspectives of Children and Parents*. Mahwah, NJ: Lawrence Erlbaum Associates.

Livingstone, S., & Helsper, E. (2007) Taking Risks when Communicating on the Internet: The Role of Offline Social–Psychological Factors in Young People's Vulnerability to Online Risks. *Information, Communication & Society*, 10(5), 619–644.

Livingstone, S., & Haddon, L. (2008a) Risky Experiences for Children Online: Charting European Research on Children and the Internet. *Children & Society*, 22, 314–323.

Livingstone, S., & Staksrud, E. (2008b) Children and Online Risk: Powerless Victims or Resourceful Participants? *Information, Communication and Society*, 12, 364–387.

Livingstone, S., & Helsper, E. J. (2008c) Parental Mediation of Children's Internet Use. *Journal of Broadcasting and Electronic Media*, 52, 581–599.

Livingstone, S., & Helsper, E. (2009a) Balancing Opportunities and Risks in Teenagers Use of the Internet: The Role of Online Skills and Internet Self-Efficacy. *New Media*, 12, 309.

Livingstone, S., & Haddon, L. (2009b) EU kids online: Final report [Online]. Available at http://eprints.lse.ac.uk/24372/ (accessed on 23 January 2010).

Livingstone, S., & Haddon, L. (Eds). (2009c) *Kids Online: Opportunities and Risks for Children*. Bristol: The Policy Press.

Livingstone, S., & Brake, D. (2010a) On the Rapid Rise of Social Networking Sites: New Findings and Policy Implications. *Children & Society*, 24, 75–83.

Livingstone, S., Haddon, L., Görzig, A., & Ólafsson, K. (2010b) *Risks and Safety on the Internet: The Perspective of European Children. Initial Findings*. London: LSE.

Livingstone, S., Haddon, L., Görzig, A., & Ólafsson, K. (2011) *Risks and Safety on the Internet: The Perspective of European Children. Full Findings*. LSE, London: EU Kids Online.

Lofstedt, R. (2005) *Risk Management in Post-Trust Societies*. New York: Palgrave Macmillan.

LTS (2010) Responsibility of all [Online]. Available at http://tinyurl.com/375dl6b (accessed on 23 January 2011).

Long, D., & Woolley, F. (2009) Global Public Goods: Critique of a UN Discourse. Global Governance, 15(1), 107-122.

Longford, G., & Patten, S. (2007) Democracy in the Age of the Internet. *University of New Brunswick Law Journal*, 56, 5–15.

Lupton, D. (1999) *Risk and Sociocultural Theory*. Cambridge: Cambridge University Press.

Luüders, M., Brandtæz, H., & Dunkels, E. (2009) Risky Contacts. In S. Livingstone & L. Haddon (Eds). *Kids Online: Opportunities and Risks for Children*. Bristol: Polity Press.

Madge, N., & Barker, J. (2007) *Risk & Childhood*. London: RSA Risk Commission.

Maduro, M. P. (2007) So Close and Yet So Far: The Paradoxes of Mutual Recognition. *Journal of European Public Policy*, 14(5), 814–825.

Marsden, C. (1999) Regulating Media Owners in Digital Television: Lessons from U.K. Analogue Policy Formation. *Cardozo Arts & Entertainment Law Journal*, 17(3), 659–690.

Marsh, J. (2010) Young Children's Play in Online Virtual Worlds. *Journal of Early Childhood Research*, 8, 23–39.

Marx, G., & Steeves, V. (2010) From the beginning: Children as subjects and agents of surveillance. *Surveillance & Society*, 7 [Online]. Available at http://www.surveilance-and-society.org/ojs/index.php/journal/article/view/beginning

Mazzarella, S. (2007) Why Is Everybody Always Pickin' on Youth? Moral Panics about Youth, Media, and Culture. S. Mazzarella (Ed). *20 Questions about Youth & the Media*. New York: Peter Lang Publishing.

McAlinden, A. M. (2007) *The Shaming of Sexual Offenders*. Oxford, UK: Hart Publishing.

McCabe, K. A. (2000) Child Pornography on the Internet. *Social Science Computer Review*, 18(1): 73–76.

McCarthy, J. (2010) Internet Sexual Activity: A Comparison between Contact and Non-contact Child Pornography Offenders. *Journal of Sexual Aggression*, 16, 2, 181–195.

McCarty, C., Prawitz, A., Derscheid, L., & Montgomery, B. (2011) Perceived Safety and Teen Risk Taking in Online Chat Sites. *Cyberpsychology, Behavior, and Social Networking*, 14 (3), 169–174.

McGlynn, C. & Rackley, E. (2007) Striking a Balance: Arguments for the Criminal Regulation of Extreme Pornography. *Criminal Law Review*, 677–690.

McGlynn, C. & Rackley, E. (2009a) Criminalising Extreme Pornography: A Lost Opportunity. *Criminal Law Review*, 4, 245–260.

McGlynn, C. & Ward, I. (2009b) Pornography, Pragmatism and Proscription. *Journal of Law and Society*, 36(3), 327–351.

McQuade, S., & Sampat, N. M. (2008) Survey of Internet and at-risk behaviors [Online]. Available at http://tinyurl.com/694fcjd (accessed on 7 March 2010).

McLaughlin, C., Byers, R., & Peppin-Vaughan, R. (2011) Findings of the comprehensive review of the literature: Responding to bullying among children with special educational needs and/or disabilities. Briefing paper for head teachers and school staff [Online]. Available at http://tinyurl.com/6gaj99p (accessed on 20 May 2011).

Mesch, G. (2009) Parental Mediation, Online Activities, and Cyberbullying. *CyberPsychology & Behavior*, 387–393.

Megee, M. (1997) Students Need Media Literacy: The New Basic. *Education Digest*, 63(1), 31–35.

Media-Awareness. (2005) Young Canadians in a wired world: Phase II [Online]. Available at http://tinyurl.com/6hjvdrt (accessed on 23 February 2010).

Mencap. (2007) Bullying Wrecks Lives: The Experiences of Children and Young People with a Learning Disability. London: Mencap.

Meredith, F. (2010) The International Market for Trafficking in Persons for the Purpose of Sexual Exploitation: Analyzing Current Treatment of Supply and Demand. *North Carolina Journal of International Law & Commercial Regulation*, 35(3), 669–722.

Metzger, M. (2007) Making Sense of Credibility on the Web: Models for Evaluating Online Information and Recommendations for future research. *Journal of the American Society for Information Science and Technology*, 58(13), 2078–2078.

Miller, M. (2003) Crime Scene Investigation. In S. James, J. Nordby & S. Bell (Eds). Forensic Science: An Introduction to Scientific and Investigative Techniques. London: CRC Press.

Hargrave, A, & S. Livingstone (2006) *Harm and Offence in Media Content: A Review of the Evidence*. Intellect: Bristol.

Ministry of Justice (2009) Circular 2009/01 on the Criminal Justice and Immigration Act: Possession of extreme pornographic images [Online]. Available at http://tinyurl.com/6bzld9x (accessed on 12 March 2010).

Mitchell, K., & Ybarra, M. (2007a) Online behavior of youth who engage in self-harm provides clues for preventive intervention. *Preventative Medicine*, 45, 392–396.

Mitchell, K., Wolak, J., & Finkelhor, D. (2007b) Youth Internet Users at Risk for the Most Serious Online Sexual Solicitations. *American Journal of Preventative Medicine*, 32, 532–537.

Mitchell, K. J., Wolak, J., & Finkelhor, D. (2007c) Trends in youth reports of sexual solicitations, harassment and unwanted exposure to pornography on the Internet. *Journal of Adolescent Health*, 40(2), 116–126.

Mody, S. (2001). National Cyberspace Regulation: Unbundling the Concept of Jurisdiction. *Stanford Journal of International Law*, 37(2), 365–390.

Moore, D. (2010) Technology Literacy: The Extension of Cognition. *International Journal of Technology and Design Education*, 21(2), 185–193.

Moore, M (2007) British police smash online paedophile ring [Online]. Available at http://tinyurl.com/6jqfgcg (accessed on 12 January 2010).

Morse, S. (1999) Neither Desert nor Disease. *Legal Theory*, 5, 265–309.

Morton, T., & Duck, J. (2001) Communication and Health Beliefs Mass and Interpersonal Influences on Perceptions of Risk to Self and Others. *Communication Research*, 28, 602–626.

Muncie, J. (2001) The Construction and Deconstruction of Crime. In J. Muncie & E. McLaughlin. *The Problem of Crime*. London: Sage Publications/Open University.

Mueller, M. (2010) *Networks and States: The Global Politics of Internet Governance*. Cambridge, MA: The MIT Press.

Murray, A. (2007) *The Regulation of Cyberspace: Control in the Online Environment*. Abingdon, UK: Routledge Cavendish.

Murray, A. (2009) The Reclassification of Extreme Pornographic Images. *Modern Law Review*, 72(1), 73–90.

Muntarbhorn, V. (2001). General Rapporteur's report from 2nd World Congress against CSEC Yokohama, Japan [Online]. Available at http://tinyurl.com/6xuxy8y (accessed on 12 June 2010).

Nairn, A., & Mayo, E. (2009) Marketing to Children on the Internet: What's Right and Wrong? *Childright, the Journal of Law and Policy Affecting Children and Young People*, 26–30.

National Campaign. (2008). Sex and tech: Results from a survey of teens and young adults [Online]. Available at http://tinyurl.com/5rxzaj (accessed on 23 March 2010).

Nathanson, A. I. (2002). The Unintended Effects of Parental Mediation of Television on Adolescents. *Media Psychology*, 4, 207–230.

Nathanson, A. I. (2004) Factual and Evaluative Approaches to Modifying Children's Responses to Violent Television. *Journal of Communication*, 54, 321–336.

NCMEC. (2009) Policy Statement on Sexting [online] Available at SEXTINGhttp://www.missingkids.com/missingkids/servlet/NewsEventServlet?LanguageCountry=en_US&PageId=4130 (accessed 12 September 2011)

NCTE. (1975) Resolution on promoting media literacy [Online]. Available at http://tinyurl.com/5vga3ja (accessed on 23 April 2010).

National Foundation for Educational Research. (2009) Children's online risks and safety: A review of the available evidence [Online]. Available at http://tinyurl.com/6ydtr6c (accessed on 24 June 2010).

Negroponte, N. (1995) *Being Digital*. New York: Vintage Books.

Nelson, P., & Dorsey, E. (2008) *New Rights Advocacy: Changing Strategies of Development and Human Rights NGOs*. Washington, DC: Georgetown University Press.

Newell, P. (2008) Legal frameworks for combating sexual exploitation of children [Online]. Available at http://tinyurl.com/64az7hg (accessed on 12 March 2011).

NGO Group for the Convention on the Rights of the Child and ECPAT International to the 2nd World Congress against Commercial Sexual Exploitation of Children (2001) Briefing notes [Online]. Available at http://tinyurl.com/6hp86jt (accessed on 12 November 2010).

Norton Online Family. (2009) Kids' top 100 searches of 2009 [Online]. Available at http://tinyurl.com/ydpu463 (accessed on 3 June 2010).

Norton. (2010) Norton Online Family Report: Global insights into family life online [Online]. Available at http://tinyurl.com/69hw5h8 (23 January 2011).

NSPCC. (2009) NGO statement on the revision of the council framework decision on combating the sexual abuse, sexual exploitation of children and child-pornography, repealing Framework Decision 2004/68/JHA [Online]. Available at http://tinyurl.com/6buehlb (accessed on 23 October 2010).

OCEANZ. (2010) Arrest in undercover operation against child sex tour operator [Online]. Available at http://tinyurl.com/6ylxg8q (accessed on 13 November 2010).

O'Connell, R. (2003). A Typology of Child Cybersexploitation and Online Grooming Practices. University of Central Lancashire, UK: Cyberspace Research Unit.

O'Connell, R., & Davidson, J. C. (2001) The Sex Exploiter, Second World Congress against the Sexual Exploitation of Children, 8, 8–9 [Online]. Available at http://tinyurl.com/66c4suo (accessed on 24 June 2010).

O'Donnell, I., & Milner, C. (2007) *Child Pornography, Crime Computers & Society.* UK: Willan Publishing.

OECD. (2002a) OECD Guidelines for the Security of Information Systems and Networks: Towards a Culture of Security. Paris, France: OECD.

OECD. (2002b) Regulatory Policies in OECD Countries: From Interventionism to Regulatory Governance. Paris, France: OECD.

OECD. (2003) Emerging Risks in the 21st Century. Paris, France: OECD

OECD. (2004) The implications of convergence for regulation of electronic communications [Online]. Available at http://www.oecd.org/dataoecd/56/24/32983964.pdf (accessed on 12 March 2010).

OECD. (2008a) OECD policy guidance on convergence and next generation networks [Online]. Available at http://tinyurl.com/5vfas5x (accessed on 12 March 2010).

OECD. (2008b) The Seoul Declaration for the Future of the Internet Economy [Online]. Available at http://tinyurl.com/6dfgvb (accessed on 23 June 2010).

OECD. (2008c) Protecting Children Online [Online]. Available at www.oecd.org/sti/ict/children (accessed on 23 November 2010).

OECD. (2009) Summary Report. APEC–OECD Joint Symposium on Initiatives among Member Economies Promoting Safer Internet Environment for Children [Online]. Available at http://tinyurl.com/5spdpdy (accessed on 12 November 2010).

OECD. (2010a) The Economic and Social Role of Online Intermediaries [Online]. Available at http://www.oecd.org/dataoecd/49/4/44949023.pdf (accessed on 23 January 2011).

OECD. (2010b) Risk and Regulatory Policy – Improving the Governance of Risk. Paris: OECD.

Office of the Children's Commissioner. (2006). *Bullying Today: A Report by the Office of the Children's Commissioner, with Recommendations and Links to Practitioner Tools.* London: Office of the Children's Commissioner.

OfCom. (2006) *Media Literacy Audit: Report on Media Literacy amongst Children.* London: OfCom.

OfCom. (2008a) Identifying appropriate regulatory solutions: Principles for analysing self and co-regulation [Online]. Available at http://tinyurl.com/6h4yu8s (accessed on 2 February 2010).

OfCom. (2008b) UK Code of Practice for the self-regulation of new forms of content on mobiles [Online]. Available at http://tinyurl.com/6jcyp8n (accessed on 25 February 2010).

OfCom. (2008c) Media Literacy Audit: Report on UK Children's Media Literacy [Online]. Available http://tinyurl.com/68nqo9u (accessed on 25 February 2010).

OfCom. (2009) UK Children's Media Literacy: 2009 Interim Report. London: OfCom.

Ofsted. (2010) The Safe Use of New Technologies. UK: Ofsted.

Office of the Attorney General. (2008), Attorneys General say MySpace response to subpoena reveals 90,000 registered sex offenders with profiles 3 February 2009

[Online]. Available at http://www.ct.gov/ag/cwp/view.asp?A=3673&Q=433228 (accessed on 20 March 2010).

Ohler, J. (2010) *Digital Community, Digital Citizen.* London, UK: Sage.

Ohler, J. (2011) Character Education for the Digital Age. *Educational Leadership,* 68(5) [Online]. Available at http://www.ascd.org/publications/educational-leadership/feb11/vol68/num05/Character-Education-for-the-Digital-Age.aspx (accessed on 23 April 2011).

Ohm, P. (2011) Massive Hard Drives, General Warrants, and the Power of Magistrate Judges. *Virginia Law Review,* In Brief 1 [Online] Available at http://tinyurl.com/6x3nexg. (accessed on 24 April 2011).

Olson, L., Daggs, J., Ellevold, B., & Rogers, T. (2007) Entrapping the Innocent: Toward a Theory of Child Sexual Predators, Luring Communication. *Communication Theory,* 17, 231–251.

Olweus, D., Limber, S., Flerx, V., Mullin, N., Riese, J., & Snyder, M. (2007) *Olweus Bullying Prevention Program: Schoolwide Guide.* Center City, MN: Hazelden.

Orndoff, M. (2010) The Secret World of Sex Tourism: Evidentiary and Procedural Hurdles of the PROTECT Act, [comments]. *Penn State International Law Review,* 28, 4, 789–814.

O'Neill, O. (1988) Children's Rights and Children's Lives. *Ethics,* 98, 445–463.

O'Neill, B., & Hagen, I. (2009) Media Literacy. In S. Livingstone & L. Haddon (Eds). *Kids Online: Opportunities and Risks for Children.* Bristol: Policy Press.

O'Neill, B., & McLaughlin, S. (2010) Recommendations on safety initiatives. LSE, London: EU Kids Online [Online]. Available at www.eukidsonline.net (accessed on 10 February 2011).

Optenet. (2010) More than one third of web pages are pornographic [Online]. Available at http://tinyurl.com/6xcwfzr (accessed on 16 June 2010).

Ost, S. (2009) *Child Pornography and Sexual Grooming: Legal and Societal Responses.* Cambridge, UK: Cambridge University Press.

Ostertag, S. F. (2010) Processing Culture: Cognition, Ontology, and the News Media. *Sociological Forum,* 25: 824–850.

OSTWG. (2010) Youth safety on a living Internet [Online]. Available at http://tinyurl.com/6g9zszf (accessed on 10 February 2011).

Palfrey, J., & Gasser, U. (2008) *Born Digital.* New York: Basic Books.

Papadopoulos, L. (2010) Sexualisation of Young People Review [Online]. Available at http://tinyurl.com/67xtoq2 (accessed on 20 November 2010).

Parliament of the Commonwealth of Australia (2010) Explanatory memoranda. Crimes Legislation Amendment (Sexual Offences against Children) Bill 2010 [Online]. Available at http://tinyurl.com/5updms3 (accessed on 10 March 2011).

Patchin, J., & Hinduja, S. (2006) Bullies Move beyond the Schoolyard: A Preliminary Look at Cyberbullying. *Youth Violence and Juvenile Justice,* 4(2), 148–169.

Patchin, J., & Hinduja S. (2010a) Trends in online social networking: Adolescent use of MySpace over time. *New Media & Society,* 12(2), 197–216.

Patchin, J., & Hinduja, S. (2010b) Cyberbullying and Self-Esteem. *Journal of School Health,* 80(12), 616–623.

Pati, R. (2011) States' Positive Obligations with Respect to Human Trafficking: The European Court of Human Rights Breaks New Ground in Rantsev v. Cyprus and Russia. *Boston University International Law Journal,* 29(1), 79–142.

Pavia, C. (2011) Constitutional Protection of "Sexting" in the Wake of Lawrence: The Rights of Parents and Privacy. *Virginia Journal of Law and Technology,* 16, 189–227.

Penman, R., & Turnbull, S. (2007) Media Literacy – Concepts, Research and Regulatory Issues. Australia: ACMA.

Perrin, B. (2010) Taking a Vacation from the Law? Extraterritorial Criminal Jurisdiction and Section 7(4.1) of the Criminal Code. *Canadian Criminal Law Review*, 13, 175–209.

Perritt, Henry H. (1996) Jurisdiction in Cyberspace. *Villanova Law Review*, 41(1): 1–128/ Perritt, Henry H. (1996) Jr. 41 Vill. L. Rev. 1.

Phippen, A. (2009) Sharing personal images and videos among young people [Online]. Available at http://tinyurl.com/6jzv9ah (accessed on 12 January 2011).

Pinheiro, P. (2006) *World Report on Violence against Children: UN Secretary General's Study on Violence against Children*. Geneva: United Nations.

Podgor, E. (2004) Cybercrime: National, Transnational, or International. *Wayne Law Review*, 50(1), 97–108.

Porter, M. (2006) Strategy and Society: The Link between Competitive Advantage and Corporate Social Responsibility. *Harvard Business Review*, 78–92.

Porter, R. (2002) Matrix of Modernity? *Transactions of the Royal Historical Society (Sixth Series)*, 12, 245–259.

Postman, N. 1983. *The Disappearance of Childhood*. New York: Vintage Books.

Powell, A. (2009) New technologies, unauthorised visual images and sexual assault [Online]. Available at http://tinyurl.com/3oadt6p (accessed on 3 January 2011).

Prensky, M. (2001) Digital Natives, Digital Immigrants. *On The Horizon*, 9(5), 1–6.

President's Working Group on Unlawful Conduct on the Internet (2000) The electronic frontier: The challenge of unlawful conduct involving the use of the Internet, Appendix C [Online]. Available at http://tinyurl.com/6j8dkzq (accessed on 21 January 2010).

PriceWaterhouseCoopers (2009) Implementation report of the European Framework for Safer Mobile use by Young People [Online]. Available at http://tinyurl.com/6xcu3kn (accessed on 12 February 2010).

Princeton University Program in Law and Public Affairs. (2001) The Princeton Principles on Universal Jurisdiction [Online]. Available at http://tinyurl.com/6xce87v (accessed on 11 March 2010).

Prout, A. (2005) *The Future of Childhood*. UK: Oxon.

Purdy, L. M. (1994) Why Children Shouldn't Have Equal Rights. *International Journal of Children's Rights*, 2, 223–241.

Putnam, T., & Elliott, D. (2001) International Responses to Cyber Crime. In A. Sofaer & S. Goodman (Eds). *Transnational Dimension of Cyber Crime and Terrorism*. Stanford, CA: Hoover Institution Press.

Quayle, E. (2010) Child Pornography. In Y. Jewkes & M. Yar (Eds). *Handbook of Internet Crime*. Devon, UK: Willan Publishing.

Quayle, E., & Taylor, M. (2002) Paedophiles, Pornography and the Internet: Assessment Issues. *British Journal of Social Work*, 32(7), 863–875.

Quayle, E., & Taylor, M. (2003) Model of Problematic Internet Use in People with Sexual Interest in Children. *Cyber Psychology & Behaviour*, 6, 93–106.

Quayle, E., Loof, L., & Palmer, T. (2008) *Child Pornography and Sexual Exploitation of Children Online*. Bangkok, Thailand: ECPAT International.

Rackow, P., & Birr, C. (2010). Recent Developments in Legal Assistance in Criminal Matters. *Goettingen Journal of International Law*, 2(3), 1087–1128.

Ray, L., & Smith D. (2001) Racist Offenders and the Politics of Hate Crime. *Law and Critique*, 12, 203–221.

Reguero Jiménez, N., & Scifo, S. (2010) Community Media in the Context of European Media Policies. *Telematics and Informatics*, 27(2), 131–140.

Rideout, V. (2007) Parents, children and media: A Kaiser Family Foundation survey [Online]. Available at http://www.kff.org/entmedia/upload/7638.pdf (accessed on 12 January 2011).

Rideout, V. J., Foehr, U. G., & Roberts, D. F. (2010) Generation M2: Media in the lives of 8- to 18-year-olds [Online]. Available at http://www.kff.org/entmedia/upload/8010.pdf (accessed on 11 November 2010).

Rosen, L. D., Cheever, N. A. & Carrier, L. M. (2008) The association of parenting style and child age with parental limit setting and adolescent MySpace behavior. *Journal of Applied Developmental Psychology*, 29, 459–471.

Royal College of Psychiatrists. (2010) Self-harm, Suicide and Risk: Helping People Who Self-harm. London: RCP.

Sadat, L. (2001) Redefining Universal Jurisdiction. *New England Law Review*, 35, 241–263.

Sacco, D. (2010) Sexting: Youth practices and legal implications [Online]. Available at http://tinyurl.com/3toh83q (accessed on 12 January 2011).

Saltzer, J., Reed, D., & Clark, D. (1984) End-to-End Arguments in System Design. *ACM Transactions on Computer Systems*, 4(2), 277–288.

Sampson, R. (2002) Bullying in schools (Problem-oriented guides for police: problem-specific guides series, guide no. 12). Washington, DC: US Department of Justice.

Schewick, B. (2010) *Internet Architecture and Innovation*. Cambridge, MA: MIT Press.

Selgren, K. (2010) Paedophiles increasingly access images from webcams [Online]. Available at http://tinyurl.com/3bbavtf (accessed on 12 April 2011).

Senft, T. (2008) *Camgirls: Celebrity and Community in the Age of Social Networks*. New York: Peter Lang.

Sepper, E. (2010) Democracy, Human Rights, and Intelligence Sharing. *Texas International Law Journal*, 46(1), 151–208.

Shariff, S. (2008) *Cyber-bullying: Issues and Solutions for the School, the Classroom and the Home*. UK: Routledge.

Shariff, S. (2009) *Confronting Cyber-Bullying: What Schools Need to Know to Control Misconduct and Avoid Legal Consequences*. Cambridge: Cambridge University Press.

Sholte, J.A. (2002) Civil Society and Democracy in Global Governance. *Global Governance*, 8(3), 281–304.

Smedinghoff, T. (2008). Defining the Legal Standard for Information Security: What Does "Reasonable" Security Really Mean? In A. Chander, L. Gelman & M. Radin (Eds). *Securing Privacy in the Internet Age*. Palo Alto, CA: Stanford University Press.

Smetana, J. G. (1995) Parenting styles and conceptions of parental authority during adolescence. *Child Development*, 66(2), 299–316.

SMH. (2011) Swedes jailed for life for Philippine Internet porn [Online]. Available at http://tinyurl.com/3oanhgh (accessed on 24 May 2011).

Smith, C. (2011) Facebook removes 20,000 underage users every day [Online]. Available at http://tinyurl.com/6gmbruc (accessed on 12 April 2011).

Smith, R., Grabosky, P., & Urbas, G. (2004) *Cyber Criminals on Trial*. Cambridge: Cambridge University Press.

Smith, G. (2010) Norwich man facing child porn charges [Online]. Available at http://tinyurl.com/3pffhfk (accessed on 19 April 2010).

Smith, J., & Hudson, C. (2009) Inside virtual goods: The US virtual goods market 2010–2011 [Online]. Available at http://tinyurl.com/yc4tsqc (accessed 20 March 2010).

Solum, L., & Chung, M. (2004) The Layers Principle: Internet Architecture and the Law. *Notre Dame Law Review*, 79, 815–948.

Sonck, N., Livingstone, S., Kuiper, E., & de Haan, J. (2011) Digital literacy and safety skills [Online]. Available at http://tinyurl.com/6cxjpc2 (accessed on 21 April 2011)

SWGFL (2010) Online Safety policy and practice in the UK [Online]. Available at http://tinyurl.com/3dq4bsp (accessed on 22 March 2011).

Spielhofer, T. Bielby, G., & Marson-Smith, H. (2009) Children's Online risks and Safety: A review of the available evidence. UK: DCSF.

Stald, G. (2008) Mobile Identity: Youth, Identity, and Mobile Communication Media. In D. Buckingham (Ed). *Youth, Identity, and Digital Media*. Cambridge, MA: MIT Press.

Staksrud, E., & Lobe, B. (2010) Evaluation of the implementation of the Safer Social Networking Principles for the EU Part I: General Report. European Commission SIP, Luxembourg [Online]. Available at http://tinyurl.com/3prs8a9 (accessed on 24 January 2011).

Stern, S. (2007) *Instant Identity: Adolescent Girls and the World of Instant Messaging*. New York: Peter Lang.

Sundar, S. S. (2007) The MAIN model: A Heuristic Approach to Understanding Technology Effects on Credibility. In M. J. Metzger & A. J. Flanagin (Eds). *Digital Media, Youth, and Credibility*. Cambridge, MA: The MIT Press.

Sunstein, C. (2005) *Laws of Fear: Beyond the Precautionary Principle*. Cambridge: Cambridge University Press.

Sunstein, C. (2007) *Worst-Case Scenarios*. Cambridge, MA: Harvard University Press.

Swearer, S. M., Espelage, D. L., Vaillancourt, T., & Hymel, S. (2010). What Can Be Done about School Bullying? Linking Research to Educational Practice. *Educational Researcher*, 39, 38–47.

Taylor, M., Holland, G., & Quayle, E. (2001) Typology of Paedophile Picture Collections. *The Police Journal*, 74(2) 97–107.

Taylor, M., & Quayle, E. (2003) *Child Pornography: An Internet Crime*. Hove: Brunner-Routledge, 2003.

Tarissan, F., Latapy M., & Prieur, C. (2009) *Efficient Measurement of Complex Networks Using Link Queries, INFOCOM Workshops*, IEEE, 254–259.

The Age (2010) Australian police unearth global pedophile ring [Online]. Available at http://tinyurl.com/3prgd4m (accessed on 20 January 2011).

Thornburgh, D., & Lin, H. S. (2002) *Youth, Pornography, and the Internet*. Washington, DC: National Academy Press.

Tippett, N., Houlston, C., & Smith, P. (2010) *Prevention and Response to Identity-Based Bullying among Local Authorities in England, Scotland and Wales*. Manchester: Equality and Human Rights Commission.

Turkle, S. (1999) Cyberspace and Identity. *Contemporary Sociology*, 28(6), 643–648.

Turkle, S. (2007) *Evocative Objects: Things We Think with*. Cambridge, MA: MIT Press.

Turkle, S. (2011) *Alone Together*. New York: Basic Books.

Ungar, S. (2001) Moral Panic versus the Risk Society: The Implications of Changing Sites of Social Anxiety. *British Journal of Sociology*, 52(2), 271–291.

UN. Secretary-General's Study on Violence against Children (2006a) [Online]. Available at http://www.unviolencestudy.org/ (accessed on 5 October 2010).

UN. (2006b) Report of the Secretary-General, A/61/270.

UN Secretary General. (2001) Promotion and protection of the rights of children, A/56/488.

UN Secretary General. (2006) Report on Violence Against Children, A/61/299.

UN Secretariat. (2010) Recent developments in the use of science and technology by offenders and by competent authorities in fighting crime, including the case of cybercrime, A/CONF.213/9.

United States Department of Labor. (2009) 2008 Findings on the worst forms of child labor – Madagascar, 10 September 2009 [Online]. Available at http://tinyurl.com/5syg8yj (accessed on 26 May 2011).

United States Department of State. (2010a) Sri Lanka, 8 April 2011 [Online]. Available at http://tinyurl.com/5syg8yj (accessed on 26 May 2011).

United States Department of State. (2010b) South Africa, 8 April 2011 [Online]. Available at http://tinyurl.com/5syg8yj (accessed on 26 May 2011).

United States Department of State. (2010c) Russia, 8 April 2011 [Online]. Available at http://tinyurl.com/5syg8yj (accessed on 26 May 2011).

United States Department of State (2010d) Madagascar, 8 April 2011 [Online]. Available at http://tinyurl.com/5syg8yj (accessed on 26 May 2011).

US Senate Committee. (2006) Hearing on "network neutrality [Online]. Available at http://tinyurl.com/zodcf (accessed on 6 October 2010).

US Senate Committee. (2010) Examining Children's Privacy: New Technologies and the Children's Online Privacy Protection Act [Online]. Available at http://tinyurl.com/43z3c33 (accessed on 12 February 2011).

Valentine, G. (2004) *Public Space and the Culture of Childhood*. Hants, UK: Ashgate.

Van Asselt, M. (2005) The Complex Significance of Uncertainty in a Risk Era: Logics, Manners and Strategies in use. *International Journal of Risk Management* (special issue on uncertainty), 5(2/3/4), 125–158.

Van Asselt, M., & Vos, E. (2006) Precautionary Principle and the Uncertainty Paradox. *Journal of Risk Research*, 9(4), 313–336.

Van Asselt, M, Vos, E., & Rooijackers, B. (2009) Science, knowledge and uncertainty in EU risk regulation. In M. Everson & E. Vos (Eds). *Uncertain Risks Regulated*. England: Routledge, Cavendish.

Walden, I. (2007) *Computer Crimes and Digital Investigations*. Oxford: Oxford University Press.

Walden, I. (2010) Computer Forensics and the presentation of evidence in criminal cases. In Y. Jewkes & M. Yar (Eds). *Handbook of Internet Crime*. UK: Willan Publishing

Wall, D. (2007) *Cybercrime*. Cambridge: Polity Press.

Ward, T., Louden, K., Hudson, S. M., & Marshall, W. (1995) A Descriptive Model of the Offense Chain for Child Molesters. *Journal of Interpersonal Violence*, 10, 452–472.

Werbach, K. (2002) A Layered Model for Internet Policy. *Journal of Telecommunications and High Technology Law*, 1(37), 58–64.

West, D. (2000) The Sex Crime: Deterioration More Apparent than Real? *European Journal on Criminal Policy and Research*, 8(4), 399–422.

WGIG. (2005) Report of the Working Group of Internet Governance [Online]. Available at http://tinyurl.com/3w2t5u9 (accessed on 12 January 2010).

Whetten, D., Rands, G., & Godfrey, P. (2002) What are the responsibilities of business to society? In A. Pettigrew, H. Thomas, & R. Whittington (Eds). *Handbook of Strategy and Management*. London: Sage.

White, G. (2004) Civil Society, Democratization and Development: Clearing the Analytical Ground. In P. Burnell, & P. Calvert (Eds). *Civil Society in Democratization*. London: Frank Cass.

White House. (2011) Conference on Bullying Prevention [Online]. Available at http://tinyurl.com/433kz7n (accessed on 11 March 2011).

Whitlock, J. L., Powers, J. P., & Eckenrode, J. E. (2006) The Virtual Cutting Edge: Adolescent Self-Injury and the Internet. Special Issue on Children, Adolescents and the Internet. *Developmental Psychology*, 42, 402–417.

Wilkinson, I. (2001) *Anxiety in a Risk Society*. London: Routledge.

Wolak, J., Finkelhor, D., & Mitchell, K. (2006) Online victimization of youth: Five years later [Online]. Available at http://tinyurl.com/44gmtp (accessed on 24 September 2010).

Wolak, J., Finkelhor, D., & Mitchell, K. (2008) Is Talking Online to Unknown People Always Risky? Distinguishing Online Interaction Styles in a National Sample of Youth Internet Users. *Cyberpsychology and Behavior*, 11, 340–343.

WC III. (2008) Adolescent declaration to end sexual exploitation [Online]. Available at http://tinyurl.com/3lwoctl (accessed on 12 January 2011).

WSIS. (2003) Declaration of principles building the information society [Online]. Available at http://tinyurl.com/3zvgadj (accessed on 12 January 2010).

WSIS. (2005) Tunis Agenda for the Information Society [Online]. Available at http://tinyurl.com/3w42cpw (accessed on 12 January 2010).

Wu, I. (2004) Canada, South Korea, Netherlands and Sweden: Regulatory Implications of the Convergence of Telecommunications. *Telecommunications Policy*, 28(1), 79–96.

Yar, M. (2006) *Crime and Society*. UK: Sage Publications.

Ybarra, M., & Mitchell, K. (2004) Online aggressors/targets, aggressors and targets: A comparison of associated youth characteristics. *Journal of Child Psychology*, 45, 1308–1316.

Ybarra, M., & Mitchell, K. (2005) Exposure to Internet Pornography among Children and Adolescents: A National Survey. *Cyberpsychology and Behavior*, 8, 473–486.

Ybarra, M., Mitchell, K., Finkelhor, D., & Wolak, J. (2007) Internet Prevention Messages: Targeting the Right Online Behaviors. *AP & AM*, 161(2), 138–145.

Youn, S. (2008) Parental Influence and Teens' Attitude toward Online Privacy Protection. *Journal of Consumer Affairs*, 42, 362–388.

Zittrain, J. (2008) *The Future of the Internet and How to Stop It*. New Haven, CT: Yale University Press.

Index